Historic Houses of Early America

ELISE LATHROP

Other Books by ELISE LATHROP

✠

EARLY AMERICAN INNS AND TAVERNS

WHERE SHAKESPEARE SET HIS STAGE

SUNNY DAYS IN ITALY

Etc., Etc.

Home of Postmaster General Gideon Granger, and later of many notable men, British and American. It is now occupied by the Arts Club of Washington, D. C.

HISTORIC HOUSES
of
EARLY AMERICA

By 𝕰𝖑𝖎𝖘𝖊 𝕷𝖆𝖙𝖍𝖗𝖔𝖕

I l l u s t r a t e d

"All houses wherein men have lived and died
Are haunted houses. Through the open doors
The harmless phantoms on their errands glide
With feet that make no sound upon the floors."
The Builders — LONGFELLOW

TUDOR PUBLISHING CO.
NEW YORK · MCMXXVII

HISTORIC HOUSES OF EARLY AMERICA

PRINTED IN THE UNITED STATES OF AMERICA

To

Helen, Mabel, and Tony
who all helped greatly

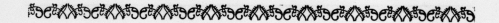

Preface

THE author does not pretend that all early houses in the United States are included in this volume. Had this been done, it would have been necessary to list so many that the book would either have resembled a mere index, or have been extended far beyond the number of pages convenient for one volume.

As a rule, only such old houses are included as have interesting stories connected with them, or those which have been the homes of interesting and famous people. A few have been mentioned whose chief claim to distinction is their age, but only when this itself is remarkable.

Nor does the author claim that all of the old houses in the United States with interesting histories have been included; merely those which to her seem the most interesting. The omissions have been made chiefly because the houses, though interesting, were too modern to come properly in the book's field. Very few of those included are less than a century and a half in age, and many are much older.

Since many of these houses have been taken over by historical or family associations, all buildings to which the public is admitted, either gratis or on payment of a small fee, have been marked in the index with an asterisk.

❧ Acknowledgments ☙

IN addition to many Chambers of Commerce, Historical and Patriotic Societies, librarians, postmasters, etc., thanks are due to the following:

Mrs. W. F. ADAMS, *Misses* LENA BARKSDALE, PATTEN BEARD; *Mr.* and *Mrs.* EDWARD BENNETT, *Miss* FANNY P. BROWN, *Mmes.* A. P. BURNHAM, L. S. COX, *Messrs.* W. H. CRAWSHAW, FREDERICK R. CURTIS, WILLIAM L. DEYN, *Miss* FLORENCE DILLARD, *Messrs.* C. FRANK DUNN, GEORGE FRANCIS DOW, JAMES L. EISENBERG; Editor of the Vineyard Haven Gazette; *Mrs.* EWING R. EMISON, *Mr.* FRANK ENO, *Mrs.* VIVIEN MINOR FLEMING, *Mrs.* W. B. FOLSOM; *Messrs.* JAMES THAYER GEROULD, WM. M. GERHART; *Mrs.* J. COOKE GRAYSON; *Messrs.* JOHN B. HICKS, GALEN W. HILL, JOHN E. HINMAN; *Miss* ETHEL G. HOYLE; *Mrs.* JAMES E. IRVINE, *Misses* ELLA C. LINDEBERG, BERTHA H. LYMAN, ANNE V. MANN, ELEANOR MOREHOUSE; *Messrs.* WM. Z. MAHON, JESSE MERRITT, LLOYD MINTURN MAYER, GEO. B. MCCORMICK, EVERETT S. MELOON, PERCY CHASE MILLER; *Dr.* ELLIS P. OBERHOLZER; *Misses* JOHANNA PETER, JANE PRATT; *Messrs.* J. S. PRICE, W. F. PUTNAM, M. H. RANDALL, EDWARD H. REDSTONE; *Mmes.* JAMES ROSS, A. G. A. SAUNDERS, EDWARD SHOEMAKER, CHAS. H. SHUART; *Misses* M. J. SMITH, L. G. STONEY; *Mr.* P. B. STINSON, *Mrs.* SUYDAM; *Dr.* CHARLES H. L. WILCOX, *Messrs.* H. L. WILLET, WILLIAM F. WORNER, and many others for great assistance.

✦ Contents ✦

ix

ᚷ Illustrations ᚷ

HISTORIC HOUSES
OF EARLY AMERICA

Chapter I

The Oldest Surviving House
in the United States

I F ONE were asked offhand where the oldest house in the United States might be found, the chances are that one of two answers would be given: either that it must be somewhere near that spot in Virginia where the first English colonists landed, or in Massachusetts, possibly in Plymouth, where the Pilgrims, after landing on Cape Cod, made their first permanent settlement.

Either or both answers would be wrong. For the oldest house in the United States one must go much further south or west. Nor will it be easy to decide between at least three rival claimants for this distinction.

St. Augustine, Florida, claims it, as a placard on one house there announces. This house is now occupied by the St. Augustine Institute of Science and Historical Society, but even after much investigation, the Society is unable to fix definitely the exact date of its building, although they have proved that it is very old.

Tradition ascribes at least a portion of this attractive building to monks who came with Menendez in 1565, and asserts that the house was the chapel and hermitage of these monks. Charles A. Reynolds, who has written a pamphlet about " The Oldest House in America," — not this but another claimant — asserts that " there were no Franciscans in St. Augustine in 1565, although there was a fortified camp." The Historian and Librarian of the Historical Society, Miss Emily L. Wilson, has furnished much information acquired after investigating

3

old Spanish documents, but first a bit of history may not be unwelcome.

Ponce de Leon landed on the coast of Florida in 1512, but he made no settlement then, nor on his return some nine years later, at which time he found the Indians fiercely hostile, lost some of his men, and was himself taken back on shipboard with an arrow wound from which he later died.

It remained for French Huguenots to make the first settlement. In 1562, Jean Ribaut landed with a body of colonists on Parris Island, South Carolina, and two years later, sent Laudonnière, one of the leaders, to build a fort on St. Johns River, Florida, which fort he called Caroline. Later, Ribaut himself went and took command there. In 1565 the Spaniard, Don Pedro Menendez de Ayllon, landed on the Florida coast, and built a fort within the present city limits of St. Augustine, "on an islet next to and close to the one where they are now," according to a translated letter of Dr. Caceres, written in 1574. The fort was moved to its present site in 1566.

The Spaniards decided to wipe out Ribaut's settlement, surprised the inhabitants, and butchered several hundred of them, some say all but eight, on the plea that they were exterminating "heretics." They even set up a monument stating: "I do not do this as to Frenchmen but as to Lutherans." This act was not approved by the French of the Catholic faith, and in 1567, the Chevalier Dominique de Gourges, a Gascon Catholic nobleman, attacked St. Augustine, and inflicted the same treatment on its inhabitants as had Menendez on those of Fort Caroline. De Gourges then set up a board, on which was inscribed: "I did not do this as to Spaniards, nor as to infidels, but as to traitors, thieves and murderers."

Laudonnière had described the Indians whom he found in the vicinity of St. Johns River as kind hearted, fine appearing people. "Both men and women were clean in their persons and in their homes — their women dressed in soft skins, ornamented, and some with woven garments, were as handsome as any of the European women, and even Christian whites would not have been kinder to these

An old room in the " oldest house," St. Augustine, Florida, and one of three claimants to be the oldest house in the United States. The picture shows the original old beams in the ceiling, beneath the plaster which, although old, was added long after the house was built.

The " oldest house in America." If not positively that, it seems certain that it is the second oldest, and many believe that it is truly entitled to its claim of oldest. Now the home of the St. Augustine, Florida, Historical Association.

Photo courtesy of the Chamber of Commerce, Santa Fe, N. M.

Ruins of the Communal Dwelling, Frijoles Canyon, Bandolier National Monument, near Santa Fe, New Mexico. This is called the first apartment house in America.

Photo courtesy of the Chamber of Commerce, Santa Fe, N. M.

One of the Cliff Dwellings, Frijoles Canyon, Bandolier National Monument, near Santa Fe, New Mexico. This shows the tiers of dwellings cut in the side of the cliffs, occupied by an almost prehistoric race.

Frenchmen than were these Indians, who up to that time, had never seen a white man." Laudonnière further wrote that they " made two crops a year, corn and peas, and had many kinds of fruits, and lived, each family, in its log and mud huts." [1]

St. Augustine then was founded in 1565, and when the English under Sir Francis Drake attacked and burned it in 1586, a map drawn by one of Drake's men shows that there was at that time a cluster of houses near or on what is now St. Francis Street, on which stands the house of Geronimo Alvarez, quarters to-day of the Historical Society. Furthermore, when the English took full possession of St. Augustine in 1763, one historian reported seeing a house with the date: 1571 upon it.

In their researches, the Society has found the report of the Spanish Governor, written after Moore's attack upon the city in 1702. This report mentions that " some of the houses were saved," and asking for money for repairs, he particularly mentions the Governor's house, the St. Francis convent and the Treasury building. The Society also possesses letters from a Spanish Governor, proving that the fort now standing was completed in 1690, at which time he employed slaves to " rebuild the official houses with stone, as they are built of wood, and in bad condition." The first stories of these houses were then built of " tabique," probably the same as the South Carolina tabby, with " thin walls and roof of shingles, as is customary in this province." He also mentions that the Governor's house was the first in the province. This building is now the Post Office, the Treasury building is owned privately. The wooden roofs of all three were burned during Moore's attack.

In 1884, the Geronimo Alvarez house, which apparently may justly claim the title of oldest in St. Augustine, or share it with that of the present Post Office, was bought by an American for a residence, the Spanish family which then owned it thinking it so old as to be valueless. The new owner covered the interior walls with wood, which the Historical Society, when they took possession a couple of years

[1] Mr. N. L. Willet, in a pamphlet on Beaufort County, S. C.

ago, had removed, baring the old stone walls, the hand-hewn beams of the ceilings. Miss Wilson describes the floors of the lower story as of tabby or coquina, " crushed and pounded to a depth of two feet with salt water." The present plan of this first story is the same as shown on a map made in 1788. The Society is now trying to get documents from Spain which will establish the ownership of the house prior to 1763, when they have the record of its transfer from one Hernandez to Jesse Fish. Miss Wilson herself, and she has made extensive investigations, believes that this house was indeed built as early as 1571 for the monks who came with Menendez, and that the coquina was put on about 1600. The Historical Society possesses a record of the building in 1598 of "a powder house of stone, a mile from the city," as ordered by the Governor at that time, showing that stone or coquina was already being used.

The three other houses claiming to be the oldest here, the Worth, Don Toledo and Dodge houses, are believed by careful investigators to date from about 1801–3, with the possible exception of the Worth house, which may have been built in 1791, and on the site of an older one.

The Governor's house, now the Post Office, has been much remodeled by both English and American Governments. The old Treasury still has a second story with wooden walls, and a balcony on the garden side, as has the " Oldest House," but beams and ceilings of the former are not so old, as it has evidently been more extensively repaired. Miss Wilson is convinced that these three were standing in 1690. The type of these is a lower story of coquina or tabby, an upper one of wood, with balcony overlooking the garden. Before 1690, stone for building purposes was allowed only to the Governors, then members of the Menendez family. Furthermore, as establishing the legitimate claim of the " oldest house " to be such, the Society owns a copy of a petition addressed to the Congress of the United States in 1824, by a number of the descendants of early Spanish families, asserting that their " descent was so well-known that it would be a waste of time for the Government to make them prove their titles," which latter went back to the 17th and 18th centuries. Among those signing this petition were Geronimo Alvarez and his son, Antonio.

The type of these houses somewhat resembles that of many old Charleston, South Carolina, residences. Very solid are the timbers used in the construction of the "Oldest House." The stone walls added later are broken in places, revealing solid timbers beneath, and the ceiling beams are equally substantial.

It seems quite probable then that this house was built originally for the Franciscans, and after they moved into a larger convent, was owned privately. When the English obtained possession of Florida, the Spaniards were given a year in which to sell their property, but a number of old families, not wishing to sell, transferred their houses and estates " in confidence " to Jesse Fish, among these families being descendants of Ponce de Leon and of Menendez. When Florida returned to Spanish ownership, the old Spanish descendants returned as well, and demanded back their property. With the King's consent, the Governor agreed to sell them back their homes at auction, if they had not already purchased them. When the houses were thus auctioned off to the original owners, the King of Spain held a mortgage on the properties until, in 1801, this was cancelled, and a clear title given the owners. Among these was Don Geronimo Alvarez, who later signed the petition to Congress, and the deed which Alvarez received at the time of the auction, in 1789, describes the house as built of coquina and wood.

All visitors to St. Augustine, in addition to the old houses, will be interested in the venerable fort, which, built solidly of coquina, in 1690 replaced two earlier wooden forts. The tablet affixed by Governor Alonzo Fernandez de Herreda, stating that the fort was finished in 1756, alludes rather to the completion of changes and repairs made. Named Fort Marion in 1821, and now a national monument, this old fort has witnessed thrilling scenes; has been attacked by the English both with and without Indian allies, and has been under the flags of Spain, England, the United States and the Confederacy. Famous Indian chiefs, the Wild Cat and Osceola, and sixty-three patriots, including three Signers of the Declaration of Independence, Arthur Middleton, Edward Rutledge and Thomas Heyward, Junior, have been imprisoned here, together with David Ramsay, Revolutionary historian, and Lieutenant Governor Christopher Gadsden, the latter kept in a dark dungeon for almost a year. Here is a secret dungeon whose existence had been forgotten until it was re-discovered by two American officers in 1835; here are the hot shot oven, and an odd, irregular but massive archway beside the broad, low stone steps which lead to the ramparts.

Leaving St. Augustine, one must travel far westward to find the next claimant to be " the oldest house in the United States."

Aside from the possible date of two such claimants within the present capital city of New Mexico, Santa Fe, there exists at no great distance a collection of dwellings whose exact age no one has yet determined, and which Santa Fe styles " the first apartment house in America." This claim can hardly be contested.

In the Canyon of the Rito de los Frijoles, but a pleasant drive from Santa Fe, these prehistoric ruins yearly attract scientists for purposes of study, as well as many tourists. Fortunately the ruins are to be preserved, for in 1916, President Wilson set aside the land on which are the most important ones as a national monument, and it bears the name of the scientist who first investigated and explored them, Adolph F. Bandelier. Those who visit them must leave motors or carriages at the top of the canyon, and by a steep path climb for some six hundred feet, either on foot or donkey back, down into the bottom of the canyon, where the Rito de los Frijoles has its course.

From the bottom one may gaze up at the ruins, the houses of several stories, built into the side of the cliff, at the strange ceremonial chamber, with its altar and opening in the roof to carry off smoke, or if willing to do more climbing, up ladders in some cases, may stand within the actual walls of a number of these dwellings, for the most important ones have been excavated under the direction of the School of American Research and the United States Forest Service.

Since there are Indian *pueblos* of the present day laid out quite in the manner of these ruins, some antiquarians declare that the Indians of New Mexico to-day are the direct descendants of these cliff dwellers. It is known that when the first Spaniards came to this part of the country, in 1595, or perhaps earlier, they found the remnants of Indian *pueblos* near where they laid out the city of Santa Fe. Ralph Emerson Twitchell, who has written a number of books and pamphlets on this section of the country and its history, states that in his opinion, none of the *pueblos* on the site of Santa Fe was inhabited when the Spaniards arrived. If so — for other historians dispute this — then the claims of a certain building in Santa Fe to be the " oldest house in America," — and barring as not strictly speaking a house, the cliff dwelling — are not positively to be maintained, but another very old residence bases its claim upon more definite data.

Close to the very ancient San Miguel church there stands to-day a house built as are hundreds of houses occupied now by Mexicans in this southwestern country, of adobe, its low, flat roof grass grown, its windows and door openings now barricaded to preserve it as long as possible, and exclude tramps or children at play. Originally of two stories, as an old picture shows, there now remains but one.

Residents of Santa Fe say that this house was once the dwelling of the Indian chief of Tiguez, the *pueblo* which once stood on the site of San Miguel church, and of other houses in this part of the city. Some dispute the assertion that Tiguez stood on this site. However, it is claimed that Coronado found this house standing when, at the head of 1100 men, he visited this country in 1540. He is also said to have made this house his headquarters until his return to Mexico in 1543.

Local tradition goes further, and asserts that on the site of San Miguel, generally conceded to be the oldest church in the United States, for although repaired and partly re-built from time to time, much of the original structure remains, a church was built at the time of this early visit. Some believe that Spaniards under Espejo founded at least a temporary settlement here at that time. Almost everyone agrees that there were *pueblos* here, but the date of the Spaniards' arrival, and whether or not they made any kind of a settlement is disputed. They did find a system of irrigation, and a people skilled in agriculture, acquainted with the cultivation of cotton, the weaving of cotton and woolen fabrics.

One can find a date varying not more than ten years according to historians, for the building of the interesting old Palace of the Governors, now a museum. The story of these early days is romantic and thrilling.

Oñate, the Spaniard, married the granddaughter of Montezuma, and in 1598 came here from Mexico " with 83 ox-wagons, 7,000 cattle, and 400 colonists," as Charles F. Lummis tells in an attractive booklet issued by the Santa Fe Chamber of Commerce. First settling where Chamita now stands, Oñate, with a party of his soldiers, stood off savage Indians, and explored the country as far as what is now Nebraska, marched over the deserts to the Gulf of California, and back again, then removed the settlement which he had founded thirty miles north to what is now Santa Fe. Save that Twitchell puts the date of the founding of Santa Fe at ten years later, or 1608, the two accounts agree fairly well.

He also explains that the church of San Miguel, and houses for Indian servants were built on one side of the river, the Royal Palace, which was also to serve as fortress on the other side, but makes no mention of the old house of Tiguez.

Whichever date is preferred, even the latest, 1609, makes this at least the second oldest surviving house in the United States, provided that the house in St. Augustine was built in 1571.

The royal palace then was built either in 1609, or a few years earlier, its *presidio* enclosed by an adobe wall. The original wall was 400 feet in length, with a tower at each end, the eastern one for a chapel, the western for storing ammunition. Adjoining the western tower were the dungeons.

The palace itself was about 120 feet long, its depth varying from twenty to seventy-five feet, with a portal fifteen feet wide. It contained a great courtroom, sixty feet long; the roof was supported by massive pine beams, the woodwork rough and heavy, and the floors were of dirt. The building itself was of adobe. There was a garden, and a small irrigation ditch supplied palace and garden with water. By 1617 there were probably, according to Mr. Twitchell, only forty-eight Spanish soldiers in the whole of this territory, and most of these lived in the palace fortress.

The Indians had been friendly enough, but the Spaniards tried to convert them forcibly to the Christian religion, and whippings and other punishments inflicted did not tend to keep relations cordial. Finally they killed some of the Spaniards, and in 1680 the Indian Pope headed a revolt, sending those messages of knotted yucca cord to Indians in outlying *pueblos;* messages both swift and effective.

Fortunately for the Spaniards, they got news of the proposed uprising before it came off, or they might all have been surprised and killed. As it was, the Indians attacked three days before they had originally planned, and killed more than four hundred of the twenty-five hundred settlers, soldiers and friars then in the territory. Refugees came in from other Spanish settlements, and took refuge in the Palace of the Governors. The enemy succeeded in cutting the water supply, and after being besieged for a week in the palace fortress, a band of a thousand, the surviving Spaniards, made a sortie, and fighting fiercely, succeeded in escaping across the desert, eventually arriving at El Paso del Norte, what is now El Paso, Texas. The Indians were left masters in Santa Fe, occupied the palace, but did not destroy it. Instead, they set up a ceremonial chamber or Kiva in the court, and made some changes in the interior construction.

Not until 1693, when Diego de Vargas recaptured Santa Fe, did the Spaniards return. The following December, one hundred soldiers, seventeen missionaries, and seventy families came back from El Paso, and settled. The Spaniards were now firmly entrenched, repaired the old palace, re-built the ruined churches, and dominated the country.

In 1708, a Viceroy reported that when he took possession, he found " five broken pine benches, six chairs, some without backs, two ordinary tables, two plain bedsteads with pine slats, and a big copper kettle, burned and battered," as furniture of the palace. This was all except ten keys!

In 1744, the entire palace was restored and rebuilt, but some of the original timbers supporting the old roof are in place to this day. All of the windows at this time were glazed, something then almost unknown from Chihuahua to the Mississippi River.

Incidentally, Santa Fe has had experience with many governments, having been ruled by Spaniards, Indians, Mexicans and Americans, while for one week the Confederates occupied the town, and their flag floated over the old palace.

This was until very recent times always the residence of the Governor, to whatever nationality he belonged. A small cemetery was originally connected with the palace, and in the dungeons now gone, Indians as well as noted Spaniards and later Americans have been imprisoned. The Spanish general who re-captured the city from the Indians, Don Diego de Vargas, was one of these prisoners, charged with many crimes of which he was later acquitted by his sovereign, Phillip III of Spain. The Americans were imprisoned under charge of violating the Spanish laws, and entering the province for trade purposes. They were not wanted in Santa Fe in those days. Among these prisoners was David Merriwether, later governor of the territory. Another, in 1807, was Major Zebulon M. Pike, of the United States Army, who was detained a prisoner in the palace by the Spanish authorities.

In the course of time, some of the original decorations were removed from the palace walls; festoons of the ears of Indians slain in the course of frequent fierce fighting, and which horrible ornamentation was arranged over doors and windows of rooms used for public business.

Here in this palace when, in 1851, Santa Fe became United States territory, many prominent natives were tried, and a few sentenced to be hanged for insurrection. Here lived the first American Governor, James H. Calhoun; here David Merriwether took up his residence as Governor not so long after occupying one of the dungeons. On the

THE OLDEST HOUSE, SANTA FE, N. MEX.

Photo courtesy of the Chamber of Commerce, Santa Fe, N. M.

A rival to the claims of St. Augustine's " oldest house," this, said to have been the home of the Tiguez Indian Chief, may be the oldest. Although this claim is disputed, it undoubtedly ranks as one of the very old surviving houses.

Photo courtesy of the Chamber of Commerce. Santa Fe, N. M.

The Palace of the Governors, Santa Fe, New Mexico. A very old house, dating from 1598 to 1609, according to differing historians. Although restored, some of the original beams are still in place. It is now a public museum.

Hill Crest, near Stateburg, South Carolina. This historic mansion was occupied, during the Revolution, by both the British under Cornwallis, and the Continental troops, and both left a prized sign of their occupancy. It was still later visited by the Federal troops, but was not damaged.

Photo by George W. Johnson

The Horry house. Modernized by the addition of the double piazzas, this house belonged to one of Charleston's old Huguenot families, members of which figured in her Revolutionary and social history.

roof of the palace another Governor, Edmund G. Ross, chose to take the oath of office picturesquely at sunrise.

A distinguished Governor, General Lew Wallace, wrote his famous " Ben Hur " in this building, while his wife wrote her book, " The Land of the Pueblos."

Not until the present century did it cease to be the Governor's mansion. Then, when the present handsome house was built for that purpose, the old building was turned into a museum, and now, filled with interesting relics of all the different governments, with old furniture, manuscripts, etc., it is visited by many tourists.

Even as late as 1846, it is said that the palace was the only building in Santa Fe to have glazed windows; something difficult to realize to-day, when visiting the charming little city, with its picturesque blending of old and new. But the first railway whistle was not heard in Santa Fe until 1880.

Chapter II

The First European Settlement

To the coast of South Carolina, and one of the group of islands near Beaufort, one must look for the second landing place of Europeans in what is now the United States — always excepting the Icelanders, if they really did visit these shores. In South Carolina one finds also the first actual settlement.

Although the Spaniards twice landed on the island of St. Helena, off the Carolina coast, they made no settlement there, merely carrying off some of the peaceful Indians as slaves. It remained for the French Huguenots, under Jean Ribaut, to land on Parris Island with a band of colonists in 1562.

This was "so notable a body of nobles and gentlemen that a French historian said of them: ' they had the means to achieve some notable thing and worthy of eternal memory.' On May 27th, 1562, we find Ribaut anchored in ten fathoms of water off what is known to-day as Parris Island, just a few miles from Port Royal of to-day."

Ribaut and his men landed, and "while they walked through the forest, flocks of wild turkey flew above their heads, and around they beheld partridges and stags. . . . On returning to the ships, they cast their nets in the bay, and caught fishes in numbers so wonderful that two draughts of the net supplied enough for a day's food for the crews of both ships." [1]

Ribaut found the Indians of what is now Beaufort County "kindly, self-respecting, and for those days quite civilized peoples."

[1] *Beaufort County, South Carolina*, N. L. Willet.

14

On Parris Island he built a fort, to which he gave the name Charles-fort, and after taking possession of the country in the name of his sovereign, returned to France to report his discovery.

"He left in this fort a garrison of twenty-six men. Not return-ing quickly on account of home wars, the garrison afterward built a ship with the aid of the Indians, using Spanish moss and rosin for caulking it. This was the first ship constructed in America, and in it the garrison sailed to Europe.

"In 1565, another French ship landed at Port Royal. Its mis-sion largely was to thank Chief Audusta for his kindness to the gar-rison on Parris Island." [2]

In 1564 the Spanish destroyed the fort on Parris Island and built another which they abandoned. This the Indians, in 1576, en-tirely destroyed. Apparently the Spaniards, as usual, made no attempt to live peaceably with the natives. In 1577 the Spaniards built still another fort " of cedar posts and tabby."

A few years ago two American officers found on this island the out-lines of an old fort of tabby and cedar, some of the ancient posts still sound. They believed this to be Ribaut's fort, and a monument to the early French Huguenot settlers was raised here shortly after the dis-covery. But some old Spanish histories recently discovered tend to establish it as the ruins of the Spanish fort, built fifteen years later than Ribaut's, while of the latter it is believed no vestige remains. A third old fort, parts of whose four foot walls still remain, was built by the English in 1731, while of their earlier one, in 1711, nothing is left, but its site is believed to have been in the heart of the town of Beaufort.

In Beaufort stands to-day, still occupied, a house more than two hundred years old, with but superficial exterior changes, including a large porch with pillars. The lower part of this house is of tabby, in which are loop-holes for rifles, and beneath them a stone ledge for ammunition.

Beaufort was settled early in the 18th century. In 1710, at a meeting of the Lords Proprietors of the Province of Carolina, it was

[2] *History of Beaufort, S. C.*, N. L. Willet.

agreed to build a seaport town at Port Royal, but this house, oldest in the section, is believed to have stood here as early as 1690. Another very old house, also of tabby, which was sold to be used for the rectory of old St. Helena's church, was the home of " Tuscarora Jack," a nickname given John Barnwell, one of the early settlers here, because he drove the Tuscarora Indians from the province. A third old tabby house in Beaufort, now in ruins, belonged to his grandson.

Although the houses in Beaufort were not destroyed during the Civil War, every one was sold afterwards by the Federal Government. Meanwhile, they had been left by their owners, and almost everything of value in the way of furniture, silver, etc., had been gradually removed by negroes or soldiers. For this reason, this section of the country is treasure trove for antique hunters.

At the small settlement known as Sheldon is a house said by some to have once been the residence of General Stephen Bull, by others of one Verdier; but in any case it is very old. Magnificent Sheldon Hall, built by General Bull, was, with the old church, burned to the ground. In the old house standing, the entire woodwork, long since repeatedly painted, is said to be of solid mahogany, and there are carved wooden ornaments or pendants on the exterior. On the occasion of Lafayette's visit in 1824 he spoke from its porch, but the house is now a barber shop.

The Bulls and the Eliots were among the most prominent English landowners here. Stephen Bull came over with Sayle, one of the early governors, bringing with him many servants. In addition to land here, he took up large tracts along the Ashley River, which remained in the family for more than two hundred years.

After Ribaut's early attempt at colonization, the first permanent settlement in South Carolina was made under the Lords Proprietors.

Charleston's first settlers came in 1670, but Charles Towne, as it was called until after the Revolution, lay on the opposite side of the Ashley River from the present city. In 1672, John Coming and his wife, Affra, gave up their land at Oyster Point, the present site of Charleston, and Mr. Henry Hughes also " voluntarily surrendered up

Photo by George W. Johnson

The Miles Brewton house, one of the most beautiful old mansions of its period. It has been used as headquarters by the British during the Revolution, and by Federal generals in the War between the States.

The beautiful old live oak avenue leading to old Tomotley Plantation, near Sheldon, South Carolina.

Known as the Lord Campbell house, that gentleman, South Carolina's last Royal Governor, occupied it, and from its garden steps he made his escape to a British frigate in Charleston harbor, at the outbreak of the Revolution.

one halfe of Oyster Poynt, to be employed in and towards the enlarging of a Towne." In 1679, the settlement was ordered moved to this site, which was done while Sir John Yeamans was governor. At this time, large estates or grants of land were called baronies, and among these were Wadpoo, Broughton, Colleton and Fairlawn Baronies, the men who received these grants often being called Landgraves.

From Charleston as headquarters, one may visit many interesting old estates in the vicinity, along the two rivers, the Ashley and Cooper, which meet in Charleston harbor. Charleston itself offers much of history, and many interesting old houses tempt the visitor to linger. It is, perhaps, the American city which has best preserved its old-time atmosphere. Even new buildings, for Charleston by no means lives solely in the past, are frequently built after the old manner. Some of the handsome modern residences on the new part of the famous Battery have been fitted with woodwork, doors, iron railings and gateways, removed from some old house demolished, or so converted for business purposes that the interior was torn out. There is a strong local feeling for keeping this woodwork, the beautiful wrought iron railings and gateways, in Charleston, and not allowing them to be purchased and shipped away.

After giving up their land at Oyster Point, John Coming and his wife lived on a large tract of land known as Comingtee, and this has remained in the family of collateral descendants, the Balls, to the present day. A brick house, believed to be one of the two oldest in the parish, still stands on the estate. The date of its erection is not definitely known, but it is possible that it may have been built by Captain John Coming himself; if not, by his half brother, Elias Ball, who succeeded to the property after the deaths of the childless Comings, somewhere about 1698 or 1699. There are notes among the family papers of repairs made to a house here in 1731, while in 1738 some changes in the garret windows were made.

Originally the house had but two large rooms on each of its two floors. Later, partitions were built in, and a large wooden addition which has now been removed. The estate was famed for its hospitality.

To quote Mrs. Leiding: " So perfect were the arrangements made for guests that in every sleeping room was to be found the old four-poster, double bed, and a trundle bed or crib." [3]

Charles Towne was built on the new site, with fortifications following the line of to-day's Water Street. By 1715, there were three forts or garrison houses in or near the parishes of St. John's and St. Stephen's, in this part of the country. One on the Cooper River, three or four miles below Monck's Corner; another on Daniel Ravenel's place, Wantool; the third on the Izard plantation on the Santee River.

What is assuredly one of the oldest surviving houses in Charleston, if not the very oldest, is that known as the Colonel William Rhett house on Haskell Street. This is admitted to be one of the first houses built outside of the old fortifications.

Colonel William Rhett came to Carolina in 1698. The next year there was a terrible epidemic, probably yellow fever, which was followed by a terrific hurricane, and in the work of re-building the young colony four men figured prominently: William Rhett, James Moore, Sir Nathaniel Johnson and Nicholas Trott. All except Moore were new comers.

This Rhett house, a square, brick edifice, covered with stucco, was built before 1722. Galleries in the usual Charleston style have been added on both sides. No longer a private residence, it is rented to lodgers, but in one of the rear rooms may still be seen a black marble mantel in which is cut the Rhett coat of arms, a lion rampant, holding in one paw a Crusader's flagstaff, on the pennon a Crusader's cross, the carving filled in with gold. In the old dining room, inserted in the centre of another black marble mantelpiece, is a tablet which it is thought Colonel Rhett may have brought from an earlier dwelling, if this one is not indeed the original, as it may be, since Johnson's Traditions speak of it as " in good condition in 1722." On the second floor is still another old black marble mantel, long ago decorated with a hand-painted design of morning glories.

From the steps of this house, in the days immediately preceding

[3] *Historic Houses of South Carolina*, Harriette Kershaw Leiding.

the Revolution, Lord Campbell heard his commission as governor read aloud to a crowd which " listened in sullen silence." Originally the grounds extended down to the water, and a gate opened on The High Way, now King Street.

Colonel Rhett has several claims to fame. During the Franco-Spanish alliance, the Governor of the Carolina settlements, Sir Nathaniel Johnson, sent a privateer to the neighborhood of Havana, to look for French and Spanish ships. This vessel returned with prisoners of both nationalities on board, and chased by four or five French vessels. Colonel Rhett, who was both soldier and sailor, was appointed vice-admiral, and sailed to attack the French fleet with but a few small vessels under his command. He defeated the larger force.

Pirates began harrying the settlements. The first of these were the mutinous crews of three French ships which had been sent in 1564 under René Laudonnière to bring food and aid to Ribaut's early colonists at Fort Royal. These mutineers were later killed by the colonists of the new French settlement at Fort Caroline. But from that day, pirates were all too frequent visitors.

At the death of the English governor, Sir Richard Kyrle, Robert Quarry, in 1684, assumed the title of governor, and allied himself with the pirates. Two months later he was ousted from his assumed office, but Joseph Morton, the new governor, invited Sir Harry Morgan, a notorious buccaneer, to the settlement. Another notorious pirate was Blackbeard, who one day sailed up the river to Charles Towne, demanded provisions and drugs for his sick, got them, and sailed away. Then came Stede Bonnet, who terrorized the coast. A former major in the English army, well educated and wealthy, he had lived at Barbadoes before taking to piracy. An expedition was organized against him, but although some of his men were taken, Bonnet escaped.

Woodrow Wilson, in his History of the American People, quotes an old narrative, possibly that of one of Bonnet's contemporaries, whose author gave what he considered an explanation of the gentleman's having turned pirate.

" This humor of going a-pyrating proceeded from a disorder in his mind, which had been but too visible in him some time before this wicked undertaking, and which is said to have been occasioned by some discomforts he found in a married state."

Colonel Rhett came to Sir Nathaniel's assistance, although the two were not good friends, and in another attack on the pirates with his own ships blocked the channel where he had caught them, and forced the pirate ships aground. Although his own *Henry* and *Sea Nymph* grounded, he fired on his opponents with such effect that they surrendered, when, to the joyous surprise of the Charlestonians, it was found that the leader was Stede Bonnet himself.

Bonnet was imprisoned in the underground dungeons of the old Wool Exchange, still standing in Charleston. Since the dungeons have now been lighted with electricity, one may inspect them and can but marvel that, despite the massive walls, Bonnet again escaped. It is said that an Indian furnished him with a woman's dress for disguise, but pursued into the sand hills by Rhett and his men, he was finally recaptured and hanged.

In 1722, Rhett died of a stroke of apoplexy, and was buried in the churchyard of the new, unfinished St. Philip's church, to which he had given a silver communion service still in use. His early companion in the colony, James Moore, died a few months later. The two men were never good friends, but a daughter of Moore married a son of Rhett, and from this couple the present Rhett family is descended.

In this old Rhett house, Governor Wade Hampton of Revolutionary fame, grandfather of the Confederate general of the same name, was born. Part of the once extensive garden remains at one side. The Colonel's granddaughter, Mrs. Thomas Smith, built and lived in the house still standing at No. 64 Church Street.

In 1707, visiting Charles Towne, John Lawson, Surveyor General of North Carolina, stated: " The town has very regular and fair streets, in which are good buildings of brick and wood." In 1720, Oldmixon mentions Mr. Landgrave Smith's house on the Key, with a drawbridge and wharf. " Col. Rhett's is on the Key, and 10 or 12 more deserve to be taken notice of."

The first Landgrave Thomas Smith came to this country soon after 1679. His son, Thomas, second Landgrave of the name, and his grandson, the Reverend Josiah Smith, are all said to have lived in their house at Goose Creek, which was wrecked by the earthquake of 1886, and later burned.

The fortifications of Charles Towne already mentioned "enclosed a parallelogram along the west bank of the Cooper, not more than four of the present squares by three broad." They were needed "not only on account of Indians by land and pirates by sea, but because this was the southern end of his Majesty's dominions, and the nearest neighbors, the Spaniards of St. Augustine were an ever present danger."

Furthermore, "there were bastions at the corners named for four of the Lords Proprietors; Granville, at the end of the East Battery; Colleton, near the present Baptist church; . . . . Cartaret, near where Meeting and Cumberland now join, (not far from the old Powder Magazine, now the property of the Colonial Dames,) and Craven, at the east end of the present Market." [4]

Charleston has suffered from several disastrous fires, as well as an earthquake, which destroyed many of the oldest houses. Among these was, it is said, the residence of Charles Pinckney, first in this country of a distinguished family.

On a corner of East Bay and Tradd Street, on the water side, stands a large building, now closed and dilapidated, but bearing distinct traces of having once been a mansion. Like many Charleston homes, the ground floor is less high-ceiled than the one above, on which is often found, as in England, the drawing room. The window arches of the second story of this house are much higher than those below. This now mournful old building is said to have been the residence of Thomas Pinckney.

The Charles Pinckney mentioned as the first to come to this country built himself a residence which must have been very near this house, if not on its site. He had three sons; Thomas, an officer in the British

[4] *Historical Sketch of the Old Powder Magazine, Charleston*, Ellen Parker.

army, died young; Charles became Chief Justice, while the third, William, was a Commissioner in Equity. The second Charles was educated in England as a lawyer, returned to Carolina, where he became successful in his profession, was later a King's Councillor, then Speaker of the House. He married, but after remaining childless for some years, finally adopted his brother William's oldest son as his prospective heir, and sent him to England to be educated, as told by Mrs. Leiding. She goes on to say:

"A romantic incident in the family annals interfered with this plan.

"In 1739, Colonel George Lucas, Governor of Antigua, arrived in Charleston with his family. The climate of the West Indies did not suit Mrs. Lucas. . . . Mrs. Lucas and her daughter were cordially received in Charleston society, but were especially welcomed in Colonel Pinckney's home. So open was Mrs. Pinckney's admiration for the young lady that she declared her readiness to step out of the way and permit her to take her (Mrs. Pinckney's) place." [5] Surely an extraordinary declaration for any wife to make. However, Mrs. Pinckney died the following year, and the widower promptly married Miss Eliza Lucas, and they had three children: Charles Cotesworth and Thomas, who both became generals in the Revolutionary Army, and a daughter, who married Daniel Horry. The Horrys were Huguenots, some of them fighting under Francis Marion in the Revolution, and the Horry house, built between 1751 and 1767, but with a recently added piazza, still stands on the corner of Meeting and Tradd Streets.

After his second marriage, Charles Pinckney "bought a whole square on East Bay, and built a handsome mansion in the centre of it, facing the harbor. The house was two stories high, with roof of slate . . . one of the rooms on the second floor was thirty feet long, and had a high ceiling. The whole house was wainscoted." This description from Mrs. Leiding's book exactly fits the old house now standing on East Bay, already mentioned.

The brother, William Pinckney, also had a house on East Bay, and

[5] *Historic Homes of South Carolina*, Harriette Kershaw Leiding.

here the first quarterly meeting of Charleston's St. George's Society was held in July, 1733.

Directly opposite this house which may or may not be the Pinckney residence, for actual proofs could not be found, stands a shabby old building on the site of an older house, said to have been the birthplace of Robert Tradd, the first white child born in Charles Towne.

A local historian states that the first Colonel Miles Brewton house, which stood on the southwest corner of Tradd and Church Streets is gone. The house now known by that name was built for the grandson and namesake, Miles, by the first Miles Brewton.

But on this corner stands a square brick house, with a two-story and evidently older brick building, with odd peephole shutters, adjoining it on Church Street. The house next to this, on the south, is said to have been the gift of the first Miles to his daughter, wife of Dr. Thomas Dale; and beyond that was the son, Robert Brewton's home.

The corner house is now The Patio, Miss Emily Barker's interior decorating studio. She has from the first been deeply interested in studying the history of the place, and learned, as did the writer from an early chronicle, that the original house on this site, with a three story coach house adjoining, was visited more than a hundred years ago by a disastrous fire, which entirely destroyed the residence, and burned off the third story of a coach house. It seems quite probable therefore that here once stood the home of Colonel Miles the First, while the lower two stories of his old coach house have survived to the present day.

The two buildings effectually shut off from the street an old courtyard, now grass grown, with but a few aged shrubs remaining of a possible garden. A former servants' house on Tradd Street has been converted into apartments, but the old wooden bridge still connects it with the corner house. Over this bridge, the valet used to pass back and forth to the master's room.

Whether or not the corner house was the original Brewton house, burned and rebuilt, it came many years ago into the possession of a German, who used it for his feed business, removing partitions which probably once divided the ground floor into a hall and two large rooms, so that now there is but one great room, with fine old woodwork, and with two similar doors surmounted by fanlights, opening one on Tradd, the other on Church Street. The German also removed the old staircase, and substituted a small one built outside from the gallery extending along the courtyard side. Later, the house was for a time a boys' school. The rooms on the upper floors still have their fine old mantels.

Robert Brewton occupied his Church Street house until 1745, in which year he succeeded his father as Powder Receiver, with the duty of seeing that powder from the old magazine on Cumberland Street was distributed as needed. Then he sold it to his sister, Rebecca, wife of Jordan Roche.

On Church Street, just beyond Tradd, is the large house once the residence of Judge Thomas Heyward, grandson of Captain Thomas Heyward, of the British Colonial Army. When the Provincial Congress enlisted two regiments, in 1775, Judge Heyward was made captain of the first company. A year later, he was one of a committee of ten to report on a form of government for the colonies, and he was furthermore one of the Signers. When President Washington visited Charleston, spending a week there in May, 1791, this house with its furnishings, then occupied by Mrs. Rebecca Jamieson, was rented by the entertainment committee for Washington's use, for the sum of sixty pounds, that "being the lowest rate at which the said house can be procured."

A tablet stating that Washington resided here is affixed to the house. The Daughters of the Revolution, Colonial Dames, and the city authorities have placarded almost all of the important old houses and buildings in Charleston, as well as the more important sites of others now gone, so the visitor can enjoy a stroll through the city, and at the same time locate the notable buildings.

At 69 Church Street stands the house occupied before 1762 by Jacob Motte, for twenty-seven years Treasurer of the Colony. His son, Jacob, married Rebecca Brewton, the heroine of Fort Motte.

The Mottes were an old and noble French family. After the revocation of the Edict of Nantes, the Marquis de la Motte went to Holland. His son, Jean, was sent by the Dutch Government as consul to Dublin, Ireland, and there he Anglicized his name to John Abraham Motte. About 1704, he came to South Carolina, received grants of several plantations there, and a few years later went to Europe to fetch his family back with him. He was one of the Commissioners of the Church Act; the next year commissioner of the first public school established in South Carolina, and was buried under the west end of old St. Michael's church.

His only son, Jacob, was one of the original founders of the first fire insurance company in America, known as the Friendly Society. He, like his father, was interested in education, and contributed to a fund for educating negroes. One of his last acts, as Treasurer, was to receive an order which was passed December 8th, 1769, by the Provincial Assembly for 10,500 pounds currency "for the purpose of aiding the American colonies in their resistance against the tyrannical measures being adopted by the British Parliament."

The senior Jacob was twice married, and of his nine children by his first wife, almost all figured prominently in the Revolutionary annals. His son, Jacob, who married Rebecca Brewton, promptly offered his services to his country, and was killed in the early days of the Revolution. Another son, Major Isaac, served in the army, represented South Carolina in the Continental Congress, and was appointed by Washington naval commander of the port of Charleston. Another son, Charles, was captain in the Revolutionary forces. One daughter, Anne, married first Thomas Lynch, Senior, then General Moultrie of the patriot army, and her sister married Lieutenant Peronneau, fighting on the same side.

Jacob Motte, Senior, married for his second wife the widow of Joseph Pinckney, and had two children by her.

Robert Brewton's son, Miles, was the first occupant of the charming old house now known variously as the Miles Brewton or Pringle house. It stands on King Street.

The second Miles, like his father and his grandfather before him, was appointed Powder Receiver. Miles became a member of the Commons in 1763, and was constantly re-elected until the Revolution changed the name of that legislative body.

This very lovely old house has remained in the family down to the present day. In 1769, the South Carolina Gazette and County Journal contained a statement to the effect that the advertiser, Ezra Waite, an English architect, had "finished the architecture and conducted the execution thereof . . . and also calculated, adjusted and draw'd at large for to work by the Ionick entablature," etc., of this house. Evidently Waite felt that his professional reputation was at stake, attacked by some one whom he "believed to be Mr. Kinsey Burden, a carpenter." Workmen to build the house were probably brought from England.

A high brick wall with large gates of iron separates the house from the street. Across the street there used to be a garden, in which was set a house once occupied by the patriot, Robert Y. Hayne, but both house and garden have now vanished. Originally the garden in the rear of the Brewton house went through to Legare Street, and a gateway on the latter was used by British officers when they occupied the house.

Along the side of the front yard is the old carriage house, with kitchen behind, and the servants' quarters above, while a second house, originally also for servants, and formerly connected with the carriage house by a wash house, pigeon house, etc., no longer belongs to the family, but has a separate entrance on another street.

The coach house and the servants' quarters are older than the big house, as is shown by the construction. While bricks brought from England as ship ballast were probably used for all the buildings, those in the former houses are laid in alternate rows of headers and stretchers — endwise for headers, lengthwise for stretchers — while in the big house they are placed according to Flemish bond, or alternately a lengthwise with an endwise brick, a newer construction. The two smaller houses still have the original roofs of English tiles. Adjoining the kitchen may be seen the old brick oven, but the room into which it once opened is gone. Walls and roof of the kitchen were badly damaged during the earthquake, and one can easily trace the new bricks used afterwards for repairs.

A double flight of steps mounts over a basement to the front portico of the main entrance of the Brewton house. The fine old doorway opens into a broad hall running through the house, and a broad staircase with low treads ascends with a landing to the second floor, on which are the drawing room and three large bedrooms. Between the drawing room and the bedroom behind it a steep, winding flight of stairs leads to the attic, where Mrs. Motte kept her pretty daughters hidden, while the British officers occupied the house. From the drawing room, French windows open on to a porch over the portico. The porch floor was once of lead, but this was removed by the Federal troops when they occupied Charleston, during the Civil War.

The drawing room, and indeed the entire house, is filled with beautiful old furniture, china, and portraits of many bygone generations. There is a portrait of Miles Brewton, first owner of the house, by Sir Joshua Reynolds, and a copy of a portrait of the first Miles by Rembrandt. The original went to another member of the family when some possessions were divided. Here is a portrait of the first owner's mother, painted by Henrietta Johnson, said to have been the first woman painter in America. The artist is buried in old St. Philip's churchyard.

The woodwork is very lovely in this drawing room, with carved cornice and carved, broken pediments over the doors, all of solid mahogany. Here, too, is a huge seachest, in which the Axminster carpet once covering the floor was shipped from England. Only one tattered fragment remains, its colors still bright, for the northern soldiers slashed it up into saddle cloths. The mantel is of white marble, with a central panel on which is carved a shepherd resting with his sheep beneath a tree — very like the one in Mt. Vernon which was a present to Washington.

Among other wonderful old pieces of furniture are two Empire chairs, bought at the sale of Louis Philippe's effects, and a secretary, whose shelved top has now been taken off, and is used as a china closet. Had it remained in place, the top would reach almost to the room's high ceiling. This piece was the work of Jacob Sass, a Charleston cabinet maker of about 1794.

The rooms on the first floor were the dining room at the right, a sitting room with library behind it on the left. The ceiling of the sitting room has decorations of London putty, which are as firmly in place, as well preserved as though the work of yesterday. A great marble slab fastened to the dining room wall was used as a table on which to set hot dishes. Its counterpart from the other side has been removed and very appropriately placed as a memorial to Rebecca Motte in the vestibule of St. Philip's Church.

In the basement are offices and a large sewing room, in which in olden times it is said that often as many as seventeen seamstresses were busy at once. The mistress of the home used then personally to superintend the cutting and making of clothing for her children, — for the boys until they were quite well grown — all of her husband's and sons' underclothing as well as that for herself and her daughters, shirts and collars for the men of the family. In addition, clothing for house servants and others on the plantation, sheets and pillow cases, etc., all were made under the watchful eye of the mistress, so it is small wonder that many seamstresses were needed. Almost all of the old Charleston householders had a plantation in the country, along the river, from which supplies were sent down by boat to the city. In this case, the plantation was Runnymede, and a boat manned by eight oarsmen, with a sail as well, was used for such transportation.

The old garden though diminished is still large. Once it contained a marble bathing pool, greenhouses, etc., but these are gone, although part of the old brick retaining wall remains. Snowdrops brought from England by the first owner still blossom every spring, and a rose planted by Louis Philippe survives. Windows upstairs on the garden side of the house have charming little iron balconies, while on the lower floor, a broad semi-enclosed piazza, like a modern sun parlor, runs across the back.

Much space has been given this old house for several reasons. In the first place, it is a beautiful example of its period; it is in perfect condition, and much history and romance are connected with it.

As has been stated, the first owner was a man of prominence, and his wife, one of the Izards, belonged to another prominent family. The last colonial governor, Sir William Campbell, married another Izard, a cousin of Mrs. Brewton, and stayed in this house while his own residence was being prepared for him.

Shortly after his arrival in Charleston, a delegation from the Provincial Congress waited on him, and requested permission to present an address. This " was brought by ten newly appointed captains and colonels, only two beside his host, Mr. Brewton, retaining their specific designations and costumes."

The address set forth that "we readily profess our loyal attachment to our Sovereign, his Crown and Dignity," but went on to enumerate certain intolerable grievances, for which they asked redress.

Sir William was "very thoughtful" after the address was read, and called Mr. Brewton from his bed in the middle of the night, and begged him to implore the Committee to use more moderate language. Mr. Brewton consulted with three of the gentlemen, but they thought it impossible to change the wording.

Then for the first time, tragedy touched the house. Shortly before the Revolution, Miles Brewton, his wife and children set sail from Charleston for New York, and nothing was ever heard of the vessel or of a single passenger. Whether they were attacked by pirates, and made to walk the plank—and at that time pirates infested these shores — or whether the ship with all aboard was lost in one of those terrible storms frequent around Cape Hatteras was never known. The house passed then to Brewton's two sisters, and one of these, Mrs. Rebecca Motte, was living in it when the British occupied Charleston. They had already seized and fortified her plantation home, Mt. Joseph, on the Congaree River. She it was who sent her three charming daughters up into the attic, for she was unwilling to have them seen by her uninvited guests. Food was carried secretly to them by a faithful old slave.

Mrs. Motte always presided at her table with all the formality of a hostess entertaining, as long as Sir Henry Clinton, Lord Rawdon and their staff remained, and the story goes that when they left, Sir Henry thanked her for her hospitality, but regretted that he had not been permitted to make the acquaintance of her family.

The three fair daughters later married distinguished Americans; John Middleton, of Lee's Legion, General Thomas Pinckney, son of Eliza Lucas, and Captain William Alston, of Marion's brigade. The latter, it is said, built the Alston house at No. 70 Tradd Street, still a residence, although its old-time appearance is marred by the addition of a modern bay window.

Mrs. Rebecca Motte is justly called a heroine. Left a widow early in the Revolution, she was living in a new house in Orangeburg County when the British arrived there, took possession of it, fortified it by digging a deep ditch around the house, topping this ditch with a high parapet, and called it Fort Motte.

Mrs. Motte and her family took shelter in a nearby farmhouse. Then came Generals Francis Marion and Henry Lee. They besieged Fort Motte, then, learning of the approach of British reinforcements, deliberated. Military tactics dictated firing the house, and thus driving out its defenders, but they hesitated to do this, because it belonged to a widow and kinswoman.

" Burn it," she is said to have urged. " Burn it. God forbid that I should bestow a single thought on my little concerns, when the independence of my country is at stake. No, sir, if it were a palace, it should go."

She went into the farmhouse, and fetched some East Indian arrows and a bow adapted for the purpose, and with the help of these, the roof of her house was set on fire, and the garrison of a hundred men surrendered. She then gave a banquet, beneath a long arbor, to the officers on both sides, and " by her gentleness, and tact soon had victor and vanquished conversing pleasantly together."[6]

A dinner guest in the Miles Brewton house before the Revolution

[6] Horry's *Life of General Marion.*

was Josiah Quincy, of Boston, who came to Charleston for his health, in 1773. He was amazed, as he wrote in letters, at Charleston's crowded harbor, the Charles Town library, founded in 1748. Charleston was one of the first cities in the colonies to establish one, and even before this the Puritans had a circulating library, the books kept in the house of one of their members, Henry Smith, of Beech Hill, Goose Creek. Books were sent back and forth by a negro slave, who carried them in a cowhide bag to protect them from the weather.

Quincy also went to a dancing assembly during his stay in Charleston, where he found "the dancing good, the music bad, the gentlemen many of them dressed with elegance and richness uncommon with us. Many of them with swords on."

The British left one permanent souvenir of their occupancy of the Brewton house. On the black marble mantel in the sitting room is scratched a profile portrait of Sir Henry Clinton. Seen in the right light, it is clearly distinguishable.

Again, in this room or the drawing room above, Mrs. Peronneau and other patriotic women appealed to Balfour and Lord Rawdon to spare the life of the patriot, Isaac Y. Hayne, then imprisoned in the basement dungeons of the old Exchange, and appealed in vain.

The great-great-grandchildren of Rebecca Motte now own and occupy this house.

From 1864 to 1865, it was occupied by the Federal Generals Hatch and Meade.

Three Charleston houses are pointed out as *the* one from which Francis Marion made his fateful leap.

Apparently the best claim to this honor is that of the old house on the corner of Orange and Pringle Streets, first owned by Colonel John Stuart, commissioner of Indian affairs in colonial days. A consistent Tory, when the Revolution was imminent, he sold the house and returned to England. In this, now known as the Pringle house, the very window of the second story corner room is pointed out as that from which Marion leaped. The story is as follows.

The gentleman then living in this house used to give sumptuous stag entertainments. He had a fine wine cellar, and in order that his guests should do full justice to the food, the Madeira and port wines, he was accustomed to lock the dining or supper room doors until he thought that a sufficient quantity had been consumed. It is said that this custom was not his alone.

Now Marion was the most temperate of men, something which must have stood him in good stead later, when he was often making a meal of sweet potatoes only, cooked under what one writer has styled as long a list of oak trees as there are beds in which George Washington is said to have slept.

At all events, Marion decided that he had drunk enough wine, and finding the door into the hall locked, and his host either unwilling to open it, or unobservant, the future " Swamp Fox " decided to escape by the window, jumped from it, and broke his leg. He was sent out to Charleston to his home to recuperate, and when the leg mended, made his way to North Carolina. Here Rutledge gave him a commission as Colonel, and ordered him to report with all the men that he could assemble to General Gates. When he and his band of shabby, ill-clad followers presented themselves, the General was not in the least impressed, and to get rid of them, ordered Marion to destroy every boat in the Wateree River which the British might use to escape from Charleston. His success made the General change his opinion of the new helper.

Francis Marion was descended from French Huguenots who settled in 1690 on the Santee River. He was born in St. John's Parish, Berkeley, South Carolina, and received but a limited education before going to sea. At sixteen, he was shipwrecked and almost lost his life in a hurricane in the West Indies, so yielding to his mother's entreaties, he left the sea, but when only seventeen was a lieutenant in Moultrie's cavalry, fighting against the Cherokee Indians.

Not handsome, with distant manner, he was none the less tremendously popular with his men, and probably harried the British during the Revolution more successfully than any other man in command of similar forces.

The Governor Rutledge house. Although the double piazzas give it a modern look, it was the home of " Dictator " Rutledge. Shortly after the War between the States, the Federal Courts met here.

The Governor Bennett house, Charleston, S. C. Although more modern than many of Charleston's old homes, this is interesting because of its builder's history, and of the events which occurred here during his lifetime.

The Washington house. This was the residence, after the Revolution, of General William Washington, kinsman of the President.

One of the best known "sweet potato stories" told of Marion narrates that a British officer, sent from the garrison at Georgetown under flag of truce, to negotiate terms, was invited to dine with him. Roast potatoes, served on pieces of bark composed the dinner, and the Englishman is said to have declared on his return that they could not hope to conquer men who were willing to live and fight on such frugal fare.

On Broad Street is the home of R. Goodwin Rhett, who has been Mayor of Charleston, and is now President of the Chamber of Commerce, but the house has claims to attention far antedating this. Three stories high, of brick with piazzas across the front on two stories added some seventy-five years ago, and apparently a fine modern residence, it none the less was the home of "Dictator" Rutledge, and was built in 1760.

The Dictator, John Rutledge, was the son of a physician who emigrated to this country from England in 1730. John and his two brothers were sent back to England to be educated, but there was never any doubt as to the side on which the young man's sympathies would be when stormy days for the colonies drew near. John was a member of the Stamp Act Congress in 1765, of the Continental Congress in 1774–75 in Philadelphia, and later a member of the Council of Safety. In 1776, he was chosen first president of the separate state of South Carolina, and Captain Barnard Elliott in his diary tells of orders that "Col. Robert's regiment of artillery and all the militia now in Chas. Towne under the command of Col. Pinckney do, at 11 o'clock this morning, draw up two deep in Broad Street, on the side opposite St. Michael's Church . . . in order to receive the Hon'ble John Rutledge Esq., constitutionally appointed by the Hon'ble the Legislature as President and Commander-in-Chief of the same."[7]

Later, Rutledge was elected Governor of South Carolina, and when the British occupied Charleston joined General Greene's army in North Carolina, was again South Carolina's governor after the war, and given absolute authority, with the title of Dictator, which title he held from

[7] *Historic Houses of South Carolina*, Harriette Kershaw Leiding.

1780 to 1782. He was a member of Congress, and also of the convention which framed the Constitution of the United States.

The present owner of the house is a descendant of the old Rhett family.

Shortly after the War between the States, in the drawing room on the second floor of this house, the United States courts were held for some time.

Two doors away is another old house, once the property of early settlers, the Izards, who also owned estates along the Ashley River. A tablet on this house states that it was built in 1827 by Ralph Izard, and bought in 1829 by Colonel Thomas Pinckney, Mrs. Izard's brother-in-law, but a house here belonged to the Izards in 1757. The family of the present owner has owned it for almost a century. It is a three story brick house, covered with stucco, with heavy old shutters still in place, and the entrance at one side.

Mrs. Brewton's sister, Mrs. Daniel Blake, owned what was later known as the William E. Huger house on Meeting Street. Here Lord and Lady Campbell lived during the brief period that he was Governor, until he left in 1775, taking refuge on H.M.S. Tamar, of Sir Peter Parker's fleet, in Charleston harbor. He was rowed from the foot of his garden down Vanderhorst Creek, and out into the harbor. His wife, "a young lady esteemed as one of the most considerable fortunes in the province," — she had been a Miss Izard, and was thus described on the occasion of her marriage by the Charleston Gazette, in 1763 — remained behind him, and later is noted as protesting vehemently when her "chariot and horses" were seized in reprisal for the taking of a sum of money by the captain of H.M.S. Scorpion, from a patriot ship bound for the West Indies. The house in which they lived was sold to Colonel Lewis Morris of New York, who styled himself Morris of Morrisania. Later, after he and Daniel Huger married sister heiresses, daughters of William Elliott, Morris sold his house to his nephew, Daniel Elliott Huger.

The house is noted for two serious accidents which happened to guests on the front steps. The first occurred when part of the bull's-eye window in the gable fell on the head of Francis Kinlock. It was he who vainly tried to rescue Lafayette from his prison in Olmutz. Kinlock after the accident was carried into the house here, and Mrs. Huger's protests against the performing of the dangerous operation of trepanning are supposed to have saved the young man's life. At all events, he recovered.

The second accident was more tragic. A young Englishman was a guest at the time of the severe earthquake of 1886. Alarmed, he ran out of the house, and on the steps was struck on the head by a piece of the parapet from the roof, and killed.

This house was built about 1760. The panels in the drawing room were mirrors, but these were removed and sent north by Federal soldiers.

Another old house, No 2 Ladson Street, was occupied at the time of the Revolution by Mrs. Tidyman. She was a Royalist, and gave a ball at which Captain Archy Campbell, known as " Mad Archy," met Miss Pauline Phelps, and fell in love with her. He made a bet of fifty pounds that he would marry her, but she did not smile on his suit. He then invited her to take a drive with him in his gig, behind his fast horse, and during a long drive over rough country roads, made furious love to her, and so frightened her that when he finally drew rein at the Goose Creek parsonage, out in the country, she was in a half fainting condition. He requested the parson to marry them, and when that gentleman demurred, declaring that the lady must first consent, Campbell drew a pistol, and held it towards the priest in so threatening a manner that priest and lady offered no further objections, and the ceremony was performed. In less than a year the wild lover was captured by patriots, and in trying to escape was killed.

Still another old house in excellent condition, built in or soon after 1768, stands on the Battery.

Lieutenant-Colonel William Washington, a cousin of the Commander-in-Chief, won renown as an officer in the Revolutionary Army until the battle of Eutaw Springs, September 8, 1781, when his regiment was cut to pieces, and he himself wounded and taken prisoner.

When the British evacuated Charleston he remained behind, and in 1785 bought this house on the west corner of Church Street and South Bay. Three years later, he was appointed a Brigadier-General, and lived here until his death.

An attractive old house on Ashley Avenue has a beautiful spiral staircase with a mahogany handrail about which a story is told. The first owner drew the plans for the house himself, called in an architect, and bade him build it while he, the owner, was absent in Europe. In vain the architect tried to interrupt the directions. Each time that he opened his mouth, the testy owner bade him build exactly according to the plans, declaring that he knew perfectly well how he wanted his house. The architect had no choice but to remain silent after these rebuffs.

When the owner returned from Europe, he was all eagerness to see the completed house. There it stood, two stories high, with an attic.

"But where are the stairs?" he cried, after entering, and finding none.

"That is what I tried to tell you," replied the architect. "You provided none."

Of course stairs had to be built, and this is supposed to explain the spiral staircase, as the only kind which could be added without changing the arrangement of rooms, but there are several other old houses in Charleston with spiral staircases.

There is also supposed to be a secret stair hidden somewhere in the walls, and what resembles a panel in the wall of the second floor, near the main stairs has been thought the entrance to such a secret passage. If there is a spring to open it, it has not been found, although the present mistress of the house hopes to discover the secret.

All of the timbers in this house, considerably more than a century old, are handhewn, and when electricity was installed, the contractor declared that he lost money on the job, so thick and hard were the beams through which openings for the wires must be cut.

In the yard still stands the two-story brick house, the slave quarters, and bells of different sizes still connect it with the main house. Each servant thus knew from what room a bell rang, and who was responsible for answering it.

A gas filling station in front of the old Manigault house on King Street partly conceals it from view. The original entrance was on the side street, facing the park which lies between King Street and the Second Presbyterian church. Doubtless this park once formed part of the grounds of the house. The original circular lodge entrance stands here, but between it and the house a lot is now fenced off, so one must pass through a break in the old wall on King Street, partly circle the house, and then mount a flight of steps to the decaying old piazza and great wide door. The house was designed in 1765 by Gabriel Manigault, architect of Charleston's City Hall, the Orphan House, Hall of the South Carolina Society, etc., for his son, Joseph Manigault, Speaker of the South Carolina House of Commons.

Gabriel Manigault for more than twenty years furnished the Charleston Library with room and book space rent free, and was for many years vice-president of the association, the Governor being honorary president. After the Powder Magazine on Cumberland Street was no longer needed for storing ammunition, Manigault used it for his wine cellar.

Opposite the front door of the King Street house, at the rear of the very broad hall, a staircase ascends, with a broad landing beneath a window set in a semi-circular bay. A large drawing room, now rapidly falling to ruin, lies at the right of the hall, and two rooms, smaller, but of good size, are at the left. Behind the drawing room space is filled with the back stairs, running from basement to attic. Even this stair has a mahogany handrail and bannisters, while those of the main staircase are beautifully handcarved, the treads of mahogany as well. Upstairs are five large rooms, and throughout the house are hand carved doors, mantels and cornices, and the ruins of once handsome ceilings. The house is in a most neglected state, divided into cheap tenements, and nothing done to keep it in repair.

From the house a secret passage, no longer open, ran down to the sea. One also led from the cellar to the roof. At the side of a closet on the second floor, beside where once were shelves, one may still see the opening into the attic above. Probably this was once entirely concealed by a panel.

It is told that when the British were advancing on Charleston, Gabriel Manigault, having lost his son, came with his fifteen year old grandson, Peter, to fight in the trenches, and defend his home.

Efforts were made to preserve this house when it had become undesirable as a first class residence, but these failed, and its survival is now probably but a matter of a few years.

The Bennett house on Lucas Street is not much over a century old, built about 1814, but there is interesting history connected with it.

Governor Thomas Bennett was wealthy and popular. During his term of office, Denmark Vesey, a mulatto, came from his native San Domingo to South Carolina. He had witnessed or shared in the uprising of the blacks on that island, and succeeded in persuading some of the Carolina negroes to rise. A few faithful slaves in Charleston learned of the plan, and went to the whites with their information. The white citizens armed, and the negro ringleaders were overpowered and taken without bloodshed. Vesey and thirty-four others were hanged to a tree which still stands almost in the centre of Ashley Avenue, which street when laid out was turned slightly to spare the tree. A number of other negroes were transported, and four white men found implicated, a German, a Scotchman, a Spaniard and one Charlestonian were imprisoned and fined.

In 1821, Governor Bennett sought to curb traffic in slaves between the states. His own slave, Rolla, had been one of the ringleaders in the planned uprising. Vesey's two chief lieutenants were Peter Popas, who had been a trusted slave, and Gulla Jack, whom the other negroes believed to be a " conjurer," and the crab claws which he distributed among them they fancied rendered them invulnerable.

It was George, a heavily built mulatto belonging to the Wilson family, a blacksmith who worked out, giving only a small percentage of his earnings to his owners, who exposed the insurrection to the whites. George could neither read nor write, but was a devout Methodist. Of the men hanged, three were Governor Bennett's slaves. As a reward for warning the authorities, George and another slave, Peter, were given their freedom, and a pension of $50 a year for life.

The ceilings in the Bennett house are twenty-one feet high, the rooms average twenty-two feet square, and there are twenty-one of them. The spiral staircase is an architectural marvel, always commented on by members of that profession, for it is not attached to any wall, merely to floors and ceilings.

Governor Bennett started lumber mills near the house which are still in operation, and aided the infant rice industry. He conveyed to his son-in-law, Jonathan Lucas, the land on West Point, in this part of the city, where stands a rice pounding mill, now for many years inactive, even as the wharves where many rice laden boats used to tie up, are deserted and rotting.

Soon after 1830, James Nicholson built the house in which is now located the Misses McBee school for girls. This place was originally an estate outside the city, known as Ashley Hall, and a small, one-story brick building still standing on the grounds is said to have been built by Stephen Bull, one of the early and prominent settlers in the vicinity of Beaufort. Both his son and grandson were Royal Governors. William Bull, the son, had enormous grants of land, and in this little building it is said that he signed a treaty with the Indians, under Attakullakulla, which lasted until the Revolution.

In this fine house are a circular staircase rising for three stories to the roof, and beautiful and elaborately carved woodwork of mahogany.

Chapter III

EARLY CHARLESTONIANS' COUNTRY ESTATES

O N THE old estates outside of the city of Charleston, along the Ashley and Cooper Rivers, some of the early mansions have survived; others have been so re-modeled as to be practically new, while of the rest, a number have entirely disappeared, or have been replaced with modern residences. Part of this country was devastated by the British during the Revolution, and again later by the northern armies during the Civil War, while other places escaped this devastation for no apparent reason.

Only a short drive from Charleston, although in part over a road most trying to automobile springs, is what is still called Fenwick's Castle.

A Fenwick commanded a company of militia during the French invasion of 1706. Another, Edward, was a member of His Majesty's Council in 1747, married one of Ralph Izard's daughters, and for second wife, Mary Drayton, of Drayton Hall, which will be mentioned again. The Fenwicks were of a titled English family, and Edward was sometimes known as Lord Ripon, but they apparently soon dropped their titles.

Turning off the John's Island County Road, the only good bit traversed on this visit, one takes a rough, deeply rutted side road, and eventually enters what must once have been a broad avenue, shaded by magnificent old trees. Some of these remain, but between them and the narrow, rough cart track, all that is left of the avenue, small trees, bushes and undergrowth have sprung up.

The house, which may be seen whenever the negro caretaker who lives nearby is at home, is of brick, two stories high, on a thick-walled high basement. In this basement or cellar is an old circular, brick lined well, and a gaping hole, the beginning of a passage running down to the river, but now so blocked and filled in that it would be very difficult to enter. It is said that this basement was an earlier building, used as a fort.

Doubtless there once were lawns and gardens sloping down to the river, but no trace of them remains. There are even no steps left by which to reach the two once fine doorways opening into the hall which runs through the house. One must use a ladder, nor does this seem very safe, for the floor and pillars of the porticoes are rotting, and there are gaps in the boards.

The doorway towards the river, not that to which the drive now leads, was probably used as the main entrance, for it is larger.

Hardly a pane of glass remains in the windows, across which the heavy old shutters are barred. On one side of the wide hall are two square rooms, on the other a passage opens, with rooms on either side, the house at that end being semi-circular. The same arrangement is repeated on the floor above. Upper and lower rooms were once paneled in cedar and pine, with mahogany woodwork. The latches and hinges were of silver and the mantels highly decorated, but unless something is soon done to prevent, there will be nothing left of the house but a brick shell. Even the fine old doors have been replaced by the cheapest of painted ones.

The place is owned by a man who has no wish to live in it — and indeed considerable money would have to be spent to make it habitable. The land is leased in small tracts to tenant farmers.

There is no trace now of the race course which Lord Ripon is said to have laid out in front of the house, so that his guests might watch the races from the windows. The story goes that one of his daughters fell in love with a young Englishman, who brought over some thoroughbred horses for her father. He would not hear of such a match for his daughter, and the couple thereupon eloped. The father, hotly pursuing the young couple, overtook them and inflicted a horrible punishment, for he hanged the young man to a tree, as he sat his horse, and compelled the unfortunate girl to lash her lover's horse from beneath him. She died of a broken heart, and probably it is her ghost that is said to haunt the upper corner room on the river side.

Edward Fenwick was a loyalist, and his estates were confiscated, which was probably the first step downward in the history of the once splendid old place.

Considered the oldest house in this part of the state, and the first one of brick outside of Charleston is Medway, home of Landgrave Smith, one of South Carolina's earliest English settlers. He came to this country soon after 1679, and there is a tradition that here he married a beautiful baroness.

Of Medway two stories are told. The first that Thomas Smith, the first Landgrave, built it for his son, Thomas, also known as Landgrave. Probably both men, as well as the second Landgrave's son, the Reverend Josiah Smith, all occupied it at different times.

The other story says that the house was built by Jean de Arsens, Sieur de Wernhaut, whose widow later married Smith. If this is true, instead of standing on a tract of land originally granted the Landgrave, it probably adjoined his grant. It would be interesting to trace the ancestry of this Sieur de Wernhaut. Who was he, and from what country did he come? Could it be from Brittany, and would that explain the curious end gables which rise in steps? There is a tradition in parts of Brittany that by building the outer walls with the effect of steps, evil spirits might be induced to walk down from the roof, and leave the house in peace.

At all events, whichever of the two men built the house, the steps remain for us to examine. Built about 1682, two stories in height, with large, low-ceiled rooms, the "inferior bricks" of its walls may have been made on the place, for it is told that most of those used in building Fort Sumter were made at Medway. It is on or near a tract of land granted to the first Landgrave by the Earl of Craven, and is fifteen or sixteen miles from Charleston. Before the War between the States, there was a race track at Medway, and the owner raised blooded horses. While many ghosts, including that of the Landgrave, are said to haunt the old rooms, there is one particularly touching story of a ghostly visitor.

Always at the season when races used to be run here, there appears a lovely young woman. Her ghost wanders through the house, and even those who have never seen her may admit that they have heard the rustle of her gown.

It seems that while the horse racing owner was alive, this young woman, a recent bride, came with her husband to pay a visit. Every afternoon, as it grew dusk, she waited and watched from a window for the return of her young husband. One day they brought him home to her on a stretcher, dead. Since her own death her ghost has haunted the house.

Landgrave Smith is buried on the old lawn, close to the house. At his death, in 1794, he left a " silver tobacco box " to Summerville Boone, who lived four miles away. Perhaps this is the box to which the Ancient Lady refers.

The Izards had estates in this section, but of their place, The Elms, nothing but ruins remain. In this house Lafayette was entertained in great state, one of the octagonal wings being fitted up especially for the occasion. This wing was always thereafter called " Lafayette's wing." In the old Goose Creek church nearby may be found a tablet to Ralph, the first Izard to come to this country, who is buried in the old churchyard here. His hatchment, said to be one of but two existing in this country, still hangs on the wall of the church.

Still nearer the church than Medway is the Oaks, a beautiful modern house in colonial style, but an old resident of Charleston assured the writer that the original, home of the Middleton family, prominent in the annals of Charleston and its environs from early times, was not as has been stated, entirely destroyed by fire, and replaced by the handsome modern residence. On the contrary, she says, part of the old house survived, and was included in the new one. At all events, no one can deny the age of the magnificent live oaks, which border the avenue leading to the door. Veiled and draped in grey moss, their beauty is such that they are not easily forgotten.

Approached by the bridge across Goose Creek, where in early days there was only a ford, the house is charmingly situated, set in a clearing, with lawns sloping down to the winding stream. It is told that a motion picture director obtained permission to film the beautiful avenue of live oaks for a picture laid in colonial times.

Arthur Middleton, one of the Royal Governors, was the first of his name to come to South Carolina. His son, Henry, President of the first Congress in 1774, married Lady Mary, daughter of the Earl of Cromartie, who was banished from England for corresponding with the "Old Pretender." After being left a widow, she died at sea, while returning in 1789 from London to Charleston. Another Middleton place in this section, Crowfield, was occupied by a member of the family until his death in 1876. This was Henry Middleton, great-great-grandson of the original "emigrant." His grandfather, Arthur Middleton, was a "Signer."

Arthur Middleton built Crowfield, naming it, so the story goes, after family property in England. His son, William, returned to England, and the place was then sold out of the family in 1776, but later re-purchased by a Middleton.

A letter written by Miss Eliza Lucas, the future Mrs. Pinckney, gives an account of this old place. She made "an agreeable tour" to "several very handsome gentlemen's seats, at all of wch. we were entertained with the most friendly politeness. The first we arrived at was Crowfield, Mr. William Middleton's seat, where we spent a most agreeable week. The house stands a mile from but in sight of the road, and makes a very handsome appearance; as you draw nearer new beauties discover themselves; first the beautiful vine mantling the wall with delicious clusters, next a large pond in the midst of a spacious green presents itself as you enter the gate. The house is well furnished, the rooms well contrived and elegantly furnished. From the back door is a wide walk a thousand feet long, each side of wch. nearest the house is a grass plat ornamented in a serpentine manner with flowers; next to that on the right hand is what immediately struck my rural taste, a thicket of young tall live oaks, where a variety of airy choristers poured forth their melody, and my darling, the mocking bird, joyned in the concert, enchanted me with his harmony. Opposite on the left hand is a large square bowling green, sunk a little below the level of the rest of the garden, with a walk quite round bordered by a double row of fine large flowering Laurel and Catalpas — wch. afforded both shade and beauty."

Still another Middleton place, Otranto, has also survived, and is now a club house. It is a story and a half building, with dormer windows on the upper floor, and a wide porch supported on heavy pillars, running along three sides. The porch was probably a later addition.

There is some doubt as to when the present house was built. Arthur Middleton must have lived here very early in the 18th century, and in 1706, as shown on old records, he donated four acres of land for the parsonage at Goose Creek. Although the old church there is in good condition, there seem to be no traces of the old parsonage, and in 1796 Otranto was occupied by the rector, the Reverend Porgson. About this clergyman Mrs. Leiding tells a delightful tale.

He was an ardent fisherman, and one Sunday set out for church, his sermon under his arm, but his rod in hand. On the Goose Creek bridge he could not resist the temptation to throw a line, and suddenly hooked a big trout. So interested in his prize did he become that all unheeded, his sermon slipped from beneath his arm, and fell into the stream.

The Otranto place was later occupied by Dr. Garden, after whom the botanist, Linnaeus, named the gardenia.

Middleton Gardens, now a Pinckney place, was originally part of the old Middleton grant. It is noted for the beautiful gardens stretching down to the river, only less lovely than the famous Magnolia Gardens, which were laid out in 1750. An old Tudor house at

Middleton Gardens was burned, but one wing was saved, and around this the present residence was built. Set back at some distance from the highroad, the gardens are behind, on the river side. Arthur Middleton, the Signer, is buried here.

Beautiful Belvidere, on the west side of the Cooper River, is now the Charleston Country Club.

Although the house is well over a century old, it is the second one built on this site. The name, Belvidere, was given it by the Shubrick family, wealthy English merchants, who bought the land before the Revolution, and built a house. Mrs. Leiding says that it was the home of three of the Colonial governors, Craven, Johnson and Glen, but in that case, a still earlier house must have stood there.

During the Revolution, at the time when Charleston was evacuated by the British, the American troops were stationed at Belvidere, and kept there until the British embarked and left the harbor, that there might be no conflict.

In 1796, on a Sunday, as the family were coming from church, they saw smoke, and when they reached home, found that it had burned to the ground. The story goes that it had been set on fire by a negro maid, who was in love with the English gardener. He had suggested that she steal the family valuables, and when she had done so, he fled, leaving her alone to face the consequences. For some strange reason, she believed that by burning down the house the theft might escape detection, but such was not the case, for the terrified woman is said to have confessed both the theft and arson, for which she was hanged. Her ghost is believed to haunt the avenue where she used to meet her faithless lover.

The house was soon re-built; it is this structure which serves as the Country Clubhouse. It is square, two-storied, of wood, with an attic, and set on a high basement of brick; two small, detached buildings are nearby. Square, high ceiled rooms, opening from a wide hall with a fanlighted entrance are found here, as is usual in houses of its period. The old dining room on the main floor has a corresponding apartment, the former ballroom, on the second floor, with decorated door-ways, and a fine mantel with an elaborate design of shells and sea-weed.

The builder, Thomas Shubrick, distinguished himself in the Revolution, and married Miss Sarah Motte — not one of Rebecca Motte's daughters, but perhaps a niece. She was a beauty and belle, and for these reasons, was selected to sit opposite Washington at the dinner given him in 1791.

Two of the sons of this couple distinguished themselves at sea, Captain Templer in fighting the Barbary pirates. He was sent home to bear news of the victory over them, but the Hornet, on which he sailed, was lost, and he perished with it. Captain Edward Rutledge Shubrick was also lost at sea, and a monument was erected to him by the officers and men of his frigate, the Columbia, in old St. Philip's churchyard.

Just why, in view of his patriotic services, the estates of Thomas Shubrick should have been sequestered is hard to understand. He did recover them, but after the death of Captain Templer, who inherited the property, his widow never lived there, and it passed through several hands before being eventually acquired by the Country Club.

A curious story is told of Mrs. Thomas Shubrick. One night she awoke suddenly from a dream in which she had seen her brother, floating on something white, out at sea. She wakened her husband and related the dream, but he reassured her, and she fell asleep again. But when she had the same dream three times, she finally insisted that her husband get up, dress, go to town, and hire a pilot boat to search the path of incoming vessels. Her husband yielded to her entreaties, but for three days the pilot boat cruised in vain. Then, when all must have been thoroughly convinced that the lady was quite mad, they spied something floating. Going nearer, it proved to be a hencoop, and clinging to it, almost exhausted, was Mrs. Shubrick's brother. The vessel on which he had sailed for Charleston had been lost at sea.

A long avenue leads up to the porticoed Hampton. Entering, there is a spacious hall, the walls hung with old family portraits; and some fine old furniture has been preserved as well. On the first floor, in a wing, is a great ballroom, with a fireplace so large that it is said that five people can stand in it at once. Some of the old landscape paper, too, may still be seen on the walls of Hampton's large chambers. Although this house was built in 1730, the original, about a mile away, is still older. Originally owned by Horrys, it has its ghost, but such a mild one! Apparently it has never been seen, merely heard, with a sound "like someone moving a carpet stealthily across the floor."

Fairfield, oldest place on the Santee, is the Pinckney estate, owned by Thomas, the first of that name to come to South Carolina in 1692. He it was who built the house on the corner of Tradd Street and South Bay, Charleston, mentioned in the preceding chapter.

Thomas, the son of Charles Pinckney and Eliza Lucas, inherited Fairfield. From here he went as Minister to the Court of St. James while Jefferson was President, and went reluctantly. His wife is said to have "been in tears almost ever since her husband's appointment." However, he served his country well there for four years, and later was Minister to Spain. Mrs. Pinckney and Martha Washington were on terms of cordial friendship. The Pinckneys visited at Mt. Vernon, and the two ladies evidently exchanged garden seeds, for a letter written by Mrs. Washington, thanking the other for a gift of "mellon seeds," still exists.

Mrs. Leiding quotes from the letters of an Englishman, who visited this country, spending three years here, and returning to England in 1824, published a book of his travels. This man, Adam Hodgson, brought letters to General Thomas Pinckney, and was entertained by him at Fairfield. Hodgson was amazed at the number and size of its windows, and comments upon the tax on panes of glass in his native country. He also says:

"My host had an excellent library, comprising many recent and valuable British publications, and a more extensive collection of agri-

Photo by George W. Johnson

Medway, the first brick house built outside of Charleston, S. C., and from bricks said to have been made on the plantation. The gables, like steps, are very unusual, and may have been built by Sieur de Wernhaut, husband of the lady who later married one of the Landgraves Smith.

Headquarters House or Fenwick Castle, John's Island. Cornwallis made his headquarters at one time in this old house now rapidly falling to ruin. It was built by one of South Carolina's early settlers, Lord Ripon, who dropped his title. Nearby, the first owner laid out a race course, but no trace of it now remains.

Mulberry Castle, with four quaint "flankers." This is one of the pre-Revolutionary estates near Charleston, kept in good repair and occupied. It was used as a refuge and fort for families in the neighborhood during early fighting with the Indians.

cultural works than I had ever seen before in a private library. In works on botany and American ornithology the supply was large."

It was not so surprising as his guest thought that General Pinckney was interested in agriculture. He inherited this interest from his grandmother certainly, and probably from his grandfather as well.

Eliza Lucas Pinckney took the greatest interest in the produce of her adopted country. She even made experiments in silk culture on her plantation, and in the Powder Magazine, Charleston, is preserved a dress of brocade in a charming design of flowers, on a gold colored background, which was made from silk which she raised. The produce of her silk worms was sent to England, and three dress patterns woven from it, one being presented to the Queen of England, another to Lord Chesterfield, and the third returned to America for Mrs. Pinckney's own wear. Another dress of "dove's neck" brocade, with a design of flowers and palms on the dove colored background, carefully preserved in the Magazine, was also Mrs. Pinckney's property, and is likewise believed, although not known positively, to have been made from South Carolina silk.

Before her marriage, she had "the business of three plantations to transact," after her father returned to Antigua, for her mother's health continued poor, in spite of the change in climate for which they had come to South Carolina. Eliza Lucas is said to have anticipated, by experiments on her plantation, the raising of several varieties of tropical fruits, and futhermore it was on her plantation, along Wappoo Creek, that the first cultivated indigo was raised in South Carolina, in 1741–42. The plant had been discovered growing wild here.

Mrs. Ravenel tells an anecdote of Fairfield as happening "while the place belonged to Mrs. Rebecca Motte." Fairfield never belonged to the Mottes, but Mrs. Rebecca's daughter married General Thomas Pinckney, the owner.

The mistress of the house was talking to a young American soldier one morning, when British soldiers were seen approaching. With ready presence of mind, she rolled the young American up in a great rug, and placed the roll against the wall, confident that it afforded a good hiding place. The soldiers arrived, and she proceeded to give her cook orders to prepare some chickens. Rashly the youth allowed his stomach to get the better of his discretion, for he stuck his head out of one end of the roll, and cried:

"Keep the giblets for me!" whereupon he was promptly made a prisoner.

Another charming old place, Drayton Hall, is in excellent condition as regards the house, but the grounds are neglected and sadly fallen from former days, since its owner visits it but seldom.

This property and the world famed Magnolia Gardens were originally one estate; then it was divided between two brothers. The old house on Magnolia was burned by Sherman's men, and a thoroughly modern one now stands in the beautiful gardens. During the season when the azaleas are loveliest, in March or early April, these gardens are open to the public.

The Draytons were early settlers here, although they did not receive their lands as an original grant, but purchased them. Entering from the highway, through fine gates, there is a long avenue, then another pair of gates, beside which is one of the fish ponds mentioned in Miss Lucas' letters, and which are characteristic of these river places. This one is now choked with waterlilies.

From the drive, one approaches the rear of the square, red brick house, with a portico to which a double flight of steps ascends. The real front is toward the river, and probably in the old days, gardens sloped down from house to river's edge. Much of the building material was brought from England, and inside the house is wainscoted from floor to ceiling.

Mrs. Leiding is responsible for the statement that the seal of South Carolina was designed by two gentlemen of the neighborhood; one side by Arthur Middleton, the other by Chief Justice Drayton. She also mentions the story that it was at Drayton Hall that Eliza Lucas met her future husband, Chief Justice Pinckney. The two Pinckney brothers and the future Chief Justice Drayton were fellow school-mates at Westminster, and later at Oxford University.

Lord Cornwallis occupied the house while its owner was attending the Continental Congress in Philadelphia, where he died during the convention sessions.

Several later generations of Draytons were physicians, and all of them took much interest in the gardens of Drayton Hall.

John Davis, in his *Travels in America* in 1798, speaks of Drayton Hall as "a venerable mansion," yet it was not then sixty years old. It had what was suspected of being a ghost, and many were the guests who, given a certain bedroom, retired, only to flee from the room with stories of the ghost they had seen. Later a more intrepid visitor did indeed awaken to see a figure in white, which vanished even as he watched it, but he discovered that the supposed ghost had left a sub-stantial impress on the bed where she had appeared to be sitting. It was discovered next day that the visitant was no ghost, but a sleep-walking daughter of the house. The gentleman " laid " the ghost, and married the daughter.

One of the descendants of the Draytons, a Grimke, was obliged to change his name to Drayton, that he might inherit the property through his mother, and thus a Drayton has always owned it.

Fairlawn, near the present village of Monck's Corner, on the Cooper River, was the seat of the only member of the Colleton family who came to live permanently in the colony, although they held large grants of land. This one was the great-grandson of the original Lord Proprietor, Sir John Colleton, named by Charles II of England as one of the grantees of the Province. Sir John and his older sons never visited the Province, but between the Ashley River and Wappoo Creek, the Waheewah Barony is supposed to be the site where Landgrave James Colleton, a younger son, built a fine residence. He was forced by his indignant subjects to leave. He also owned another barony, Wadpoo, on the Cooper River, where he had a fine stone house.

In 1726, the Honorable John Colleton came to live on Fairlawn Barony, which also belonged to the family. Here he built what was said to be a magnificent mansion. This was burned by the British during the Revolution, to drive out Marion and his men, for they had been greatly annoyed by this gallant band, who lay in ambush for them behind the great cedars of the avenue leading to the house. The British first used it for a time as a storehouse, burning it when driven out in 1781. Brick ruins remain, showing it to have been one of the largest houses of its time in the state. A rare book, printed in 1821, by Mrs. Graves, the daughter and heiress of this Sir John, tells of the destruction of her home.

"They burned down the mansion . . . and destroyed every building, including a Town built on the Barony for the residence of several people belonging to the estate, with the granaries, mills, etc. On this occasion, in addition to the furniture, paintings, and books, plate, etc., a large sum of money which was in my father's strong box, and my jewels, were lost, either destroyed or plundered."

The land on which Yeamans' Hall stands is said to have been purchased from the family of Governor John Yeamans by Governor Thomas Smith, and given to his son. In any case, a Governor Smith lived there as early as 1693. The old house stood in good condition until the earthquake of 1886, when it was severely damaged, and later burned. It has recently been repaired, a story and a half old building, and a number of bungalows have been built near it, all serving as living quarters during the summer and hunting seasons for a club of gentlemen of Charleston and the vicinity.

Mulberry Castle, the Broughton estate on the western branch of the Cooper River, was built in 1714, on land transferred six years earlier to Thomas Broughton by Sir John Colleton. It comprised 4423 acres, part of the original tract granted to Sir John's father, Sir Peter Colleton. There was some misunderstanding about the boundaries of the Broughton tract, and when Mr. Broughton began building, it was found that he had unwittingly encroached upon Sir John's estate of Fairlawn. The matter was easily adjusted between the two gentlemen by simply exchanging three hundred acres of each plantation.

The curious old house which Broughton then built on his land, for which he retained the early name of Mulberry, is said to be a replica of the old Broughton home at Seaton, England, as depicted on the Broughton family tree which they brought over to America with them. Thomas Broughton was the first of the Royal Lieutenant-Governors, and one of the signers of the Church Act, separating Church and State.

A two-story house, with dormer windows, the original Dutch roof now replaced by a mansard, it has at each corner a detached room, oddly known as a flanker. As is often the case, the bricks of which the house is built are said to have been brought from England. There does not seem to have been much clay suitable for brick-making in this part of the State. Medway seems the first of the Carolina estates in connection with which brick-making is mentioned.

The strongest house in this section of the country, on a high bluff, overlooking the river, Mulberry Castle was used as a refuge for women and children when Indians threatened, being one of the three " forts " mentioned as existing during the Indian wars of 1715.

Each of the flankers has a trap door in the floor, and beneath, a deep cellar, stone paved, in which ammunition was stored. Not many years ago, a small cannon, thought to pre-date the Revolution, was dug up in a field near the house.

Colonel Thomas Broughton figures prominently in the history of the Colony. He, Robert Gibbes and Fortescue Turbeville were deputies. The Governor, Tynte by name, died, and two sessions were held to elect his successor. Turbeville voted for Gibbes, who was thereupon proclaimed the Governor, but almost immediately thereafter Turbeville had an apoplectic stroke, and died. It was then discovered in some manner that he had voted at the first session for Broughton, but before the second had accepted a bribe, and cast his vote at the later session for Gibbes. Thereupon Broughton claimed the office, and came from Mulberry with an armed force to take possession. Gibbes closed the city gates, raised the drawbridge, but apparently Broughton's men gained entry, for there was fierce fighting in the square at the foot of Broad Street, Charleston, in front of the watch house, now the old Exchange, and in the "half moon opposite old St. Philip's," where now St. Michael's stands.

During the Revolution, Colonel Broughton, because of outspoken dislike of the British — this must have been the son of Thomas mentioned above — was " disciplined " by Cornwallis, and had a troop of horse stationed at Mulberry.

Colonel Broughton himself had a narrow escape from the British soldiers; his life probably, his liberty certainly, being saved by one of his negro " patroons " or shipmasters. The British were approaching Mulberry, and he could hardly have escaped them, but one of his rice boats lay at the landing in the river. To this boat Broughton ran, the negro made him lie flat on the deck, then covered him with a small boat. Although the soldiers searched the vessel, it apparently did not occur to them to lift the small boat, or the negro managed in some way to divert their attention. After their departure, Broughton was able to get away safely.

Thomas Broughton's ghost is said to walk up and down the stairs of Mulberry Castle, and along its corridors, but no explanation of the uneasy spirit wanderings has ever been given.

Two miles from Mulberry Castle, the old house known as Exeter is still standing. It, too, was built on land transferred by Sir John Colleton in 1767, to Mary Broughton, adjoining the tract already transferred by him to Thomas and Nathaniel Broughton. None the less, the house is supposed to have been built in 1712. Sir Nathaniel Johnson is believed to have lived here at one time, but the house has another interesting bit of history connected with it. It was the home of " Mad Archie " Campbell, whose exploit of carrying off the lady of his choice, and marrying her at the point of a pistol, has already been told.

" Mad Archie," who assuredly deserved his sobriquet, was descended from the royal house of Argyle. He was an ardent loyalist, and his early death came about in this manner:

A battle was fought at Videau's Ridge, between the British cavalry under Coffin, and the American troops under Colonel Richard Richardson. The Americans were at first victorious, and took a number of prisoners, among these " Mad Archie " who was captured by two Venning brothers. One of them took the prisoner on his horse behind him, and when Campbell attempted to escape, shot him dead.

Exeter is another of the two-story brick houses, the bricks laid in Flemish bond style. Several Revolutionary skirmishes occurred near the old house.

Adjoining Mulberry on the south is Lewisfield, standing on another part of the original Colleton grant, which was transferred in 1767 to Sedgwick Lewis. According to Johnson's *Traditions of the Revolution,* Miss Sarah Lewis in 1774 married Keating Simons, and it was this couple therefore who owned the place during the Revolution. When Charleston was taken by the British, Simons was allowed to return to his country home on parole. One day, Lord Cornwallis, on his way from Camden to Charleston, sent a courier to announce that he and his " family " would dine with Mr. Simons the following day.

" Accordingly Mr. Simons provided amply for his reception; killed a lamb for the occasion and poultry and other plantation fare in abundance, and arranged his sideboard in accordance. But his lordship had his own cook and baggage wagon with him, and was well served by those who knew his inclinations. Accordingly they killed the old ewe, the mother of the lamb; and on Mr. Simons telling the Scotchwoman, the cook, that this was unnecessary, and showing the provisions, she replied that his lordship knew how to provide for himself wherever he went."

Mr. and Mrs. Simons were kindly invited to have dinner with their unbidden guests. Mr. Simons accepted for himself, but announced that he " could not think of his wife becoming a guest instead of presiding at her own table," and told his lordship that his wife was "otherwise engaged." Mr. Simons had provided some of his best wines, but Cornwallis " enquired of his aides if they did not bring with them some of his old Madeira, and called for a bottle or two."

It proved afterwards that this Madeira had been carried off from Mr. Mazyck's plantation when Cornwallis visited it.[1]

Mrs. Leiding tells another good story about this old place.

At about this time, General Wade Hampton was paying court to Mr. Simon's sister. One day, arriving on horseback to visit the lady of his choice, he found a party of British, who had landed from two boats which had gone aground on the river bank. Hampton wheeled his horse, galloped back and shouted to his command; they came up, engaged the enemy, taking a number of prisoners, and burned the two boats. The British instantly suspected Mr. Simons, whether justly or unjustly does not appear, of complicity in the matter, and a company of Black Dragoons was sent from Charleston to capture him, and bring him in dead or alive. Simons learned of this, escaped to the swamp, and joined General Marion, with whom he remained until the end of the war.

Lewisfield is now a clubhouse for a group of Charleston gentlemen.

Where the Cooper River divides, forming two branches, on the point thus formed, Captain John Coming, already mentioned as an early landowner in Charleston, settled and named his place Coming's Tee. His wife, Affra Harleston, of well connected English folk, came to this country as a bondwoman, and one writer has thought to trace a romance here, namely, that the well-bred English girl fell in love with the captain, and took this step to join him, since her parents did not consider him good enough as a husband for their daughter. However this may be, the two were married shortly after their arrival in the new country.

They had no children, and at their death the property passed to Captain Coming's half brother, Elias Ball, who married one of Affra's sisters. She died about 1720, and eleven months later, the widower married Mary Delamere, who was about the age of his eldest daughter. They had seven children, four of whom died, and the property has remained in the Ball family ever since.

[1] *Historic Houses of South Carolina*, Harriette Kershaw Leiding.

An old brick house, built either by Captain Coming or Elias Ball, is still standing on the property.

A history of the Ball family describes the original house as having but two rooms on each of the two stories, with great old fireplaces, carved cornices and paneling. In 1833, an addition as large as the original house was built on by John Ball, who then owned it.

The grounds run down to the river, and it may also be approached by either of two avenues leading from the highroads along the two branches of the river.

There was a wedding here in 1750, when Henry Laurens married Eleanor Delamere, in " a splendid room, carpeted with crimson and black, set round with crimson covered chairs and tables . . . a pure white ceiling, bordered by gold . . . a shower of glass drops, hanging in silver chains from the centre was shimmering with little soft tapers." The son of this couple was Colonel John Laurens, of the Revolutionary Army.

In 1781, this Colonel Laurens was sent to France to negotiate a loan with the French Government. He was put off on one pretext and another, from March until May, when he became impatient, and resolved to take matters in his own hands, and wait for no more diplomatic dawdling. The Count de Vergennes, in an interview, spoke of the favor that Laurens was asking, but the Colonel refused to admit that it was a favor, and observed:

" But as the last argument I shall use with Your Excellency, the sword which I now wear in defense of France as well as of my own country, unless the succour I solicit is immediately accorded, I may be compelled within a short time to draw against France as a British subject."

The next day, he followed up this speech by himself handing a memorial to the King at a public function, to the astonishment of the monarch, and dismay of his courtiers. However, this manoeuvre was successful, and the following day, Baron Neckar told him that the Count de Grasse, with twenty-five ships, was on his way to America, and that a loan of 1,500,000 *livres* had been granted.

At Yorktown, when Colonel Ross complained for Lord Corn-wallis of the harshness of the terms that the Americans were demand-ing, namely, that the British troops should march out of the camp with colors cased, and drums beating a British or German march, Laurens replied:

"You seem to forget that I was a capitulant at Charleston, where General Lincoln, after a brave defense of six weeks in open trenches, by a very inconsiderable garrison, against the British Army and Fleet, was refused any other terms than marching out with colors cased, and drums *not* beating a British or German march."

James Burchell Richardson, Governor in 1802 of South Carolina, was a son of General Richard Richardson of Virginia, who came to South Carolina from Virginia in 1725. The General received a grant where now is Clarendon, and from 1754 to 1760 was member of the Assembly for Prince Frederick. He was Justice of the Peace, Colonel of militia, and during the Snow campaigns against the Tories, in 1775, quelled the revolt, for which he received the thanks of the Provincial Congress. Despite his age, he was a Brigadier General in the Revolutionary Army, and with the Hon. William H. Drayton, was commissioned by the Committee of Safety to "make progress through the back country to explain the causes of the present dis-pute between England and the Colonies, and secure a General Union of the people." He was more than seventy years old when Tarleton took him prisoner, dragging him from his home, and setting him on a horse behind a trooper, sent him to a British prison ship in Charleston harbor. While prisoner, Cornwallis offered him titles and offices under the Crown if he would join them, but he refused, and left the ship only to die before the end of the war. Soon after his death, Tarleton visited Clarendon, and with his own hand applied the torch, burning it to the ground, while he had General Richardson's body disinterred and left until the entreaties of the family finally persuaded him to allow it to be re-buried. No old Richardson place has survived.

A Richardson married Richard Manning, first Governor of South Carolina of that name, from 1824-26. This couple were the parents of John L. Manning, Governor in 1852, hence the former Miss Richardson was the wife, mother, sister and daughter of a governor, and had she lived long enough, would also have been the great-aunt of a third Richard Manning, the War governor, six of whose sons served in our army overseas. The house built by John L. Manning at great expense, still stands near Clarendon, but is no longer owned by the family.

Continuing towards Wedgefield, an old house known as Melrose, although sadly fallen from a former estate, deserves mention. It is the original house built by the " emigrant," Colonel Matthew Singleton, who was born in England in 1730, and came to this country as a youth, and was married here when but twenty years old. About the time of his marriage he built this house, a simple structure, with three rooms on each of two stories, and a great chimney at each end. Later it was enlarged, but the fine home which Colonel Matthew built for his son, Captain John, a few miles further up the road, when the son married Rebecca, daughter of General Richard Richardson, although it survived the Civil War, was burned shortly after that through the carelessness of a refugee family, allowed to take shelter there.

The same fate befell Home Place, another Singleton house built for Captain John's son (in which his daughter, Angelica, who married President Van Buren's son, and presided at the White House, was born), so only the oldest of the three Singleton houses survives. This family made a large fortune by shipping indigo and cotton down the river from Manchester, a thriving town near their estates, but it would be vain to search for any trace of Manchester now. It disappeared with the coming of the railway, even the chimneys of the old houses having been carried away.

Both Captain Singleton and his father served in the Revolutionary Army. The elder was one of those who drew up resolutions to be presented to the General Assembly of South Carolina, reading in part:

"Resolved to maintain our Constitutional Right at the hazzard of our lives and fortunes, and this to be laid before the General Assembly." He and the father of his daughter-in-law, General Richardson, were also delegates to the Congress of the Province of South Carolina, assembled in Charles Towne on January 11th, 1775.

Matthew Singleton was with Marion, and at one time, when near his home, Melrose, was stricken with smallpox. He concealed himself in the swamp but a few miles away, and was tended by a trusty slave. In the swamps the Americans, who alone knew them well, were fairly safe from discovery by the British. The question of food for the sick man was solved by sending the slave every night to Melrose. Here, according to instructions, he tapped at a lower window pane, whereupon Mrs. Singleton opened the second story window above, and lowered a basket of food, at the same time receiving and sending messages.

The captain recovered to fight on to the end of the war, but died in 1787. His son died in 1820, when sixty-six years old.

Although the son John's house burned, and although a later descendant cut down the beautiful hedge of hawthorne and crabapple, which had been planted English-fashion to separate the estate from the road, two things remain from the days of its builder, Captain Matthew, and the occupant, John.

First, the highroad here was originally very bad in wet weather, for the soil was clay. Captain John tired of seeing the big wagons on their way from North Carolina, laden with pitch, tar and turpentine, get stuck in the roads; he tired of hearing the wagoners cursing and swearing. So he had many loads of sand hauled, and this mingled with the clay produced an excellent road which lasted until recent times. A northerner who came to this part of the country, and brought with him a trotting horse accustomed to roads near New York City, declared that this stretch of road passing old Midway, as the second Singleton place was called, was the only place where his horse could trot in all that countryside.

The other remnant of days long past is the fine old avenue of trees which led from the highroad to the mansion. They were still standing a few years ago at least, and with them is linked Midway's ghost. The ghost, apparently, made but a single appearance.

It has been told that the Singletons had large cotton interests, and Captain Matthew sent his son to England on one of his sailing vessels, with a load of cotton, as soon as he reached manhood.

Following family custom, Captain John duly sent his son John, eldest of the family. Finally the day when the ship might be expected to arrive in Charleston on the return voyage drew near. In those days, with sailing vessels, of course the date could be but approximately fixed; nor would news of its safe arrival in port be obtained until some one arrived at Midway from the city. To have quick means for the son of the house to reach home and his anxious mother, his own saddle horse was sent down to Charleston in charge of a negro, several days before the earliest day when the young master might be expected.

Then, one bright moonlight summer night, Mrs. Singleton was awakened from sleep by the rapid hoofbeats of a horse coming up the long avenue. She left her bed, hurried to the window overlooking the avenue, and saw her son on his horse. As he rode around the house towards the stable, he looked up directly into her face, and waved his hand. She hurried to rouse her husband, and he descended to open the house door for his heir, but there was no one in sight. Finally he alarmed the groom, and bade him open the stable door, but there was no sign of either horse or rider.

The negro was the first to grasp what had happened.

"Oh, Miss," he wailed, "you'll never see Marse John again. That was his ghos!"

She never did see her son again, but when several days later the ship safely reached port, the captain came himself to bring sad tidings to the Singleton household. On the very night that his mother had seen him, bright moonlight, the captain told, the young man had gone on deck for a last walk before turning in for the night. He never was seen again, and it was supposed that in some sudden toss or roll of the ship he had gone overboard.

Near Stateburg is a place always known as The Ruins, although those visiting the house may well wonder at the name, for there are no ruins in sight.

Long ago, on the hill near this house, stood the residence of General Sumter. Mrs. Sumter, a helpless paralytic, was living here when the British appeared, and was alone in the house with her niece. Her husband was away with his men; her nephew, a boy of thirteen, had fled at news of the soldiers' coming to hide his thoroughbred horse in the swamp, which he did successfully, and then from a hiding place in the top of a tree, watched what was happening at his home.

Had it not been for her niece, Mrs. Sumter might have been burned to death, for the soldiers were preparing to set fire to the house, and she could not move. The girl persuaded them to carry the invalid out in her chair, which they did, depositing it on the lawn, from which Mrs. Sumter watched the destruction of her home and all of her belongings. One soldier, feeling sorry for her, presented her with a ham from her own smokehouse, hiding it among the cushions and blankets of the chair, that it might not be seen and taken by his comrades. General Sumter was called by the British "the greatest plague in the South," and they had no pity for his family.

After the soldiers left, Mrs. Sumter is said to have taken refuge in the neighboring Hill Crest.

It was not from the ruins of General Sumter's home that the place derived its present name. After the Revolution, General Sumter sold it, and the new owner built the present house, but not on the old site. After living in it for many years, the family moved west, the house was unoccupied, and rapidly falling to ruins when the present owner bought it. While repairs were being made, she used to remark that she was driving up to The Ruins to see how work was progressing. The name has persisted ever since.

Hill Crest, on the opposite side of the road, survived attacks in both the Revolution and the Civil War.

Its exact age is not known. In the early days of the Revolution,

Mr. and Mrs. Thomas Hooper came from Charleston, probably for greater safety, and purchased the house then standing from Adam F. Brisbane. Mr. Hooper was a brother of William Hooper, one of the Signers. His wife's father was Captain Benjamin Heron, who after serving in the Royal Navy, settled on Cape Fear, and married the great-granddaughter of the colonial South Carolina Governor James Moore. Later, he went to England, and it seems possible that to her father Mrs. Hooper may have owned the sparing of herself, her family and home from molestation by the British, for Captain Heron had been prominent in the colonial government, in addition to his naval service, having been deputy auditor and secretary, and clerk of pleas and of the Crown, an office with extensive patronage and perquisites.

He was also for many years chairman of His Majesty's Council, and when he died, in 1770, was buried in Windsor Castle, and tribute paid to his valuable and efficient services. It would seem that the British who soon appeared near Mrs. Hooper's home, knew of this gentleman, for although Cornwallis made Hill Crest his headquarters, the only damage done was the now prized mark of a musket butt on one door. Cornwallis was here in pursuit of General Sumter and his gallant band.

Later, the house was headquarters for General Nathaniel Greene, and the Colonial troops burned the initials: C.A., for Continental Army, on another door, this mark being still more prized by the present owners.

On the estate is a great tree, known as the Tory oak, because a tale has it that a Tory spy was hanged to its branches.

When the Hoopers bought the place, the house was built of laths and plaster. Their niece, who lived with them, married Dr. William Wallace Anderson, of Maryland, whose father was Colonel Richard Anderson, of the Continental Army, while the bride, Miss Mackenzie, traced her descent from a brother of the great Scot, William Wallace.

To this couple Hill Crest passed, after the deaths of the Hoopers. Dr. Anderson had already done much to beautify house and gardens, and became fascinated with *pisé* construction because of its soft coloring. He accordingly tore down both wings of the house, and re-built them of *pisé*, leaving the central portion as originally. Five outbuildings on the estate, and the church at Stateburg, not far away, are also of *pisé*, said to be the only group of that construction in the country.

Dr. Anderson's three sons served in the Confederate Army; one became a general, another Surgeon General, the third, who was killed early in the war, a captain. The second married Miss Virginia Childs, daughter of Brigadier General Thomas Childs, of Massachusetts. This lady was none the less thoroughly in sympathy with the Confederate cause.

She was living with her children in Wilmington, North Carolina, when General Sherman came to that town. Now her father had been Sherman's commanding officer, and as a child she had known Sherman well. Recalling this, Mrs. Anderson determined to ask protection for her children, herself and her home, so lest one miscarry, she dispatched three notes by three different messengers to the General. It happened that all three reached him, and in time he rode to the house of his former young friend. Rather severely he remarked:

"Do you know that you have written me three notes to-day?" Then: "What do you want, Virginia?"

"Protection for my family and house," promptly.

"Where is your husband, Virginia?" continued Sherman.

"Fighting for his country."

"What would your father say to you, Virginia, with a husband a rebel?"

"My father would say my place was with my husband, but what would my father say to you, Tecumseh," with spirit, "fighting women and children?"

A guard was sent by the General to protect Mrs. Anderson's house, but as her daughter said, in telling this: "He could not protect the chickens in the back yard." After a time, there was an exciting scramble between the Federal soldiers and the Anderson children as to who should first get the chickens.

Mrs. Anderson, Senior, was at Hill Crest when General Potter's raiders passed through the country, and they swarmed over the place, helping themselves to whatever they could carry off, and damaging some of the furniture. Of course they also bagged chickens, but spared the house, which is still occupied by the descendants of Dr. Anderson of the Confederate Army. It is in beautiful preservation, a fine specimen of a colonial house, and the grounds and garden are charming.

The Hon. Joel R. Poinsett, after whom the beautiful flower introduced into this country from Mexico is named, died at Hill Crest, while on a visit in 1851 to his friend, Dr. Anderson.

Chapter IV

The First English Settlement

For many years it was believed that the sole surviving fragment of the buildings which once stood on Jamestown Island, the first English settlement in the United States, was the lonely old tower of our first Protestant church. There it stood, isolated, square, still substantial, draped with ivy, and close to the river which winds around the low-lying island on which the first English settlers landed. Time has proved that this belief was a mistake.

In 1901, excavations revealed the foundations and brick arches of the old church, the aisles and chancel tombs. The owners of the island had given the twenty or more acres, upon part of which tower and church stand, to the Association for the Preservation of Virginia Antiquities, that the excavations might be made. It is now known that while a church was built here in 1607, the tower probably belonged to the third, or even the fourth one built on this site, the latter in 1647. Further excavations revealed more, for the foundations of three brick houses, probably the first built here, and perhaps as early as 1607, were later uncovered.

It will be recalled that these English colonists sailed from England December 19th, 1606, and after lingering in sight of the English coast for six weeks, because of " unprosperous winds," finally made the trip across that unknown waste of water, the Atlantic ocean.

They landed on Jamestown Island, and although the settlement had less than a century of life, the climate proving too " insalubritious," here they built a church and held regular services daily, for they had come to the new world to extend the doctrines of the Church of England, not to escape religious persecution.

The houses whose foundations have been uncovered by the excavations are those mentioned in the Ludwell patent in 1694, and show that the buildings, as proved by the foundation walls, were three in number, apparently adjoining, the length being two hundred and forty feet, the depth varying from twenty-four to forty-six feet. These walls were found from one to five feet below the surface, and are believed to be the foundations of " Philip Ludwell's country house," the state house and one other. James Towne was, it is thought, never more than a straggling settlement of perhaps a score of houses.

Here in James Towne, on July 30th, 1619, more than a year before the Mayflower sailed into Cape Cod Bay, the first general legislative assembly ever held in America met, and the day after assembling, petitioned the London Company, under whose direction they then lived — the British Government had not yet taken over the province — for workmen to build a university at Henrycropolis, further up the James River. This university was begun, the first English educational institution on American soil, but all traces of the buildings were wiped out in the Indian uprising and massacre. In 1624, Virginia became a royal province.

Eight years later, Dr. John Pott secured a patent for 1200 acres of land at the head of Archer's Hope Creek, probably adjoining the tract on which William and Mary College was built, and a year later, a palisade six miles long was built across the peninsula from the head of Archer's Hope to that of Queen's Creek, the former a tributary of the York, the latter of the James River. On the ridge between the two rivers, close to the palisade, a settlement known as Middle Plantation was made. Even before Jamestown was burned to the ground during the Bacon revolt in 1676, some of the settlers had begun moving up the river to the newer and healthier site.

At the mouth of Gray's Creek is the Smith Fort farm, where the outlines of old earthworks, built under the direction of Captain John Smith, in 1608-09 may still be traced. The brick house fifty feet long

standing here is said to be the oldest in Virginia, the land having belonged to Thomas Rolfe, son of Pocahontas. He is said to have sold
the land to Thomas Warren, who built in 1654 the house now owned
by a negro. But it is also asserted positively that the old chimney,
which is of different construction, actually belonged to the house in
which John Rolfe and his wife, Pocahontas herself, lived. Bishop
Meade is one of those who believed this when he visited the spot, some
time between 1838 and 1857. He says that the material of which this
chimney was built was of " marl, mixed with seashells crushed in a kind
of cement, extremely hard and durable."

Four miles from Jamestown the ruins of Green Springs, former
residence of Governor Berkeley of the Virginia Colony, exist, with
outlines of some of the high arched window frames. In the fine house
once standing here were entertained many cavaliers, who took refuge
in the loyal colony after Charles II was banished from England.
Nathaniel Bacon stopped here on his way to Jamestown, and again,
after burning that town, on his way back, making it his headquarters,
for Berkeley had taken refuge on a ship in the river. Since the
state house in Jamestown had been burned with the other buildings,
the first Assembly held after Bacon's revolt met in this Govrnor's
house.

After Sir William's death, his widow, Lady Frances, married
Philip Ludwell, whose Jamestown " country house " had burned
with the others. Her cousin, Lord Culpepper, rented Green Springs
from them while he was Governor of the colony. It passed to the Lee
family when Hannah Phillips, daughter of the third Colonel Ludwell,
married William Lee, who served as United States Minister to Vienna
and Berlin. The second house on this site, now ruins, was built by their
son, William Lee, but there still survive some of the apple, cherry and
peach trees which Governor Berkeley planted. Although his widow
married again, on her tombstone in Jamestown was inscribed: Lady
Berkeley.

Near Smithfield, Surry County, there is still standing on the James
River an old red brick house known as Bacon's Castle. But although

Tazewell Hall, home of Sir John Randolph, Attorney for the Royal Commonwealth of Virginia. Peyton Randolph was born here, as was Edmund Randolph, later Governor of Virginia. It stood on one of the four converging plantations on the site of what later became Williamsburg.

The Moore house, Yorktown, Virginia, home of the Royal Governor Spottwood. In this house the Articles of Agreement were drawn in 1781, between the Americans and the English.

Home of John Blair, Senior, President of the Council of Virginia and Acting Governor of the Colony; also of his son, John Blair, Junior, appointed by President Washington on the first Supreme Court of the United States. The old doorstep was brought here from Williamsburg's first theatre, long since gone.

Home of the Hon. Peyton Randolph, First President of the Continental Congress, which met in Philadelphia in 1774. He was also Provincial Grand Master of Masons, Virginia. This old Williamsburg house is in excellent preservation, and still a private residence.

this house figured prominently in Bacon's Rebellion, Bacon himself never occupied it or owned it.

It was built of bricks brought from England in 1655, by Arthur Allen, and for those days was a mansion, with large, high-ceiled, paneled rooms. At each end are three chimneys, set close together, a curious arrangement said to be unique in this country. Although modern owners have made some changes and additions, these have been done so as to affect the general appearance but little, with the exception of a modern porch, and the old house is still a residence.

During Bacon's rebellion, it was seized and fortified by three of his followers, Lieutenant Colonel William Rookings, Captain Robert Burgess and Captain Arthur Long, and for nearly four months stood off all attacks. Finally, in December, 1676, it was taken by a force from the ship, Young Prince, lying in the river, under command of Robert Morris. Probably at that time the small brass cannon were mounted in the attic windows, remaining there until comparatively recent times. From that same period must date the love letter scratched with a diamond, covering with fine writing several panes of glass in a window of a barred dungeon in the cellar. No one knows now who the writer was, or to whom the letter was addressed.

Bacon's own place is said by Mr. T. Beverly Campbell, writing recently for the Richmond *Times Dispatch*, to have been the Curle's Neck plantation, further up the James River. As this place was owned at an early date by the Randolphs, it is possible that they bought it in when it must have been confiscated by the Royal Governor. Bacon is also said to have owned a place called " Bacon's Quarter," within the present city limits of Richmond, its site now occupied, as Mr. Campbell states, by the American Locomotive Company's plant, and the small stream nearby is still known as Bacon's Quarter Branch.

Nathaniel Bacon, leader of the rebellion, was a wealthy man, a graduate of Cambridge University, England. The uprising was a protest of the colonists against the adminstration of the governor, Sir William Berkeley, and an act of the British Parliament, recently passed, directing that all goods intended for Virginia must be sent to

England first, and there re-shipped in English vessels. There was also objection to intercolonial duties, and especially there was dissatisfaction when, in 1673, all of the revenues of the colony were turned over to Lord Culpepper and Lord Arlington, the two nobles to whom Charles II had given over the colony. Furthermore, the Virginians considered that Governor Berkeley had done nothing to protect them against the Indians.

Bacon was a member of the Colonial Council, and finally, at the head of a band of colonists, he attacked the Indians and captured their fort. He was appointed commander of the Virginia forces, but Governor Berkeley refused to sign his commission, although he later yielded to popular demand, and did so. The two men were now enemies, and before long Bacon was proclaimed a traitor, and took up arms against the Governor and his forces.

When he attacked Jamestown, Berkeley fled to a warship, and the town was, as mentioned, burned, but shortly after that Bacon died, his followers lost heart, and Berkeley returning established himself in power. He took such cruel revenge on Bacon's followers that his sovereign, Charles II, is said to have exclaimed: "That old fool has taken away more lives in that naked country than I for the murder of my father."

Meanwhile, Middle Plantation had grown, and in 1676 was the meeting place of a convention called by Bacon to protest against Governor Berkeley.

In 1698, since Jamestown had not been re-built, and had long been thought "insalubritious," Governor Francis Nicholson made Middle Plantation the seat of government, and the following year an act was passed, providing for the building of a capitol, the chief street was named Duke of Gloucester, in honor of Queen Anne's oldest son, a name retained to-day, and the town became known as Williamsburg, oldest incorporated city in the United States. It remained the capital of Virginia until after the election to the Presidency of Thomas Jefferson, when, through his influence, it was succeeded by Richmond. The old office of the Secretary of the Colony, now a private residence, a story and a half brick building, used from 1705 to 1776 as the office, still stands near the Green on which is the site of the old Capitol, burned in 1832.

In the early days, while the settlement was still called Middle Plantation, four plantations centred in the town site, each with a dwelling built in the adjoining corners, so that the occupants were near neighbors. These four houses were Bassett Hall, Tazewell Hall, Garrett's and Wheatland. Mrs. Bassett and Martha Washington were sisters.

Bassett Hall is a fine old house, still a private residence, and in excellent condition. Set well back from Francis Street, an avenue bordered with fine trees leads to the front door. There is a wide hall paneled, with broad staircase mounting by two landings to the second floor, and rail and bannisters are hand carved.

The dining room in the rear is filled with old family portraits, silver and fine old furniture; the front rooms are respectively drawing room and library. At the time that he succeeded to the Presidency, John Tyler was living in this house, and was in the library when a messenger arrived in Williamsburg to notify him of the death of President Harrison, and Tyler's consequent succession. Washington was often entertained here in the early days, and it is said that the Irish poet, Tom Moore, wrote his poem, " The Firefly," while visiting here. The house has a romance connected with it as well.

Before the Civil War, Custer, later as General to meet a tragic fate, and Lieutenant Lee were bosom friends. The war found them on opposing sides, and Lee was wounded and nursed back to health in Bassett Hall. His nurse was Miss Burfey; patient and nurse fell in love, and became engaged to be married. The wedding day was set while Williamsburg was besieged by Federal troops, but Captain Custer came through Federal and Confederate lines under a flag of truce, to be best man at his friend's wedding.

Tazewell Hall had a narrow escape from being torn down. It was wished to extend England Street through the grounds of the old house, and the house itself was in the way. But moved aside, and turned half around, it is now firmly fixed on new foundations, occupied, and doubtless will have many more years of existence.

Although another house is now known as that of the Randolphs, this was the home of Sir John, Royal Commonwealth Attorney, and first of the name to come to this country. Here Peyton and Edmund Randolph were born, and Sir John's son and namesake also lived in it. This John Randolph must not be confounded with the other John of Roanoke, grandson in the sixth generation of John Rolfe and Pocahontas. The Williamsburg John was brother of Peyton, and father of Edmund. Peyton "gave early signs of a too independent spirit to be very acceptable to the English Government." Sent to England " on account of some of our complaints, and speaking his mind too freely for the Court and Cabinet, he was displaced from his office, and his brother John, who had acted during his absence, took his place. At the outbreak of the Revolution, John went to England, but bitterly repented this, and directed that his body should be taken back to Virginia for burial." (Bishop Meade.) John's son remained with his uncle.

What is always known as the Randolph house was probably built about 1750, the exact date uncertain, for all the records were burnt. Of massive, hand hewn timbers, the entrance hall runs across the front of the house, instead of through it. Behind the hall is a big old drawing room, with large fireplace, and hand carved mantel, and at either end of the hall, doors open into wings. From the drawing room one descends steps into a kind of central hall, from which stairs lead to the second floor, and further in the rear is a modern addition. The house has all the signs of having been built at several periods, and is in excellent condition. It is occupied by a family whose members, although from quite a different section of the country, are deeply attached to the old house, and delight in its age and history.

Edmund Randolph studied at William and Mary College, and became a lawyer. He helped frame the Constitution of Virginia, was the first Governor of the state, a member of the convention which framed the Constitution of the United States, and while at work on this, was appointed by Washington Attorney General. Five years later, he was Secretary of State, which office he resigned after the signing of the Jay treaty with England, and found himself practically ruined, because, while holding that office he had incurred responsibility for funds provided for foreign service. He resumed his law practice, but was compelled to assign his land and slaves.

Peyton Randolph also occupied this house. He was Attorney General of Viriginia, Speaker of the House of Burgesses, and first President of the Continental Congress.

The Governor's Palace stood at the far end of what is still called Palace Green. In front of the site is now a modern schoolhouse, deplored because of its modernity by some old residents. Indeed, as a rule, Williamsburg has preserved much of the old time atmosphere, many of the modern buildings being of the same light colored brick, and along the general lines of the old survivors.

On the actual foundations of this palace, from which Lord Dunmore was driven, now stands a one-story building, used in connection with the school, and some of the old bricks were used in its construction. The monument erected to commemorate the old building is quite screened by the schoolhouse, and one must go around to the side to find it. Then one may learn that the Palace, which originally consisted of a house probably two stories in height, with a smaller building at each side, one an office, the other the guardhouse, was destroyed by Federal troops during the War between the States, at the time that the property was owned by Letitia Tyler Semple, daughter of the President.

In 1706, Williamsburg already had a free school, Mattey's, and in 1716 the first theatre in the United States was built here by William Levingston, but all traces of the theatre have disappeared, save that its stone steps, imported from England, serve now for the Blair house.

Williamsburg may not boast the oldest college in the United States, for that honor is justly claimed by Harvard, since the earlier Virginia one at Henrycropolis was entirely wiped out. But William and Mary was, with one exception, the first American college to have chairs of Law, Political Economy, Modern Languages and History, and in 1693, at the time when Harvard had a President and two professors only, the Virginia college had a President, six professors, and a master. The architect of the early buildings is said to have been Sir Christopher Wren. The Indian building on the campus was built in 1723, and Mr. Ratcliffe, an Englishman, gave £45 a year for its support as a school for the Indians. It is now Brafferton Hall, and used by the college.

The main building of the college is the fourth to stand on this site, three previous ones having been burned to the ground. The President's house, built in 1732, was occupied by Cornwallis about the time of the siege of Yorktown, and later was burned by the French during the struggle. It was then re-built by Louis XVI of France, at his own expense, so that the present house, still occupied by the college President, is more than a century old.

The Galt house on East Francis Street is said to be the oldest in town, for it was spoken of as " more than a hundred years old at the time of the Revolution," but its age is its chief claim to mention, nor is that definitely established.

Near the college, on the grounds of the Hospital for the Insane, stands a small building of one room, the kitchen, all that is left of the large dwelling on the " Six Chimney Lot " plantation of Martha Washington when she was Mrs. Custis, and close by is a tree which she is said to have planted.

The kitchen is the usual one of southern plantations, with a huge fireplace, but some interest attaches to the hospital itself, in that it was the second in the world — the first was in France — to be built with the plan of curing if possible, rather than merely imprisoning the unfortunate insane.

The Blair house on Duke of Gloucester Street still stands, and on the same street is the Paradise house, an old stone building, unoccupied in the autumn of 1926, and apparently doomed to remain so unless much repairing is done. Some of the once fine old woodwork remains, but has been painted an ugly brown.

The Blair house was the residence of John, President of the

Council of State, Acting Governor of Virginia. After his death in 1771, his son John lived here until his death in 1800. He was Justice of the United States Supreme Court. It was also occupied by John Blair's son-in-law, Professor Andrews, and by John Marshall when a student here.

Of the Paradise house, the following is told. The mistress of the house was always called Lady Paradise, as she insisted, although she had no claim to such a title. She dressed her hair so elaborately that she could not or would not put bonnet or other head covering upon the structure, but whenever she walked abroad in Williamsburg, behind her always followed a small page, carrying a suitable head covering displayed upon a pillow.

Most striking of the houses on the old Palace Green is that of George Wythe. Fairly well preserved before, it is now insured a long lease of life, for through the untiring efforts of Dr. Goodwin, rector of Bruton Church, it has been purchased for a parish house, and save for an addition in the rear for parish purposes, has been carefully restored to its original state.

This was the home of a famous man, one of the Signers of the Declaration of Independence, the first law professor in America, who had for students such men as Thomas Jefferson, James Monroe, Chief Justice Marshall, Henry Clay, Edmund Randolph, and many other later distinguished men. Wythe designed the seal of the United States, and lived in this handsome house for many years. During the Yorktown campaign it was for a time Washington's headquarters, and in it Lafayette was entertained on his last visit to America. Ellen Glasgow described this house as the residence of Judge Bassett, in her novel: *The Voice of the People*.

The old house has the unusual distinction of three ghosts.

In Judge Wythe's room, any occupant is liable to be awakened by the touch of a cold hand on his forehead; George Washington may be seen walking in the hall on moonlight nights, but on these alone, while Mrs. Skipworth, who was Elizabeth Byrd, often descends the old staircase.

A fine brass knocker hangs on the front door, the broad hall runs through the square house, and a flight of low, broad stairs, with hand carved bannisters, mounts to the second floor, while another almost as fine descends beneath to the cellar. There are many HL hinges here on doors and window shutters, but some of these, though old, may have been placed here recently. One front room on the first floor has broad window seats, and there are peephole shutters, and rimlocks with the seal of England cut in them all over the house. An upper room in the rear was a billiard room, and here Washington is said to have played many a game.

On the other side of the Green is a low white cottage with dormer windows, the early home of Governor Page. It has a paneled hall and parlor, with small window panes, on one of which may be read, scratched with a diamond: " T.B. 1790, Nov. 23. O fatal day." No one knows who scratched the words or why, so anyone may invent a romance to fit them.

This house is now, rather to the annoyance of its owners, quite generally known as the Audrey house, because Mary Johnson chose to make it the setting for her novel of that name. The rooms have the great old fireplaces of the time when it was built, and a fine old hedge of box in the garden behind the house is another survivor of days long past.

The great front door, its solid outer boards lined with another thickness of diagonals, to defend its inmates from Indians, is another relic of the past, and old H hinges abound. A number of interesting relics are also cherished here by the devoted owners, and include Powhatan's stone axe.

At one time Page cottage was the home of Rebecca Byrd, whose fiancé, as their wedding day drew near, had himself sent to prison on some trumped up charge to get out of the marriage. Despite this mortification, the lady eventually married another.

The home of Governor Dinwiddie, square, with broad portico supported by white pillars, faces on Palace Green, opposite the Page house. The St. George Tucker house, very long, low and rambling, which stands on the street leading from Palace Green to the Court

Beautiful "Carter's Grove," built for another of "king" Carter's sons. Three pirates are buried in its cellar, and their ghosts are said to haunt it.

Garden of the Old Stone House, Richmond, Virginia. This is said to have been laid out exactly as the garden in which, also in this city, Poe courted his wife.

Old Stone House, Richmond, the oldest in the city, now a memorial to Edgar Allen Poe.

House Square, but not facing the latter, is said to have been Lafayette's headquarters. Here in Williamsburg is also the Cary house, home of two sisters, one of whom Washington vainly wooed for she married George Fairfax instead. This by no means exhausts the list of old houses, but merely the most important, or those with most interesting associations have been mentioned.

The substantial build of the earliest of them, the beauty and charm often found, need surprise no one. Virginians lived well from the early days of the settlement. They very soon possessed stores of pewter, plates, dishes and platters, which were gradually followed by those of silver. China and glass were imported at an early date from the mother country, and they brought with them or imported silver chafing dishes, sack cups, porringers, etc. Their family portraits brought with them were often the work of artists of European renown. Turkish rugs covered their floors at an early period.

In early colonial days there is mention of such furniture as "parlour beds, trundle beds, dressers and chests of drawers;" of looking glasses, later pier glasses, and finally of chimney mirrors. They had Holland blankets, dimity coverlets, crickets, stools, chairs, harpsichords, spinets, and "joined dining tables."

John Davis, a Welshman who visited Virginia at an early date, wrote:

"The higher Virginians seem to venerate themselves. I am persuaded that not one of that company would have been embarrassed at being admitted to the presence and conversation of the greatest monarch on earth."

On the excellent road from old Williamsburg to almost equally old Yorktown, is a beautiful old place, one of many belonging to the family of Carter, which name will be frequently encountered in any chronicle of old Virginia.

Of this old mansion it is impossible to speak without superlatives. Built in 1722, by "King" Carter, as a wedding present for his daughter Elizabeth, who married Nathaniel Burwell, the house itself is in a perfect state of preservation, and cries aloud for some wealthy buyer who will fill it with guests, and once more revive its past splendors.

About five miles from Williamsburg, one turns from the high-road, and for perhaps half a mile, traverses a neglected but not impassable road between fields. If ever it was an avenue no trace now remains. But after half a mile, comes a double row of splendid old cedars, set well back from the road, and after these, always proceeding in a straight line, one enters an avenue bordered with a double, in some parts triple row of locusts, magnificent old trees, fortunately untouched by axe. The red brick house is at the end of this avenue, with what was once a lawn in front, while behind, terraces once descended to the James River, half a mile away, and there are traces of a sunken garden.

Mounting a short flight of semi-circular stone steps, each massive as millstones, one is confronted by a heavy door with great lock. This is really the rear entrance, for steps descend to the cellar just within a very broad hall, running through the house to another great door, and portico without. The entire hall from floor to ceiling is paneled, the floors are of dark wood, partly black walnut, partly hearts of pine, while the beautiful carving of cornice, door and window frames is of mahogany. A recent owner painted this exquisite hall in red, white and blue, but a later owner removed this disfigurement, and restored it to its original beauty. The ceilings throughout are very high.

From the hall an unusually broad staircase, with low treads, rises, turning with a landing on the rear wall, and lighted by an enormous window. The great square hall is separated upstairs by an enormous archway from what was once a library, with windows overlooking the river. Paneled from floor to ceiling, bookcases line every inch of the lower part of the walls not occupied by doors or windows. The frame of this arch, the cornices, the exquisite delicately carved bannisters of the staircase, are all of mahogany. There are four large rooms on each floor, and the last owner to occupy the house connected the dining room with the old kitchen, formerly a detached building. On the other side of the house a brick building similar to the kitchen was the bachelor quarters.

After members of the Carter family no longer owned it, it was falling out of repair when an elderly gentleman bought the place, put it in perfect order, installed a heating plant, and settled down to enjoy his beautiful home. He lived only two years, and his widow sold it. It was then bought by several men together, who farm the rich lands, but the house is occupied only by a caretaker and her family. Visitors are admitted upon payment of a fee, and the house is kept in good order, but one would gladly see it fully occupied, refurnished with the old portraits and furniture long since scattered, or if not these, at least with substitutes.

Down in the cellar, so the story goes, three pirates were buried many years ago, but their restless spirits do not trouble the present occupants.

On the mahogany stair rail are many scars made during the Revolution by the savage General Tarleton. One story says that while occupying the house as his headquarters, he ordered some of his men who were upstairs to come down, and when they did not obey promptly enough to suit him, he rode up the broad, low stairs on his horse, hacking at the bannister rail with his sword as he rode. He and his men of course plundered the place before leaving.

The house is put together with wooden pegs, many of which may still be seen, and it has strong inside shutters which could be closed to give protection from Indians. When these shutters are closed, the old brick walls are exposed to view in the recess. Brass locks and hinges, silver plated, are throughout the house. The walls are at least two feet thick.

The paneling and woodwork of the first floor rooms are painted white, as so often in old houses, except in the dining room and hall, where all is in the natural finish. In the drawing room overlooking the river is a marble mantle, said to be the first ever brought to the United States. This is one of the Virginia drawing rooms claiming to be the scene of Washington's proposal to the Widow Custis.

In 1751, this house was the home of Rebecca Burwell, the "Dying Belinda" who refused Thomas Jefferson and married Jaquelin Ambler.

Of old Yorktown but little remains. The hotel, more than a century old, the church nearby re-built on a much older foundation, and the office of the county clerk are set among modern houses and buildings, but on the way to the monument commemorating the surrender of Cornwallis, close to the road, are the historic Nelson house and a still older one next door, both with gardens in the rear.

The first house of wood which "Scotch Tom" Nelson, first of his family to come to America from Penriff, Scotland, built for himself here in 1715 is gone, as is a third one, built ten years later for his son. The present, built in 1740 for William Nelson's eldest son, Thomas, the Revolutionary general and grandson of "Scotch Tom," was occupied by the owner at the time of the British bombardment. A butler while serving dinner was struck by a shot and killed, his silver tray in his hand. Nelson left the house under a flag of truce.

This Thomas, the grandson, was one of the Signers, a Governor of Virginia, a Major General in the American army, but died a poor man, having given almost everything that he possessed to the American cause. He was educated in England, and there took up smoking "filthy tobacco, also eating and drinking, though not to inebriety, or more than was conducive to health and long life," as Bishop Meade quaintly and rather obscurely comments.

The Nelson house, a private residence, is no longer owned in the Nelson family. It has a hall paneled with very wide planks, and painted white. The dining room is also paneled, with capitals carved in a pattern of roses and acanthus leaves surmounting fluted columns in half relief. Each of the two stories has four large rooms, and there is a high attic. On the first floor, the original rooms were the drawing room, with General Nelson's office behind it, a library and a dining room, all except the dining room paneled to the ceiling. The

Parlor in the home of Chief Justice Marshall, Richmond, Virginia.

Dining room in the home of Chief Justice Marshall. The house was built by him in 1789, and is now the property of the Society for the Preservation of Virginia Antiquities, who opened it as a museum on March 27, 1913.

View of the James River from Westover. The boulder marks the exit of a tunnel leading from an outhouse near the mansion, and built for escape when Indians threatened.

The fine iron gates of Westover, ordered by its builder, Colonel Byrd.

Dementi Studio

The "White House of the Confederacy," Richmond, this is now the Confederate Museum, filled with many interesting relics of that period. Jefferson Davis' only son died by falling from an upper balcony now removed.

old fireplaces have been left, but otherwise the interior has been much re-modeled, and the house is never shown to strangers. In the outer wall may be seen one of the cannon balls embedded there during the seige of Yorktown. A large garden and grounds are on three sides of the house, and the brick wall surrounding the whole has been carefully repaired where needed, and is draped with festoons of clinging old ivy.

The place was considerably damaged during the siege, the one cannon ball still remaining by no means representing the extent of such damage. Nelson is said to have told Lafayette: "Spare no particle of my property so long as it affords comfort or shelter to the enemies of my country."

The house of the General's uncle, who was known as the Secretary, was destroyed during this bombardment, and when he was brought to town under a flag of truce, and saw this, he, equally patriotic, is said to have congratulated the American officers on the destruction that their bombardment was effecting.

The oldest house in town is probably the Shields, formerly the Sessions house, designated as one of the twelve surviving very old houses west of Chesapeake Bay. It has been but little modernized.

One story and a half high, with the quaint dormer windows on the upper story found in the old Virginia houses of this type, it has great chimneys, and many HL hinges, chiefly found in New England. Whether southerners were not, like the northern settlers, afraid of witches is a moot question, but while H or L hinges are plentiful, the combination is quite rare in the south.

This house was built between 1691 and 1699 for Thomas, son of "Scotch Tom." He married Mary Read. Bishop Meade in his *History of Early Virginia Churches and Families*, the greater part of which deals with the early part of his ministry, or soon after 1838, mentions Miss Tomasia Nelson as living here at that time.

It has a charming, box-bordered, ivy grown old garden, and the front door is a so-called Christian door, although not of the same type found in the Old North Church, Boston, and the Webb house in Wethersfield, Connecticut. This one has two upright crosses, but the same tradition clings to it, namely, that it was good for driving away witches from the house.

The death of General Nelson left his widow in the big house next door almost penniless, the house and a tiny income being hers only through the kindness of her husband's creditors, who allowed her the use of both until her death.

Three quarters of a mile from Yorktown, on Temple Farm, is the old Moore house where the papers for the surrender of Cornwallis were drawn up and signed. Part of this house is very old indeed, and was the residence of Colonel George Ludlow, a member of the Colonial Council, and a relative of Edmund Ludlow, one of the regicide judges. Furthermore, the house stands on the site of one built more than a century before the Revolution, the home of Captain Nicholas Martain, ancestor of Washington and Nelson, prominent in the first "rebellion against tyranny," in Virginia, when, in 1634, the colonists deposed from office the unpopular governor, Sir John Harvey, and shipped him out of the country. Captain Martain died in 1657.

Here lived Lucy Smith, granddaughter of Major Lawrence Smith, who surveyed York and Gloucester Counties, and laid out Yorktown. Lucy married Augustine Moore, said to have been a grandson of Governor Spottswood. Temple Farm was chosen by the Royal Governor of Virginia as his residence, probably on account of the beauty of its situation.

Motoring from Williamsburg to Richmond, one passes over what is practically the old colonial road. At Bottom's Bridge, Cornwallis is said to have stationed troops when he raided Richmond, and it was also the site of a camp during the war of 1812.

The name, Providence Forge, commemorates the site of an early iron foundry, owned and worked by Colonel William Byrd, whose name figures so prominently in Virginia history.

The site of Richmond was explored in 1607 by Captain John Smith, but not until 1742 was a town incorporated here, built, like ancient Rome, as the inhabitants are fond of telling, on seven hills, although later another was included within the city limits.

Richmond suffered too much destruction during the War between the States for one to find many very old buildings, but a few remain in what is practically a modern city.

The oldest house in town, on Main Street, now called the Poe Memorial, and a shrine to that poet, was built in 1737, by Jacob Ege. Of stone, with very thick walls, a story and a half high, it contains but four small rooms, two on each floor, with a tiny passage between; from the lower one steep narrow stairs mount to the upper. Sometimes called Washington's headquarters, there is no authority for believing that Washington ever occupied it.

A charming garden behind the house, with a summer house and fountain, is said to have been laid out in facsimile of the garden belonging to the Allen house on Second and Franklin Streets, Richmond, in which Poe courted his wife.

The old house contains many interesting relics of the gifted and unfortunate poet. Here, too, is preserved one of the first British red coats made in this country, its colors almost as bright as though but recently dyed.

Richmond became the capital of Virginia in 1799, and the Governor's mansion on Capitol Square was built that year for Thomas Jefferson, the Governor. The present house standing on the original site, dates from 1811, save for a recent addition in the rear which contains the present dining room. The broad hall and large rooms on the ground floor open with broad archways into each other, suggestive of Monticello, and admirably fitted for state and entertaining purposes. Unfortunately a fire caused by a Christmas tree a couple of years ago damaged some of the valuable old furniture and portraits, although these have been as far as possible restored. The fire did not injure the walls of the house.

In 1818 was built what is now known as the White House of the Confederacy, a three-story brick building covered with grey stucco. For many years, it has been a Confederate museum, and is filled with most valuable and interesting relics of that period. Here are, to mention but a few, the seal of the Confederacy, the original provisional constitution of the Confederate States, many portraits, battle flags, uniforms worn by prominent generals including that of the beloved commander, Robert E. Lee, and many of his little personal belongings. Among these is the beautiful sword presented to him no one now knows by whom, for all efforts to learn the donor's name have thus far failed. Here, too, is the *uniform* in which Jefferson Davis was captured, not as some old northern schoolbooks used libelously to declare, a woman's dress and hoopskirt.

The balcony from which the little Davis son fell and broke his neck has been removed from the house.

The different rooms are named after the Confederate States, and the societies of each state collect relics, etc., under the direction of a state regent.

After the surrender of General Lee, the Federal troops occupied the city, and their commanding officer made this house his headquarters. In what is now the Georgia room, President Lincoln was received, but remained in Richmond only a few hours. After the troops left, it was used as a school, until finally the Confederate Memorial Literary Society obtained possession, and devoted it to its present use.

Most interesting is the Chief Justice Marshall house on the corner of Ninth and Marshall Streets, now preserved as a memorial by the Association for the Preservation of Viriginia Antiquities. To this society are due the preservation and maintenance of many interesting and historic houses and buildings, but unfortunately there are not nearly sufficient funds as yet to carry out all that they hope to do, for buildings in Virginia which ought to be preserved are very numerous.

Marshall's fine house, built in 1795, is entered by so small a door, opening into so narrow an entry that visitors are not surprised to learn that the real main entrance is at the side. It seems that Marshall accepted the architect's plans for the house, and then went to Europe. On his return, he found that through some odd mistake, the house had been set at right angles to the original plan, so the small side door became the entrance from the street, the drawing room, which should have overlooked the extensive grounds which then lay behind the house, had instead its windows overlooking the two streets. The old detached kitchen which stood behind the house has now been removed, the fireplace in a rear room filled in, and covered with a paneled wall, otherwise few changes have been made.

The small entry opens into a large hall running across the house, divided in the middle by an archway, with a fanlight above. The dining room, largest of the three on the first floor, has a beautiful old mantel, and shutters made of one length of board, with butterfly hinges. A portrait of Washington painted from Peale's miniature, and not much resembling those with which we are most familiar, hangs here. Another interesting portrait is that of Fielding Lewis, who married Betty Washington. Their third daughter, Margaret, married Thomas Marshall in 1809. She was a great invalid for most of her married life, but Marshall was devoted to her always, and after her death, would never again occupy their bedroom above the drawing room.

Marshall was a law student, as mentioned, at William and Mary, but there are those in Richmond who will tell that he never attended but four law lectures there. One can but marvel, if this be true, at the remarkable lectures which those four must have been, to say nothing of the mental equipment of the student who listened to them.

Richmond is an excellent centre from which to visit various interesting places. A pleasant drive southward brings one to Petersburg, where there are a number of interesting old houses. The town itself is historic.

Captain John Smith explored this territory, which the Indians called Appomatuck, and here it is claimed lived King Powhatan, father of Pocahontas, so Petersburg likes to believe that on its site the Indian princess saved the white explorer's life. The maiden's real name was either Matoax or Matoaca, the name Pocahontas being given her by her fellow Indians, it is said, when naming her to the white men, because of a belief that no one whose true name was unknown could be killed. Powhatan's true name was Wahunusukak, which surely offers difficulties of pronunciation.

In Petersburg's Central Park is preserved Pocahontas' stone wash basin. Confronted with this, who would deny that she lived here?

Major Peter Jones, a comrade of Colonel William Byrd, founder of Richmond, established a trading post here in Petersburg, on the river, as early as 1675, when it was called Peter's Point, but long before that it had been a camping ground for both Indians and white men. The actual town was not founded until more than fifty years later, but a two-story stone structure on the river, now used as a seed storage warehouse, is pointed out as the original Peter Jones trading station.

Folly Castle, built in 1763 by Peter Jones, great-grandson of the major, still stands. It received this name because it was thought most foolish for a childless man to build so large a house.

The old colonial home of Colonel John Bannister still stands on High Street. He was prominent in the days immediately preceding the Revolution, was a colonel in its army, and also took active part in the second war with Great Britain. He was the first mayor of Petersburg.

Marks on the floors of rooms in this house are said to have been caused by Revolutionary soldiers as they grounded their arms, but this tale is doubtful. In 1781, the great French traveler of those days, the Marquis de Chastellux, was a guest here.

In the heart of the city are three hills, Bollingbroke, Center and West by name. A small frame house, all that remains of the former Bolling mansion on the first hill, was occupied by the British General Phillips as headquarters, and here Benedict Arnold, the traitor, Tarleton and Cornwallis also stayed. General Phillips fell ill shortly before Lafayette arrived to check Lord Cornwallis' advance, and was brought to Bollingbroke a sick man. He is said to have cried out: " Can they not let me die in peace? " during the bombardment. He died in the house, and was buried in Blandford cemetery, now within Petersburg limits. A week later Cornwallis, whom Jefferson described as " the proudest man of the proudest nation on earth," arrived and made his headquarters in the Bolling house.

During Lafayette's cannonading from Archer's Hill, shots were aimed at Bollingbroke. It is told that Arnold was crossing the yard outside when a ball passed close to him, so he ordered the occupants of the house to take to the cellar for safety. Two balls struck, one of which killed Molly, the cook, as she stood in the kitchen doorway.

General O'Hara, who after he came to America in 1780 was in command of the British forces, is said to have made his headquarters at this time in Long Ornery tavern, one mile west of Petersburg. There he was visited by Mrs. Bolling, who requested the return of negroes and horses which had been taken from her, and were then in the tavern. O'Hara refused to return them. It was he who surrendered Cornwallis' sword at Yorktown.

On Center Hill is a house just over a century old, which was used in 1865 as headquarters by General Hartsuff, of the Federal forces. In it, too, was held the reception given President Taft, when the monument to the Pennsylvania soldiers of the War between the States was dedicated.

An underground passage led from house to river, and more than fifty feet of it are still open. A cannon ball remains embedded in a wall, and many bullet holes mark attic doors, testimony to the fierce fighting that went on around Petersburg during the Civil War.

The third of the three hills was the site of a house now gone, said to have been built for stewards of the Bolling estate.

Across the river stands a fine old house on Dunn's Hill, which was occupied by Lafayette while he directed the shelling of Bollingbroke. A wonderful old box hedge still survives.

Nearby is Violet Bank, a pre-Revolutionary house which originally contained twenty rooms, many of which have been removed, until now there are few, but these make up for lack of numbers by size. Entering the wide hall, on the left is an enormous room, square, high-ceiled, which once served as General Robert E. Lee's office. On the lawn near the house is a huge umbrella tree, which is said to have sheltered the

General's tent. Another story goes that the tree itself sprang from a riding switch carried by Peter Francisco, and carelessly tossed aside, with no thought that it might take root.

This same Peter Francisco, while sitting in one of these rooms unarmed, saw a British soldier enter, who demanded "those massy buckles which you wear on your shoes."

Francisco replied that they were the gift of a dear friend, and he would not give them up. "Take them if you can," he added.

The dragoon placed his sabre under his arm, and advanced to take them, whereupon Francisco seized the sabre, and literally cut the man's head in two. There are many tales of this Francisco's great strength.

The house is solidly built, its heavy doors of mahogany, the floors wonderfully well laid, joining tightly even to-day.

This by no means exhausts the interesting old houses around Petersburg, all of them private residences. To name a few, here is Appomattox, home of the Eppes family, the estate on which it stands having been granted by the British Crown to Colonel Francis Eppes in 1635. The house which still stands, built in 1715, was set on fire by Arnold's men, was twice fired on by northern gunboats.

Cobbs, home of the Bollings, stands on the left bank of the Appomattox River. Kippax was the first home here of this family, which, like one branch of the Randolphs, claims descent from Pocahontas.

At Cawson's, was born John Randolph, whom Bishop Meade describes as "a most talented, eccentric and unhappy man," and refers to his "peculiar and unhappy temperament, his most diseased body and the trying circumstances of his life and death."

Randolph had the courage, at a time when duels were all too frequent, to decline General Wilkinson's challenge, declaring that he would not stoop to Wilkinson's level. He endured the abuse and vilification which Wilkinson heaped upon him without changing his stand.

In 1799, he was elected Member of Congress, and distinguished himself by his wit and eloquence. He opposed the War of 1812, and thus lost his seat, but two years later returned to Congress, and in 1825 was elected Senator. In 1822 and 1824 he visited England, and attracted much attention because of his eccentricities of dress and manner. He was a member in 1829 of the convention for revising the Constitution of Virginia, was Minister to Russia, and died in Philadelphia.

All along the James River on both sides, lie these historic homes, some of them still occupied by members of the original family to own them, others purchased by the wealthy from distant states, still others, saddest of fates, now rapidly falling to ruin. Yet so staunchly were they built that it is hard to destroy them, and the visitor can but hope that some one may yet come to restore their vanishing loveliness.

With one of the most noted, this very thing is in process.

Brandon, the historic estate of the Harrison family for more than two hundred years, seemed doomed. The house was almost in ruins, the road to it practically impassable for automobiles. Then quite recently it was purchased from the heirs by Robert Daniel, now of New York City, but originally of Richmond. He is a great-great-grandson of Edmund Randolph, so that the place passes into the possession of a descendant of one of Virginia's oldest families.

The new owner is having it restored as nearly as possible to the old state, and it will soon be what it once was, a show place on the James River.

The land here was first granted to John Martin, who came to America with Captain John Smith. Martin was a member of His Majesty's first council in Virginia, and his place was then known as Martin's Brandon. He either sold or gave up the grant, for in 1635 it was conveyed to John Sadler and Richard Quiney, merchants, and William Barber, mariner. Quiney's brother, Thomas, married William Shakespeare's daughter Judith. Richard left his share of the land to his son, and from the latter it passed to his great-nephew, Robert Richardson. In the year 1720, according to one account, Richardson sold it to Nathaniel Harrison, a Burgess, councillor, naval officer, County lieutenant of Surry and Prince George Counties, and auditor general of the county, an important person, as this list of offices shows.

Other authors state that the place passed to Lady Frances Ingleby, and that she sold it to Harrison. The first Nathaniel had a son of the same name, who was a member of the Council of State, and this Harrison's son Benjamin married Evelyn Byrd; not the beauty of Westover, but her aunt. The eldest of their sons, George Evelyn, a member of the House of Burgesses, inherited Brandon.

Upper Brandon, not far away, was built in the 19th century by William Byrd Harrison, younger son of the first Benjamin.

The oldest part of Brandon, the southeast wing of the present house, was built by Nathaniel Harrison about 1712, and a few years later he added the other wing, both built of red bricks brought from England. When the first Benjamin married Evelyn Byrd, she brought with her family portraits painted by Godfrey Kneller, Sir Peter Lely, and one said to be by Van Dyck. The house was paneled and wainscoted with rare woods, and is a beautiful specimen of the elegant Virginia mansion of the period. On its window panes many distinguished visitors had scratched with a diamond their names. The hall has triple arches supported by Ionic columns.

Brandon was saved during the Civil War by a happy chance.

In 1863, the occupant, Mrs. Isabella Harrison, was advised to leave the place, as it was considered too dangerous with the approach of the Federal troops for longer occupancy. She went to Richmond, her brother, Dr. Thomas Ritchie remaining. The troops soon drew near, and Dr. Ritchie was carried off to one of the Federal gunboats in the river. The soldiers then proceeded to plunder the place.

They tore out the beautiful wainscoting, probably looking for hidden treasures; broke the windows, with their valuable autographs, destroyed all of the outbuildings, but fortunately did not burn the house; being called off for other duties, they announced their intention of returning shortly and finishing it.

It happened that President Lincoln's physician and close friend was the husband of Mrs. Harrison's sister, and he interceded with the President for Brandon. Lincoln knew Dr. Ritchie by name and reputation, and dispatched telegraphic orders to Fortress Monroe that Brandon be spared.[1] But the portraits and old furniture, with everything else portable of value had been carried off; the old window shutters, built to resist attacks of Indians, had been hacked by bayonets, and riddled with bullets, and many bullets were embedded in the front door, where it is to be hoped they will be allowed to remain.

Flower de Hundred is another old place on the river, and no one seems able satisfactorily to explain the name.

The first owner, Sir George Yeardley, was that Governor of Virginia who called and presided over the first free legislature that ever met in the American colonies, the Assembly of 1619, held in the old church in Jamestown. His nephew, Edmund Rossingham, and John Jefferson, ancestor of the President, represented Flower de Hundred in this Assembly. The Governor lived in Jamestown, but in 1621 he built on this plantation the first windmill in America. Here in 1622 six people were murdered by the Indians, the property was sold, and then changed hands several times until in 1725 it was purchased by Joseph Poythress, and has remained in the family ever since.

The oldest part of the present house was built more than a hundred years ago by John Vaughn Wilcox, who married the widow, Susan Peachy Poythress. This was a small building of but three rooms, and was used by Wilcox when he came to superintend the planting of the land. His son finished the present building. In June, 1864, General Grant, on his march to Petersburg crossed the river here. His men did much damage to the old house, hacking magnificent mahogany woodwork and furniture, tearing up floors and smashing marble.

On the opposite side of the James River, about eight miles from Richmond, on the road to Curle's Neck, one may turn from the highway, and by a practicable road approach a house that fairly pleads for a wealthy owner, anxious to restore it to its former beauty and occupy it, which the present owner does not care to do, preferring the city.

Like almost all of the homes along the river, Wilton faces on the James, and one approaches the rear from the road. Here one sees a square brick house, two stories high, disfigured by a modern porch,

[1] Article in *The Homemaker Magazine*, by Marion Harland.

already crumbling to decay, and at one side an equally disfiguring two-storied wooden addition. Passing around to the river side, where once the grounds sloped in terraces and gardens to the water's edge, not more than an eighth of a mile away, another less conspicuous disfigurement, a square, brick railed porch has been added, which like the rear one, though better, is wholly out of keeping with the beautiful Georgian entrance, the white pediments and pillars, and the hand carved white cornice below the eaves.

But worse awaits one inside.

A very broad hall runs through the house, with two rooms on each side, and the same plan is followed on the second floor. From floor to ceiling, halls and all of the eight rooms are paneled in what seems to be black walnut, and the broad staircase with its low treads, its finely carved bannisters, and unusual hipped railing, are all of the same wood. The last owner before the present gentleman bought it so covered the paneling with paint, while although he did not paint the staircase, except the stair treads, which are green, he so coated everything with varnish, that it is difficult to determine just what the wood is. The floor boards are as close, the heavy doors swing as easily and close as tightly as ever, and a few of the massive brass rimlockers remain.

It is bad enough downstairs, where the paneling is touched off with red and green and yellow, but what can one say of the beautiful rooms upstairs, the walls entirely painted over in ugly greens and yellows?

Another owner tore out the secret staircase which led from one of the lower rooms facing the river to the bedroom above, making closets of the space, while upstairs a hall was made of part, to connect the addition.

A secret passage led from somewhere in the cellar down to the river, for use in case of Indian or negro uprisings. A depression on the lawn quite plainly indicates part of its position, and the farmer living on the estate is so interested that he intends to open it again, being quite sure that he has located the river end, beneath a great boulder. In the cellar floor, now covered with concrete, but probably once flagged, two brass spikes project several inches, and he thinks that possibly some kind of a wrench once fitted over these, and turning, raised the flagstones over the entrance to the passage.

There is also a story that a button in one of the hall panels when touched pressed a secret spring, which opened a passage, but there seems now no trace of such a button.

The drawing room and dining room have white marble mantelpieces such as one finds in many old Virginia mansions, and probably imported from England. Old shutters with H hinges, very thick, still remain on the lower floor windows.

The exact age of this beautiful house is not known. It was built for William Randolph, a son of Colonel William, the first of the family, who came to Virginia in 1744, married Mary Isham, and settled on Turkey Island. The house there has long since disappeared. The owner of Wilton died in 1761, so it is reasonable to suppose that it dates from the 1750's.

Unfortunately more damage than disfiguring paint, removing a romantic staircase and blocking a secret passage has been done. Fine trees have been cut down and others left to die for want of care, but some still survive.

At Ampthill, opposite Wilton, the first iron works in America were established in 1619, under Governor John Berkeley, but after the Indian massacre three years later, they were abandoned and finally destroyed by Tarleton's men, during the Revolution.

The house at Ampthill was built in 1722, by Henry Cary, who superintended the building of the Governor's Palace and the State House of Williamsburg. Ampthill passed to his son, Archibald, a patriot, who introduced in the Virginia convention the resolution moving for entire independence of Great Britain.

Beyond Wilton lies Curle's Neck, a very old estate owned at an early date by Richard Randolph, who married the only child of Pocahontas and John Rolfe. Richard was another of Colonel William's numerous family.

The old house here has long been gone, and there now stands a beautiful brick residence, built quite in the old style, although thoroughly modern within. According to the best authorities, this house is between thirty and forty years old. It is owned by a northern gentleman who occupies it for but a short period of the year.

Continuing in the same direction, fine old Shirley is reached. This, like the majority of the river places, is a private residence.

Three stories high, of red brick, and set on a slight elevation, the grounds sloping down to the river, the plantation was at an early date the property of Colonel Edward Hill, a member of the House of Burgesses. He died childless, and his sister, Elizabeth, succeeded to the property. She married John Carter, and a descendant of theirs, Anne, married Light Horse Harry Lee, of Revolutionary fame, and was the mother of Robert E. Lee, beloved Commander-in-chief of the Confederate Armies.

The first of the Carter family in America, John, was the father of the famous " King " Carter, the title having been given him because of his wealth, and magnificent mode of life. When John Carter died, he left what was an immense fortune for those days; 300,000 acres of land, 1,000 slaves, and 10,000 pounds sterling in cash. Shirley was the home of one of the " King's " numerous sons, Charles, who had twenty-three children, one of whom, Dr. Robert, married Mary, the daughter of General Thomas Nelson.

Shirley is still occupied by the descendants of the original owners.

The large house has but three great rooms on the lower floor, and a hall running across the house. In this hall, a staircase runs around a great square opening to the roof, and some recent owner installed a curious elevator, hung on chains.

The entire lower floor is paneled from floor to ceiling in great wide boards which have been painted many times. The walls are literally covered with old family portraits, including a large one of " King " Carter in his gold-laced red coat, doubtless his uniform in the royal militia, and the portrait of one of his three wives. The King looks as though he thoroughly enjoyed good living.

The first house at Shirley was built in 1650, and altered in 1770, when the present porticoes at front and rear were added, and the hipped roof changed to the present mansard.

The doorways are lovely, topped by hand carved pediments, and over the hand carved mantels are immensely broad panels. Peale's full length portrait of Washington is one of the art treasures on these walls.

The estate of Berkeley adjoins Westover, but in the autumn of 1926 it seemed deserted, nor was it possible for an automobile to approach it by the drive turning off the highroad, so reluctantly a visit was abandoned.

The land here was granted in 1618 to Sir William Throckmorton, Sir George Yeardley, Richard Berkeley, and John Smith. In 1622, George Thorpe, head of the Virginia Committee for the proposed college at Henrycropolis, was murdered here with eight other white men by the Indians.

Later, the land where the present house stands came into the possession of John Bland, a London merchant. His son, Giles, lived here until he was hanged in 1676 by Sir William Berkeley, for taking part in Bacon's Rebellion. The property then passed to the Harrison family. A governor of Virginia, one of the Signers, a general in the Revolutionary army and a president of the United States were all born here. The first Benjamin Harrison to live here was Attorney General, Speaker of the House of Burgesses and Treasurer of the colony. His sons were Benjamin and Nathaniel, the latter the founder of the Brandon family. Berkeley descended to a Benjamin Harrison for several generations.

The fourth of the name was for many years a member of the House of Burgesses, and he built the present house at Berkeley. His son Benjamin was also a member of the House of Burgesses, and of the committee that ratified the Declaration of Independence, of which he was a Signer. His son William Henry born in Berkeley, was our ninth President, but the place passed to his elder brother, another Benjamin. Before the Civil War it was sold.

It is said that every president from Washington to Buchanan has stayed here, and here came General William Henry Harrison, " Tippecanoe," to write his inaugural address as President in his mother's room. The house was used as headquarters by McClellan, and the cellar served as a prison for Confederates.

Beautiful Westover, most carefully cared for of all the estates along the James, restored and loved by its present northern owners, is not open to strangers, save that they are allowed to see the gardens, now being restored as nearly as possible to their original condition, when lovely Evelyn Byrd used to wander in them.

This place was twice ravaged by Benedict Arnold and once by Cornwallis during the Revolution, while during the War between the States, General McClellan and his soldiers camped near the house.

On the river side, the real front, are a number of beautiful old tulip trees, survivors of a long row, and one of these has been kept alive by most extensive and skilled tree surgery. Until far above the ground, a great cavity in the trunk has been filled in with cork and cement, such a cavity that one would think a tree could not survive. Yet not only does it leaf out each spring, but marvelous Nature is gradually growing new bark, so that the edges are slowly closing over the cement framework.

William Byrd and his wife came to Virginia in 1674, first making their home at Belvidere, then coming here to Westover. Byrd held many important offices in his adopted country. He was High Sheriff of Henrico, a member of the House of Burgesses, and in 1687 the King appointed him Receiver General of His Majesty's revenues for the Colonies, in which office at his death he was succeeded by his son. The first William began collecting the fine library to which his son added. In 1688, he bought land and began building Westover.

The first house was destroyed by fire through the carelessness of a housekeeper in 1749, but William's grandson, another William, rebuilt it.

The son of the first William, Colonel Byrd, nicknamed the Black Swan, married Lucy Park, daughter of one of Marlborough's aides.

Dementi Studio

Westover, on the James River. Once the house of the Byrds, a portrait of beautiful Evelyn Byrd still hangs in the library, and her ghost is said to wander through its halls.

Brandon, home of the Harrisons, the family which gave two Presidents to this country. Although it long since passed from the ownership of that family, and was threatened with ruin, it has recently been purchased by a descendant of another great Virginia family, the Randolphs, and is now being thoroughly restored.

Byrd was educated in England. Their daughter, the beautiful Evelyn, was taken to England and presented at court when but sixteen. The Earl of Peterborough fell in love with her, and asked her hand in marriage, and she seems to have returned his love, although the Earl was over sixty, and a roué. The father would not hear of the marriage for his beloved daughter, and brought her back to Virginia, where she pined and finally died of a broken heart. When the Colonel was left a widower, he married twenty-eight year old and widowed Maria, born a Taylor.

The grandson who re-built Westover, with Peter Randolph was appointed by the Governor to visit the Indian tribes of southern Virginia, including the Cherokees, and try to arrange a treaty with them. The two men accomplished this successfully. Later, Byrd was a member of the House of Burgesses. He married Elizabeth Carter of Shirley, and when she died, Mary Willing of Philadelphia. She was related to Benedict Arnold's wife, which proved unfortunate for her, for Arnold, after going over to the British, landed at Westover with nine hundred men, on his way to attack the patriot forces, and Mrs. Byrd was held responsible. However, she succeeded in convincing her accusers that she was in no way false to the American cause.

In 1782, the Marquis de Chastellux was a guest at Westover, and thus wrote of it in his Travels:

" There are magnificent houses at every view, for the banks of the James River form the garden of Virginia. That of Mrs. Byrd surpasses them all in the magnificence of the buildings, the beauty of its situation, and the pleasures of society. . . . She takes great care of her negroes, makes them as happy as their situation will admit, and serves them herself as a doctor in time of sickness. She has even made some interesting discoveries on the disorders incident to them, and discovered a very salutary method of treating a sort of putrid fever, against which the physicians of the country have exerted themselves without success."

The third William, a very popular man like his father, was unfortunately an inveterate gambler, and the estate passed out of the family. Arnold stayed here in 1781, and Cornwallis during the same year, while at a time when the French officers were guests in the house, they expressed the greatest admiration for the lovely daughters of their host.

Evelyn's room is still pointed out to visitors, and here she is said to walk, while the tap of her high-heeled slippers, the rustle of her silken gown may sometimes be heard on the stairs. She is buried not far away.

There are four rooms on each of Westover's three floors, the main building is paneled from floor to ceiling, the panels painted cream color now, and who can say how many times they have been painted? The front left hand room as one looks over the river, and the adjoining wing which contains a ballroom, were badly damaged by fire some years ago, before the present owners bought the place, and this necessitated some new woodwork, but the old has been carefully matched. The wing on the other side of the house connected by pantries, etc., contains the kitchen, laundry and servants' quarters. In the smaller drawing room on the left in the rear hangs the three-quarter length portrait of the beautiful Evelyn Byrd.

The first Colonel Byrd was educated at Oxford, a great friend of the Duke of Orrery, as is duly set forth on his monument in the old garden, where he is buried at the intersection of two walks. Here in the garden some of the old box borders still survive, supplemented where needed by new plants, for everything is done to restore but not change the place. Here, too, is a rare Judas tree, with lovely pink blossoms in season.

Westover has its passage to the river, and a curious one. Although the entrance close to the water's edge may be plainly seen, it would be difficult now for a grown person to enter, as much earth has choked it; but a police dog belonging to the family often goes in apparently for a considerable distance, when taking refuge from guests whom he does not like. The other end of the passage is at the bottom of a dry well in an outhouse, some rods from the house, and by lighting a torch and staring down, or climbing down the ladder which reaches within a couple of feet of the top, the two brick arches through which one entered the passage to the river, and another to the cellar of the house, may be seen. A former owner had the latter passage bricked up, for she was afraid that snakes came through it. Originally one could accordingly go from the house to the river, or end the trip at this out-house, as he chose.

Tuckahoe, no longer belonging to descendants of the original owners — indeed it has changed hands repeatedly — has decided interest, even although one may find it difficult to obtain permission to visit it.

The odd name is said to be derived from the Indian word for an edible root which grew in abundance here.

Thomas, one of the many sons of the Randolph of Turkey Island, came into this property, and his father built a house here for him. Every room was paneled in either black walnut or hearts of pine. On the estate a small building is said to have served as a schoolhouse, and here Thomas Jefferson studied with his cousins, the little Randolphs.

After the death of their father, Jefferson's father was their guardian, and took his duties so seriously that he removed to Tuckahoe with his own family.

Two ghosts haunt the place, or so it is said; one that of a murdered peddler, appears in the southeast chamber; the other, a bride, wanders with floating hair, wringing her hands, along the eastern side of the garden, near the wall.

Chapter V

A GOOD motor road runs northwest from Richmond to an interesting section of Virginia, the neighborhood of Charlottesville. As one travels along this highroad, before leaving Louisa County, one may see at the right a square, red brick house, quite modern in appearance and well kept. None the less, although now a private residence, this was the Cuckoo Tavern, from which, on learning of the approach of the British General Tarleton and his men, Jack Jowett, or Jouette — the name is variously spelled — began his long ride to Monticello, to warn Jefferson and the members of the Virginia Assembly, recently removed from Richmond, of the advancing troops.

At the Jowett Tavern, kept by Jack's father, and now the Red Lands Club, Charlottesville, within a stone's throw of the Monticello Hotel, he ended his journey of forty miles. In order to outdistance Tarleton, he took unfrequented lanes and side paths, through thorns and brambles, and it is said that, to the day of his death, Jack Jowett's face was scarred from cuts and scratches received on his ride.

Thomas Jefferson afterwards introduced in Congress a resolution that a pair of pistols and a sword be given the heroic rider. Only the sword was given, and not until eight years later. It is treasured by Jowett's descendants to this day.

After warning Jefferson and his guests at Monticello, Jowett rode to Castle Hill, or perhaps stopped there on the way. Some believe that Tarleton was delayed at the latter estate not merely because his soldiers ate up two breakfasts intended for the General, but that Mrs.

Walker, mistress of Castle Hill, had given orders that everything possible be done to delay him, like Mrs. Murray of New York, when by detaining the British at her home, she gave the Americans time to escape from Manhattan Island.

The elder Jowett came to what is now Charlottesville in 1773, bought one hundred acres of land, and built his tavern, The Swan, in which the legislators several times met. Jowett laid out High Street, and kept tavern until his death in 1802. Another of his sons, Matthew, a captain in the Continental Army, was killed at the Battle of Brandywine.

The present Albemarle County, much smaller than the original, was set off in 1744. Before that year it had been explored by Robert Walker, William Randolph, Nicholas Meriwether, Robert Lewis, and Peter Jefferson, father of the President. All of these names recur in any chronicle of old estates in this section. The river now known as Rivanna was named River Anna, after Queen Anne, and the entire range of the Southwest Mountains was explored by Jefferson and Walker. When Goochland County was separated from Albemarle, it was Peter Jefferson who made the survey.

The first homes here were but one or two-roomed log cabins, with stone chimneys. These cabins were in most cases replaced by houses of rough boards, hand hewn, with hand wrought nails, and having high peaked roofs. Early settlers molded their pewter spoons for daily use.

After Peter Jefferson married Jane Rogers, he built, about 1737, the first house at Shadwell, named for the English birthplace of his wife's mother. This house was burned in 1770. Shadwell was part of the "Punch Bowl Tract," which Jefferson bought from Randolph of Tuckahoe for "Henry Weatherbourne's biggest bowl of Arrach punch." The Randolphs had already acquired lands in what was then almost a wilderness, the mountainous Albemarle County.

Colonel Thomas Mann Randolph, son of the master of Tuckahoe, owned the plantation called Varina, as well as Edgehill in this section. The latter place he left to his son, Thomas Mann Randolph, Junior, and probably built the first Edgehill house, about 1790. This, a story and a half structure, with wings, contained nine small rooms, the upper ones lighted by dormer windows. The younger Randolph married Thomas Jefferson's daughter, Martha, and in 1828 built on the site of the first Edgehill house another which now forms part of the present one. Here eight years later, his daughter opened a school for girls. Descendants of Colonel Thomas Jefferson Randolph introduced a bill in the Virginia Assembly, providing for the gradual emancipation of slaves.

Dr. Charles Everett, one of Jefferson's physicians, later bought Edgehill, and dying, willed it to his nephew and namesake, directing that his slaves be freed, and transported back to Liberia. Fortunately for them, by a codicil the nephew was permitted to use his discretion as to the destination of the freed slaves, and decided to send them instead of to Liberia, to Mercer County, Pennsylvania. In 1852, Everett built a new house on the Edgehill plantation, and moved the old one back, dividing it into two outhouses. The new one burned down in 1883, and the two parts of the old house were once more united on the original site.

Castle Hill is one of the many estates near Charlottesville which once formed part of the huge grants given early settlers. For more than a hundred years it has been the property of the Rives family, and is now the home of the author, Amelie Rives, Princess Troubetzkoy.

Nicholas Meriwether, one of the earliest explorers of what is now Albemarle County, received a grant of more than 30,000 acres here. His widow, Mildred, married Dr. Thomas Walker, a well-known local character, and thus the Castle Hill property came into Walker's possession. He is said to have been the first white man to enter Kentucky, in 1750, and his hatchet with the initials: T. W., was found not long ago in that state. He won the friendship of the Indians there and in Virginia, and was one of those who drew up a treaty with them in Lancaster, Pennsylvania, in 1744, which treaty gave to the colonists all the territory in Virginia claimed by the Indians. He was also one of a group of men who purchased 6,000,000 acres of land from George Croghan, who had bought them from the Indians. Walker had charge of the commissary department under Braddock, and when he returned from that ill-fated expedition, brought back with him a stallion which, according to local chroniclers, lived to be forty-eight years old.

Walker was a student at William and Mary College.

One of his agricultural experiments was the grafting of a Newton pippin from New York on the wild Virginia crabapple, thus producing the Albemarle pippin, a delicious variety of apple.

The Castle Hill estate originally included Cismont, Castalia, Music Hall and Belvoir. The houses on the first two are less than a century old; at Music Hall, oddly named, the first house, built about 1783, has practically been torn down and re-built, while at Belvoir, the old house burned down, and a later owner of the place cut down so many of the fine old trees that the Hon. William C. Rives, commenting upon the destruction, is said to have remarked:

"The man should have left one upon which to hang himself."

The first house on the Castle Hill property is believed to have been built about 1764 by Thomas Walker, into whose possession the estate had then come by his marriage to Mildred Meriwether. This house forms the rear of the present one, built in 1824 by the Hon. William C. Rives, United States Senator from Virginia, and Minister to France. He, too, owned the estate through his wife, Judith Page Walker, a descendant of Thomas Walker. This Mrs. Rives, like her descendant, was an author, two of her books being " Home and the World " and an " Epitome of the Bible for Children."

A long drive of nearly a mile from the highroad brings one to what is the most remarkable feature of this fine old estate, something absolutely unique, as those learned in trees and shrubs have many times declared. From the road, one turns into a driveway which, in the shape of a long oval, takes cars or carriages to the house on one side, and away on the other. All of the lower end of this oval is en-closed between walls of box trees — walls nine or ten feet thick, and almost impenetrable, towering to the height of at least thirty-five or forty feet. It is difficult for one who has not seen this marvel to credit it. Box hedges nine or ten feet high, though rare, do exist, but anything like this wall would be, according to all accounts, impossible to duplicate. Visitors from foreign countries are amazed. There are no records of the planter of this wonderful box wall, but undoubtedly it is very old. The upper portion of the drive is without such wall, but here and there, at the sides, are isolated trees rising to almost if not quite the same height. From the front portico, one gets a beautiful view of mountains in the distance, through a cleverly cut opening in the box, leaving beneath a hedge of goodly height, and allowing the towering walls on either side to frame the panorama effectively. Those interested in psychic phenomena declare that an atmosphere favorable to these is also conducive to the growth of box.

The old portion of the house consists of a broad hall with a large room on either side, and an upper half story, lighted by quaint dormer windows. Mr. Rives built on the larger front part in such a way that through the front entrance one passes into a hall which joins the old one almost imperceptibly. The rear door is directly opposite the front one, and through both may be had a beautiful view of the mountains in the distance. A more modern staircase in the newer portion supplements the old one still remaining in the old building.

At right and left of the front door, large rooms open from the hall. The one on the left has the green Empire furniture bought for it by Mr. Rives, and the Erard piano, still of good tone. The walls of both rooms are covered with old family portraits, while in the hall hangs a charming portrait of the present owner, painted by her husband.

From the green drawing room opens another room which, when there are several guests staying in the house, is used as a bedroom.

One night a guest was to occupy it, and the family retired to the second story. Prince Troubetzkoy told the writer that he was awakened from sleep by his friend's voice, calling him frantically from the lower hall. He hurried down to find that gentleman in a state of excitement.

" What is the matter? What has been going on here? " the friend demanded.

The host, who had heard nothing, asked what he meant.

"Why, for a half hour or more, there has been the greatest commotion down here, people coming and going, doors opening and shutting, chairs pushed back in the drawing room."

There was no trace to be found of any nocturnal visitors, and one is free to explain it as he chooses, although many in the neighborhood will smile, and murmur: "The family ghost!"

This is not the only ghost story connected with the place. Not far from the entrance drive, on the other side of the road by which it is approached, is a hollow. No horse can be induced to pass through this hollow after dusk. At all events, the mistress of the house admits that although an excellent rider, she was thrown when she vainly tried, after several previous failures, to force her mount to take this direction.

A party of children of another member of the family, picnicking in here, lingered until the sun was setting. None of these had ever heard any tales of a haunted hollow, but suddenly one of the children glanced up, and remarked: "What a funny looking carriage." A moment later, she added: "And see how funnily dressed the ladies are."

The others saw nothing, but later the child described minutely what she had seen, and the description was that of an old fashioned coach, the costumes those of long ago.

Ghosts are no novelty in this state.

Here at Castle Hill, at the time that Tarleton was being delayed by the wily mistress of the house, it is told that finally, becoming indignant at the length of time that he was kept waiting for his breakfast, he went to the kitchen, only to be told by the cook that she could do nothing. His soldiers had already eaten up two breakfasts that she had prepared for him. Finally she advised him to keep his men out of her kitchen if he wanted breakfast. Anyone familiar with colored cooks can form a picture of Mammy, and her righteous indignation.

Tarleton is said to have become so furious that he had the offending soldiers tied to cherry trees outside the kitchen, and severely whipped. Eventually he got the third breakfast, ate it, and started on his way, but too late.

Breakfasting at Castle Hill that morning, and surprised by the arrival of Tarleton are said to have been William and Robert Nelson, and Francis Kinlock. They started to make their escape, and the first two succeeded, but one British soldier recognized Kinlock, and called out:

"Stop, Cousin Francis. You know I could always beat you running."

The two had been at school together, and Kinlock, knowing this to be the truth, allowed himself quietly to be taken prisoner.

Nearer Charlottesville is the estate known as Clover Fields, the property for many years of a branch of the Randolph family, descendants of the original owner. Although the present house is not more than eighty years old, it stands on the site of a much older one, built in 1760, and on land which was granted to Nicholas Meriwether in 1730. The original grant hangs in the hallway of the house. This curious document sets forth that "for divers good causes and considerations, but more and especially for and in consideration of the sum of 21 pounds of good and lawful money for our use paid to our Receiver General of our Records in this our Colony and Dominion of Virginia . . . unto Nicholas Meriwether of Hanover County, Gentleman, one certain tract or parcel of land containing 17,952 acres beginning with the white Oak, marked with several letters, 13,762 acres of this tract being granted to the said Nicholas Meriwether, and to Christopher Clark by patent . . . witness our trusty and well beloved William Good, Esq., our Lieutenant Governor and Commander-in-Chief of our said Colony and Dominion at Williamsburg."

The name was originally written Merry Weather, and the family were Quakers, personal friends of King George II, who gave Nicholas more than 11,000 acres of land in addition to those mentioned in the deed.

The first house, long, low, with dormer windows in an upper story, and tall chimneys, was replaced by the present two-story, square house of bricks, covered on the outside with weatherboarding. It has massive old doors, one of which when closed gives a prolonged musical note. A small story and a half cottage near the house is at least a century and a quarter old.

Clover Fields eventually was inherited by Captain W. D. Meriwether whose daughter married Thomas Jefferson Randolph of Edgehill. The house passed to the Randolphs when two Miss Meriwethers in turn married a Randolph.

The first Nicholas Meriwether helped build what was known as Walker's Church, on the site where now stands Grace Episcopal church, about two miles from Clover Fields. Colonel Nicholas had a brother Charles. One of the latter's grandsons, during the War between the States, saw a party of horsemen approaching, and thinking them Confederate soldiers, greeted them cordially. He found out his mistake when one of the riders relieved him of his watch.

One of the Meriwethers lived at Cismont, but only the old kitchen of the original house survives.

Cobham Park, close to the railroad station of that name, is another estate which formed part of the original grant to Nicholas Meriwether. A beautiful square Georgian brick house stands on the summit of a hill, reached by a winding drive from the highway. The house is not very old, but most attractive, with a box enclosed flower garden.

The Creek, in this same section, now known as Maxfield, is a really old house, outwardly not much modernized. It is one of those story and a half clapboarded cottages, with dormer windows, and big rooms, but was moved here from its old site to make room for the canal, now no longer in use.

In 1764, Colonel Thomas Walker built this house on Belvoir estate. Another replaced it in 1790, the old one being moved to the estate now known as Maxfield, while the second Belvoir was replaced on the same site by a third, as late as 1836.

To the first house Tarleton sent half his men, looking for Colonel Thomas Walker, but he was not there.

Colonel Walker's granddaughter, Eliza Kinlock, inherited Belvoir in 1809. She married Judge Hugh Nelson, and their son Thomas became Governor of Virginia. In 1836, when the second Belvoir burned down, the old English organ which it contained was saved by being taken apart and carried out. Afterwards it was given to Grace Church, and used for many years.

Only the site remains in present day Charlottesville of The Farm, the house where Captain Nicholas Lewis and his wife, Mary Walker, known as "Captain Moll," lived. Near the town of Ivy is Locust Hill, where Meriwether Lewis, of Lewis and Clark fame was born, but the present house is not the original.

During the Revolution, a British officer, one of the prisoners sent to Charlottesville, where they were well treated, and hospitably entertained from time to time by various residents, including Jefferson, wrote letters home to England. In one of these he speaks of "an abominable liquor called peach brandy, which if drunk to excess the fumes raise an absolute delirium." Thomas Ambury, another early English visitor to this section, declared: "There is something peculiar in the climate of Virginia that should render all classes of so hospitable a disposition."

Three miles from Charlottesville, on the top of a mountain which had to be leveled to make space for a house, stands Monticello, home of Thomas Jefferson, begun by him when but twenty-one years old. Shadwell was his birthplace.

Monticello came into the possession of the Jefferson family by a grant in 1735, and was owned by them until the death of the ex-President in 1826. Young Jefferson had no architect, and made his own plans, slaves doing the work of building. He laid out bridle paths, planted gardens, etc., but the house was not finished for thirty years, partly because the builder often changed his plans. Although Jefferson had begun building in 1770, when he fell in love with a young widow, Martha Skelton, daughter of Isham Randolph of Dungeness, another of the sons of the Turkey Island settler, and brought his bride home, only the so-called Honeymoon Lodge, a one room brick building, was finished.

Most people are familiar with the story of the young couple, setting out after the wedding in a blinding snowstorm for their new home. The chaise broke down, they were forced to ride double on a horse, and eventually arrived at Monticello at two o'clock in the morning. The story that they could not get into the house, so had to spend the night in this lodge is false, since there was no house.

When Jefferson began his home, it is said that there was not another brick building in existence outside of Charlottesville in the whole section. The bricks were all made on the place except later, when he brought some of the finest for decorative use from Philadelphia. He built a saw mill, a grist mill and a nail factory. The house was finished in 1802.

Whatever one may think of the final result — and there are widely differing opinions — no one can deny the marvelous beauty of the site, with views of the exquisite mountain scenery on all sides; nor that the first floor of the house is both impressive and admirably fitted for entertaining.

Monticello is now the property of the Jefferson Memorial Association, and visitors are admitted daily on payment of a small fee.

From without, the second story, not as yet shown to visitors, almost disappears, dwarfed by the height of the lower floor with its twelve rooms. The upper story is low ceiled, ill ventilated, cut up into small rooms. Servants' quarters are in a long, low building in the hill, below the house level. These, divided into separate lodgings, each with its own entrance, are connected by a roofed, flagged porch across the fronts. In the end nearest the house, the old kitchen, a gift shop has been installed. A covered passage, mostly underground, connects the quarters and kitchen with the basement of the large house, and a similar passage extends from the latter in the opposite direction to the ice house. A third brick building near this is Jefferson's old office, and across the lawn a similar building is the so-called Honeymoon Cottage.

Entering the main building by a circular vestibule, one comes into a large hall, and from this, through a wide doorway, into the drawing room overlooking the lawn. Monticello has entrances on all four sides.

The double doors opening from the lower hall are examples of Jefferson's ingenuity, for by closing one the other moves shut automatically.

Over the front entrance is a clock with faces within and without the house. It has not been going for years, as no one now knows how to repair it, but still indicates the weather on its inner face, connected with the outer weathervane. Nearby is a ladder which was used for winding it, and which folds up into a pole. The woodwork throughout is of beech, walnut and wild cherry, some of the flooring eight inches thick, and put together with double tongued grooves, not a single nail. Nails used in building here were made on the place, in a little building passed as one drives up to the house.

In the dining room, at the side of the fireplace is a small dumbwaiter, whose door forms part of the woodwork, and would never be noticed. This was used to bring bottles of wine up from the cellar for guests at table.

A curious feature is found in the bedrooms. There were no bedsteads, beds being built into alcoves in the thick walls, and in one room, linen closets are built above the bed space. There is a suggestion of the Island of Marken here. Still more odd is the opening some five feet deep, and more than six feet broad, between Jefferson's own bedroom and private study. In this was fitted a bed which could be drawn up to the ceiling, giving free passage back and forth during the day from one room to another. From the study, in a closet a staircase mounts to an upper room, where at times Jefferson had a guard stationed. Three oval openings in the upper wall here are said once to have been filled with portraits, removed by a later owner, but they could have served for peepholes for the guard. The revolving chair and table invented by Jefferson, a model of which was shown at Philadelphia's Sesquicentennial, stands in his study.

There is as yet but little old furniture here, but the Association hopes soon to furnish the entire house with that of the period of its illustrious owner.

One exception to the small bedrooms on the second floor is a large room known as the ballroom, although no balls were ever given in it. It is said to have been intended for a billiard room, but by the time that it was finished Virginia had passed a law forbidding billiard tables in private homes, so none was ever brought here.

Everyone will surely comment: "Where are the stairs?" expecting to see a broad flight in the front hall. Instead, in each of the narrow passages which lead off at right angles from the central hall are little narrow winding staircases. Two going down to the basement are thirty-one inches broad; two going upstairs, are only two feet in width. One cannot picture a lady in hoopskirts using these stairs, and they must have been uncomfortably narrow for anyone. The story goes that Jefferson intended to build a suitable staircase, but during his travels abroad observed that at parties there was a tendency to block the stairs with lingering groups, so determined that his should never be thus crowded.

The lower floor has a drawing, dining and breakfast room, two studies, two conservatories, very like modern sun parlors, and bedrooms enough for the grown members of the family and a couple of guests. Jefferson's daughter, her husband and children almost always lived with him, for no sooner did they decide to have a home of their own at Edgehill and leave, than he would implore them to return.

Another myth will be exploded when this house is visited. Jefferson did not, when warned by Jack Jowett of the approach of Tarleton and his men, escape by an underground passage, as so often told. By means of that passage it would indeed have been difficult to escape, if not impossible, for it is nothing more than a small tunnel, through which buckets of refuse were conveyed on rollers from the house to an opening in the side of the hill behind, whence slaves took and emptied them. In one of the lower bedrooms may be seen the drop in the floor beneath which stood one of these buckets.

Jefferson lingered after the others had gone, and after making his preparations, gathering up his papers, etc., left the house on foot but a few minutes before Tarleton's men entered it.

Among other guests and members of the Legislature who were at

Monticello when the warning was given, was General Stevens, who had been wounded, and had not fully recovered. He might have been captured, but Tarleton's men saw a scarlet coated individual ahead of the plainly clad General, and believing the former to be an officer, allowed the General to escape while they pursued the red coat. This rider was none other than Jack Jowett, who, after coquetting with his pursuers, and allowing them almost to come up with him, suddenly spurred his blooded horse, and easily left them behind.

Jefferson went to the Randolph estate, probably to Edgehill. Two faithful slaves, Martin and Caesar, busied themselves in hiding valuables beneath the floor boards of the front portico, and were so busy that Caesar, who stood below, receiving the articles that Martin handed down to him, had no time to escape. Martin replaced the boards over his head, and there Caesar remained for eighteen hours, without food or drink, and without making a sound that might betray the hiding place. Martin received the leader of the soldiers, who locked Jefferson's study door, and handed the slave the key. Nothing was touched except a few things in the cellar.

One of Tarleton's men put a pistol at Martin's breast, and said that he would fire it unless Martin told him where the valuables were hidden.

" Fire away then! " cried the faithful servant, but his officer called off the soldier.

Crowds flocked to Monticello in 1809, after Jefferson's retirement from public life, and he wrote: " Political honors are but empty torments." Guests were no novelty here. The Duke de Laincourt spent seven days with Jefferson in 1796; the Marquis de Chastellux, Lieutenant Hall, of the English Army, and William Wirt, the historian, were a few early visitors.

Jefferson's daughter Martha, the housekeeper, must have had some trying times, for after her father became President, guests were even more numerous than ever, and always hospitality was lavish. In the latter years, the old steward sometimes complained that he would " cut up a fine beef, and two days later it was all gone," while once,

Monticello, three miles from Charlottesville, Virginia. This house of Thomas Jefferson, built according to his own plans, was thirty years in building. Now owned by the Jefferson Memorial Association, it is being gradually furnished with pieces which once belonged to the great man.

An interior at Monticello, showing two mirrors which once belonged to Thomas Jefferson.

A cottage 125 years old at Clover Fields, near Charlottesville, Virginia. The original house here has been replaced by one but 80 years old, but it and the cottage stand on part of the original great tract of land granted to Nichilas Meriwether, in 1750.

The tavern kept by Jack Jowett's father in Charlottesville, Virginia. Now the Red Lands Club. It was to this house that Jowett rode, after warning the members of the Assembly and other patriots at Monticello and the neighboring estates, of the approach of Tarleton and his men.

when Mrs. Randolph was asked what was the largest number of guests for whom she had ever provided beds for the same night, after some deliberation, replied: " Fifty."

Since even Monticello with its thirty-five rooms could not accommodate such an army, in addition to the large family, beds were found for some at the homes of neighbors. Undoubtedly, the enormous demands made on Jefferson's hospitality, ungrudgingly as he gave it, were at least partly responsible for his dying a poor man, his elderly daughter being compelled to leave her lifelong home. Before his death, Jefferson had become so poor that he was forced to sell many of his books, and finally subscriptions were taken up among his friends and admirers to pay his expenses until his death.

At his death, James Barclay bought the entire place for $7,000. Much of the furniture, etc., was removed, but the room in which Jefferson died had been left just as it was at the time of his death, even to the crumpled bedclothes.

Finally, hearing that the place was again for sale, some admirers in Philadelphia raised $3,000, and dispatched this sum by a young Virginian to purchase Monticello, intending to give it to Martha Jefferson Randolph for her lifetime. A fellow traveler in the stage coach with the young Virginian, as told in her pamphlet on the place by Mrs. Martin W. Littleton, was Uriah P. Levy of New York, who had been captain in the United States Navy.

The young Virginian talked too much, drank, and lost a day thereby. When he went to make the purchase, he learned that his fellow traveler had bought Monticello for $2500. At his death, Levy left the place to the people of the United States, but his relatives had the will set aside. Jefferson M. Levy inherited part under the new legal ruling, and purchased the rest. Finally the Association was formed, and succeeded in buying the property, but money is still needed for endowment purposes, and to furnish the house properly.

This by no means exhausts the list of old estates in this section, or even those with interesting histories. An entire volume might be written on them alone. Mention of a few must suffice.

To Montpelier, about thirty miles from Shadwell, in Orange County, and not far from the famous Virginia Hot Springs, James Madison, the future President, was brought by his father when a small child. The house here, built in 1756, but re-modeled in 1809, was said to have been the first brick house, that is with brick exterior, in the neighborhood. James Madison, Junior, the President, enlarged it, and a later owner added wings.

In 1820, Madison wrote that they had " ninety persons to dine with us at our table fixed on the lawn, under a large arbor." Fortunately for host and hostess, only six of the company remained for the night.[1]

Scotchtown was bought in 1771 by Patrick Henry for his home, but later passed to John Payne. This was the home of Dolly Payne, afterwards the wife of President Madison, and one of the most famous White House ladies. During the Revolution, Tarleton and his raiders are said to have ridden on their horses up the broad stone steps, and through the wide hall of this house.

Rosewell, the Page manor house, begun in 1725, and finished five years later, is a square brick building, with imported marble casement frames. The rooms are exact cubes, the hall wainscoted in mahogany, with a fine balustrade carved to represent baskets of fruit. Jefferson frequently visited here, and is said to have drafted the Declaration of Independence at Rosewell, before going on to Philadelphia and making the final version.

The place was sold to a Mr. Booth for $12,000, and in 1838, he changed the flat roof, covering it with galvanized iron, after removing and selling the lead. Then Rosewell was sold again.

A letter from Edmund Randolph still exists, in which he urges Governor Page to accept pay from Congress for the lead weights removed from the windows, and used to make American bullets. A later owner cut down all the fine old cedar trees near the house, tore out and sold the mahogany wainscoting, but spared the staircase, only to paint it white.

[1] *Historic Shrines of America*, John T. Faris.

Bishop Meade remarks on the extravagance shown in building Rosewell and other Virginia mansions, where "richly carved mahogany wainscotings and capitals and stairways abound, and every brick is English." He also mentions Rosewell's shingle roof, covered with lead.

At Salisbury, fourteen miles from Richmond, is the farmhouse which Patrick Henry rented for his family in 1784, when he was elected Governor of Virginia. His landlord, Thomas Mann Randolph, sold the property to Dr. Philip Turpin, a graduate in medicine and surgery of Edinburgh University. During the Revolution, Turpin was taken prisoner by the British, and kept as ship surgeon aboard one of their war vessels. At first he was believed by his fellow countrymen, when this absence continued, to be a Tory but eventually officers on the vessel testified that he had been no willing prisoner, while other friends in Virginia vouched for his patriotism, so his estate, which had been confiscated, was restored, an unconditional release of his property being granted, largely through the influence of Thomas Jefferson.

Red Hill, Patrick Henry's last home, in Charlotte County, and purchased by him in 1794, was recently destroyed by fire.

A fine new house long since replaced the two small wooden cottages, the home of John Randolph in Roanoke.

Up in the peak of Virginia, the northernmost portion, is another of the King Carter places. Their number is not so surprising, for the "King" had a large family, and provided each of his children with an estate.

Lewis Burwell came to Albemarle County in 1640, and settled on Carter's Creek. His son, Nathaniel, married Elizabeth Carter, one of the "King"'s daughters. Their son lived at beautiful Carter's Grove, and for a time his son, Nathaniel, lived there also, but later moved to this Carter Hall, in Clark County.

He married Susan Grymes, but was left a most disconsolate widower, and begged his friend, Governor Page, to send for his half sister, the young and beautiful widow, Mrs. George Baylor, that they two might marry. The Governor sent for his half sister, and on her arrival, the plan was unfolded. She promptly refused to accept a suitor thus provided, whereupon she was informed that the two friends had settled the match between them, and in consequence she had nothing to say about it. She actually married Burwell, and immediately after the ceremony, he remarked:

"Now, Lucy, you can weep for your dear George, and I will weep for my beloved Sukey."

Mt. Airy, in this part of the state, is the home of the Tayloes, and has never passed out of the family.

The first owner was one of the Knights of the Golden Horseshoe, who in 1716 made an expedition from Williamsburg to the summit of the Blue Ridge Mountains, a tremendous undertaking then, as it meant traversing wild country and thick forests. The expedition was led by Governor Spottswood, and the little company crossed and re-crossed the Rappahannock River. Afterwards they formed themselves into this Society of Knights, and each member received from the Governor a golden horseshoe set with jewels, as souvenir.

The house at Mt. Airy was built in 1747, of brown stone, quarried on the place, and with trimmings of sandstone from Aquia Creek.

During Lafayette's visit to this country in 1824, Mrs. Tayloe used to send him in February fresh raspberries from her greenhouses.

A few miles from the town of Culpepper stands a house with a curious history.

Built in 1742, it is typical of old houses in this section, square, with four rooms on a floor, a wide hall running through the middle and at either gable end a big old chimney, in which fireplaces open across corners of the adjacent rooms. The wife of one of the family now owning the place vouches for the following:

In taking pictures of the old house, no matter from what angle, one of the two chimneys cannot be found when the picture is developed. At best, it may appear as a nebulous something in the film, but disappears entirely when that is developed and printed. This is not the result of a single amateur photographer's efforts, she declares, but *no one* has ever yet succeeded in getting a picture of this chimney, although there is no difficulty in getting one of the house, and of the other similar chimney. She does not attempt to explain this.

In days long gone, the house was occupied by the Reverend Thompson, rector of St. Mark's Parish, Culpepper. He called it The Grange. Thompson wooed the widow of Governor Spottswood, then living at Germanna, not many miles away, but she spurned his suit, declaring with some vigor that Lady Spottswood was so superior in rank to a mere parson, that it was presumption on his part to ask her hand, and that the widow of Governor Spottswood could not demean herself by accepting him. The clergyman replied at length, arguing that as a clergyman he was above kings, and finally concluded his letter somewhat to the effect that since he had now answered all of her arguments satisfactorily, there was no longer any reason why they should not be married.

The lady must have found his reasoning conclusive. At all events, she married him, and went to live at The Grange, bringing the clergyman quite a fortune.

Many years ago, when the place came into the ownership of the present family, they changed the name to Salubria.

Salubria somewhat resembles Kenmore in style, but was built before that house. It has the usual drawing room paneled from floor to ceiling, and so enormous a fireplace that chairs may be placed in opposite corners at the same time.

While Thompson rests in the parish graveyard, his grave appropriately marked, no record exists — or at all events, none has yet been discovered — of either the death or the burial place of the former Lady Spottswood, who was a lady of importance. What became of her, and what explains the story of the house that follows, may be left for the reader to decide to his own satisfaction.

After the clergyman's death without children, the property passed after several generations, about 1830, to three sisters named Hansborough. Of these three, one jumped in the well near the house, and drowned herself; a second hung herself to a walnut tree in the yard, and the third hanged herself by a hank of yarn to one of the rafters in the attic. One of the three is said to have killed a slave, and buried the corpse in the cellar.

In 1840, the grandfather-in-law of the lady responsible for this narrative bought the place. His son succeeded to it, and this gentleman's son brought his young bride while on their honeymoon to visit his father and stepmother. The bride came from another state, and had heard no stories about her husband's old home.

On the evening of their arrival, they went to their room upstairs, and it being a warm night in June, the young husband took a pitcher, and announced his intention of fetching some cold water from the well in the garden.

The bride, seating herself in front of the toilet table, over which hung a mirror, began to let down her hair.

Suddenly she felt that there was someone in the room.

"I assured myself that it was nonsense," she tells, "and would not turn my head, or look behind me, but the feeling persisted. All at once the mirror in front of me began to cloud over, and then I could stand it no longer, but left my seat. When my husband returned, I was sitting on the side of the bed.

"'What is the matter?' he asked. 'What have you seen? You are as white as a sheet.'

"I would not tell him then, for I dreaded being laughed at, but merely said: 'Don't you ever leave me in this room alone again.'

"The next day he confessed that he had perhaps been unkind. He knew that I had never heard any of the stories current about the house, and had wished to find out for himself if I should see or hear anything, as so many had insisted that they had done.

"My stepmother-in-law has never admitted that she has ever seen or heard anything. Probably she never has. But I have had other experiences. We were staying there on a visit some years later. Extra supplies of sugar were kept in a big green wooden clothespress at the top of the stairs, since the lower floor was rather damp. A number of guests having arrived unexpectedly for supper, my stepmother-in-law wanted more sugar, and gave the bowl to the two little boys of the family, bidding them go upstairs and fill it for her. They went willingly, but in a few minutes we heard a great noise, and rushing out into the hall, found them and the sugar bowl at the foot of the stairs, down which all three had rolled together. Questioned, they declared that they had seen 'a lady all in white, her hair hanging down her back, walking in the upper hall.'"

The narrator added that she had often thought of writing some of her own experiences in the house, and telling this once to a clergyman, that gentleman remarked:

" Well, if there are ghosts, that certainly is the house in which to find them, and I admit that I myself have passed some very uncomfortable nights there."

One more story.

The lady already mentioned left by train from Charlottesville with her husband one March day for Salubria. After leaving the train, a drive of several miles was necessary. It was evening when they reached a hill from which they could plainly see the old house. Every window seemed ablaze with light, and knowing that their hostess was not in good health, the lady remarked to her husband:

" Strange, the house must be full of company."

As they approached, however, the lights disappeared, and when they mounted the steps all seemed in utter darkness. They knocked repeatedly, to no effect, until, just as they were wondering what to do, the massive old mahogany door, three inches thick, with great strap hinges, swung slowly open. As they stepped into the broad hall, they saw a single small lamp burning, so dimly that its light had been invisible outside. The door, untouched, closed silently behind them, and then, and then only, an inner door opened, and their hostess came out to greet them, explaining that she had heard the knocking, but did not dare to face the wind, blowing not against the door, however, but in another direction, so had waited for them to open it. All the servants had gone, for not one will stay in the house after dark, although in the daylight they are not afraid.

In a house in Charlottesville occupied by one of the University professors, a ghost with a peg leg is said often to be heard walking up and down, but apparently no one has ever seen this nocturnal promenader.

Of still another old house nearby they tell of one room in which it was impossible ever to keep a light burning, but this house has burned to the ground.

Chapter VI

Houses Connected with the Washington Family, and Other Virginia Estates

ONCE more returning to Richmond, the fine highroad connecting that city with Washington passes through delightful Fredericksburg. Here are a number of old houses with interesting histories, several of them directly connected with the Washington family.

Augustine Washington, father of our First President, settled in Stafford County, where his first wife died. He then moved to Wakefield, and here George Washington was born. This house was burned to the ground on Christmas Day, 1780. The Wakefield National Memorial Association has been formed, and hopes soon to build a replica of the house on the original site, and to restore the old gardens as well.

After Wakefield, the Washingtons lived for a time at Mt. Vernon, where Augustine Washington owned a tract of land, and a house which forms part of the present one. Then the head of the family bought another place known as Ferry Farm, across the river from Fredericksburg, and two miles lower down. Here his four sons and only daughter, Betty, spent their childhood, and here his second wife, Mary Ball Washington, lived for a number of years after her husband's death, and only after much persuasion, yielded to her son's and her daughter's urging, and removed to the house in Fredericksburg now known by her name.

On the site of Ferry Farm it is said that the Indians smoked a pipe of peace with Captain John Smith, but of the original buildings occupied by the Washingtons, only a single outhouse now remains.

There seems almost a fatality about early houses connected with them, for the home of Mary Ball, at Epping Forest, Lancaster County, also burned to the ground.

Ferry Farm was the scene of the famous cherry tree story. Apropos of this story, one lady in Fredericksburg expressed herself to this effect:

"It is not for me to prove the cherry tree story and similar tales true. It is for those who do not believe them true to prove them false. This they have not done as yet, and until they do, I, for one, shall continue to believe them."

On the same side of the river as the Ferry Farm, George Washington went to school at Falmouth, to Master Hobby, next door to the church. Both church and schoolhouse have disappeared. Later, when fourteen years old, he crossed the ferry, near where the present bridge stands, to the home of Parson James Marye, there, together with other young Virginians later to become famous, to continue his education at the school kept by the clergyman. The present Baptist church stands on the site of Parson Marye's house.

A bit of Fredericksburg's early history may be of interest.

Captain John Smith sailed up the Rappahannock River as far as the Falls, in 1608. When he and his companions left their boat at the foot of the Falls, landed, and proceeded to look for possible minerals, etc., they were attacked by the Indians with a storm of arrows, and in defending themselves, wounded one of the Indians, who was left for dead by his comrades. Mosco, Smith's friendly Indian guide, wished to kill the wounded man, but Smith bound up his wounds, and through this man negotiations were begun on the following day which ended in the pipe of peace, smoked near what was later Falmouth town.

Tradition says that a settlement was made here as early as 1622. In 1635, Major Lawrence Smith took up land, and is believed to have built a fort. Smithfield, four miles below Fredericksburg, is supposed to have been named for this family. Lawrence Smith's nephew, Augustine, is connected with the neighborhood as early as 1700, but from the time when the fort was built, and two hundred soldiers and their families settled nearby, until the coming of Governor Spottswood, but little is known.

Spottswood had fought with Marlborough in Europe, and coming to this country in 1710, brought with him the writ of Habeas Corpus, greatly desired by the colonists. He induced a number of Protestant Germans, ironworkers, who had come over at the invitation of Baron de Graffenreid, to settle in what became the town of Germanna, built them a fort, and opened up the iron mines in that section. When he left Williamsburg, Spottswood settled in Germanna, built himself a castle, and here, in 1732, Colonel William Byrd of Westover visited him.

With the settlement of Germanna, Fredericksburg had become an important trading post, named for Crown Prince Frederick, son of George II. Byrd speaks of his visit to " Colonel Henry Willis' new town of Fredericksburg," and that at the time of his visit, " besides Colonel Willis, who is the top man of the place, there are only one merchant, a tailor, a smith, an ordinary keeper, and a lady who acts both as doctress and coffee woman."

Governor Spottswood was deeply interested in the iron works at Germanna, the first in America, and is said to have made as much as £5,000 a year from them, which gave him the nickname of " The Tubal Cain of America."

He was a broad minded man withal, and established a school for Christianizing the Indians, giving a thousand pounds towards a college for that purpose.

He was, as mentioned in the preceding chapter, the leader of the expedition of the Knights of the Golden Horseshoe. The knights derived their name from the fact that horseshoes, not needed in the country around Williamsburg, had to be provided for their horses when going into the wilds. The golden horseshoes which Governor Spottswood presented to the knights after their expedition was over, were set with jewels, and bore the inscription: *Sic Juvat Transcendere Montes*. Needless to say, these souvenirs were highly prized, and handed down in the families of their owners for generations.

The expedition started from Williamsburg on August 20, 1716, stopped at Austin Smith's in Fredericksburg, and dined on the 24th, then left Germanna on the 25th. They drank His Majesty's health on the summit of the Blue Ridge, went on to the Shenandoah, which they called the Euphrates, and were back in Germanna on the 15th of September.

This settlement did not survive. The Germans moved first to Fauquier County, later to Madison, near the railway station of that name, and founded what is now Germantown. Nothing now remains of Governor Spottswood's "castle."

After this digression, returning to Fredericksburg, the very names of the streets, Hanover, Princess Anne, Duke of Gloster, Prince Edward, Charlotte and Sophia testify to the founders' devotion to their sovereigns. Here early customs were long retained. Not until 1742 was an ordinance passed that, because of frequent fires, no more wooden chimneys might be built, and all those not replaced within three years by others of brick or stone should be torn down by the sheriff. An old resident told Mrs. Fleming that her grandmother used to tell her that " she saw Peggy, a noted termagant, as tied in a gig that had been improvised into a ducking stool, she was pushed along through the streets polluting the air with her foul oaths, and surrounded by a clamorous crowd of men and boys. . . . She was pushed along to the old baptizing place and into the river . . . the water over her head. They drew her out, but she was more vituperative than ever. Again they pushed her in, and she came out spluttering anathemas, but the third submersion silenced her. She returned through the same streets, in the same gig, quiet as a lamb." [1]

Until the early days of the 19th century, a whipping post and a ducking stool existed in the town.

The oldest house now standing in Fredericksburg is on Princess Anne Street, between Amelia and Lewis, a story and a half cottage in excellent condition, built in 1745 by Charles Dick, Commissioner of the Gunnery, of which more later. Until a few years ago, down close to

[1] *Historic Periods of Fredericksburg*, Mrs. Vivien Minor Fleming.

the river stood an old stone building with barred windows, later used as a tobacco warehouse, but thought to have originally been a jail. Some say that African slaves were taken directly there from the boats which brought them up the river. It has been pulled down, and some of the window gratings are now used as gates in the yard of the Old Quarters Antique Shop. This jail stood on the Leaseland Settlement, the oldest part of the town, near the coffee house of Mrs. Sukey Livingston, " doctress and coffee woman," a landowner.

Augustine Washington became one of Fredericksburg's trustees in 1742, and about that time bought lots there, but he died the following year, and his widow did not occupy the house now known by her name here until 1775.

Very probably this house was originally intended for an overseer's dwelling, and at the time that Mary Washington occupied it, was a small cottage, a story and a half high, with but two rooms on each floor, and an outer kitchen, connected by a brick walk.

The front and largest room was Mrs. Washington's bedroom, and here she died. Behind was a living room, and above two small, low-ceiled bedrooms. Some years later, an addition was built on, and this is now occupied by the caretaker, installed by the Association for the Preservation of Virginia Antiquities, which owns the house.

Some articles of furniture used by Mary Washington, her work table, favorite chair, some of her pictures, are treasured in the house, with other pieces of the same period, if not actually used by her. Here are the table at which Washington and Lafayette dined, and a piano which belonged to the Samuel Washington family.

In the little garden still grows box that Mary Washington planted. The house was to have been torn down, at the time of the Chicago Exposition, but an urgent appeal from the women of Fredericksburg for its preservation brought instant response, and through the generosity of Mrs. Bryan of Richmond, it was purchased for $4,000 and saved.

The women of Fredericksburg did Mary Washington's memory another service. Tired of the rumors that she could neither read nor write, although at the time in which she lived this would not have been remarkable, they hunted and inquired until something in her handwriting was discovered; her own will. This they had photographed, and one of the photographs is now shown in the Rising Sun tavern as proof that such statements were calumnies.

To the front door of her little house went Mrs. Washington to receive the note which her son dispatched by messenger at the time of the surrender of Cornwallis. A resident of Fredericksburg, a man named Keimer, to the day of his death used to tell how as a small boy, voicing the interest of the neighbors, he hovered near her as she opened the note with the scissors hanging at her waist, read it, and then glancing up, spied the boy.

" My young man, what is it you want? "

He explained.

" Tell the gossips that George has sent me word that Lord Cornwallis has surrendered," she announced.

On another occasion, when her son had not visited her for some time, too much occupied with public affairs, an orderly appeared suddenly, and announced that " His Excellency " was on his way to visit her.

Turning calmly to her faithful colored maid, she remarked:

" Patsy, George is coming to see me. I shall need a white apron."

When Lafayette arrived after the Revolution was over to pay his respects to the mother of his beloved commander, she was no less unperturbed. Greeting him, she remarked:

" Come right in. George has told me all about you," and proceeded to entertain him with her own gingerbread and home-brewed punch, or mint juleps, according to two versions.

The recipe for gingerbread which she used has been preserved, and by the sale of gingerbread made according to it, money was earned to buy the Mary Washington chair in the D. A. R. Building, in Washington, D. C.

When Mary Washington died, she was buried in what was then a part of Kenmore, now a public park on Washington Avenue. A monument to her was begun in 1833, but never finished. Four pillars had been erected, and these and their base were a target for both armies in the fighting around Fredericksburg in the War between the States. Two of the fragments are now preserved in the Mary Washington house.

In 1880, women of the city formed an association, with branches all over the country, and by 1894, a beautiful granite shaft was unveiled above her grave, the only monument to a woman, erected by women.

At the outbreak of the Revolution, Fredericksburg furnished two of the first three Virginia regiments. Half of the generals in that war are said to have come from Virginia, and Fredericksburg and the vicinity furnished seven of these, together with the naval hero, John Paul Jones.

On Main Street, near the railway station, stands the frame house in which William Paul, his brother, lived and kept a grocery store. Oddly enough, there is a grocery store here to-day. A plain, two-story frame house, here the future hero lived with his brother, and here he added to his name that of Jones, some say in honor of his friend, Wylie Jones of North Carolina. Another story tells that John Paul commanded an English merchantman on a voyage to Tobago, when his crew mutinied, and the leader was killed by Paul in self defense. In Tobago, he was tried for manslaughter, and honorably acquitted, but returning to England, he heard rumors that he was to be tried again. Indignant, he departed for America, and thereupon added Jones to his name. From this frame house he went to offer his services to the Continental Army.

Another old square house on the corner of Main and Charlotte Streets stands little outwardly changed. Early in the 19th century this was the home of Joanna Glassel, who returned to Scotland with her father, married the Duke of Argyle, and thus was grandmother to the Marquis of Lorne, husband of Queen Victoria's daughter, Princess Louise. The Scotch considered this marriage a great distinction — for the Princess.

On Main Street, beyond the railway, stands a private residence known as the Sentry Box. It was given this name because from it such a fine view up and down the river could be had that it was used as a lookout in three wars. Modernized within, it yet still presents some of the old features. The old staircase still mounts from a broad hall, the rooms are lofty and spacious.

The exact date of this building is not known, but it was about 1750. It was to be the home of Dr. Hugh Mercer, and his wife lived here during the Revolution, but it is doubtful if he ever did, and he was killed before the war was over. Before alluding further to this distinguished man, mention should be given another house, not far from the Sentry Box, and still occupied as a private residence. This was once the home of Dr. Charles Mortimer, the physician of Mary Washington. A square frame building, it is shut off from the street by a stone wall, overgrown with ivy.

On the corner of Main and Amelia Streets stands an old, low rambling wooden house in which was Mercer's apothecary shop, where he sold drugs, besides attending to the duties of a practising physician, from 1763 until the outbreak of the Revolution. It is known that during those years he lived on Amelia Street, and since no record of another residence has been found, it seems reasonable to suppose that he and his family lived in the house in which was located his shop. Certainly there was room enough.

At present it is closed, its windows boarded up, and looks dilapidated, but it was recently purchased by the Association for the Preservation of Virginia Antiquities, and awaits only enough money to put it in good repair, when it is to be opened as a museum.

Dr. Mercer had a most interesting history. He was born at Aberdeen, Scotland, in 1725, descended on his father's side from a long line of ministers, on his mother's side from the Munros.

Mercer joined the Pretender's army as assistant surgeon, and when the Stuart cause was hopelessly lost left Leith, in 1746, for America. He first settled in Greencastle, now Mercersburg, Pennsylvania, practised medicine, and acted as apothecary, as was the custom.

Serving as captain in Braddock's disastrous expedition, he was severely wounded, and left behind for dead by his own army. Wounded as he was, after a tramp through trackless forests, he succeeded in re-joining his comrades. Later, he was captain in one of the military organizations formed for protection against the Indians. In 1756 he was given command of Pennsylvania territory, with headquarters at McDowell's Fort. Fighting desperately with Indians, he was again severely wounded and abandoned by his comrades. Hiding in the hollow trunk of a tree, he heard Indians searching for him, and discussing plans for scalping him when they found him. They did not find him, however, for he managed to march over a hundred miles, through the woods, eating roots and herbs, and it is said that his heartiest meal on this journey was a soup made from a dead rattlesnake.

Recovered, he was again wounded in fighting Indians, and in recognition of his services, received from the corporation of Philadelphia a note of thanks and a medal.

By 1757 he was a major, in command of the forces of Pennsylvania west of the Susquehanna, and the following year was associated with General Forbes, at Fort Duquesne. Either here or earlier, under Braddock, he made the acquaintance of Washington, and it may have been at the latter's suggestion that he came to Fredericksburg, where William and John Paul were at the time probably living. Mercer was a fellow Mason with Washington in Lodge No. 4, A. F. and A. M., still located in Fredericksburg, although probably the original building is a small brick structure in the rear of the present lodge.

In 1775 Mercer enrolled as a minuteman, and at the time that Governor Dunmore removed the colonial store of powder from the magazine in Williamsburg to the British man of war, Magdalen, was made colonel, and offered his services to the Virginia Convention in these words:

" Hugh Mercer will serve his adopted country and the cause of Liberty in any rank or station to which he may be assigned."

He went to Williamsburg the next year as a Brigadier General, and Washington appointed him to take charge of the troops at Paulus Hook, New Jersey.

He was severely wounded at the Battle of Princeton, January 3,

1777, and was apparently a mark for special fury on the part of the enemy, for after being wounded, he was beaten in the head as he lay helpless from his wounds. Perhaps had it not been for this he might once more have recovered, but although removed to a farmhouse nearby where everything possible was done by his own men for him, he died on January 12th.

In 1784, Thomas Jefferson introduced a bill in Congress, and an appropriation was made for the education of Mercer's youngest son, Hugh. This son died in the Sentry Box in 1853, and his son, Hugh K. Mercer, was a noted Confederate general.

Every president from Washington to Buchanan has been a guest in the Sentry Box.

The old Rising Sun tavern, built by Charles Washington, brother of the President, and also the town postmaster, was kept by Hugh Weedon, who afterwards distinguished himself in the Revolution, and became a general. This house, too, is cared for by the Association for the Preservation of Virginia Antiquities, and is interesting for many reasons.

Noted men have slept in the two small, low rooms upstairs, and noted men, including Washington, have gathered in its lower rooms. Here Washington often joined the patriots, who made this their meeting place — it was looked upon before the Revolution broke out as a "hot bed of sedition" — and here he played cards with them. It was here that, as he mentions in his diary, he played cards and "lost as usual," adding that he feared that those Fredericksburg men were "too smart for him."

Here, arriving in town late one night, and not wishing to disturb his mother at that hour, he intended to spend the night, but news of his arrival circulated, and his mother dispatched a servant with the message: "Tell George to come home at once."

The Irish Weedon before the Revolution proposed this toast: "May the Rose grow and the Thistle flourish, and may the Harp be attuned to the cause of American liberty!"

In this tavern, James Monroe early argued for freedom for the slaves, and Weedon " forever talked sedition with Mercer, the Scotch-man," who, obliged to leave Scotland with the ruin of the Pretender's cause, had no love for England. Weedon and Mercer married sisters.

On Princess Anne Street, near the railway, stands a small frame house, bought by President Monroe or given him by his uncle, in order that he might become a property owner, thus qualified to vote, and to be a candidate for the Virginia Assembly. He never lived in the house, but on Charles Street was his law office, now marked by a tablet.

At one end of Princess Anne Street is Hazel Hill, built by General John Minor, who in 1782 first in America advocated in the Virginia Assembly the freeing of slaves. The old slave block used in selling them is still standing on a Fredericksburg street corner.

Near the other end of Princess Anne Street is a large red brick house, well over a century old. The interior still has some old land-scape paper made by Dufour about 1813 remaining on the walls. The house has no special history save that it and the little office near the gate have always been occupied by a physician, from the time of building in the 1750's, by a Dr. Stevenson, down to the present day.

In the yard at the rear stands a two-storied brick house, the original slave quarters of the residence, with great fireplaces, HL hinges, thick walls, etc. It has now been charmingly converted into an antique shop.

A frame building on Charlotte Street, in which Matthew Fontaine Maury lived between the years 1836 and 1842 is still standing. Although not as old as most of the houses mentioned heretofore, it seems worthy of being included because not enough is known of this distinguished man.

Born in 1806, he married Ann Herndon of Fredericksburg. An-other house in this city was also at one time occupied by them. In 1825, Maury was a midshipman in the American Navy, and six years later, master of the sloop Falmouth, he was ordered to take his ship to the Pacific. He found that no charts, no records of currents to be encoun-tered on this long voyage existed, and was forced to make them for himself. In the Charlotte Street house he wrote his "Letters from a Luck Bag," which first brought him into prominence. Here also he wrote a "Treaty on Navigation."

In time, many honors came to him. The Pope sent him a complete collection of papal medals, an unusual honor, and since he could accept no presents from foreign governments without the consent of Congress, they made valuable gifts of jewels to his wife. At his death, it was wished to make her a gift of money from the American people, as a token of appreciation, but this she refused.

On Hanover Street, a fine old colonial house, filled with rare old furniture, and with handsome carved mantels, is Federal Hill, so named by its owner, Governor Robert Brooke, who lived here in 1791. It was used by the northern army as headquarters during the Civil War, when the town was occupied. The great porch is paved with flag-stones, and old box borders still survive. Upstairs, a room said to have been occupied by Lafayette is believed to be haunted.

One of the most interesting, and certainly the most beautiful house here has been left for the last.

Kenmore, home of Betty Washington, would have been torn down had it not been for the exertions of Fredericksburg women, and especially of Mrs. Fleming and her daughter, Mrs. H. H. Smith.

It is not the first house on the estate, for one built by its owner, Fielding Lewis, was burned down, whereupon he built the present one in 1752. Four years earlier, he was living on Charles Street. The son of John Lewis of Gloucester, his first wife was Catherine Washington. When she died, he married George Washington's only sister, Betty, for whom he built the new Kenmore house. Washington surveyed the land when Lewis bought it, and planted thirteen horse chestnut trees on an avenue between his mother's home and Kenmore, one of which, suitably marked, survives to-day on Fauquier Street, between Charles and Prince Edward Streets.

George Washington took a great interest in the house that was being built for his sister, and besides planting the horse chestnut trees, set out many of the trees and shrubs on the grounds.

" There was only sixteen months difference between her and her brother George, and always they were playmates and companions. When he cut the cherry tree down, threw the stone across the river, and broke the neck of his mother's colt, she was right there, faithful and admiring, with sunbonnet tied on tight, sheepskin mittens, and perhaps a flannel mask to preserve her complexion. We do not know that she went to school to Master Hobby in Falmouth, but we know that when George and Samuel crossed the ferry to Parson Marye's, she went with them to a Dame School, where she was taught French, English, the use of the globes and fine stitchery." [2]

The Lewis family descended from one of Virginia's earliest settlers. General Robert Lewis, son of Sir Edward, received a grant of 33,333⅓ acres of land in Gloucester County, Virginia, and came to this country about 1650. His son, Colonel John, probably built Warner Hall, " like a baronial castle," on part of this grant. The Colonel was a member of His Majesty's Council, and his son John was the father of Betty Washington's husband, Fielding.

Another son of the Colonel, Robert, married Jane, the daughter of Colonel Nicholas Meriwether, of Clover Fields, and other adjoining lands. Robert served in the Revolution, and later settled at Belvoir. It was his son, Nicholas, who married Mary Walker, nicknamed " Captain Moll."

The first habitable building on the Albermarle County tract belonging to Robert Lewis, a log house built in 1747, near a spring, is said still to be standing.

Marmion, in King George County, has a house, said to have been built in 1674, by William Fitzhugh. Eventually this place came into the ownership of George Lewis, one of Fielding and Betty's sons, and has remained in the family ever since. The beautiful drawing room, with decorated panels, etc., is now owned by the Metropolitan Museum of Art, New York City.

Fielding Lewis was a wealthy man at the time that he built Kenmore; a colonel of militia, member of the House of Burgesses, vestry-

[2] *The Story of Kenmore*, Mrs. Vivien Minor Fleming.

man of St. George's Church, a successful merchant, and the owner of large estates, while Betty Washington had a goodly dowry from her father, who had both lands and mining rights.

In 1922, after having passed through many hands, Kenmore was to be sold again, and the grounds had already been staked off into building lots, when the two women mentioned before determined that it should be saved. Other Fredericksburg women responded to their appeal, and a promise from the owner was finally obtained that Kenmore should be theirs for $30,000, provided that $10,000 of this sum be paid within four months. It seemed almost a hopeless undertaking, but the money was raised, Colonel I. N. Lewis, inventor of the Lewis gun, and a collateral descendant, contributing the first $1,000. Efforts are now being made to raise an endowment fund to keep the house in repair, and furnish it more fully with appropriate articles.

It is a handsome square brick building, the walls two feet thick, set well back from what is now Washington Avenue, almost opposite the monument to Mary Washington. Originally there were small buildings at each end, one an office, the other the kitchen. The latter is being copied in a new structure, which will serve as quarters for the custodian, and the other will be replaced, as soon as funds permit, with a fireproof room to contain records, etc. The outward appearance of Kenmore will then be as when built.

Entering a broad hall running through to the rear, the stairs ascend with landings, and beneath them, opening from a narrow side corridor, is a small room, perhaps an office. Four large rooms are on the first floor, and one in the rear has an elaborate ceiling in stucco work, said to have been done by two Hessian prisoners sent for this purpose by Washington himself, after the Battle of Trenton. Over the mantel is an elaborate design suggested by him for his sister's children, and executed by these Hessians. It depicts the fable of the fox, the crow and the piece of cheese, and teaches the dangers of flattery. This work was, of course, done years after the house was built.

Across the hall is another room with the ceiling elaborately decorated in four sections, representing the four seasons, with palms for

Spring, grapes for Summer, acorns for Autumn, and mistletoe for Winter, probably done by the same workmen. Another room contains the Washington coat of arms, the head of the swan now gone, doubtless removed by some vandal. The two Hessians are said to have done work at Mt. Vernon as well.

The great doors at Kenmore have the original brass rimlocks, brought from England, and all of the windows have great shutters. In the Fox and Crow room Betty Washington is said often to have sat with a book. This room overlooked the walk by which her mother daily came from her home to that of her daughter. Betty was fond of novel reading, of which her mother disapproved, so when the old lady came in sight, the novel was slipped behind one of the great shutters, and all was serene.

In the wide hall, Washington was greeted by his mother and sister, on his return after the Battle of Yorktown. Some say that in one of Kenmore's lower rooms the patriots gathered when news arrived that Lord Dunmore had removed the store of powder from the magazine in Williamsburg, and that here they drew up a resolution of protest, ending with the words: "God save the liberties of America." This was on April 29th, 1775. When Washington took command of the Continental Army, two of Betty and Fielding's sons went with him.

Upstairs there are four more large square rooms, and already some fine old furniture has been assembled.

It was in 1775, that the Virginia Convention established a manufactory of " small arms " in Fredericksburg, the first in the colonies, and appointed Fielding Lewis as one of three commissioners to head this. Land near the town was purchased with " a noble spring " on it, still known as Gunnery Spring, and the factory was built. In less than a year, they were repairing old guns and turning out new ones which were said to be as good as any.

" The running expenses were estimated at £2,958 annually, which included stock, a master workman, and thirty others, besides negroes to do the drudgery and work the garden, rent for the mill and extras.

" All the workmen took their dinners daily at the Gunnery, hence the need for a 'spacious garden.'" The factory "turned out one hundred stand of arms a month, besides much repair work."

Colonel Lewis and Charles Dick, then living in Fredericksburg's now oldest surviving house, staked their own fortunes to run this factory. At one time, Lewis advanced "seven thousand pounds, all that I had at that time on hand." He had already contributed over £40,000 to the Revolutionary cause, for he equipped and maintained three regiments. This amount, secured by mortgaging Kenmore, was the cause of his widow's being compelled later to sacrifice the place.

Old men, women and children worked in the factory making ammunition.

After her husband's death, Betty Lewis sold lot after lot from the estate, to satisfy creditors, and finally, in 1794, the house went also, Mrs. Lewis left Fredericksburg, never to return, and made her home with her married daughter, Elizabeth Carter, in Culpepper County, where she died three years later. About this time, the house was bought by Samuel Gordon, remaining in his family for sixty years. Then it became a boys' school, and about forty years ago was bought in a dilapidated condition by W. Key Howard. His son labored lovingly and with skill to repair the damages to the beautiful stucco ornamentation, but in 1914 it was again sold, and its fate seemed evident. Only a miracle could preserve it, but fortunately for all lovers of the beautiful and historic, the miracle was wrought.

One of the ladies responsible for saving Kenmore tells of a visitor who became deeply interested in hearing of the gun factory, and the money advanced by the original owner of the beautiful house that she was then inspecting.

"Oh, yes," eagerly she observed, "Colonel Lewis. He is the man who invented the Lewis machine gun, of course."

Although she confused the two men, the earlier Colonel's guns were used effectively in the battle of Yorktown, but their maker died on that very day.

Just outside of Fredericksburg, the house on Willis Hill was probably built by the grandnephew of the first of the family to come to

Virginia. The pioneer died in England in 1691. The grandnephew, Henry, married for his third wife, even as he was her third husband, Mildred Washington, aunt of George and his brothers and sisters.

This Henry was " the top man of the town " alluded to by Colonel Byrd, and the son, Lewis, was Washington's constant boyhood companion.

Byrd Willis inherited the place, and married Mary, one of the eleven children of Fielding and Betty Lewis. The daughter of Byrd Willis, Catherine, married for her second husband Prince Murat.

Part of Willis Hill was sold, and in 1818 the Marye family built Brompton there. This house was headquarters of the Confederate Commander during the fierce fighting here, known as the Battle of Marye's Heights, and by that name, instead of Willis, the hill is now known.

Just across the river from Fredericksburg, reached by a bridge now, instead of the old ferry, stands Chatham, a white brick colonial house, no longer in the ownership of the family which built it, but carefully restored and tended. This is another place which is never shown to strangers.

It was built by William Fitzhugh, and if a brick picked up near one of its old chimneys, and bearing the date: 1721, indicates the year when it was set up, the builder must have been the second William, son of the " emigrant," who came to Virginia in 1670, was a renowned lawyer, and published a book in England on Virginia law. This first William's will was probated in 1701 in Stafford County.

Other chroniclers declare that the house was built here by the third William Fitzhugh, grandson of the second, and son of Henry of Eagle's Nest, who married Lucy, another of " King " Carter's children. In any case, it was the third William who gave the place its name, after his friend, the Earl of Chatham, and made it famous by his lavish hospitality, excellent wines, and private racecourse. This William married Ann Randolph, and their daughter married George Washington Parke Custis, Washington's step-grandson, and adopted son.

The courtship of George and Martha Daindrige Custis is said to have taken place under the old trees, or in the paneled rooms of

Chatham, as well as at a later date, that of Robert E. Lee and Mary Custis.

The gardens of Chatham are very lovely, and the house has a paneled hall more than twenty-five feet square, but much of the original paneling and woodwork of mahogany was torn out by the northern soldiers. On the place is an Indian cave, and along one of the walks a lady in white is said to stroll at times, wringing her hands, but the cause of her grief as well as her name, have both long been forgotten.

Whether or not Washington courted his wife here, for other places claim this honor, his frequent visits to Chatham were, according to his own testimony, " among my most interesting memories," and he thoroughly enjoyed Mr. Fitzhugh's " good dinners, good wine, and good company."

In the early days of the 19th century, the house was owned in turn by two brothers named Jones. Still later, Washington Irving dined in the old house on a spring day, on " jowl, turnip salad, poached eggs and corn pone, with dried cherry roll and hard sauce for dessert." Surely a strange menu, but Irving was " charmed and charming." [3]

On the day before the Battle of Fredericksburg, the house was occupied by Federal troops. At that time it was owned by General Lacey, and he urged General Lee to train his guns on it, but Lee refused, for it was associated with his courtship and many happy memories.

On the lawn here, Clara Barton is said to have begun her nursing.

Not far from Chatham still stands Traveler's Rest, where more than a hundred years ago, Catherine Willis went as a child bride with the owner, Atcheson Willis. Later, a widow at fourteen, she went to Florida, and it was there that she met Prince Murat.

Belmont, on the outskirts of Fredericksburg, now the home of the distinguished artist, Gari Melchers, was built for Susanna Knox, by her father, Fitzhugh of Chatham.

Stratford, forty miles from Fredericksburg, on the same side of the river as Chatham, is the ancient home of the Lees. Even those not interested in genealogy will perhaps pardon a digression here, for once

[3] *Historic Periods of Fredericksburg*, Mrs. Vivien Minor Fleming.

one enters Virginia, if never before, the great prominence of this family is realized.

In 1642, Richard Lee patented 1,000 acres in Westmoreland County, and began building Stratford. His son John inherited it, but died without heirs, and it passed to his brother Richard, who was educated at Oxford University. Richard's fourth son John was living in the house in 1729, when it burned down, his wife and child having to be thrown from an upper window to save their lives, while he himself was " much scorched."

Queen Caroline of England liked and admired Lee so greatly that she sent him " a bountiful present from her privy purse," and he built the present house. It contains more than twenty rooms, with a central hall twenty-five by thirty feet. In this great apartment it is said that sessions of the courts were at one time held, as well as religious services, and this explains why the hall was built so large.

Thomas, son of Colonel Richard Lee, the second of that name, was very prominent in the Council, and also at one time was acting Governor of the State. The last Lee to own the property, Major J. Henry, died in France in 1837.

The Lee family contributed to Virginia while it was a province, one governor, four members of the Council of State, and twelve members of the House of Burgesses. To the colony of Maryland they gave two Councillors and three members of the Assembly. Four Lees were members of the Convention of 1776, two signed the Declaration of Independence, and one of the leading cavalry officers in the Revolution was Light Horse Harry Lee.

After the Revolution, the family was no less prominent, for among its members were an Attorney General, several Members of Congress, two governors of the State of Virginia, and one of Maryland; in the Civil War, in addition to the famous and beloved Commander-in-chief, Robert E. Lee, there were three Major Generals and one Brigadier General of the name, while in the Spanish War, General Fitzhugh Lee, at the time of its outbreak Consul General in Cuba, became a Major General in the United States Army.

Ditchley, on Chesapeake Bay, was another place belonging to a Lee, the first to come to this country, and his seventh son, Hancock, is buried there. The original house was built by Hancock Lee about 1687, the present one in 1765, by his descendant, and the place remained in the Lee ownership until 1789, when it was sold to James Buell, Junior; but as he married Lettice Lee, it did not really go out of the family, and has remained the property of their descendants ever since.

Still another Lee estate is Chantilly, Westmoreland County, the property of Richard Henry Lee. Cobbs, one more of the Lee estates, was two hundred years old, according to Bishop Meade, when the house was removed in his day.

Another old place on the north side of the Rappahannock, Sabine Hall, was one of the holdings of the omnipresent Carter family. It was not an original grant to them, but was bought by Colonel Landon Carter, one of the " King " 's grandsons, early in the 18th century, and the house was built in 1730. Landon married first a Miss Armistead, then Maria Byrd of Westover, and built Sabine Hall for her, having his own brick kilns.

Landon was a determined man. It is told that he and others of the neighborhood did not like the minister who had been sent to them, so they locked him out of his church, compelling him for some time to hold services in the churchyard.

Robert, another of " King " 's sons, known as the Councillor, had on his estate at Nomini a veritable army of workers in various trades, such as blacksmiths, colliers, a stocking loom maker, a cabinet maker, ten carpenters, three coopers, and two postillions to ride with his coach and four. He is said to have owned sixty-two male slaves, and twenty-seven women and children.

Leaving the vicinity of Fredericksburg, on the way to Washington, and but a few miles south of that city, is Gunston Hall, the home of George Mason. Close to old Pohick church, which both Mason and Washington attended, one leaves the highroad, and winds through the woods for four miles, until the beautiful house is reached.

The George Mason who built it was the son of another George, one of the Knights of the Golden Horseshoe, the third generation of the name in Virginia. The first George Mason came here in 1657, and was known as the Cavalier. The builder of Gunston Hall, close friend of Washington, married Ann Eilbeck, said to have been one of Washington's early loves, but this made no difference in the friendship of the two men.

Built about a century and a half ago, the house was a favorite visiting place for many noted men. George Washington was often rowed down from Mt. Vernon in a four-oared gig, manned by negroes in livery, to visit his friend, or take Sunday dinner with him. In the house are pointed out the Jefferson room, and Lafayette room, occupied by them on visits, while in the library, Jefferson and Mason are said to have made the first rough draft of the Declaration of Independence. The same story is told of Rosewell.

This lovely house and its charming grounds had a very narrow escape. After passing out of the Mason family ownership seventy years ago, various persons had from time to time bought and sold it, making changes, or allowing lack of repairs to effect others, until a few years ago it was again put up for sale. A dairyman seemed about to acquire it, and boasted that he intended to " tear down all that old stuff," and convert it into a first class dairy farm, for which it was well suited as far as location and natural advantages went. Fortunately he did not get the place. Instead it was purchased by a couple from Massachusetts, with both the means and the taste to put it back into its present perfect condition.

The new owners employed twenty workmen for an entire year to restore it to good condition. The glass paned doors of the old cupboards on either side of the big old fireplaces in the lower rooms had been broken or torn off, sometimes leaving a fragment by which it was possible to have replicas made. There had to be much removing of paint, re-painting, and even changes, to restore the original appearance within and without. One late owner had built a disfiguring tower on the house, and another had erected an ugly brick building which entirely shut off the beautiful view in the rear.

The house is a story and a half high, the upper rooms lighted by dormer windows. A wide hall runs through from front to back, with big old doors, the stairs mounting with a landing half way up, at the rear of the hall, and supported as they turn by an archway beneath which one passes to the rear door.

There are the usual four rooms on the lower floor, all large, square, high-ceiled, with exquisitely carved cornices, mantels, and other wood-work. That in the front room at the right, the drawing room, is said to be the finest existing example of Chinese Chippendale. Across the hall is the library, its cupboards on either side of the fireplace now serving as bookcases, as they may have done in Mason's time. Over the carved mantel hangs a photograph of his Bill of Rights, photographed by per-mission of Congress from the original, preserved in Washington. This seemed to the present owners a highly suitable decoration, for here in this room that paper was drawn up. Behind the library is the dining room, and another sitting room, or possibly " the chamber," lies be-hind the drawing room.

By the rear door, one steps out on a porch, from which a brick walk, bordered with wonderful old box hedges, nine or more feet high — the finest which the writer has ever seen save for the remarkable wall of box trees at Castle Hill — runs down to a pavilion, from which is a truly exquisite view. Directly below, reached by a flight of steps, is the old flower garden, now with a new lease of life, since it is carefully tended, and beyond, looking over a gentle slope, may be seen the blue Potomac.

Former owners have cut down many of the old trees which once shaded the beautiful grounds of Gunston Hall, although one passes through a grove of quite large trees before reaching the circular drive-way in front of the house, but fortunately no one thought of selling or destroying the beautiful old box hedges, loved by the present owners as they must have been by those who planted them — probably George Mason himself — and watched them become things of beauty. Down this old box-bordered walk, and through the old rooms many distin-guished guests have strolled in the early days of our Republic.

The house is, of course, not open to the usual visiting stranger, but the writer was privileged to see the lower rooms and the exquisite old garden under the guidance of the gracious owner.

George Mason was responsible for the separation of Church and State in this country. The State used to determine the amount that each citizen should contribute to the support of the former. Mason brought about the change which left it to each one's conscience and choice to determine the amount of church contributions.

Back on the highroad to Washington, shortly after leaving Pohick church behind, there may be seen on a hill at the left, some distance from the road, Woodlawn, a fine old brick house, home of Nellie Custis, Martha Washington's granddaughter, and her husband, Major Lawrence Lewis, Washington's greatnephew.

In sleepy, old Alexandria stands the Ramsay house, oldest in the city, as a tablet affixed by the Chamber of Commerce states.

The house stands on a corner, only a stone's throw from the Carlyle mansion, and like the latter, the garden originally must have run down to the river. Now a dilapidated board fence shuts off what is left of both gardens from the street in the rear. William Ramsay built the house in 1751, and his son, Dennis, was a compatriot of Washington during the Revolution, serving as a colonel. He was also one of Washington's honorary pallbearers. Mrs. Annie McCarty Ramsay collected money to aid in the financing of the Revolution, as is also stated on the tablet.

The frame building is of two stories and attic, now very shabby and dilapidated, with a store on the ground floor, unoccupied in the autumn of 1926, nor did the house show signs of life. It is undoubtedly doomed soon to disappear.

To visit the Carlyle mansion, or as it is often called the Braddock house, one must cross the hallway of a modern apartment house, and passing out by a rear door, part of the old stone paved walk leads to the original flight of steps and front door of this historic old residence, which may be seen daily on payment of a small fee.

John Carlyle came to this country about 1740, and settled in Dumfries, Virginia. By 1744, he was located at Bellhaven, which four years later was incorporated as Alexandria. In 1752 he built the Carlyle house, on the corner of Fairfax and Cameron Streets. Some say that it was built over an old fort, whose rooms are now called the dungeons.

In 1758, Carlyle was appointed Royal Collector for South Potomac. He married Sarah, daughter of William Fairfax, a grandson of Henry, fourth Lord Fairfax, of Denton, Yorkshire, England. At twenty, William Fairfax served in Spain, under his cousin, Colonel Martin Bladen. He was then appointed agent for his first cousin, Thomas, sixth Lord Fairfax, and went to live at Belvoir, on the Potomac. His son by his second wife, Brian, became the eighth Lord Fairfax.

John Carlyle was a prominent man, a member of the Committee of Safety, and took part in the Revolution. He was twice married, and by his second wife had an only son, George William, born in 1765. Had the latter lived, he would have inherited the title of Lord Carlyle, after the death of his first cousin, the Reverend John Daere Carlyle, who died without sons in England, in 1804. But George William when not yet seventeen, joined Light Horse Harry Lee's Legion, and was killed at the Battle of Eutaw Springs, South Carolina. His father had died the year before, and the estate went to the young cadet's nephew. His half sister, mother of the heir, was the daughter of Sarah Fairfax. The heir's granddaughter married her cousin, Thomas, ninth Lord Fairfax.

The Fairfaxes and Culpeppers also intermarried. Thomas Fairfax married Lord Culpepper's daughter, and was the seventh Fairfax to become Lord Cameron. During Cromwell's time, or soon afterwards, the Fairfax family records were hidden for safe keeping, and lost. They remained lost for nearly two hundred years, when a box was found, apparently filled with tiles. Someone removed a layer of these, and there underneath were the records.

The Carlyle house is called Braddock, because of the council which that General held there before undertaking the expedition against Fort Duquesne, which was to result in his death, as well as because for some time Braddock made it his headquarters. The council was attended by

One of the fine mantels in beautiful Kenmore, Fredericsburg, Virginia. Here Betty Washington and her husband Fielding Lewis lived. The plaster work of this mantel was done by two Hessian prisoners, sent by George Washington to decorate Kenmore, and the design, showing the Fox, the Crow and the Cheese, teaching the dangers of flattery, is said to have been drawn by Washington himself.

the colonial governors of five states, including Robert Dinwiddie, Lieutenant-Governor of Virginia, Robert Hunter Morris, " whose thankless task it was to get war votes out of the Pennsylvania assembly of Quakers and lethargic German farmers; Horatio Sharpe, the brave and energetic gentleman who was Governor of Maryland; James De Lancey of New York, and William Shirley, Governor of Massachusetts — who although past sixty years of age, was as strenuous as Dinwiddie, and eager for the field, though he had been bred a lawyer." [4]

Here also came Benjamin Franklin, Richard Henry Lee, Colonel William Johnson, Commodore Keppel, Peter Halkett, many British officers, and George Washington, then a young lieutenant, who attracted Braddock's attention at this time. Here was planned the expedition which led to Braddock's death.

It was from the Carlyle house that Braddock wrote to Sir Thomas Robinson, urging the imposing of a tax on tea on the colonies, to repay the British Government for sums spent on the war with France.

In 1785, another conference was held in this house between Washington and the Governors of Maryland and Virginia, to settle the boundary line between the two commonwealths, and other differences. From this meeting came the call for an assembling of delegates from all of the colonies to meet in Philadelphia in 1787. This convention framed the Constitution of the United States.

Colonel Carlyle and his family were frequent visitors at Mt. Vernon, even as Washington was often a guest at the Carlyle home, Alexandria.

Arlington, now a naval and military cemetery, is interesting only for visitors to its graves; the house is a mere shell, all of its old furnishings long since removed. A bill was passed a year or more ago by the House of Representatives to provide money for its upkeep, but has not yet passed the Senate. It is the hope of those behind the movement to refurnish the house in harmony with the period of its building, and make it a museum.

It was built in 1802, by George Washington Parke Custis, grandson

[4] *History of the American People*, Woodrow Wilson.

of Martha Washington, and the President's adopted son. After Martha Washington's death, Mary Custis and Robert E. Lee were married in the drawing room at Arlington, and when Mary inherited the place, on the death of her father in 1857, they lived here. At the time of the marriage, Lee was in the United States Engineers.

John Custis, the first of the family in America, came to Virginia in 1640 from Rotterdam, where he is said to have kept a hotel which was very popular with English travelers. He had six sons and one daughter; the latter married the son of Governor Yeardley, so the family was early connected with prominent Virginians. The most conspicuous of his six sons, John, was made a Major General at the time of Bacon's Rebellion.

Mt. Vernon is too familiar to be described here, but something of its early history may be of interest.

John Washington, the first of his name in America, settled at Bridge's Creek, Virginia, in 1656, and there is found the old family burial ground. He was a member of the House of Burgesses, and the parish received his name, Washington. He married three times. No trace of his house remains.

His grandson, Augustine, built the house already mentioned on the west side of Pope's Creek, in which the First President was born, and which burned to the ground. To his first wife's son, Lawrence, Augustine Washington gave a tract of land now known as Mt. Vernon, upon Lawrence's return from a campaign in the West Indies, under Admiral Vernon. The son named his place after his old commander. George Washington frequently visited his half brother as a boy, and eventually inherited the place.

Another Washington estate, Bushfield on the Nomini, the home of George's youngest brother, John Augustine Washington, has disappeared.

That our First President liked luxury, is shown by an order sent to London before his marriage to Mrs. Custis. This order called for " a mahogany bedstead with carved and fluted pillars, and yellow silk and worsted damask hangings, window curtains to match; mahogany chairs with seats of yellow silk and worsted damask, an elbow chair, a fine, neat mahogany serpentine dressing table, with a long mirror and brass trimmings, a pair of fine carved and gilt sconces."

The piazza at Mt. Vernon is floored with stone flags, imported from Lord Lonsdale's estate near Whitehaven, England.

Martha Washington was no idle lady of leisure. She rose at dawn all the year round, and always retired to her room for one hour after breakfast, for private prayer.

Washington once compared Mt. Vernon to " a well resorted tavern." Mr. Faris quotes from a letter written by him to George Lewis, which has a strangely modern note: the servant question.

" This running off of my cook has been a most inconvenient thing for the family, and what rendered it more disagreeable is that I had resolved never to become the master of another slave by purchase, but this resolution I fear I must break. I have endeavoured to hire, black or white, but am not yet supplied." This letter was dated November 13th, 1797.

How the belongings of Washington were scattered is shown by the following extract from Bishop Meade's *History of Old Virginia Churches and Families*. He says in part:

" In a way I need not state, I got Washington's coach about fifteen years after Washington's death. It was too heavy to use, and began to decay and give way." The Bishop thereupon " caused it to be taken to pieces, and distributed among the admiring friends of Washington, — and also a number of female associations for benevolent and religious objects." It was then cut up and made into walking sticks, picture frames and snuff boxes, and " about two thirds of one wheel yielded $140," as the Bishop naïvely remarks, apparently with no sense of regret that the valuable relic had not been preserved complete. He himself " kept the hind seat on which the General and his lady were wont to sit," and used it for some time as a sofa in his study.

Washington, the national capital, although a new city, has an old history.

Accounts of this section of the country were published in England as early as 1621. Captain John Smith explored it in 1608, and speaks of the Patawomeke, and praised the location and climate. Washington and Major Pierre Charles L'Enfant met at a house in Georgetown to discuss the latter's plans for the city. Here they learned that in 1663 one Francis Pope had a vision, in which he saw a stately building on what is now Capitol Hill. He bought the land, and called it Rome, while a stream at the foot of the hill was given the name of the Tiber. These names appear on an old map. It was from Pope's descendants that the land was acquired.

L'Enfant was removed before his plans were entirely carried out. He refused tardily offered compensation by Congress, and spent the last years of his life on the various estates of the Bigges family, and dying, was buried on the estate of Chillum Castle Manor, near Bladensburg.

The first mistress of the unfinished White House was Mrs. John Adams, who accompanied her husband there in 1800. Congress had voted $6,000 for furnishings, but these had not arrived. Most members of the Government then had to live in Georgetown.

Mrs. Adams liked her new home none too well. In a letter, she calls it " this great castle," while, although it was " surrounded with forests," wood was " not to be had, because people cannot be found to cut and cart it — the great unfinished audience room I make a drying room of, to hang up the clothes in. The principal stairs are not up, and will not be this winter."

After the War of 1812, when it was burned by the British, to rebuild and refurnish the White House cost $300,000, and on January 1, 1818, the first New Year's reception was held in it.[5]

John Tayloe, of Mt. Airy, Virginia, in 1798 commissioned Dr. William Thornton, the architect, to build him a Washington home, and three years later it was finished.

This, known as the Octagon house, at the corner of 17th Street and New York Avenue, N. W., has a large circular vestibule, opening into a hall paved with black and white marble, at the rear of which a fine

[5] *Historic Shrines of America* John T. Faris.

staircase mounts with a landing. Some of the old garden and its enclosing brick wall remain, and bits of the old box hedges once bordering
the walks.

Mr. Tayloe was a worthy son of Virginia, and maintained his state's
reputation for hospitality. When the White House was burned by the
British, he offered the Octagon house as a residence to the President,
who accepted the offer. In an upper room, on the famous table, with its
curious triangular drawers, the so-called " Treaty table," the Treaty of
Ghent, marking the close of the War of 1812 with England, was signed
on February 18th, 1815.

For a time used for a girls' school, the house came down in the world
as years passed, until eight or ten colored families occupied it as a tenement. The table had been purchased by a San Franciscan, and was in
that city during the earthquake and fire of 1906. The owner saved it
by wrapping it in sheets, and taking it with her when she was obliged
to leave her home. Then the San Francisco chapter of the American
Association of Architects bought it for $1,000, and when the general
Association bought the Octagon house for their headquarters, after first
occupying it on a lease, the San Francisco architects sent on the table,
which is now in its old place.

No. 2017 I Street, N. W., residence of Gideon Granger, Postmaster of the United States from 1801 to 1814, was begun in 1802,
but sold in 1808 by him.

James Monroe lived in this house while Secretary of State, Secretary of War, and for a few months after he became President. President Madison, Secretary of State Monroe, and Secretary of War Armstrong held a grave conference here on August 14th, 1814, when the
Battle of Bladensburg was in progress. The British advanced so rapidly
that it is told that Monroe galloped on horseback through the halls of
the house in order to escape, but this story seems unfounded.

The façade was changed in 1881, an additional story added, and it
is now the home of the Arts Club of Washington.

The house is of red brick, the lower floor has three windows across
the front, with a door at one end, and these three windows are all in

the spacious reception room, opening with a great archway into another large square apartment. These two, with the hall, occupy the entire main part of this floor, but there is a rear extension, with kitchen and other rooms. Broad, low stairs, mahogany railed, lead to the second floor, where are two more large connecting rooms, and a smaller one over the front of the lower hall. The old drawing room measured fifteen by thirty-two feet. The lower hall has the usual black and white marble floor of the period, and a handsome lunette over the front door. When occupied by Monroe, the house contained twenty rooms.

General James Maccubbin Lingan, a distinguished officer in the Revolution, " either from prescience or coincidence," in January, 1791, a few months before the site for the city of Washington as the Capital was selected, purchased this lot. In 1802, he sold twenty-five feet frontage on the west, and three years later, an additional frontage of seven feet to Timothy Caldwell. Caldwell first built a small house which now forms the rear portion of the present building, and when he secured additional land, built the main portion in front of the first house. He intended to build the " handsomest house in the city near Washington Circle." Caldwell was a brickmaker, and had lived on Race Street, Philadelphia, his brickyards being in Hickory Lane.

After Caldwell, the British Minister, the Right Honorable Stratford Canning, occupied the Granger house from 1820 to 1823. He and his attachés could not get into the White House to attend President Monroe's second inauguration, because of the crowd.

Canning gave a unique ball, but was not in good health, and at public dinners, drank the healths proposed in toast and water, which habit was much criticised.

The Hon. Charles Richard Vaughan, the next British Minister, also occupied the Granger house. The Mayor of Washington, rather tactlessly, one would say, invited Vaughan to the Fourth of July celebration, but the latter tactfully replied that " he would be indisposed on the 4th of July."

A New Year's crowd of President Jackson's admirers so filled the White House, that Vaughan, who had gone with the intention of paying his respects, on arriving, exclaimed: " This is too d—d democratic for me! " and went home.

In 1828, the civil marriage ceremony between Marcia Van Ness and Sir William Gore Ouseley, who at the time was attaché of the British Legation, was performed in this house.

Virgil Maxey, while Solicitor of the Treasury, also lived in it.

Alphonse Pageot, Secretary of the French Legation, Baron de Mareschal, Austrian Minister, Charles Francis Adams, from 1857 to 1861, while Representative for Massachusetts, Silas Casey, a Civil War General, were other occupants, and then it was used for St. John's School.

Samuel Harrison Smith, editor and proprietor of *The Intelligencer,* writes his wife, his " dearest Margaret," that he had just returned from a dinner party at General Dearborn's, where he met Mrs. Madison and Mrs. Duval. " Mr. Granger, who was present, and who is a very agreeable man, after a few bottles of champagne were emptied, on the observation of Mr. Madison that it was the most delightful wine when drunken in moderation, but that more than a few glasses always produced a headache next day, remarked with point that this was the very time to try the experiment, as the next day being Sunday, would allow time for a recovery from its effects. The point was not lost upon the host, and bottle after bottle came in, without, however, I assure you, the least invasion of sobriety. Its only effects were accumulated good humor, and uninterrupted conversation."

Mrs. Benjamin Crowninshield, wife of the Secretary of the Navy, wrote " Dec. 1, 1815. I think I told you we were to dinner at Mrs. Monroe's, I Street, the day before yesterday. We had the most stylish dinner I have ever been at. The table wider than we have, and in the middle a large perhaps silver waiter, with images like some Aunt Silsbee has, only more of them, and vases filled with flowers, which made a very showy appearance as the candles were lighted when we went to table. The dishes were silver, and set round this waiter. The plates were handsome china — the forks silver, and so heavy that I could hardly lift them to my mouth; dessert knives silver, and spoons very heavy.

Mrs. Monroe is a very elegant woman. She was dressed in a very fine muslin worked in front and lined with pink, and a black velvet turban close and spangled. Her daughter, Mrs. Hay, a red silk sprigged in colors, white lace sleeves, and a dozen strings of coral round her neck. The drawing room was handsomely lighted — transparent lamps, I call them — all the furniture French, and andirons, something entirely new." The six year old grandchild, dressed in plaid, was also apparently present at this " stylish dinner," for she, too, is mentioned in this letter.

The house once occupied by Stephen Decatur, at F Street and Jackson Square, has one window bricked up. But on the anniversary of his death, the figure of Decatur may, it is said, be seen at a certain hour, standing at, and gazing out of the bricked-up window.

In West Virginia, but in Virginia before the Civil War, Charles Town is historic. George Washington probably surveyed the site, which was on his brother Charles' estate, and it was named for the latter. Incidentally, it was in Charles Town's Court House that John Brown was tried and convicted.

Five miles from the town is Claymont, first known as Happy Retreat, built about 1820 by Bushrod Washington, nephew of the President. A long, low, colonial house, connected with the main portion by long passages are two smaller buildings, servants' quarters and the office of the master of the estate.

Harewood, mansion of the President's brother, Samuel, is said to have been built under supervision of the former. To this house Dorothy Todd came from Philadelphia in Thomas Jefferson's coach, to be married to James Madison, Light Horse Harry Lee being present at the ceremony. Lafayette, Louis Philippe and his two brothers were guests at Harewood, and this place, too, has remained in the family of the original owner.

Chapter VII

⚜ THE EARLIEST COLONIAL HOUSES NOW STANDING ⚜

ALTHOUGH the Virginia settlement is thirteen years older, and again although Virginia has a goodly share of not merely old but very interesting houses, after Florida and New Mexico it is to Massachusetts that one must turn for the next oldest survivors, and which also have interest aside from their age. Here again are two rival claimants for the title of oldest, and both are venerable. But since it forms a convenient centre, before visiting these two houses, let us stop in Boston.

Every visitor here will surely wish to see the Paul Revere house, as may be done on any week day by paying a small fee. If strolling anywhere in the vicinity, possibly with no thought of paying such a visit, attention will be called to it. A little group of children will appear from side streets, almost one might fancy that they sprang from the very sidewalks. These children, almost all of Italian parentage, although they would proudly proclaim themselves Americans, will surround one, will urge, entreat, admonish.

" Aren't you going to Paul Revere's house? " " Have you been to Paul Revere's house? " or: " Let me take you to Paul Revere's house," they cry, and proffer printed descriptions. One smiling Italian woman was even teaching her lisping baby to say: " Paul Revere's house," as she stood and watched the would-be guides.

His former residence stands directly on the street, its threshold almost level with the sidewalk; beside it is an old hitching post, while a wooden drain pipe still leads from the eaves, although now emptying into a modern city drain.

From the street, the substantial old house seems of but two stories, for there is no sign of the attic in the steep roof. The windows of the front façade are filled with small leaded panes, reproductions of one old window found in the attic when restorations were begun.

Passing into a small entry, one comes into a large room running across the rest of the front, with a window in the rear, opening on what was doubtless once a large garden, now merely a small yard, hemmed in by modern buildings. The room has the great fireplace that one expects to find in so old a house. Behind the front room is a small one, and there are two similar rooms above, the stairs ascending steeply from the entry. Over the entire house is an attic. Built in 1670, its most distinguished resident, Paul Revere, lived in it from 1770 to 1800.

Paul was skilled in twenty-two trades, and became the father of sixteen children. Before his first marriage, he was second lieutenant in the artillery, and took part in the expedition against Crown Point in 1757. He was one of the party, disguised as Indians, who threw the famous cargo of tea into Boston Harbor, and before the ride which Longfellow helped make famous, had already made two others of almost equal importance. The first was on the occasion of the Tea Party, the second after the Boston Port Bill was enacted four months later, when he rode to Philadelphia with the news, making the trip in six days. Then, on April 18, 1775, came the third, when he rode to alarm the Lexington patriots.

Fortunately the Revere house was purchased by the Daughters of the American Revolution, and has been carefully restored, the four rooms filled with interesting old furniture, bedspreads, candlesticks, etc., with original letters written by Revere, and other rare old documents. Only a few of these articles, save the letters, belonged to him, or were originally in the house, but a fine old carved chest in the lower front room was his.

Most of the woodwork and floors are the original, and in making the repairs, a bit of old paper like that once covering the walls of the lower room was found in the attic, was carefully copied, and used, the pattern showing St. Mary's-le-Bow, on the Strand, London.

As in all modern cities, growth and increasing population have meant in Boston the disappearance of old landmarks, so one must not expect to find many survivors to-day. Aside from the disastrous fire of 1872, which destroyed a number, the widening of old streets, the change of residential sections into those devoted to business, account for the disappearance of others. When in 1912 a list of " Forty of Boston's Historical Houses " was published by the State Trust Company, even then the majority of the forty had already been torn down. A few still survive.

The Capen house, at 41–45 Union Street, was standing at least in the autumn of 1926, and used as an oyster house. Capen was a town officer, Sergeant in the Ancient and Honorable Artillery, and a shop-keeper. It was to him that Benjamin Thompson, the future Count Rumford, was apprenticed as a boy.

The home of Josiah Quincy, of the distinguished family which will be mentioned at length later, stands on Park Street. He was Mayor of Boston, President of Harvard College, and a prominent citizen.

The Hotel Touraine occupies the site of the John Quincy Adams house, in which Charles Francis Adams was born. The latter illustrious man was Member of Congress, United States Minister to England, and under President Lincoln was appointed to represent the United States in the Alabama Claims Tribunal, which met at Geneva.

Leaving Boston, at Dorchester one finds a house which Baedeker styled the " second oldest house in the United States," the Pierce house. Although, as has been seen, this is not true, it probably is second oldest in the Colonies. Standing on a site which will soon be very valuable, since the city is rapidly extending in that direction, its demolition is only a question of a few years at most. Marion Harland (Mrs. Terhune), in *Some Colonial Homesteads*, gives the date of building of the oldest part as 1640, but others say that it is three hundred years old.

In 1630, on the ship Mary and John, Robert Pierce set sail from England for the Massachusetts colony. John Pierce, presumably his father, had a patent of land in that colony as early as 1621. Robert first settled on Pine Neck. Then, in 1640, according to Mrs. Terhune, he built his house in Dorchester, one of but two in the county.

It was owned by the Pierces until quite recently. Some years ago, they built a fine new house on the opposite side of the street, and into this they moved, taking with them much of the old furniture from the old homestead. Then ill fortune came, and the last Pierce owner was obliged to sell the new house, which, although standing a year ago, was to be torn down almost immediately. Meanwhile, the old one had survived, occupied by an elderly lady and her son. The latter was so interested in it that he spent much of his leisure time in repairing it.

The oldest part, a two-story building, is not used by mother and son, but the old addition of two stories and attic, under a long sloping roof, probably thought very elegant when built, is their home. It has the low ceilings, small entry, with steep winding stairs, and it also has the solid old timbers of early days, for the frame of the house is of black oak.

John Pierce married Ann Greenway, daughter of one of the early settlers, and when he came from England brought with him his coat-of-arms. Mrs. Terhune tells the following story of his grandson, John, showing how strictly the Puritans observed the Sabbath. It was, she explains, hardly customary for men to shave oftener than once a week, and this in preparation for the Sabbath and church services.

John had been busy, or had put off his Saturday afternoon shave so late that the sun set as he finished shaving just one half of his face. Since the Puritan Sabbath began at sundown, he wiped his razor, removed the lather from his face, and the following day went to meeting with one side smoothly shaven, the other with a week's growth of beard upon it.

John left seven children, and eight others died in infancy.

His grandson, Samuel, married at the outbreak of the Revolution, and the day marked three important events for him: his marriage, the receipt of a commission as captain from the King's Government, and that of a colonel from the Continental Congress. He chose the latter.

It was Colonel Samuel who built the addition to the house.

The parlor in the newer part had nine doors. Here, when one of the big fireplaces was being altered, a cavity was discovered in the masonry, and within a little pair of satin slippers, but there was no one to say to whom these had belonged.[1]

Further from Boston, in the same general direction, is Dedham, a suburb with wide streets, beautiful lawns, and fine old shade trees. Dedham claims to have the oldest frame house now standing in the United States. It well repays a visit.

This, the Fayerbanks house, preserved by descendants of its builder, although the name is differently spelled now, is said to have been built in 1636, so it apparently antedates Dorchester's relic by four years. It has never passed out of the family, and eight generations lived in it before the descendants formed themselves into a corporation, which intends to see that the old house is kept in good repair, and that, barring accidents, it shall stand as long as its stout timbers endure.

Not far from the road, surrounded by lawn, shaded by venerable trees, it is a rambling, low, shingled house, resembling three connected buildings, and that is what it really is. Of the eight windows on the front, no two are of the same size, and the same irregularity is noticeable in the clapboards, some being four, some twenty-one inches wide.

The pleasant mannered caretaker, herself a descendant of the Fayerbankses, lives next door, and is always ready to show visitors over the old house, these paying a small fee towards its upkeep. One first enters the oldest part of all, with its high-pitched roof coming down to within a few feet of the ground. From a small entry, we pass into the old kitchen, with walls of overlapped white pine boards, now darkened by age. Here is a great chimney and open fireplace, in which the old crane still hangs. Here, too, is the old brick oven, although no longer usable. The ceiling beams are all old ship timbers of English oak, chamfered. This room was never plastered, and although many years ago the overhead rafters were painted, time has now almost wholly removed the paint.

On the other side of the entry is the parlor, to which after the first part of the house was built, an additional six feet of space was added.

[1] *Some Colonial Homesteads*, Marion Harland.

The ceiling is barely six feet high, but this room has been plastered. Behind it, a leanto contains a former bedroom, and another long apartment, known as the milk room, with its own outside door.

From the little front entry, stairs around the great chimney lead to two old bedrooms, and a ladder gives access to the attic over this oldest part. The timbers here are finely shaped, even ornamented, and are believed to justify the family claim that they were brought from England, as were the diamond shaped panes of glass set in leaden frames.

The first Fayerbanks to come to America and settle, Jonathan, came from England in 1633, with a wife and six children, and after looking about, located in Dedham, then called Contentment. He brought with him timbers for the frame of a house, and these reposed for three years in Boston, while he was seeking a favorable site. A door has been cut downstairs in the old part of the house to admit to the eastern wing, believed to have been built by Jonathan for his eldest son, John, on the latter's marriage in 1641. The wing was then a separate house, with two rooms downstairs, one a small bedroom, and one upper room, reached by its own staircase. This part has been somewhat modernized, having been plastered and papered a hundred years ago.

The western wing, built in 1654, connected with the main portion by a door, never had a chimney, and with its second story rooms reached by a third staircase, probably served as sleeping quarters for men hired to work on the large farm which once surrounded the old house.

The last male Fairbanks to occupy the old homestead was Ebenezer, father of eight children, a member of the Congregational Church choir, and in some demand from singing schools of neighboring towns. He had five daughters, two of whom married, and when he died, the three unmarried sisters occupied the house, and took turns, a week at a time, doing the housework, but the local tale that each used her own stairway is laughed at now. The last of the sisters died in 1879, more than eighty-four years old, and a niece, Miss Rebecca Fairbanks, continued living in the old house until frightened by a severe thunderstorm, when a bolt of lightning passed through the room which she occupied at the time, and killed her dog. The next winter she removed to Boston, and for the first time in its history, the house was let to strangers. Miss Rebecca returned the following summer, and lived there until the Fairbanks Association was formed to buy and maintain the old place, the President of the Association being of the ninth generation of the Fairbanks family.

The Association has collected by gift and purchase many interesting pieces of old furniture, cooking utensils, spinning wheels, etc., all of which merit closer attention than the average visitor gives.

East of Dedham, in Quincy, formerly part of old Braintree Township, is what is familiarly known as the "Dorothy Q." house, preserved and maintained by the Colonial Dames.

Set well back from the road, in extensive grounds, shaded by fine trees, this is a beautiful old mansion.

The first permanent settlement in Braintree was made in 1634, and the oldest part of this house was built in 1636, so it rivals as to age the Fairbanks house. The original portion into which the door now used by visitors opens, in the rear of the present house, consisted of a very large room on the ground floor, and two smaller rooms above, reached by a narrow staircase. The former was kitchen, living room, and meeting place for the neighbors.

The old part was built by William Coddington, who came to Massachusetts in 1630, with the Governor and Charter. He was several times Assistant of the Colony, its Treasurer, and was spoken of by an early chronicler as "munificent and upright." This did not save him from trouble when he became a convert to what the Puritans styled the Antinomian heresy, due, it is said, to the reasonings of the remarkable Ann Hutchinson, "a woman of great gift of speech and powers of mind." She was later a fugitive, and settled in what is now Pelham, New York, where she and all but one of her children were shortly afterwards massacred by the Indians.

In the year 1637-8, a warrant was issued for Coddington to leave the Colony, because he was a follower of Wheelwright, another of the Antinomians. Edmund Quincy, first of his name in America, bought the house from Coddington. His youngest son, Edmund, was born in it in 1681, a man of note, member of His Majesty's Council, Justice of the Supreme Court of the Colonies, etc., but died and was buried in England. The second Edmund's son, Edmund, married Dorothy, ancestress of Oliver Wendell Holmes, and it is from Holmes' poem, "Dorothy Q." that the house has taken its name. From the picture, photographs of which may be seen in the Hancock house, to which we shall come later, the poem would seem to describe the second Dorothy as well as her mother, with the "high, square brow, from which the hair rolled back," the "compressed lips, tapering fingers and slender wrists."

The father of the future Mrs. Hancock lived like an English squire, had fourteen children by his first wife, and three by his second, so there was much difference in age between the oldest and the youngest. This explains how Dorothy Second's oldest brother, Daniel, could be the grandfather of Abigail Adams, who was five years older than Dorothy herself. It was Dorothy's father who enlarged the house, which was certainly necessary with seventeen children.

Returning to the kitchen and living room, here are the great beams, wooden sheathed walls, and huge fireplace characteristic of the time when it was built. The fireplace may have been even larger than now, for a closet on the outer end is thought to have been made from the original. At the other side of the chimney, behind the old brick oven, is a secret passage which connected by an underground tunnel with the river. By means of a thirty-foot ladder, the attic could be reached as well. Close to the oven, a panel opens, revealing a long shaft, through which food might be passed up from the kitchen to those hidden in the attic. Very inconspicuous this panel, its existence would not be guessed.

One may follow the secret passage in the wall by mounting the old stairs, but some small openings in the wooden sheathing are not, as might be fancied, air holes or for lighting it; they are merely knot holes, from which the knots long since dropped.

That secret passage was often used. It not only constituted a refuge from marauding Indians, but it is said that the regicide judges of Charles I of England, whose movements will be noted in Connecticut,

Design of the old paper in the dining room of the Dorothy Q. house, Quincy, Massachusetts.

Design of old paper on the walls of the parlor, Dorothy Q. house, Quincy, Massachusetts. This paper was imported from France, and placed on the walls in preparation for the marriage of Dorothy, daughter of the house, to John Hancock. But when the wedding occurred, it was not here, but in Fairfield, Connecticut, that the ceremony took place.

The Maynards, Waban, Mass.

The John Alden house, Duxbury, Massachusetts.

The Maynards, Waban, Mass.

The kitchen and huge fireplace in the John Alden house, Duxbury, Massachusetts.

also came from the Quincy River up through the tunnel, and were hidden in the attic.

When Dorothy's father enlarged the old house he made of it a mansion. A hall leads from the new front door back to the old kitchen, and on either side are large handsome rooms, finely paneled, and with plenty of old H and HL hinges on the doors. In the drawing room is a beautiful hand carved, shell top china cupboard, such as are found only in houses of distinction. The walls are still covered with paper brought from Alsace, and hung here in 1773, the first paper ever made in rolls, instead of the small sheets printed from blocks, as previously.

Great preparations were made about this time to beautify the drawing room, for here the daughter of the house, Dorothy, was to be married to John Hancock. Since he was born in a house across the street, his father, the Reverend John Hancock, being minister of Braintree's First Congregational Church, the young couple had probably known each other from early childhood. But John was an ardent patriot and a marked man, and when the wedding day drew near, it was not safe for him to be so close to Boston, even while his duties with the Convention in Philadelphia, of which he was President, called him away. Accordingly, Dorothy, duly chaperoned by her aunt, went to the home of " Auntie Burr " in Fairfield, Connecticut, where later they were married. She only returned to her old home as a visitor.

In the drawing room, the present sufficiently large mantel swings back in a great door in the paneling to reveal the much larger original fireplace. A later addition to the house, separated only by an archway from the drawing room, is the music room, and behind this lies " Tutor Flint's study," with a staircase winding to the tutor's bedroom above. This has a recess for the bed, really an early example of a wall bed, and here, too, are fine strap and HL hinges. In the study is treasured the chair used by John Hancock, when he was inaugurated Governor of Massachusetts.

Over the drawing room and dining room across the hall, are two large bedrooms added at the same time, one of which has an old powder closet. The whole house is filled with charming old furniture, china and ornaments of the period when it was built, collected by the Colonial Dames, gifts from many friends.

In this house were entertained such distinguished guests as Benjamin Franklin, Sir Harry Vane, Judge Sewall, of witch trial notoriety, Sir Harry Frankland, beautiful Agnes Surriage, and many others.

Like Edmund, Josiah is a Quincy family name, and they had a joke that the house " descended from 'Siah to 'Siah." One of the Josiahs was Mayor of Boston and President of Harvard College, and occupied the house on Park Street, Boston, already mentioned.

Another old house in Quincy was built in 1730 by Leonard Vassall, whose son, Henry, married a Royall, as will later be mentioned. The house was beautifully finished with panels of solid mahogany. Leonard had also a Boston home, now gone. John Adams bought this Quincy house when it was confiscated, after Leonard's grandson, John Vassall, to whom it had descended, went to England at the outbreak of the Revolution. Both John Quincy Adams and Charles Francis Adams celebrated their golden weddings in this house; Brooks Adams, the latter's youngest son, lived in it until his recent death (1927), when the Adams Kin Association was formed. This plans to buy and open it as a museum.

In what is now called Quincy Adams, practically one town with Quincy, are two Adams houses, both open to visitors. The first, in which John Adams, second President of the United States was born, is believed to have been built in 1679, and then consisted of two rooms only, with a later leanto on the ground floor, and four small rooms with an attic above. Bricks for the chimney were brought from England, and there is one of the convenient secret passages to the attic connecting with both front and back bedrooms. The house was later enlarged by John Adams, and some of the paper still on the walls is said to have been bought by him. Here is an organ used by his nephew, Henry, the tone still sweet, a few old pieces of furniture and other articles have been added, but the interior of the frame building is quite bare.

The northside kitchen is part of the original house, with a great fireplace which the future President is said to have closed when he made other alterations. In this room is preserved part of the trunk of a cedar tree, which stood on Merry Mount Hill at the time that Captain Morton landed there in 1625, and until 1898, when it was blown down.

Merry Mount was that settlement founded by Captain Wollaston, with thirty companions from England. Wollaston began building a house near this one of the Adamses. Later, he returned to England, but Thomas Morton remained, and the settlement doings and merrymakings scandalized the Puritans. The Mount is on the farm later owned by John Quincy Adams.

Morton made friends with the Indians, but when he and his companions set up a Maypole, adorned with bucks' horns, and drank and danced around it, the people of the Plymouth Colony were outraged. Morton told them that they were merely envious, but they finally set upon and captured him, intending to send him back to England. He escaped and returned to " Mere-mount," through the woods. Again he was attacked, and this time his enemies succeeded in shipping him back to England. In 1629, he returned, but two years later was again sent back, his house burned, his lands confiscated, by order of the General Court.[2]

John Adams fell in love with Abigail, daughter of the Reverend William Smith of Weymouth, and Dorothy Hancock's greatniece, but the clergyman did not look at all favorably upon Adams as a son-in-law. He was a lawyer, and that seemed sufficient condemnation. The reverend gentleman even preached a sermon from the text: " Mary hath chosen the better part," in an attempt to convince his daughter, Abigail, of her folly. But that maiden merely requested her father to preach another sermon from a text of her own selection, namely: " John came neither eating nor drinking, and ye say he hath a devil."

Abigail carried her point, married her John, destined to be distinguished, while her sister Mary's husband is chiefly known through

[2] *History of Old Braintree and Quincy*, William S. Pattee.

his brother-in-law. The young couple went to live next door to Adams' parents.

This second house, built in 1716, was originally a mere tiny cottage on land granted by the Indians. It had one room serving as kitchen and living room, and a bedroom above. From the living room a door whose panel is made from a single great plank, still leads down cellar, but its curiously named " corpse door " has been boarded up.

Later, probably as the law business prospered, a larger, better kitchen, with huge fireplace and oven, with a much better cellar below was added in the rear, a sitting room across from the little front entry, and two bedrooms above, while the old kitchen became Adams' law office. In the larger of the two new bedrooms, on July 11th, 1767, John Quincy Adams was born.

The laths in these two old houses are all hand made, and it may be interesting to learn that 300 constituted a day's work, for which the workman received the equivalent of 62½ cents.

In the enlarged cottage, Abigail and her husband lived until after the Revolution. Here she wrote memorable letters to him, and always she spoke of the " humble cottage " with affection. When he was sent to England to represent his country, she went very unwillingly, and when her son, John Quincy Adams, future sixth President, accompanied his uncle as secretary to Russia, she admonished him not to let his head be turned by the glimpses of wealth and luxury he encountered.

Here she wrote in letters to her husband, breathing lofty patriotism: " Courage I know we have in abundance, conduct I hope we shall not want, but powder — where shall we get a sufficient supply? " and again: " I scarcely know the taste of biscuit or flour for these four months, yet thousands have been worse off, having no grain of any sort." The Minute Men were soon melting pewter spoons, or any pewter articles that they could find, and John Quincy Adams alluded to seeing them running the dozen or two spoons owned by his parents into bullets in the kitchen. Many of the soldiers stopped at this hospitable house, and were fed and lodged wherever room could be made for them.

The house was taken over in 1896 by the Quincy Historical Society, and restored by them, since when it has been open to visitors.

Hingham has a number of old dwellings, one of which, a garrison house, is said to date from 1640. Another built in 1680 is now the Wampatuck Club house. The home of Major General Benjamin Lincoln, who received Lord Cornwallis' sword at Yorktown stands, and so does the home of the Reverend Daniel Shute, built in 1746, but as these are occupied by the descendants of the two men, and private residences, visitors could hardly gain admittance.

The home of Susan B. Willard was, however, left by her to the Hingham Historical Society, and this is shown.

Daniel Webster's home in Marshfield burned down nearly fifty years ago, although his garden study was spared. Between Marshfield and Green Harbor is the old Winslow house, on an excellent highroad. It is in fine condition, and maintained by the Historic Winslow House Association. An addition built to harmonize with the old part is leased as a tea room and restaurant, only the old kitchen of the original house being used for these purposes. This room was probably originally a shed, or summer kitchen, and had wide outer doors through which a team of oxen bringing great logs for the fireplaces could be driven. The old well was close by, now under the tea room.

Built in 1669, this is truly a mansion. Downstairs in addition to the room mentioned, are a winter kitchen, from which stairs descend to a dark cellar, paved with square bricks, probably brought from England; four worn stone steps lead to another, always cool cellar, and a third flight mounts to the rear of the second floor; a living or dining room, a bedroom, and a real drawing room, with beautiful plain wood paneling. The outer walls of the house are of wood, "clinked" with brick, then with an inner board lining on which the first papering was fastened directly. Later were added split laths and plaster, the paper applied to the latter, as nowadays, but there is preserved one bit of the old wall, with distinct traces of early paper. The winter kitchen had a splashed ceiling, dark stains applied to the timber, an evident attempt at decoration, like the spatter work floors in the old Bottle Hill Tavern in Madison, New Jersey, or the herringbone ceiling in the Buckman Tavern, Lexington, Massachusetts.

In the winter kitchen, with its huge fireplace and oven, sixty-five pies are said to have constituted a day's baking. Four different fireplaces were removed when the house was being restored, before the original great one, with its rare rounded instead of right-angled corners at the back, was finally discovered.

The front door of the Winslow house has a double cross, one on the upper part, another on the lower. HL hinges have replaced older ones of the strap variety, judging from the marks in the solid old wood.

From the front entry, a real Jacobean stairway ascends. Only the finials are modern, otherwise every bit of stairs and balustrade is as originally, and wooden pegs still hold it in place. This balustrade was doubtless brought from England, for certainly the houses of the period in this section which were built entirely in this country show nothing similar, but the continuation of stairway and balustrade from the second floor to the attic was made here at a much later period.

In restoring this fine old house, it was found necessary in some of the rooms to remove thirty-four coats of paint.

Above the sitting room is a large bedroom to which John Winslow brought his bride. It has a great fireplace, with wall cupboards on each side, the right hand one masking a secret passage in the back, which led both up to the attic, and down to the cellar. The passage was recently explored by small boys, who reported that there was plenty of room. Traces of the tunnel which it is believed once led from this passage in the cellar to the sea have thus far been sought in vain. The passage must have been useful, if it really existed, for this was a Tory household.

Across the entry is another large bedroom above the drawing room, with a powdering closet opening out of it. The room was once used by Dr. Isaac Winslow as his office, the powdering closet as a store room for his drugs. It has some fine paneling added in 1760 by General

John Winslow, after he returned from Nova Scotia, where he had been sent to expel the Acadians. Here is carefully preserved one genuine Winslow chair; the rest of the furniture in the house has been collected from various sources. Three small back bedrooms upstairs, not now shown to visitors, complete the list of rooms.

The home of John and Priscilla Alden stands close to the electric railway in Duxbury, in plain sight from it and from the highroad.

John and Priscilla were married in 1623, but they came to this house, which was built for them by their third son, Jonathan, only after the first cabin home burned. Although not the original home that Alden built for his bride, the lines from the poem describe it almost equally well:

" Solid, substantial, of timber rough-hewn, from the firs of the forest." [3]

It has always been owned in the family, and at present, Mr. John Alden, of Hyde Park, Massachusetts, holds it on a twenty years' lease.

He is an enthusiastic collector of antiques, and has loaned many beautiful pieces of furniture, china, pewter, old ornaments, etc., which add greatly to the interior. A few original articles also remain, such as the old corded bed in which the first couple slept, and in which both John and Priscilla died.

From the small front entry open two large rooms, the one at the right a fine apartment, in which many distinguished guests have been entertained. In the rear is an old kitchen, which at one period of its existence was plastered, but the plaster has now been torn off, showing the original rafters, the very broad planks of walls and floor. The large front room at the left opens into the small bedroom used by the first owners, and upstairs are six more, as well as an attic, in which wooden pegs still hold the roof in place.

In the largest room downstairs may be seen an old trap door in the floor, and it is believed that through this people used to take refuge in the cellar beneath, at the approach of Indians.

All of the walls are covered with reproductions of old papers; the

[3] *Courtship of Myles Standish*, Henry Wadsworth Longfellow.

old fireplaces remain, and a fine corner cupboard, while in one room may be admired a twenty-seven inch plank in the woodwork. Many butterfly, HL, hatchet and arrow hinges are on the doors, and upstairs, on a cupboard door in the largest room, is a rare rat-tail hinge. Among interesting articles are two " Courting Mirrors." A suitor would take one of these with him when calling upon the maiden whom he wished for his wife, and would lay it on the sitting room table. If the maiden picked up the mirror, this signified that she was willing to accept him; if she did not, there was nothing for the hapless lover but to pick up his mirror and depart.

Kept open and cared for by the John Alden Kin Association, its members hold an annual meeting here on July 28th.

Reached by shady roads, running between handsome estates, at South Duxbury is the Myles Standish house, down close to the water, and now a private summer cottage. It has four rooms downstairs, and the steep stairs dividing into two half as wide, branching flights, often found in old New England houses. Some of the old doors, big fireplaces and cupboards beside them remain. The house is now quite off the beaten track, with no near neighbors.

It, too, is the " simple and primitive dwelling," through whose rather small rooms " strode with a martial air, Myles Standish, the Puritan Captain." [4]

Here, after his wife, Rose, died, Standish thought to bring the fair Priscilla; from this house he dispatched John Alden, who loved her also, to court her, since he, Standish, believed himself too unskilled in wooing to win a young maiden, and to this house from Plymouth, " not far off, though the woods are between," [4] John returned with the news that he had failed to win the Captain a bride, but that Priscilla had admitted a liking for himself.

From Duxbury, the next stop of interest will be Kingston.

This town is two hundred years old. In 1726, it had but fifty houses, but none the less, it petitioned to be separated from Plymouth on the grounds that it was too far to go to meeting. Many of the inhab-

[4] *Courtship of Myles Standish*, Henry Wadsworth Longfellow.

itants lived six or seven miles away from Plymouth's meeting house, and this seems always to have been a weighty reason with the mother colony for allowing settlements to break away from her.

Kingston was duly allowed to separate. The house of the first minister, Mr. Joseph Stacey, stood on the point between the modern Boston and Bridgewater roads. The terraced garden and trench of the Sever house, an early one, are believed to have been made by Acadian refugees, who came to Kingston in 1755, the first being a French family, allowed to take shelter in the schoolhouse, and furthermore supplied with firewood. Others followed. In 1802, Kingston proved itself one of the pioneers in woman's education, by appropriating $100 for a girls' school, one of the very first in New England.

The first roads in this section were mere Indian trails and wading places across the streams.

Governor Bradford's house in Kingston was acquired in 1921 by the Jones River Village Club — the old name of the settlement was Jones River. It had been greatly modernized by recent tenants, plastered, painted, etc. The club had all of this modern paint and plaster, the modern spruce woodwork removed, disclosing the old rafters and planks. In one rear room had been dumped much of the wood that had been torn out to be replaced by new, so this and the fireplace frames have been restored. The house was built either in 1674 or 1675, for during King Philip's War, when the Indians were burning and fighting, a runner came here from Halifax, Nova Scotia, to warn the settlement. The men took the women and children to the garrison house, located where now is Bay View Park, the railroad practically following the old highway.

They then returned to their homes for food and clothing, and saw smoke arising, apparently from the Bradford house. On Abram's Hill, stood a solitary Indian, who called out at sight of them: " Chocwaug! " (the white men are coming!) They fired, and the Indian fell, rolling down behind the hill. There were no signs of any other Indians, so the men went on to the Bradford house, and found that the Indians had poled two or three loads of hay against it, and set fire to it. But the timbers were so green that they did not burn, merely charred, and it was the smoke from the hay which they had seen. (Fifty years ago, in repairing the old house some charred timbers were uncovered.) After extinguishing the fire, the men looked for the Indian whom they had shot at in the swamp of cedar and pine, at the foot of the hill, but although they found his traces and blood, they could not find the Indian, and finally gave up the hunt, concluding that his fellows had carried him off.

After peace had been made between Indians and white settlers, an Indian came one day to the little settlement on Jones River, and re-called these incidents. Asked how he knew so much about them he explained that he was the Indian fired at, and showed the scars of serious wounds. He then told that he had lain hidden in the swamp under leaves, during all the time that they had been hunting for him, and that they had passed back and forth several times, almost stepping on him. After they had given up the search, his fellow Indians had returned, and carried him off. This could not have happened later than 1676, thus the approximate age of the house is established.

Governor Bradford's manuscript history of the early days was willed by him to his eldest son, Major William Bradford. (The site of this son's house is now marked by a tablet.) The Major left it to his son, John, and it was in the old Bradford house between the years 1723–28, when it was loaned to Judge Sewall of Boston. Then came the Revolution, and the manuscript disappeared, together with Governor Bradford's notebook, " written with a blue pencil," as had previously been noted in referring to it. Manuscript and notebook seemed hopelessly lost.

Late in the 18th century, a man discovered that a butcher in Halifax was using paper from a notebook in which to wrap purchases, and furthermore, that there was writing in blue pencil on the pages. Investigation showed that this was the actual Governor Bradford notebook, in which he kept copies of all the letters he wrote. Some three hundred pages were recovered.

Still there was no trace of the manuscript history, until much later, when an English author quoted from a history of the colonial days by Governor Bradford. More investigation and inquiries finally resulted in the information that this manuscript was in the library of the Bishop of London, and that dignitary refused to give it up. However, while a very popular American, Thomas F. Bayard, was our Ambassador at the Court of King James, aided by the representations of Senator George Frisbie Hoar, of Massachusetts, he prevailed upon the Bishop to send the manuscript back as a gift, and it is now in the Boston State House.

The western end of the Bradford house is the oldest; the east end, a large front room downstairs, with hand hewn and planed wood, the marks of the plane still distinguishable beneath the paint on boards over the big fireplaces, and another room were added sometime between 1720 and 1740. Here the Governor entertained a Catholic priest, and out of courtesy to his guest, served a meatless dinner on the Friday that the priest was under his roof. Furthermore, when Protestant services were being held in the house on Sunday morning, the Governor suggested to his guest that he would probably feel more at ease if strolling in the garden, while these services were in progress.

Much later, when some Irish emigrants arrived in Kingston, they were quartered here, and again, when a place was needed to conduct the first Catholic mass ever said in Kingston, it happened to be empty. After no other place could be found in town whose owners would consent to mass being said there, General Joseph Sampson allowed it to be celebrated in the Bradford house.

In this interesting survival of early colonial days are the very steep old stairs, with no trace of a handrail, and the last two or three steps dividing into two half as wide. How did small children ever come safely down such stairs? Here are also the great open fireplaces, the broad planks in the floors, massive rafters supporting the upper floor, and a few of the windows have reproductions of the original tiny leaded panes of glass. The newest room downstairs has the plain woodwork which, at the time of its building, was beginning to appear as a first decorative touch, instead of the merely necessary boards.

Older than the Bradford, is the Willett house, in the northwestern end of the town. This was built in 1653, but is empty, owned by an old gentleman who lives nearby. Probably it will not long survive.

The house occupied in Revolutionary days by Major General John Thomas is standing, a private residence. In what was once an old tavern is now located the telephone exchange, and still another, much modernized, is a private residence.

Major General Thomas was born in Marshfield, in 1724, and moved to Kingston when very young. He served through the French and Indian wars, receiving his commission as Colonel, and assisted General Winslow in removing the unfortunate Acadians from their homes, then settled in Kingston, practising medicine and surgery, and taking an active part in town affairs. Immediately after the Battle of Bunker Hill, he was made a Brigadier General, one of the first eight appointed by Congress, and in less than a year, was promoted to Major General.

Dorchester Heights was fortified under his direction, and he was chosen to head the rescue of the American Army in Canada. John Adams, writing to General Thomas of this appointment, declares that this is considered by some " the most important post in America," and John Hancock, in enclosing his commission to Thomas, wrote that " the Congress have been anxious to fix upon some general officer, whose military skill, courage and capacity will probably ensure success to the enterprise. In Major General Thomas they flatter themselves they will not be disappointed."

When Thomas reached Canada, he found the army in a serious condition, smallpox raging. He contracted the disease, and died at Chambly, twelve miles from Montreal. His son, John, became a colonel in the Revolutionary Army.

Continuing south, at North Plymouth, on the left side of the road, is the William Cross house, white, square, two-storied, now a well-kept private residence, not open to the public, but with a placard to state its extreme age. The interior has been entirely made over, and only the outer walls and some of the staunch timbers of the old building remain. In the Harlow house, Plymouth, is an old stone sink which was taken from this Cross house, and enthusiasts used to declare that " it came over in the Mayflower." As one skeptical New Englander remarked: " It is highly improbable that the Mayflower loaded up with such cumbrous cargo." Doubtless an early colonist brought it over from Holland, for it was recognized as typical by a Hollander, who visited the Harlow house.

In Plymouth, the Howland house, owned and kept up by the Howland Kin Association, is really the oldest now standing, but has at different times been so altered and modernized that it now has far more the appearance of a house built in the middle of the 18th century, than of 1666, when the original part was set up. It was then of the salt box type. From the front entry, good sized rooms open on either side, with a smaller room behind each, and there are big old fireplaces. Steep stairs mount to the upper rooms, and in one of these, whose sole window affords a good view of the harbor, the floor beside it is visibly worn by the feet of anxious watchers for the return of ships on which were fathers, husbands or sons.

In the attic may still be seen some of the wooden pegs holding the roof in place.

The house is furnished throughout with antiques collected by the Association, and is open to visitors on payment of a small fee, throughout the summer.

The Harlow house, second oldest in Plymouth, built in 1677, has been so restored to its original shape that it has the appearance of a far older house than the Howland. Plymouth is indeed fortunate in possessing three houses which picture three different periods of colonial life; the Harlow standing for the 17th century, in the latter part of which it was built, the Howland for 1750, the Antiquarian, representing the period of its building, 1809.

In the Harlow, may be seen some of the original wooden walls and timbers of the old fort used during the French and Indian wars by the settlers. The modern laths and plaster have now all been removed, and as soon as possible, the modern joists which now divide the two large downstairs rooms will follow. It appears that the carpenter engaged to remove the modern additions could not believe that the owners really wanted everything of the kind taken out, so one day when he was not supervised, he carefully replaced the joists, evidently supposing that new laths and plaster were to be applied. He was stopped before he had added the laths, and the society only awaited funds to have the joists removed again.

The room beyond the tiny entry, with its steep, unguarded stairs, here, too, dividing at the top, contains an enormous fireplace, the brickwork extending far out into the small room behind, thus furnishing a convenient shelf on which to stand milk pans, or put bread to rise in cold winter weather. In this house has been assembled a most interesting collection of furniture and utensils belonging to the daily life of its early existence. Here is the long-handled shovel, given every bride, to use in putting in or pulling out her bread and pies from the big Dutch oven. There are pots and pans, all kinds of cooking utensils, a loom on which rugs are still woven, appliances for winding and carding wool; a cradle, standing box for a little toddler, and small rocker for an older child; one of Tabitha Plaskett's school benches, and a few pieces of table silver. One spoon, much worn on the edges, and so discolored that it hardly seems silver, was found in a wall when repairs were made.

In the chimney here, as usual, a stick of green timber, called a "Trammel stick," or long pole, was fastened across in the upper part to hold pots and kettles. Of course in time the pole charred through, and sometimes did more, for charred timbers in the wall near this fireplace show that there was danger that the house itself might take fire. Nor did the timber always fall without serious injury.

In *Old Times in New England*, published by the Association for the Preservation of New England Antiquities, an extract from the *Boston News Letter*, for Nov. 25th, 1742 is reprinted:

"We hear from Leicester that on a Wednesday Evening last Week, a very sad Accident happened in the Family of Capt. Daniel Denney, viz: A large Kettle of boiling Water (or Wort) being over the fire, and the Trammel stick happening to be burnt the Kettle fell down, and spilt the Liquor upon four Children who sat or lay upon the hearth, (some of whom were asleep) which scalded them in so terrible a manner that one died presently after, and another's Life is despaired of."

The Tabitha Plaskett house, built in 1722, is now an antique shop and tea room. Tabitha is described as " the first schoolmistress in New England," but a present day Plymouthian indignantly denied that this could be true, demanding to know whether anyone believed that New England children went untaught from 1620 for more than a century, or until the days of Tabitha. She added that a certain clergyman of the early days was known to have taught some children. Still he was not primarily a school teacher.

At all events, Tabitha taught in Plymouth at an early date. She used to spin and wind wool as she heard her pupils' lessons, and if a child was naughty, or did not pay as close attention as she thought proper, Tabitha would throw one of her skeins of yarn around his or her shoulders, and hang the culprit up therewith to a peg in the wall.

The first dinner given by the Plymouth Old Colony Club, in honor of the landing of the Pilgrims, was on December 22, 1769, at 2.30 P.M. The menu comprised:

" A large baked Indian whortleberry pudding," served first of all.

" A dish of sauquetash," (this not the dish made of corn, beans and a bit of salt pork with which we are acquainted, but containing besides corned beef, potatoes and turnips, a meal in itself.)

" A dish of clams
" A dish of oysters
" A dish of codfish
" A haunch of venison
" A dish of sea fowl
" A dish of frost fish and eels
" An apple pie, a course of cranberry tarts and cheese." [5]

[5] *Reminiscences of an Antiquarian*, William T. Davis.

Winifred Cockshott, in her *History of the Pilgrim Fathers*, tells that in 1641, a pair of red silk stockings attracted much attention on the streets of Plymouth until it was learned that they were stolen from Boston.

The so-called Antiquarian House, maintained by Plymouth's Historical Association, as is the Harlow House, is a fine mansion, now painted in colonial buff and white. It originally stood on Main Street, on part of a tract granted in 1623 to Edward Winslow, Francis Eaton and Captain Myles Standish. Threatened with demolition, when its site was required for the new Court House, the women of the town busied themselves, and finally money for its purchase and removal to a nearby site was raised.

The beautiful entrance hall, with drawing room and keeping room are all octagonal. A fine broad staircase leads upstairs, and in the rear is a long, three-storied ell, in which, on the first floor are the dining room, kitchen, pantries, etc. A back stairway leads to all three floors, or they may be reached from the front by going up and down various short flights, passing through several rooms.

The house was built by and for Major Hammett, who had two daughters and two nieces, all four of whom were married about the same time. For the four young couples he gave a grand reception in the house. Downstairs, opening off a passage from the main hall and underneath the stairs, is a large closet, apparently once a pantry, for a slide opens from it into the rear hall. An architect who examined the house carefully declared that the kitchen was a separate building in the rear, and one of the members of the Historical Society says that her grandfather built on the ell. Yet the kitchen looks old, so possibly the more modern looking brick portion of the ell was built to connect kitchen and house. If an outside kitchen seems odd for New England, one is assured that here, too, several of the early occupants were slave owners, which may explain it.

The mansion is filled with beautiful things; with Chippendale and Phyfe furniture, rare old china, one of the first grand pianos ever manufactured in this country, a fine old secretary or writing desk, with

The Myles Standish house at Duxbury, Massachusetts. Standing practically as when built, this is now a private summer cottage, quite removed from the highroad.

The south room in the John and Abigail Adams Cottage, at Quincy, Massachusetts. When John Adams prospered, this became his law office, and he built on an addition of several rooms for family use.

Photo by Stiff, Provincetown, Mass.

The " Hooked Rug " house, called the oldest in Provincetown. Once the home of Seth Nickerson, who left it to go to the Revolutionary Army, it is at least 150 years old, and if not the very oldest, as claimed, is one of the two or three oldest of the old Cape town.

The old Fairbanks house, Dedham, Massachusetts (built 1636). This, in reality consisting of three houses joined, is one of the very oldest frame houses in the United States. It is now maintained by the Fairbanks Kin Association.

ingeniously hidden secret compartments, portraits of some of the early owners, etc.

Leyden Street is the first street in Plymouth laid out by the Pilgrims, and near its foot a tablet placed on a house marks the site of the very first building. A house stood at least recently on Sandwich Street, some of its timbers having come from the old fort on Burial Hill at the close of King Philip's War, and there are a number of other survivors, including the John and Edward Winslow houses, but so modernized as hardly to be recognized as old.

Down on Cape Cod one will find many old houses. Barnstable, the county seat, which disputes with Sandwich the distinction of being the first town on the Cape, is quaint and pretty, with a broad, shady main street, the Cape highroad. Here is the public library, which was the "new house" of John Lothrop, Barnstable's first clergyman to have a church. His predecessor had preached from the top of a large boulder on a hill nearby, which boulder, broken up, built the county jail.

Mr. Lothrop came here from Scituate about 1639, having spent his first five years in this country in that settlement, and five years later, built his "new house." The original part is the left hand side, strong, substantial; although with modern windows, the big old fireplace remains. The other side of the house, later but still old, is the library proper, and the building was left to the town by the Sturgis family, which had several times intermarried with the descendants of the Reverend John. Barnstable was served by Captain Myles Standish, he having been one of a commission appointed to establish the boundary line between that town and Yarmouth.

At North Truro, much further down the Cape, is Highland Light, one of the oldest and most powerful lights on the coast. For more than a century, the Government has owned this tract of land, now diminished by the action of the sea, and the fierce storms common here, from the original ten acres to but five.

The lighthouse keeper has been a member of the same family for all these years, and he has also conducted a hotel business here, from the time when he merely lodged and fed such travelers as passed, to the present day, with a larger building supplementing the first hotel, now an annex. The old farmhouse still stands, and in 1926 was given a new lease of life, re-shingled and generally repaired. It is a low, solidly built house, covered with unpainted shingles.

Chatham has a house which is believed to have been built about 1752, and recently a campaign for funds with which to buy and preserve it was inaugurated by the Chatham Historical Society. They will use it for meeting rooms and also as a museum.

The library at Hyannis is housed in a quaint little low house, decidedly old, and with a half story reached by ladder-like stairs.

Provincetown, beloved of artists, is well known, but some of the history of the old whaling town may be less familiar.

Every motorist has cause to remember its very narrow, winding main street, formerly always known as Front Street, while the other parallel one was Back Street. Now they are known as Commercial and Bradford, but are no wider than in the old days. Provincetown's other streets hardly count, as they are mere lanes, connecting these two.

Until 1830, Provincetown had no actual street, the Bay was its chief thoroughfare, on which residents rowed " up along " or " down along " to do their shopping, or pay visits. If not rowing, they walked on the sands. But when, in 1830, Provincetown was granted quite a sum of money by Congress, as her share of damages sustained in the War of 1812 by shipping, the enterprising young men proposed to lay out a sixty foot wide street where is now Commercial Street, thus insuring ample roadway and sidewalks on both sides. The older men objected violently. They and their forefathers had always walked on the sands, and what had been good enough for them was good enough for the younger generation. But the younger generation persisted, and as a compromise, a twenty-five foot wide street was laid out. Now it would be difficult indeed to widen it, involving, as it would, the removal or tearing down of half of the houses and buildings along the entire length of the town.

Many droll stories are told of Provincetown's early settlers. The soil here was very poor, so when her captains sailed to distant ports, with their cargoes of fish, whale oil, etc., they usually brought back earth as ballast, knowing well that if they did not want it themselves for a garden, there would be neighbors only too glad to have it. Almost all of the Provincetown gardens are due to imported soil, even as many of her old trees were imported.

A certain captain returned from one trip with a load of rich earth, which he hastened to spread on his garden plot, congratulating himself on the fine garden that he would have. But he had not reckoned with the Cape Cod gales. One morning he awoke to find that his rich earth had all been blown over on his next door neighbor's garden. He went and demanded it back. The neighbor refused to give it. Much arguing and quarreling followed, and finally the matter was taken to the Court. The learned judge decided that undoubtedly the soil belonged to the man who had brought it from overseas, but even as the captain was triumphing, the judge added:

" But if you go over on your neighbor's land to remove it, you will be liable for trespassing."

The captain ruefully digested this opinion, and then remarked that there seemed nothing for him to do but wait for a wind from the opposite direction to blow the soil back again, and begged the judge to enjoin the neighbor from planting anything to hold the soil down. The story neglects to say whether the judge granted this injunction or not.

Many of the oldest houses here were originally located on the actual point of the Cape, where now stands the lighthouse. The storms were so severe, however, that eventually the houses were towed across the bay to the present sites in town.

Provincetown natives think little of such removals. Nor, during the War of 1812, did the British frigates in the bay long keep the Provincetown fishermen penned. Since they could not sail out into the bay, and around the Cape to New York, to exchange their fish for much needed supplies, they sailed close to the shore down to Sandwich, and there carted their boats across the Cape to Buzzards Bay, thence, by alert manoeuvering, they sailed to New York.

A house more than a hundred years old perches on the top of a hill in Provincetown, and is still owned by the family that built it. A daughter of the house married Thomas Lothrop, a descendant of the Barnstable clergyman, and the husband came to live in his wife's town. What followed is typical of Cape Cod.

The business of Provincetown was fishing; her captains sailed to many ports, but there had never been a wharf. Mr. Lothrop proposed building one, but received no encouragement from his fellow towns-men. Quite the contrary. No wharf could be built, they assured him, or if it were built, it would be washed away by the storms of the very next winter. But Mr. Lothrop persisted, built his wharf, and it lasted through many winters. After this, others followed his example. Mr. Lothrop also is said to have organized the first Masonic Lodge in Provincetown.

What is now known as the Hooked Rug Shop is said to be the oldest house in town, but its exact age is unknown. It is known, however, that from it Seth Nickerson, the owner, left to join the Continental Army. In addition to its display of rugs, it houses a collection of old ship models, including the one commanded by Captain Samuel Samuels, who claimed that he sailed from Sandy Hook to Queenstown in nine days and some hours.

Another old house nearby shows the original style and position of Provincetown dwellings, for it faces the beach, which early residents used as street. The ell on the present street is more modern than the main part, which is known to be at least one hundred and thirty years old.

As early as 1641, the Cape towns of Sandwich, Yarmouth, Barn-stable, Seekonk and Nauset, the mainland towns of Scituate, Taunton and Duxbury were in existence.

Chapter VIII

⬥ The Royall Mansion and Slave Quarters ⬥

A TRIP either by train or motor in a northerly direction from Boston will take one to a number of interesting old houses, some of which are open to visitors.

The Craigie, more generally known as the Longfellow house, is familiar at least by picture to many who have never been in Cambridge. It is open as a museum.

The handsome old mansion was built by John Vassall, in 1760, and was then surrounded by a park of one hundred and fifty acres. This family were almost universally strong Loyalists, which is odd when their history is studied. The first John Vassall of whom there is mention was an alderman in London, England, and in 1588, he fitted out two ships, and joined the Royal Navy in the expedition against the Spanish Armada. His sons, Samuel and William, were both original patentees of lands in the Massachusetts Colony, and although Samuel never came to this country, he has a monument in King's Chapel, Boston, which proclaims that he was "the first who boldly refused to submit to tax tonnage and poundage imposed by the crown." He was imprisoned and his goods seized because of this protest, and Cromwell's Parliament voted him more than £10,000 damages.

Vassall seems to have received but little of this sum, for in 1657 he (or his heirs) claimed that more than £3,000 were due for "service of one ship," and another, the Mayflower, had, "when laden and manned, been taken and made use of against the enemy." One would not expect to find this man on the side of the Crown, and probably had he come to the colonies, he would not have been.

His brother, William, was the first to come. With his wife and six children, he set sail in 1635, and first settling at Roxbury, he later removed to Scituate. In 1646, he returned to England in aid of a petition for redress of wrongs. No blind Loyalist this man. He never returned to Massachusetts, but went to Barbados, and died there.

His son, John, lived in Jamaica, but the latter's son, Major Leonard Vassall, born on that island in 1678, removed to Boston before 1723. He brought with him a wife and some of their sixteen children, and when the wife died, married in New England, and had another daughter.

Major Leonard attended Christ Church, Boston, built the year he settled in that city, and was one of its wardens. In 1727, he bought an estate on Sumner Street. He also built the house in Quincy.

Of the Major's numerous children, four sons are of interest. Lewis, who settled in Braintree, where he bought two houses with lands, and like his father, was church warden. Colonel John, who settled in Cambridge, where his son, John, probably built the Craigie or Longfellow house; William, who also lived in Cambridge, purchased an estate in Bristol, Rhode Island, and in 1744 bought a house and lands on Queen Street, Boston, long since replaced by modern buildings.

William was the most prominent of the family, and was warmly praised by Adams, who found no fault with him except for his " excessive garrulity." His estates were all confiscated during the Revolution.

The fourth brother was Henry, who married Penelope Royall. He is said to have bought the Cambridge house from his brother John, but if so, it was a house built before the one now standing. Apparently Henry's nephew, John, purchased his father's place back from his uncle, and in 1760 built " a splendid mansion," probably the present one. Henry married an Oliver, of the same family as the last royal governor, Thomas Oliver, who married Elizabeth Vassall, sister of the four brothers.

Photo by Burr A. Church

The old kitchen, Hancock-Clark house, Lexington, Massachusetts. In this, part of the oldest portion of the building, has been assembled a most interesting collection of colonial articles and furniture.

The front and rear drawing rooms, Royall house, Medford, Massachusetts.

The beautiful staircase of the Royall house, Medford, Massachusetts. The stair-rail, including that topping the newel post, is cut from a single tree.

This family history has been given at such length because it is interesting that all of the Vassalls alive during the Revolution should be ardent Loyalists, when they descended from men who had not submitted tamely to authority. Almost all, if not all of the Vassalls returned to England shortly before or during the Revolution, and the family accordingly disappears from this side of the Atlantic.

The Longfellow house was confiscated from the Vassall owning it in 1778, but three years earlier, an American regiment had camped in the park.

From July, 1775, to April, 1776, the house was used by Washington as headquarters, and courts-martial and war conferences were held within its walls. It is told that the room on the second floor, later used by Longfellow as his study, was the scene of these meetings.

On August 3, 1775, General Sullivan wrote to the New Hampshire Committee of Safety, after one of the councils of war held in this house:

"To our great surprise, we discovered that we had not powder enough to furnish half a pound a man, exclusive of what the people have in their homes. The General was so struck that he did not utter a word for half an hour."

It needs little imagination to guess at the General's thoughts during that silent half hour.

After Andrew Craigie and his descendants occupied the house, it was purchased by Longfellow in 1843, and here he spent the rest of his life. Here the tragedy of his wife's death occurred, when she was burned so severely that she died. The house is now filled with the poet's belongings.

A big square building, with a classic portico, pillars supporting a pediment, topped by a fanlight, it is too familiar to require description.

Another famous old Cambridge house, still a private residence, was built in 1767 by Thomas Oliver, the Governor. To this house came several thousand men, during the troublous days immediately preceding the Revolution, and ordered the Governor to resign. He wrote: " My house in Cambridge being surrounded by about 4,000 men, I sign my name, Thomas Oliver." He and his wife went to England.

Burgoyne made his headquarters here for a time. Later, it was used by the Continental Army as a hospital, and then the Government sold it at auction. Arthur Cabot bought it, and it was later owned by Governor Gerry. Then the Reverend Charles Lowell lived in it, and here James Russell Lowell was born in 1819, and lived for many years.

From Cambridge, following the route taken by Paul Revere for his ride — the present motor road at least approximates the old country road — one soon comes to houses in Lexington suggestive of the past, even although they are surrounded by modern buildings.

Lexington is proud of her patriots, and a number of houses once occupied by Minute Men bear tablets, stating the name of the occupant on the day when these men assembled. One of these tablets is attached to a house next door to the historic Munro Tavern, which played a prominent part in the history of that April day long ago. The Reverend Thomas Parker, when making an address in 1851, in Lexington, spoke of: " a tall man, with a large forehead, under a three corner hat, who drew up his company of seventy men on the Green. Only one is left now, the boy who piped the men to the spot." This boy was Jonathan Harrington, the fifer, who, last survivor of the Americans engaged in the Battle of Lexington, lived in this house. It is still a private residence.

Further along, facing the ancient Green, a square white house bears another tablet, proclaiming that it was the home of Marrett and Nathan Munroe in 1774. The Munroe family as well as the tavern figured prominently in the history of the battle, for of the seventy-seven Minute Men who participated, sixteen bore the name of Munro, as it was then written.

Walking around the beautiful old Green, with its ancient trees, one comes to another house with affixed tablet. This was on the memorable day the home of another Jonathan Harrington, older than the

boy fifer. A magnificent elm planted by this man's father is still standing in Lexington.

To the door of this house Jonathan Harrington dragged himself,
after doing his part with the others, and died at his wife's feet. This
house is also a private residence, but through the courtesy of its owner,
the writer was shown the lower floor.

Changes and renovations have been made; the old fireplace in the
dining room has been covered with white paneling, harmonizing with
the period of building; extra windows have been cut, and contain
modern plate glass, doorways have been broadened, but something of
the old remains. In the beautiful drawing room, probably originally
two rooms, the old fireplace and wall cupboard survive. Outwardly
there is little change.

Continuing on Hancock Street, a few minutes' walk brings one to
the interesting Hancock-Clark house, now owned and preserved by
the Lexington Historical Society. It is not on the original site, for it
stood across the street, threatened with demolition when the Society
bought it. When moved, it was turned, so that the door at the side
by which visitors enter is really the "new" front door, built when
other additions were made to the original house. It has also been placed
on new strong foundations, a cellar dug beneath, so that it not only
rests firmly, but is kept from dampness, and the installing of a heating
plant made possible.

A two-story and attic building, now painted brown, the original
floors remain throughout save in the kitchen, where a new one was
needed.

Entering a small hall from which stairs ascend with a landing, at
the right one passes into the sitting room and from it into the kitchen,
one of the two original apartments on the first floor, and with a great
fireplace and cupboards. Opening from this is a small room which
was used by the Reverend John Hancock as a study and probably also
as bedroom, for the first house had but two small attic chambers,
reached by a steep and now worn staircase from the kitchen.

The Reverend John lived here from 1697 to 1752. In one of the small low chambers upstairs, his son, John, was born, who, like his father, became a minister, and settled in what is now Quincy. John, son of the second Reverend John, was the first American Governor of Massachusetts. Another son of the first minister, Thomas, became one of Boston's wealthiest merchants, and enlarged the old house, adding in 1734 two fine large rooms on both floors, and the " new " door, entry and staircase. One of these rooms has a large fireplace framed in old tiles, given by an interested citizen from his own house, when the Hancock house was repaired, to replace those once set here. The room has the original white pine window shutters, very light and thin, with molding on the panels, now dark with age and polishing.

The other added room across the hall is charming. Large and square, with a great fireplace set in a wall paneled from floor to ceiling in native white pine, now the color of old English oak, the wood is kept beautifully polished by the caretaker, who worked hard to restore it after years of neglect. A fine four-post bedstead and some old furniture are here, although not the original pieces which stood in this best chamber on the night that Samuel Adams and John Hancock slept here, with a bounty on their heads placed by the British, and when Paul Revere rode through the town. It had not been thought safe for the two bold patriots to remain in Boston, so they had come to Hancock's grandfather's old house, then occupied by the Reverend Jonas Clark, husband of a cousin of Hancock's father. Clark was the parish minister, and as such lived here until 1805.

Upstairs, in the fine large bedroom over this best room or state parlor, on this memorable night, John Hancock's wife, Dorothy, and Mrs. Thomas Hancock, wife of the wealthy Boston merchant, were sleeping.

The story goes that when Revere rode up, and began knocking, a member of the family, disturbed from sleep, requested that the noise cease.

" Noise! " Revere is said to have cried, " You'll have noise enough before long. The Regulars are coming, and almost here."

The other upper room served the Reverend Jonas as his study and

The wonderful old Royall Mansion, Medford, Massachusetts. From this home, Isaac Royall the Second left one Sunday morning to attend service at King's Chapel, Boston. He never returned here, but, unwilling to cast his lot with the patriots, sailed for Nova Scotia, and then for England, where he died.

The old Slave Quarters of the Royall house, Medford, Massachusetts. Here were housed the twenty-seven slaves whom Isaac Royall the First, their owner, brought with him from Antigua, West Indies, where he made his fortune.

probably bedroom as well. In the four new rooms were entertained
many distinguished guests from time to time; Presidents of Harvard
University, Governors of Massachusetts and other states passed up the
broad new stairs, with their hand carved bannisters. Here are several
Christian doors, so efficacious for keeping away evil spirits, and the
original front door, now opening into the old kitchen, has twelve panels,
something quite unusual.

Portraits of the Hancocks and Clarks hang on the walls of the old
house, and a photograph of the portrait of Dorothy and John Hancock, their two children, neither of whom lived to grow up, and one of
Dorothy's sisters, the original being owned elsewhere. Hancock is extremely handsome as shown here, with a gentle expression, while his
wife is beautiful, but with a stern, repressed beauty, although from all
accounts she could be merry enough. This is quite the Dorothy described by the poet, even if he was actually writing of her mother.
Here are the:

" — womanly air;
" Smooth, square forehead, with uprolled hair
" Taper fingers and slender wrist —
" Dorothy Q. was a lady born,
" Ay, since the galloping Normans came
" England's annals have known her name;
" And still to the three-hilled rebel town
" Dear is that ancient name's renown,
" For many a civic wreath they won,
" The youthful sire and the gray-haired son."

This second Dorothy Hancock was the daughter of Judge Edmund
of the Quincy house, niece of Josiah, " young patriot and orator," who
died just before the American Revolution, of which he was one of the
most eloquent and effective promoters. His son, Josiah, first Mayor of
Boston, lived to a great age, and was " one of the most useful and
honored citizens of his time."

The Historical Society has built a fireproof room on the Hancock
house, to guard some of its most precious relics, such as: the drum used

to assemble the patriots of Lexington; the tongue of the bell which rang from Lexington's belfry that day — the old belfry has been replaced by a replica — interesting old documents, etc.

Concord was settled by a little group of families who came from England in 1635, with this spot as their definite goal, the tract of land " hereafter to be called Concord," having already been granted them.

There is a local tradition that the settlement was spared, during King Philip's War, from much of the destruction wreaked upon other Massachusetts settlements because the Concord minister had the reputation with the Indians of having decided influence with the " Great Spirit." The chief is said to have observed of this clergyman: " He great pray."

Revere did not himself ride to Concord. On the way he and William Dawes, who had met in Lexington, and started together for Concord, were overtaken by Dr. Samuel Prescott, returning from a visit to his fiancée. The three were stopped by British outposts sent to intercept them, but Prescott escaped by jumping his horse over a wall, and carried on the news.

In Concord are many old houses, although some of those which attract most attention from visitors are connected with more recent days and people. Among these latter, for instance, is Orchard House, where Louisa M. Alcott wrote her *Little Women,* and the earlier Alcott residence, Hillside, which Hawthorne, after living in a rented house, bought in a dilapidated condition, repaired, and named it Wayside House. He added the tower to serve as his study, and it is said that the only means of access was a ladder, which he pulled up after him, thus insuring privacy. The little narrow staircase on which the Alcott children played " Pilgrim's Progress " still remains.

The Old Manse, to which, in 1842, Hawthorne brought his bride, was built in 1765 for the Reverend William Emerson, grandfather of the noted author. It is told that, after Prescott brought the news of the British advance, and the gun and belfry sounded the alarm, the clergyman was the first man to respond, appearing in the bright moonlight which preceded the dawn of that momentous day.

He did not leave the ranks until they marched past his house later, when he dropped out to remain and protect his wife and baby girl. Together the three watched the fighting from an upper window. In this gloomy looking dwelling Ralph Waldo Emerson wrote his first great book, *Nature*. A placard at the gate announces that the house is not open to visitors.

Almost opposite the Old Manse is a low house, with the quaint " side chamber " windows on the second floor. In 1775, this was the home of Elisha Jones, and in the cellar on the morning of April 19th, had been stored much of the patriots' ammunition. Jones hid his wife and children there, and then stood guard over all while the British searched in vain for much of the stored goods. When he heard the firing, Jones could not remain in the cellar, but ran upstairs, and was only restrained by his wife's entreaties from firing on the fleeing British. One of them paused long enough to take aim at Elisha, and the bullet pierced the wall near a first story window in the ell, missing Jones by three feet. The spot is marked.

Visitors must not expect to be admitted to these historical homes merely on request, no matter how politely worded, but if they come provided with letters of introduction, they will find their owners cordial and obliging.

The large, square white house at the corner of the Lexington and Concord roads, in which Emerson lived from 1835 until his death, is always known as the Emerson house. After his death, his daughter, Miss Ellen, lived there until she too passed on. She was a firm believer in village life, and disliked to see Concord divide into different social strata, so she was accustomed to invite different sections of the town in turn to her house, for a lawn party. Everyone in the section chosen would be invited; young and old, rich and poor. After a social period, they would be regaled with strawberries, biscuits, cocoa and cookies.

She also formed a group of young high school girls to meet once a week at her home, there to hear read aloud such books as her father had considered profitable for the young. Very dull the modern girls found these books, but it speaks well for their deference to Miss Ellen that none the less, they went to the house. Sometimes after reading aloud for some time, Miss Ellen would hand the book to one of the girls, and excusing herself, would cross the hall to the parlor, where stretched on the hard horsehair covered sofa, she would take a ten minute nap; then, returning, would resume the reading. Occasionally, as a great honor, the group was invited to stay to tea, which meal included cocoa, biscuits and fruit.

Emerson's study, with two walls lined to the ceiling with shelves, containing all kinds of books, is just as during his lifetime, and so is the sitting room in the rear, opening on the garden.

A curious story was told by a lady who rented this house furnished one summer. She and her daughter selected a large bedroom on the second floor for their own. On the first night, they were awakened by something which sounded like a pistol shot, and seemed to come from the old secretary which stood at the head of the bed. In the morning they examined this secretary, but could find nothing to explain the sound, nor was there anything in the drawers or pigeonholes.

The same thing happened for several nights, and then they changed their room. Meanwhile, several neighbors had called, and all asked, with apparent interest: " In which room do you sleep? "

The new occupants thought this strange, but gave no particulars. Other members of the family arrived, and to these the story was told. Inclined at first to ridicule it, they had the same experience when occupying that room. Then came a young man friend to spend the week end. Telling him nothing of their experiences, he was given the room. When he came down to breakfast the next morning, almost his first words were:

" What's the matter with that room, and the old secretary? I could not sleep for the noise, like a pistol shot."

They decided to use the room no more. There were no odd sounds elsewhere in the house. Finally they learned from one of the neighbors that in that room Emerson died. The lady who told this story added:

" I am used to old furniture, and the sounds it sometimes makes but this was not in the least like those."

The local chapter of the Daughters of the American Revolution is suitably installed in one of Concord's oldest houses, on Monument Square. This house is said to have been sixty-seven years old at the time of the gathering of Concord's Minute Men, which gives it to-day the venerable age of two hundred and eighteen years.

On this same square is the Antiquarian Society house, another old survivor, and open to the public at certain hours. Here is an interesting collection of old furniture and other Colonial articles, while one room is devoted solely to Thoreau. Among other personal belongings of this writer, is the bed with ropes for springs, which Thoreau slept on in the hut where he wrote *Walden*.

Behind this Antiquarian house, on the ridge, part of the Concord men were stationed on the 19th of April. The house itself was at that time the home of Reuben Brown, one of the patriots who responded to the call.

Another old white house on Main Street, next to the old burial ground, marks the site of an early blockhouse, refuge from Indians of the early settlers, and possibly some of the old building is included within the more modern edifice.

The Concord Art Association occupies a house almost opposite the Green, and which was standing on the day that the patriots assembled. Although the interior has been re-modeled to serve the Association's purposes, the front rooms are practically the same, and the exterior is little changed.

As the booklet giving the history of Concord's Art Centre explains: " the original tiny panes of glass, of curious rose and blue tints, are still to be seen in the vestibule." Behind the great main chimney rising through the centre of the house is a secret chamber, now part of a large closet, and in it slaves are believed to have been hidden in the days preceding the Civil War. The entrance to this room was originally from the upper story, through a trap door, and its secret had been forgotten when, in 1915, it was discovered by accident, while workmen were making an opening in the great chimney. A cannon ball, powder horn, candle snuffers and a three-tined fork were found in this room, whose full history will probably never be known.

The third story had contained a large hall, which in 1802 was used for Masonic Lodge meetings. When the building was re-modeled, curious painted beams were uncovered. Furthermore, a loose stone in a retaining wall behind this house when removed revealed a cave, probably used as a hiding place during the Revolution, and there are said to be seven of these caves nearby, each site indicated by a large tree.

An unknown compiler gives this interesting account of what takes place in Concord each April:

" A week before Memorial Day, a detachment of British soldiers, some Scotch kilties with their bagpipes, and veterans of the Great War march to the music of the drum and fife and the bagpipes, under their flag and ours, to the old Battle Ground, where, in the shadow of the pine trees planted by Ralph Waldo Emerson and the school children, they lay wreaths on the graves of the unknown British soldiers who fell at the Bridge during that short engagement with the Minute Men. The little company then returns to the village square, and there is met by a group of representative men, one of whom makes an address of greeting, the commanding officer replying briefly. It is indeed a sight long to be remembered, and though in itself a small thing, signifies the real bond existing between the two nations, and strengthened by their affiliation in the Great War."

The same booklet also tells that: " Mrs. Edward Hoar, a venerable lady now deceased, told of having knelt as a child by the window in the vestibule to watch the festivities in front of the First Parish Meeting House in honor of Lafayette, during his second visit to America, in 1825. Mrs. Hoar's aunt was the young girl chosen to present Lafayette the bouquet of flowers, the customary tribute in those days to an honored guest."

In Billerica will be found old houses, one on the Chelmsford Road, kept open by the Manning Association. Their ancestor, Samuel, was one of the very early settlers in this section, and probably built this, long known as the Garrison house, used by the settlers when threatened with an attack by Indians. Such houses usually had brick lined walls, for greater protection. An early decree here directs that " there shall be a house built of stone and brick, with a chimney at ye west and — ye roofe of ye house to be sawne stuffe, covered with bords chamfered and shingled."

The Manning house is usually open to the public on payment of a small fee.

Returning to Boston by a different route, in Woburn is the Baldwin house, part of which is the original, dating from 1661. Here lived Loammi Baldwin, third generation descendant from one of Woburn's first settlers, Deacon Harry Baldwin, who came here in 1641. His son, Loammi's father, was a master carpenter. Loammi and his school friend, Benjamin Thompson, later Count Rumford, were anxious to attend lectures at Harvard University, but had little money, so walked there and back daily. In 1775, Loammi enlisted in the Continental forces, soon became a colonel, and was with Washington at the crossing of the Delaware.

Later, while surveying land, he noticed that woodpeckers were continually flying back and forth, and followed them to an apple tree. Tasting the fruit, he found it of excellent flavor, and finally grafted shoots from it on a number of his own trees, eventually producing what is now the famous Baldwin apple.

The Baldwin family still occupies the old house.

Meanwhile, Thompson, who lived opposite Loammi in boyhood days, would seem to have been most unfortunate. He was accused of treason because of a letter which he admitted writing, but always vehemently denied that there was anything treasonable in his conduct. Since he defended himself in vain, found himself still suspected, he departed for England, and lived there during the Revolution. Charles Frederick, Elector and Duke of Bavaria, later invited him to that country, and for a number of years Thompson lived there greatly honored.

In 1796, during the war between France and Austria which followed the French Revolution, he even headed the Bavarian troops, and received the title of Count Rumford of the Holy Roman Empire, taking the name of the village now Concord, New Hampshire, in which he was married. He received many other tokens of esteem and appreciation for his services from the Duke and Elector, but after the war, found his popularity diminished. He had often expressed the desire to re-visit his native land, and while Thomas Jefferson was President, received a formal invitation to do so. Rumford deliberated this, but for some reason decided not to come to America, and died in his villa at Auteuil, in 1814.

Medford must surely be visited.

On the corner of Main and George Streets, one will notice a large square, with a double row of trees through the centre. This, part of the original Royall property, has recently been purchased by the City of Medford for a park, so the approach to the beautiful old Royall mansion can never be ruined by buildings intervening between it and the street.

The first settler in this part of the country by the name of Royall was a cooper, granted a tract of land in 1629, which was known as Ryal's Side, a name still retained. This land was on the site of the town of Beverly. In 1635, Royall took his family to the shores of Casco Bay, Maine. His son, William, settled in Yarmouth. Finally the Royalls found the Indians too near and dangerous neighbors for peace, so removed from Maine to Medford, when Isaac Royall, the builder of this mansion, was three years old.

Isaac grew to manhood, engaged in the shipping business, went to the West Indies, and prospered. He married the daughter of another English settler, and three children, one of whom died in the West Indies, were born. Then he and his wife decided that the remaining boy and girl should be educated in New England, so in 1737 they returned to Massachusetts.

Isaac, Senior, then purchased land in what is now Medford. This land had historic interest. It formed part of the immense tract granted in 1631 to John Winthrop, first Governor of the Province of Massachusetts, part of his " Ten Hills Farm," running down to the Mystic

River, on which he built his own home, on what is now Temple Street, Somerville.

On that portion of the grant where Royall was to build his mansion, there were in the early days dense forests, peopled with wild animals, wolves and bears, as well as haunted by Indians. To rid himself of some of these troublesome neighbors, Winthrop decided to have the tract cleared, its heavy timber felled, and on part of the site of Royall's later house, a brick farmhouse was built for the workmen to occupy while doing this clearing, possibly by the first John Winthrop, if not, by his son, and before 1677.

At the time that Royall bought the property, it no longer belonged to the Winthrop family. His intention was to found an estate on the style of old English estates. His brother, Jacob, took charge of the construction of a fitting dwelling, and this, as it stands to-day, was built around the old brick farmhouse. On the outer wall may clearly be distinguished the outline of the earlier structure, and inside, its beams run through the mansion, supporting the rear wall of the front rooms.

When the house was finished, Colonel Royall, as he was always styled, moved in with his wife, bringing from Antigua, their West Indian home, twenty-seven slaves. Royall lived in his beautiful home but two years, and dying in 1739, was buried in a marble tomb in Dorchester.

His son, Isaac, Junior, succeeded to the property at the age of twenty, and married Miss Elizabeth McIntosh, of Surinam, South America.

Isaac, Junior, like his father was a colonel, a member of the Artillery Company of Boston. In 1761, he was made the first American Brigadier General. For nine years, he served as deputy to the General Court, always returning his salary to the treasury, and for twenty-two years was a member of the Governor's Council; for sixteen years served as Chairman of the Selectmen of Charlestown, and when his estate was set off as part of Medford, he held the same office in that community. In 1763, he was one of a committee of three to purchase by subscription the first fire engine ever owned by the town of Medford, and which was called " The Grasshopper."

He was a member of famous old King's Chapel, Boston, but also kept a pew in the Medford church, to which he gave three pieces of silver for a communion service.

Entertaining with lavish hospitality, his many friends were perhaps equally divided between Patriots and Tories. Then came the Sunday before Revere's ride.

In his coach and four, Royall set out for service at King's Chapel, and never returned to his beautiful home. General Gage sent soldiers to take up a stand at the doors of King's Chapel, a Tory stronghold, warning those of the congregation who lived outside of Boston that it might be dangerous for them to return that day to their homes, as there would probably be some slight trouble, and the roads were full of soldiers. Doubtless none of the Loyalists believed that this trouble would be long-lived or serious, but Royall decided to remain for a few days in Boston, where he had many friends. Perhaps not without a struggle did he make up his mind on which side to cast his lot. He evidently would have preferred to remain neutral, for he decided to go to the West Indies, look after his property there, and wait for the storm to blow over. But it happened that there was no ship sailing just at that time for the West Indies.

Royall's two daughters were married into strong Tory families; Mary to Sir William Pepperell, of whom more will be said later. The other, Penelope, had married Henry Vassall, and although he died in 1769, his brother William, his nephew John, both living, as did the widow, in Cambridge, and her sister-in-law, Mrs. Thomas Oliver, wife of the Governor, doubtless used their influence.

At all events, there was a ship sailing for Halifax, and Royall was persuaded to go there, sailing just three days before the Battle of Lexington, although his daughter, Penelope Vassall, remained in Cambridge, where she lived for some years to come.

After arriving in Halifax, Royall sailed for England with his other daughter and her husband, Sir William Pepperell, and died there before the Revolution was ended.

Perhaps he regretted his decision; wished that he had cast his lot with those who fought for independence. At all events, he felt kindly towards his native country, for by his will he left a tract of land to Harvard College, to found the Royall Professorship of Law, from which grew the Harvard Law School. He also requested in this will that " provision be made for a Hospital for the Poor and Infirm in Medford or Cambridge, the poor of Medford to have preference." His father had made by will elaborate provisions for keeping the estate in the family, English fashion. The second Isaac had but two daughters, and one, Lady Pepperell, died on the voyage to England, leaving a daughter, Harriet. Nor had his daughter Mary, sons. By 1778, Isaac Royall's estates had been confiscated, and he himself forbidden to return to America.

General John Stark occupied the house as headquarters for one year after the evacuation of Boston. On the same side of the mansion where may be traced the outline of the earlier farmhouse, a small square, high above the third story windows, between the two great chimneys, may be seen. This was originally a window reached by a winding flight of stairs from the third story. Whatever its original purpose, during Stark's occupancy, many times his wife, Molly, watched from this lofty window the movements of British troops on the plain below, and several times she was thus able to get useful information which she sent to her husband in the field. Generals Lee and Sullivan also occupied the house at different times. Washington visited it, and in the old summer house, now gone, he is said repeatedly to have held councils of war.

After the Revolution, it was for two years the home of Colonel Cary, whose own home at Charlestown was burned during the Battle of Bunker Hill. In 1790, it was used for a boarding and day school. In 1806, it was returned to Isaac Royall's heirs, who sold it, and after that it was owned by several people, until in 1860 the family of Jacob Tidd occupied it. Mrs. Tidd's brother, William Dawes (ancestor of the Vice-President), who rode through Cambridge while Revere was riding to Lexington to give the alarm, was a frequent visitor here after Tidd bought it.

After 1860, the old house seemed destined to come down in the world, if not to disappear. Then, in 1896, the Sarah Bradlee Fuller Chapter of the Daughters of the American Revolution rented it for chapter use, and at once began agitating for its purchase. At last, through their efforts the Royall House Association was formed, and in 1908 the house and three quarters of an acre of land around it were purchased, the deed being passed on April 16th, the very day on which its builder had sailed away from his native land.

Since then, the Colonial Dames, several chapters of the D. A. R., and the Girl Scouts have made themselves responsible for different rooms, and have aided in filling them with fine old furniture of the period when the place was the scene of brilliant social life.

The low building through which visitors now enter, was the slave quarters for Colonel Isaac's twenty-seven Antiguan slaves. Here in the great kitchen, with its enormous fireplace, measuring ten feet across, having hooks from which pots and kettles were hung, they prepared their own food, and that which was eaten by the Royalls as well. A door opposite the entrance opens directly on the courtyard of the mansion. By this courtyard, those arriving on horseback, or with coach and four, entered; the large door in the rear of the mansion is as broad and fine as the front one, looking out over what is now Medford Park. Across this courtyard food was carried to the house from the slave kitchen.

This kitchen was restored as a memorial to Mrs. Charles M. Green, wife of the President of the Royall House Association. At the side, a door admits to a large room now rented for entertainments, but which originally was the lower floor of three separate slave houses, each with its own outer door on the courtyard. All of these outer doors have big old hinges, and several have the wooden latches and latchstrings which, when hung outside, raised the latch, but if drawn inside, made it impossible to open the door from the outside. The second floor of this building is now the home of the custodian.

Passing across the old paved courtyard, separated by a replica of the old fence from the garden, we enter the beautiful house through a side door into the kitchen. On this side is a fine piazza, the roof supported by old columns, only one of which it was necessary to replace. The kitchen has a great fireplace, although visitors are assured that it was not used for cooking during Royall's time. All sorts of old cooking utensils and other furnishings are now assembled here, and an old inn signboard is sure to attract attention. The colors and gilding are very bright, the board of solid old oak, and it hung outside the Royal Oak, Medford. Later, the place was known as Jonathan Porter's Tavern. When the fifty-nine Minute Men sent by Medford returned after Concord and Lexington fighting, one Medford man remarked that he had one bullet left, and had found a mark for it. Saying this, he fired at the sign, the bullet passed through it, and the hole may be seen to this day.

From the kitchen, back stairs ascend to the second and third stories, and one may further climb a narrow flight to Molly Stark's window, or going into the beautiful hall running through the house, with the fine old doors each with great HL hinges, may ascend the broad flight of stairs here. Its handrail, including the curve over the newel post, is cut from a single tree; the spindles are all hand-carved, in three different patterns, one of each on each of the broad, low treads.

Downstairs, the room at the left of the front entrance was the dining room, beautifully paneled, with great fireplace, and containing one piece of furniture which is believed originally to have stood here. When the property was confiscated, all of the furniture was sold at public auction, and on the old inventory which was discovered there was mention of a cellarette. The one now here had come down in one Medford family from about the date of the sale of Royall's goods, and it is believed that possibly it was purchased then.

In this dining room, when the house was restored, a door was cut in the paneling to show the old brick wall, the great beam of the original brick Winthrop farmhouse. In the thick wall, too, probably by Isaac Royall, a niche was dug out for a safe, and above this a cupboard to hold other papers. The door which reveals these is concealed in the paneling, opened by touching a spring close to the floor. Here are also cupboards with fine old H and HL hinges, and a great fireplace framed by at least some of the original Dutch tiles. When the house was taken over by the D. A. R., the old fireplace was found boarded up. Removing the boards old tiles were found thrown carelessly in a heap. Some were broken, but others were intact. The latter were re-set, the broken ones replaced with new ones made after the old design, and now one can hardly tell which are new, which old.

On the opposite side of the hall are two drawing rooms, separated by doors which when folded back into the deep archway are scarcely distinguishable. It is impossible to avoid superlatives in speaking of these two rooms. Each has a broad fireplace surrounded by fine old tiles; each has two large windows, with carved framework. From the front room opens what was perhaps a powdering closet, now used to display some rare old china; in the rear room, at each side of the fireplace set in deep recesses are windows with seats beneath. Both rooms are paneled exquisitely, and the carving in the rear room is singularly lovely. The three-leaved shutters close tightly over all windows; the great boards in the wall paneling were cut from the virgin timber near the mansion, and one of these measures forty-three inches.

Passing up the broad staircase, there are four large bedrooms on the second floor, the one over the rear drawing room the state guest chamber, with the same deep window recesses as below, the same beautiful woodwork, here a wainscoting, instead of reaching to the ceiling. Above the wainscoting the walls of this room were hung with leather, on which birds and foliage were depicted in brilliant colors. Against the white woodwork, this must have been most effective. The three-leaved shutters here have each a six-pointed star peephole, near the top. The molding over the windows is carved in a beautiful design of roses and acanthus leaves. Once a four-post bedstead stood here, with crimson silk damask coverings, and perhaps a similar one may sometime be found for the room. All of the old furniture now here has been collected or contributed by friends.

In another bedroom stands the four-poster in which President Pierce was born. The Association is further fortunate in owning a small quantity of tea from the Boston Tea Party, said to have been collected from the boots of one of the participants, and for years treasured in his family.

Four more rooms on the third story, reached by the back stairs only, include a loom room.

Among the papers issued by the Medford Historical Society, is one last bit of history connected with the Royall family, or rather with one of Isaac's slaves.

When he departed at such short notice for Halifax and England, his slaves must have been left with little or no provision, and so we find that in 1783, Belinda, an aged African, one of them, begs the courts for maintenance for herself and her more infirm daughter. She states that she, Belinda, had been a slave for fifty years, and her master was " an absentee in England, from whence at that time he could not return." In consequence, she was in want. The courts allowed her fifteen pounds and twelve shillings per annum.

Upper Medford was the birthplace of Governor Peter Brooks. His father, Caleb, built a house here in 1715, and for 167 years it stood at the turn of the road. In 1882, the owner, Marshall Symmes, built himself a new house, removed the leanto from the old one, and moved the two-story building itself a few feet behind his barn, at the same time turning it around. The old front door was taken off, and the opening closed, but the solid oak timbers, even the old shutters remained, defying time. No longer a dwelling, it was used for storing apples and farm implements, and at least a few years ago still stood.

Medford has several other interesting old houses, now private residences. Up Bradlee Road, stands one of brick, known as the Garrison house, built in 1680 by Major Jonathan Wade. It has been considerably altered and re-modeled.

The Isaac Hall house, originally one of a row of five, built in 1727, all occupied by members of the Hall family, is the only survivor. At this house Paul Revere stopped on his ride to rouse Isaac Hall, Captain of the Minute Men, and every year now the drama is re-enacted. A man impersonating Revere knocks at the door, and another wearing a nightcap, sticks his head out from an upper window, and calls: " Who's there? "

The Craddock house on Riverside Avenue, once called Ship Street, is another survivor. People used to be told that this was the two-story brick house built by Matthew Craddock's agents, in compliance with his directions, in 1634, and it was called "the oldest brick house in America." It is now more generally believed that the original house was replaced by the present one in 1680, by the first Peter Tufts, but first occupied by the second, Captain Peter.

Matthew Craddock, who owned the land, never came to America. The building is often called the Fort, because of its thick walls, eighteen inches, close outside shutters, and small port holes. Even if one refuse it the earlier date, it is still venerable.

Chapter IX

SEVERAL days could easily be devoted to Salem's old houses, both numerous and beautiful. Even when strictly private residences, there is much to admire by merely strolling past, and staring with as little violation of good manners as possible, at the fine façades, doorways, and noble proportions. Salem's disastrous fire in 1913 spared most of the old houses, destroying the business and more modern section.

Of the residences to which only personal acquaintance would secure admission, may be mentioned the Pickering house on Broad Street. Set in a square of grounds, and always owned by the family of Pickering, the old house unfortunately has been sadly disfigured by additions and changes, and painted a slate grey, instead of the probably original white. The ugly jig-saw ornamentation, beloved of the 1850's, abounds, the old gambrel roof was years ago replaced by a pointed one of slate.

The Pickering family is distinguished. Timothy, born here in Salem, in 1745, took part in the Battle of Lexington, and the following year joined the Continental Army, in command of seven hundred men, was appointed Adjutant General by Washington, and from then until the end of the war, was Quartermaster of the Army. He then served his country as Secretary of War under President Washington, and is buried in the old Broad Street burial ground. His son, John, born in Salem, distinguished himself as a philologist, and two of Timothy's great-grandsons won reputations as astronomers.

Built before 1685, the house in which Nathaniel Hawthorne was born in 1804, still stands on Union Street. The Home for Aged and

Destitute Women, on Derby Street, was the Benjamin Crowninshield residence, built in 1811. Six years later, President Monroe and many notable guests were entertained in it. From 1825 to 1849, it was the home of General Miller, of Lundy's Lane fame.

The Bertram Home for Aged Men, also on Derby Street, was built in 1806–7 by Captain Joseph Waters.

Another beautiful old mansion not open to the public is the Cabot-Endicott, on Essex Street, but one may admire in passing the very beautiful old door. The house was built in 1748 by Joseph Cabot, and later became the home of Supreme Court Justice William Crowninshield Endicott, Secretary of War during President Cleveland's administration.

On Federal Street, the Assembly House may easily be distinguished by its size and ornate façade. Corinthian pillars support the porch roof, and in the same design square, half-relief pillars extend across the façade of the second story. Lafayette was given a ball here in 1782, and two years later, Washington was guest of honor at another ball.

Another fine old house close by was built in 1816 by Captain Samuel Cook, and given to his son-in-law, General Henry Kemble Oliver, who composed the familiar old hymn tune, "Federal Street," within its walls. Much of the interior fittings of the Derby mansion was purchased to use in this interior. The Derby mansion, very magnificent for its day, was built in 1799, by Elias Haskett Derby, at what was then the enormous cost of $80,000. He died that same year, and as no purchaser could be found for so expensive a residence it was torn down. Market House was not built on the site until 1816.

If time in Salem is limited, it would be best to spend it at the Essex Institute, for even if one does not care to inspect the valuable collections of old costumes, coins, pottery, valuable documents, old portraits and furniture, here may be seen one of Salem's oldest houses, and parts of several others.

Passing through the main building into the garden at the rear, here is the house of John Ward, built in 1684. Just who Ward was, save that he was an early resident, the Museum people have been unable to

When built in 1818, this house was said to be the most expensive in New England.

Next door to the Museum is another handsome house, built in 1810 by John Gardner, one of the last pieces of work of Salem's famous architect, McIntire. In 1830 Joseph White, who then owned it, was murdered by a man hired by his nephew, and it is supposed that the story of this murder suggested to Hawthorne Pyncheon's death in *The House of the Seven Gables*.

Every visitor to Salem, however hurried, will surely visit the House of the Seven Gables, and the fact that Hawthorne expressly denied that the house now standing was the one described in his romance makes little difference to the many tourists who annually visit it. Certainly, even ignoring any connection with the story, it more than merits a visit. Standing close to the water, with lawn sloping down to a sea wall, it is most attractive, and at all events, Hawthorne visited here. His portrait hangs above what is said to have been his desk, with his favorite chair before it. The house *has* seven gables, it *has* a secret staircase, and is a fine specimen of architecture, so what more could be asked?

Standing in what is now almost wholly a foreign quarter, it is fitting that it should be devoted to community and social settlement work. Hawthorne's description of the scene of his romance certainly quite describes this old house.

" On every side, the seven gables pointed sharply to the sky, and presented the aspect of a whole sisterhood of edifices, breathing through the spiracles of one great chimney. The many lattices, with their small, diamond shaped panes admitted the sunlight into hall and chamber, while, nevetheless, the second story, projecting far over the base, (some license must be excused here) and itself retiring beneath the third, threw a shadowy and thoughtful gloom into the lower rooms. Carved globes of wood were affixed under the jutting stories." These may be seen both on this and on the Hathaway house mentioned later. Even Hawthorne's description of the locality fits to-day.

" The street in which it upreared its venerable peaks has long ceased to be a fashionable quarter of the town; so that, although the old edifice was surrounded by habitations of modern date, they were mostly small, built entirely of wood, and typical of the most plodding uniformity of modern life." [1]

Visitors enter the house by a side door, opening directly from the street, and may fancy themselves in Hepzibah's old cent shop, now an office, and serving for the sale of souvenirs, but probably never until now was there really a shop of any kind here. From this, one is shown into the fine old dining room. Beside the old fireplace a door opens into a wood closet, but a spring pressed, a door in the back opens, revealing the secret staircase. Visitors may mount this staircase, now lighted by electricity, and climb narrow, steep and winding stairs, until by the time the top is reached it is dark, for one has come two stories, and the light is far below. Suddenly a door is opened by the guide, and one steps out into a small bedroom, entirely paneled in dark wood. When the door is closed, it is impossible to find it, for the panels are closely joined. This, of course, is Clifford's chamber. The secret passage had long been lost, and was re-discovered only twenty-five years ago.

Other rooms on this floor are used by the settlement workers. From a skylight in the sloping roof a fine view may be had of the harbor. We now descend the main stairs, and are shown a beautiful " grand chamber," looking out from the second story over the lawn and water. Here is a fine old fireplace, with wall cupboards, the chimney wall paneled, the rest of the walls wainscoted. Woodwork and paneling were probably added in 1720. In this room is a bed in which Hawthorne slept when visiting here, several portraits of him, and the desk and chair mentioned.

Below is the beautiful drawing room, also finely paneled. The china cupboard beside the great fireplace, has a finely hand carved inner shell top. On the iron fireboard behind the andirons in the old fireplace is this curious 16th century inscription: " An Ape will never be a Man." Was this in answer to an early precursor of Darwin?

The front door of the house is a reproduction of the original, heavily studded with nails. Repairing, re-modeling and re-building

---

[1] *House of the Seven Gables*, Nathaniel Hawthorne.

Clifford's Bedroom, showing sliding panel at right of fireplace opening out onto the secret staircase in the House of Seven Gables.

House of Seven Gables, Salem, Massachusetts.

Retire Becket house, Salem, Massachusetts.

The Hathaway house, Salem, Massachusetts.

were done at various times, for the house was built in 1668, but much of the old still remains. The Ingersoll family, whom Hawthorne visited here, first owned it in 1782, but the lovely drawing room and bedroom above had much the present appearance before then.

Several old buildings have been brought from their original sites to the grounds of the House of the Seven Gables. An old barn has been made into an attractive tea room, and either here, or in the charming old fashioned garden, now carefully restored, luncheons and teas are served in the summer for the benefit of the settlement work.

The "Old Bakery" is another building, moved here, and dating from 1683. Still another is the Hathaway house, built in 1683, its beams brought from England by Roger Conant, leader in 1626 of the first settlers, and commemorated by a statue facing the Common. Conant first went to Gloucester, but not caring for the climate, the beams were then brought to Salem, and used in building by Governor Endicott. When his house was torn down, they were given to Hathaway.

The original house seems to have consisted of the large front room, its walls of natural colored wood, with a big old fireplace, and one room above. The door opening from the small entry has three glass bull's-eyes set near the top, through which the visitor might be examined before the door was opened. A loom two hundred years old standing in this room is still used by pupils of the settlement for weaving rugs. The small entry and square room behind were added later, about 1735, the paneling and other woodwork brought from a house which stood on the corner of Federal Street, where now is a theatre. The second story and attic, used for settlement work, are not shown.

The charming old Retire Becket house is now entirely furnished with antiques for sale, which make the interior very harmonious. Three Dutch doors open from without, although the lower floor now consists of but a single room and small entry, from which the stairs ascend. Probably there were originally three small rooms here, as the ceiling beams would seem to indicate. The house was moved here from Becket Street, when threatened with being torn down.

John Becket built it in 1655, and it descended in the family until his great-great-grandson, Retire Becket, a famous Salem shipbuilder, owned it. Tradition says that additions were often made to the old house, and then, as children married and went to homes of their own, torn away.

Still a fourth outer door opens into the entry, papered with a reproduction of a rare old ship pattern. In the upper hall, the worm-eaten but still strong old beams and rafters may be seen.

Last of the interesting little group of buildings is a small, one-roomed counting house, used by the various shipowners who lived in the dwelling. An interesting old desk is here, with six secret compartments, or drawers, the existence of at least three of which is hardly to be suspected.

The Witch House, said to be oldest in Salem, was at all events built before 1675, and some say as early as 1635. Ship carpenters built it, of swamp oak, and the floors are laid with over and under lap, like a ship's deck. A modern store on the street corner half conceals it from sight, and only two rooms of the second story, now occupied as an antique shop, are shown, but these are well worth a visit. Originally the house consisted of two large rooms on each of the two stories, with the small entry and stairs between the rooms. An addition in the rear was made later.

The stairs wind up curiously, and are broader than is customary in so old a house, while but three of the treads are straight. One may admire broad planks in the original floors, old fireplaces and cupboards, with strap and HL hinges.

No witch trials were ever held in this house, but it derives its name from the fact that Judge Corwin, who conducted these trials in 1692, lived here, and some of the preliminary examinations may have been conducted in it. The Judge's portrait hangs in the Essex Museum; that of a severe, narrow-minded looking elderly man.

The Peirce Nichols house is open, through the courtesy of its owner, on Wednesday and Saturday afternoons, upon presentation of a card which may be obtained from the Essex Museum. It is a most beautiful example of its period, built in 1782, from designs by Samuel McIntire,

Salem's famous architect, for Jerathmeel Peirce, a wealthy Salemite. McIntire himself is said to have done the carving on the front door, and in the large room at the left of the hall, while for the more ornate drawing room opposite he had the aid of his brother and nephew. In 1801, one of Mr. Peirce's daughters married a Mr. Nichols, and at her death, her sister married him. There were no Peirce sons, the house descended in the Nichols family, and has belonged to them ever since.

The front door is exquisite, with its double cross panels, its flutings, which are also carried all along the top of the washboard in the broad hall running through the house. Pineapples, signifying hospitality, figure prominently in the carvings of door frames.

In the sitting room at the left are paneling, a large fireplace and wall cupboards, all carved. A door opening into a side entry has a curious arrangement of two brass rings, one of which when turned unlocks, the other locks the door. Behind the sitting room is the dining room, and both are filled with fine old furniture.

The drawing room, which it is said was eighteen years in the making, is beautiful. Its four deep recessed windows have small sofas built so as exactly to fit into the recesses, and two others, similarly fit on each side of the big fireplace with its paneled mantel in the rear wall. A mirror specially imported from France fills a prepared niche above the mantel. The first Miss Peirce was married in this room, and no expense or pains were spared to make it a beautiful setting for the ceremony.

The handsome old staircase in the hall — it is impossible to speak of this house without adjectives — leads up to the second and third stories. The Chippendale handrail above the hand carved spindles of the balustrade, is like them, of solid mahogany, but it is oddly cut in short lengths, supposedly to imitate Chinese bamboo, Chippendale having a weakness for things Chinese. The upper floors are not shown, but visitors may stroll in the old garden, sloping down in a series of terraces to what was in early days the harbor, now a filled-in street. Once a wharf extended from behind this house, and many ships landed there. The first cargo of coal, that strange new fuel, which people declared would never burn, any more than rocks, was landed at this wharf, and in the sitting room is one of the first stoves used in Salem for coal.

The Ropes Memorial, for five generations occupied by the Ropes family, with its old furniture, china, portraits, etc., is open to the public on Tuesday, Thursday and Saturday afternoons. One could spend hours studying the collections in the eight large rooms which visitors are shown, or in strolling in the beautiful old garden. A fund was left with the house for the " maintenance of botanical lectures."

This house was built about 1719, and purchased in 1768 by Judge Nathaniel Ropes. His grandfather came to the Colonies from England about 1642. Judge Ropes was a strong Loyalist, and on March 17th, 1774, while he was ill in this house, it was attacked by a mob of patriots, and he died the next day, partly due, it is thought, to the excitement. The last of the family to live here were Nathaniel Ropes 5th and his three sisters. The house was moved back from the street and an ell added by the last owners, and at their death it passed to the city.

Leaving Salem reluctantly, it is but a short drive to the old town of Beverly, where is a fine three-storied brick house, now occupied by the Beverly Historical Society. It was built in 1781 by John Cabot, and judging from pictures preserved in the Society's rooms here, those of his two brothers were equally handsome; George's, where Washington was entertained in 1787, and Andrew's, built in 1784, have disappeared. The former was replaced by a gas filling station, the latter, sold for a town hall in 1841, was torn down to make room for the present new building. The house of the brother's mother, Elizabeth, was moved from its original site, the fine staircase and paneling torn out and sold.

The three brothers were all born in Salem. George came to Beverly as a child, and in 1770 was town delegate to the Provincial Congress at Concord. In 1788, he was a member of the State Convention, and in 1793, United States Senator, and removed to Boston.

Andrew, a year older, in 1779 chartered to the Provincial Government his ship, the Defense, for an expedition against the enemy in Penobscot Bay. The ship was lost.

John, the third brother, was Representative of the General Court in 1792, and it was he who built the house which is now standing.

This survivor has a fine hand carved staircase, leading from the front door to a landing, where it meets a similar flight starting from the rear, and the latter continues to the third story. The house is finely paneled, and filled with interesting relics and furniture belonging to the Society or loaned, including two autograph letters of Washington, costumes of bygone days, etc., but nothing which belonged to the Cabots.

At the other end of the town is the very old Balch homestead, which has belonged in the family of that name ever since it was built in 1639. It is now owned by the Balch Family Association, and is being gradually restored to its original state. John Balch, founder of the family in America, was born in Bridgewater, England, in 1579, and landed on Cape Ann in 1623, coming to Salem three years later, and then to Beverly.

At present there is little here but the old walls, roof and floors, but the modern plaster is being removed, and in time it is hoped to restore it completely, and furnish it with suitable pieces of its original period. Not the least of the good work already accomplished is that done on a magnificent old tree beside the house, which by means of cork filling, chains and rivets, will, it is hoped, be preserved for many years.

Going far afield now, in the northwestern part of Massachusetts is a town filled with old houses, every one of historic interest, while the town itself has had a thrilling history.

Everyone knows Deerfield, and has read of the devastating Indian attacks, but even before white settlers came, blood was shed here.

In 1664, on the site of Deerfield there stood in a clearing a fort belonging to the Pocumtuck Indians. Here they were attacked, their fort stormed and captured by the fierce Mohawks and their allies. The "Apostle Eliot" had for some time been petitioning for a grant of land in the wilderness, and in 1665 this was finally given him, meaning that he was permitted to purchase the land from the Indians. In that same year, a party of four men rode from Dedham, and found the clearing made by the Pocumtucks a good place in which to found a new settlement. Eliot is said to have purchased 8,000 acres here in 1671, and the town was laid out, old Deerfield Street to-day occupying the "Town Plot." In deeding the land, the Indians reserved the right to fish, hunt, and pick up nuts on it.

Samuel Frary was probably the second settler, and had cultivated land in this section as early as 1669. At first, when the Indian outbreak of 1675 began, Deerfield was not molested, but hardly had two or three houses of the little settlement been slightly fortified, than Captain Lothrop and his eighty men, who had come to guard the removal for greater safety of a quantity of grain to Hadley, were surprised by the Indians, headed, it was said, by King Philip himself, set upon, and only seven escaped.

They were avenged by a detachment under Captain Moseley, who arrived too late to rescue Lothrop and his men, but finding the Indians engaged in pillaging the bodies, surprised them in turn, and falling on them, killed about a hundred, and chased the rest back and forth across the swamps until they fled. Of these troops but two were killed, and six or eight wounded. The settlers in Deerfield, however, scattered. By 1677, they were back again, Frary apparently among them, and then or soon afterwards, the oldest part of the present Frary house was built, the oldest in Franklin County.

King Philip had at first been friendly with the settlers, but his treachery was terribly punished. A curious story is told of him, to the effect that he went in disguise so perfect that even his closest friends could not penetrate it, and that he never slept in the same place for two consecutive nights.

None the less, he was killed by an Indian whose brother Philip had killed. This Indian and a white ally tracked him down, and both took aim, but it was the Indian's bullet which found its mark.

Philip's wife and child, taken prisoners during the war, were sold into slavery in the West Indies.

In 1682, the Indians attacked Deerfield again, but were driven off, and six years later there were sixty landowners in the settlement.

King William's war brought renewed attacks. In 1694, Baron

Castine with an army assembled in Canada, tried to surprise Deerfield, but was driven back. Still another army organized in Canada turned back after the Deerfield scouts discovered them.

By the time of Queen Anne's War, there were three hundred inhabitants. They were repeatedly warned of impending Indian attacks, but as they were no longer quite such a frontier town, and as they had strongly fortified Meeting Hill, they escaped them, save that two men were captured and taken to Canada.

Then in 1704, French and Indians under Hertel de Rouville, killed or captured almost the entire garrison, burning every house except that known as Ensign Sheldon's, and the Frary house, the ell of the present one. Frary was killed, his wife taken prisoner. Later, the house was owned by the Barnards. In 1746, when one of these Barnards was off to war, he went to a neighbor's to say goodbye and, noticing a little girl in her cradle, is said to have remarked: " Keep her until the war is over, and I will marry her." Twenty years later he did marry her, Elizabeth Nims.

About 1763, the beautiful ballroom was added to the Frary house, and it became a tavern. In 1775, Benedict Arnold, then a loyal Patriot, rode up to this tavern, sent for Thomas Dickinson, made him Assistant Commissary, and ordered 15,000 pounds of beef to be sent on after him, then hurried to Ticonderoga. Arrived there, he found that the fort had already surrendered to Ethan Allen. Dickinson and his brother followed with the cattle, for which Dickinson's only personal pay was the glass of liquor given him by Arnold in the tavern.

In 1890, a descendant of the Frary family bought back the house. Now a private residence, when in August, 1926, many of Deerfield's old houses were thrown open to the public, in honor of the 250th anniversary of the town, punch was served over the old bar of tavern days.

When de Rouville and his forces attacked Deerfield, killing forty-nine men, women and children, they took as prisoners twenty-seven men, twenty-four women and fifty-eight children. These captives they collected in the house of Ensign Sheldon until they were ready to march them to Canada, and this may be the reason why this house was not burned. It stood until 1848, during the latter part of its existence known as the Indian house, and the door, always called the Indian Door, showing marks of Indian hacking and firing, is now preserved in Memorial Hall, Deerfield.

Just when this Sheldon house was built seems uncertain, but in 1703-4 it stood, a fortified or garrison house, and within it a number of settlers had assembled for greater safety when the attack was made. Captain John, son of the builder, was sleeping with his wife in a second story room. They jumped out from the east window, hoping thus to escape, but Mrs. Sheldon injured her ankle so badly that she could not go on, and finally induced her husband to leave her, and make his own escape. Meanwhile, Mrs. Sheldon, Senior, in the lower room, had been killed by a musket ball, fired through a hole which was cut by a toma-hawk in the front door. The enemy came in through a back door left open by a boy, who escaped through it during the attack, and it is thought that had it not been for this the inhabitants might again have defended themselves successfully.

On the march to Canada, twenty of the prisoners were killed, in-cluding Mrs. Williams. After peace was made, and friends sought news of them, some of the children preferred to remain in Canada. In 1722, there was another Indian outbreak, but save that five men were killed, and one boy and a girl taken prisoners, Deerfield escaped.

Of the attack in 1703-4, the account of an eye-witness has come down to us. Hannah Sheldon's youngest son, Remembrance, survived, was taken prisoner, and returned to write his reminiscences, which have recently been transcribed and published.[2] Among other interesting details, he tells:

" In October, Godfrey Nims' two sons had been carried off by Indians while they were searching the meadows for their cattle." Play-ing Indian was at that early time a favorite game with the little boys, too young to remember, as some of their parents could, the attack made in 1693 on the settlement. In February, 1704, Remembrance's

[2] *Story of Remembrance Sheldon*, transcribed by Matilda S. Hyde.

father started for Hatfield on business of his own, and to buy medicine
for the sick. Remembrance wonders if he would ever have started had
he heard the rumors then beginning to circulate, as to the presence of
large numbers of Indians in the neighborhood.

Then came the fatal night.

His mother aroused him, bade him hand her her clothes, and dress
himself and little Mercy. Indians were at the moment hacking at the
door, made of double thicknesses of oak, which it was hoped might
withstand the attack. The boy did as he was told, when there came
another sound. Turning to his mother, he called her, but she was dead,
shot through the heart by a musket poked through a hole in the door
which the attackers had succeeded in making. Hannah, the young wife of
John Sheldon, Remembrance's older brother, loaded muskets bravely,
while Mary, a sister, melted and molded shot. Remembrance tells
that he was " something of an adept at throwing the knife," from
much practise, and he now threw one to such effect that one of the
Indians, as he was bursting into the house, fell with a cry.

As has been told, the back door in the leanto was found to have
been left open by an escaping boy, and through that door the attacking
party now entered. Remembrance always suspected that this lad was
" Coffee, the slave," or else " why should he shrink from me to this
day? " although he, his wife, and " little Coffee " were then living
under the Sheldon roof. (This of course was years later, when Remembrance and others of the family had returned from their captivity.)

He tells how it goes against the grain for him to see " Mary and
Ebenezer in the last ten years dispense hospitality at Deerfield tavern
to scores of Mohawk Indians, whom they durst not turn away, giving
them free bed and board because, forsooth, of having lived captive in
their lodges." He is " very glad his father moved to Hartford, leaving
the two young people to keep the tavern, which he did so soon as ever
he had got Parson Williams' family settled again in Deerfield, with
the hundred and more other captives he had redeemed."

Mrs. Sheldon, Junior, who injured her ankle, was taken prisoner, and after two years and a half was released. Possibly the Sheldon house, built about 1708, near the north end of the street, and still standing, was her new home.

One of the little garrison in the house, Bridgman by name, hid in the garret under some bark, at the time of the attack. He was discovered, and marched down into the cellar by his captors, as they explored the building. Here he loitered behind, and was apparently forgotten, but decided that they might take worse vengeance on him if they suddenly remembered him than if he voluntarily rejoined them, so did this. An Indian cut and twisted off one of his fingers, but did him no other harm, and when the northward march was begun, by again loitering behind, he managed, though badly hurt, to escape.

Ebenezer Sheldon was among the captives, and his rescue was effected thus:

Major Dudley, the Governor's son, was in Canada in 1706, after the close of the war, arranging for the redemption of prisoners, when he noticed the boy, and asked him if he were not English. The child answered that he was, and when further asked if he did not want to go home, replied that he did.

The Major sent for the Indian chief who owned the boy, and demanded if he would accept $20 for the child, at the same time displaying the money.

As he had thought, the Indian could not resist the sight of it, and agreed to relinquish the boy. The Major promptly sent Ebenezer on board one of the English ships in the harbor, waiting there to take the redeemed prisoners home, for he feared that the Indian might change his mind. This did happen, but when the chief returned with the money, begging to be given back the boy, he was told that the child had already gone, and thus Ebenezer returned to his home to " dispense hospitality " which so angered his younger brother.

Ebenezer had learned to speak the Indian tongue fluently, and after he returned to Deerfield, married and settled there, his former Indian master came to visit him.

In 1744, Ebenezer sold the house of Jonathan Hoyt, whose father,

David, with his wife and four children, were taken prisoners by the Indians, while one girl was killed. One of the boys stayed with the Indians when other captives were ransomed. In 1803, the Hoyts added to the old house.

In 1686, to " incourage Mr. John Williams to settle in Deerfield," and to induce him to become their pastor, the inhabitants of that town agreed that they " will give him 16 cow commons of meadow land, with a home lot that lyeth on the meeting house hill . . . they will build him a house 42 feet long, 20 feet wide, with a lento on the back side of the house," and also to " finish said house, to fence his home lot, and within two years . . . to build him a barn." His salary was to be " sixty pounds a year for the present, and four or five years after this agreement " they would " add to his salary and make it eighty pounds."

When the Williams family, like others, were aroused from slumber by the yells of the savages, two infant children and a black servant were instantly killed. John Williams, his wife and the remaining children were taken prisoners. Mrs. Williams, sick and feeble, with a baby only a week old, when she was dragged from her bed, and made to begin the long march to Canada, could not keep up with her captors. Growing tired of her lagging steps, the Indians tomahawked her at the foot of a hill in the present town of Greenfield, Massachusetts, and before her captive huband's very eyes.

Eunice, a little girl, and her brother Eleazer, were the only two of the Williams children who survived to reach Canada. Eunice grew up among the Indians, adopted their ways, and when offered a chance after the war was over, and arrangements were being made to ransom the captives, refused to return. Remembrance Sheldon declares, however, that at first she longed to return, but hearing that she had a stepmother, and being told by the priest who had baptized her that she would " damn her soul " if she went, she decided to remain in Canada. Here she married one whom Remembrance calls " Arosen, the finest Indian I ever knew." When she was persuaded years later to visit her family, he accompanied her. But although she shed tears at parting with her sister (this must have been a half-sister or sister-in-law), nothing would induce her to remain, and she and her Indian husband returned to Canada, never to be seen again by her Deerfield relatives.

Eunice must have been something of a trial to her relatives during that visit. Although they did persuade her to don civilized dress and attend church service once, she tore off the clothes as soon as she returned to their home, and resuming her blanket, could never again be persuaded to leave it off. Nor would she sleep in a bed, but stretched herself on a blanket on the floor.

Eunice was re-christened Marguerite, when baptized by the French Catholic priest, and although she married an Indian, her children were always called by the name of Williams, and her daughter's son was known as Eleazer Williams. He was one of those who claimed to be the dauphin, Louis XVII of France, apparently basing his claim solely upon what is said to have been a remarkable resemblance to the royal family of Bourbons.

The Williams house was among those burned, as were all save the two mentioned, and the log church, spared presumably by the French members of the attacking force. When, in 1707, the " Redeemed Captive," as John Williams called himself, returned to Deerfield, a new house was built for him. This stands to-day, moved back from its original site, and is now behind Deerfield Academy, and owned by that institution.

It was two stories high, with four rooms on a floor, and there was a secret staircase around the chimney, running from cellar to attic. Some say that Williams himself, remembering his capture, insisted upon this staircase, and that he himself furnished the funds for building it. A shell top cupboard from this house is treasured in Memorial Hall.

Original Lot No. 10, Deerfield, was drawn by Peter Woodward, Junior, together with lots 16 and 24, but apparently he never came to build on them. In 1674, they were sold to William Bartholomew, who before coming to this country, had attended in London the First Congregational Church of the Reverend John Lothrop, who later settled in Barnstable. William's son William lived in Deerfield, and presumably built the first house on Lot 10.

When on August 25th, 1675, sixty Indians suddenly appeared in the new settlement, Bartholomew's wife and six children fled to Quentin Stockwell's palisaded house, one of those early garrison houses almost always to be found in early New England settlements. This one was on Meeting House Hill. The Indians burned crops, and probably some of the houses then, but eleven days later, they made another attack, and six days later came what has always since been called the Bloody Brook Massacre, when Captain Lothrop and his little band were almost wholly exterminated.

The Bartholomews then departed for more peaceful scenes, and in 1685 sold the house to Daniel Belding. The Beldings lived here but a year when the Indians returned. Daniel, his son Nathaniel, and his daughter Esther, were taken prisoners, his wife and three other children killed, another child, Samuel, struck in the head but not killed, and his daughter Sarah managed to hide, while her sister, Abigail ran to the fort, and although wounded in the arm, escaped with her life.

In 1698, the captives returned, but in 1704, Daniel's second wife, his daughter Sarah, and her husband were taken prisoners, and never heard of again.

The widower once more married, and in 1723 built another house. He also owned the lot next door where the Deerfield Inn was later opened. When Daniel Belding died, he left his house to his son Samuel. Samuel died in 1750, after a full share of adventures, and eleven years later, his heirs sold the house to Joseph Stebbins, Senior, husband of Lucy Frary. In or about 1772, he built what is still known as the Stebbins house, two stories and attic, with a high hipped roof, a fine private residence, filled with beautiful old furniture and other treasures. It is sometimes known as the Bunker Hill house, because from it Colonel Stebbins went to join the patriot forces at that battle. He also took part in the Battle of Saratoga, and in 1781, was commissioned Lieutenant Colonel. The house has remained in the Stebbins family ever since.

The old front door still has the original great iron hinges, more than three feet long. The house is large and square. At the left of the entrance is a room with great fireplace set in the wall paneled from floor to ceiling, with a bed press built into the wall. At the right, is the best room, with cupboards in the paneled wall on each side of the fireplace, and here is a portable bed press, with HL hinges. From the first room opens a small hall, whose outer door is hinged longitudinally, so that it may be folded back, and occupy less space.

On the second story, one of the four rooms has a stencil border all around the floor, and although restored, it has been there for many years, perhaps since the house was built.

There is a great attic, really two stories high, for there are two rows of windows in the gable ends of the high-pitched roof. This garret used to be the spinning room, and Mrs. Sheldon tells that one afternoon, when Colonel Stebbins went up to the garret to see how many spinners were there at work, he found such a gathering of girls and women that, going downstairs, his report was such that a lamb was killed and roasted for supper. [3]

A great cellar, more than six feet high, extends beneath the entire house.

The Henry house was built where, before 1693, stood one occupied by a man named Broughton. He, his wife and child were killed by the Indians in the first massacre, and the house was then occupied by the family of Lieutenant Wells, who had died three years earlier. His widow married the thrice married Daniel Belding, and was killed on the march to Canada. In 1790 a house was built on the site of the old one, which had been destroyed by the Indians, by David Dickenson, a major in the Continental Army. In this house was born the Reverend George H. Houghton, of New York's "Little Church Around the Corner."

On the site of the house of Joseph Barnard, Deerfield's first town clerk, who was killed in 1695, a house still standing was either built in 1752, or one already there was enlarged and repaired by Captain

[3] *Evolutionary History of a New England Homestead,* Mrs. J. M. Arms Sheldon.

Thomas Dickinson, commissary and officer in the Continental Army, appointed by Benedict Arnold, and alluded to previously. Just south of Captain Dickinson, lived at one time Dr. Thomas Williams, brother of the founder of Williams College.

Godfrey Nims was another early settler, and built a house before 1704. There were many soldiers in the family, but local histories do not give the fate of Godfrey. His wife and five of his children were killed in the massacre of 1704; two other children were captured, and carried off to Canada, but the eldest son escaped. Of the two little prisoners, the following romantic tale is told.

The son, Ebenezer, married Sarah Hoyt, presumably one of David Hoyt's four children taken prisoners at the same time. They were trying to marry her to a Frenchman in Lorette, Canada, when she cried out that she would marry anyone of the band of captives. Ebenezer stepped forward and they were duly married. Mrs. Sheldon, in telling this story, adds that doubtless this was less spontaneous than it seemed on the surface, for the two might well have been boy and girl sweethearts back in Deerfield.

However this may be, when in 1714 they had duly been "redeemed," and were about to return to New England with their child, the Indians begged them to remain, or if the elders would not do so, at least to leave the child with them. Of course the parents did not consent to this, and in due time the trio arrived in Deerfield, where, four years before, a new Nims house had been built. This remained in the family for more than two hundred years, and is still standing.

Meanwhile, the other little Nims captive, Abigail, was taken to the French Catholic mission of Sault au Recollet. Josiah Rising, a small captive from Connecticut, was lodged in a house opposite that where lived Abigail. The children were baptized by the priest, and given the names of Elizabeth and Ignace. When Elizabeth was fifteen, the two were married, and six years later were given by the priests a tract of land on which, it is said, their descendants are living to this day.

Just who was the Stephen Nims of whom Remembrance Sheldon tells the following is uncertain. At all events, he was one of the prisoners taken in 1704 by the French and Indians, and carried off to Canada. After he was "redeemed," and returned to Deerfield, Remembrance comments that whereas, before his captivity, he was "small and puny, and over much given to books. Now on snow shoes he is tireless, he can outswim us all." He was furthermore an expert trapper, of deadly aim with either gun or arrow, and "I believe from two sticks he could kindle a fire in a deluge." However, once when Remembrance questioned him as to his feelings toward his captors, he showed some dreadful scars on his toes, and declared that those scars were imprinted upon his heart, and that never, never would he forget.

Mrs. Bunker was an early Deerfield landowner. In 1722, there was a house on her lot, owned at that time by the Widow Beaman, the school teacher. In 1694, her husband was a soldier at the fort, and while Mrs. Beaman was teaching school, a boy noticed the approach of Indians, and came to give the alarm. Mrs. Beaman gathered the children about her, and they all ran for the fort, and succeeded, despite arrows and bullets flying around them, in reaching it safely. Beaman was captured in the fighting of 1704, and carried off to Canada, but escaped. Probably this house on Mrs. Bunker's lot was built soon after his return.

When the widow sold it, it was purchased by the Allens. In 1737, there is record of an allowance paid to Samuel Allen for boarding a poor sick Indian boy and his mother. These two occupied a wigwam near the Allen house, and the Allens used to take food to the sick boy, and also kept his mother's best blankets, moccasins, and supply of wampum in safety in their attic. The Indian boy finally died, and was buried near the Allen house. When war between France and England was imminent, thus involving the colonies, the Indian woman dug up the bones of her son, and with them and her belongings in a pack on her back, set out on the long journey northward.

Eighteen months later, the families of Samuel Allen and John Hoyt were surprised by Indians while in the Deerfield hayfields. Five men were killed, one girl wounded, and one boy captured. The boy was Sammie Allen. He was carried off to Canada.

The Frary house, Deerfield, Massachusetts. The oldest portion of this house, now an ell of the main building, and the Sheldon house were spared when the Indians burned Deerfield.

The Willard house, Deerfield, Massachusetts.

The Maynards, Waban, Mass.

The Williams house, Deerfield, Massachusetts. This was built for Parson Williams the "Redeemed Captive," after he was ransomed from captivity in Canada, and returned to his home. It is now the property of Williams College.

After peace had been made, Sammie's uncle, Sergeant Hawks, with a companion, set off on snowshoes through the cold winter weather for Canada, to find and redeem his little nephew and other captives. For a long time, he could find no trace of the boy, despite his offer to the French authorities of a ransom and a French officer in exchange. Then one day while Hawks was at Government House, the blanketed head of an Indian woman was thrust into the room, and almost instantly withdrawn. This action was repeated several times, until Hawks, suspecting something, followed the woman outside.

" You come for Sammie Allen? " she asked him. " Indian woman know his father. Indian woman know his mother. Indian woman bring Sammie to white uncle."

She was as good as her word, and it then was learned that the child had been adopted, and treated as his own son, by an Indian whose own boy had died. At first, Sammie acted like a wild thing, did not know his uncle, or want to have anything to do with him. Gradually Hawks won him over, but uncle and nephew were closely guarded by the French until they could leave, for it was feared that the Indian would try to regain possession of his adopted son. The two finally reached Deerfield safely.

Sammie's home stands to-day; not the one from which he was stolen, for it was burned by the French and Indian allies, but another on the same site, probably built soon after the destruction of the first. It is solid, substantial, with a great fireplace, and has never been painted.

The former owner of the lot on which stands the Willard house, now known as The Manse, was killed at Bloody Brook. Samuel Carter owned the first house which stood here in 1704, inside a stockade. His wife and several children were massacred, four other children carried off to be redeemed later by him for " 24 pounds borrowed money." Carter sold the house to Samuel Allen, and left Deerfield. The next owner after Allen was Samuel Barnard, of Salem, Massachusetts. He left the land to his nephew, Joseph, who spent thirteen years in selecting timber with which he either built a new house, or added a new front to an older one, finishing it in 1768. The story that the ell was built before 1694 cannot be true, for only one house and one ell, the house Ensign Sheldon's, the ell the oldest part of the present Frary house, survived the conflagration of 1704, but it may have been built by Samuel Allen immediately after that disaster.

As built or re-modeled by Joseph Barnard, it has a great fireplace in which logs six feet long can be burned, and the woodwork is beautiful.

" Lawyer Samuel " Barnard inherited the property, and one Sunday morning, his three eldest daughters, " all alike in blue-gray silk gowns and pink bonnets were married in the parlor, and went to meeting " immediately thereafter.

After eighty years, the Barnards sold the house. Dr. Willard, for many years pastor of the First Meeting House here, and for forty of those years partially or totally blind, lived in it save for a brief absence, from 1807 to 1859. He has been called the Father of Unitarianism in New England.

The " Pink House," which Mrs. Sheldon says once was red, was built about 1754, by Colonel David Field. He was a distinguished patriot at the time when Deerfield was a Tory stronghold, and her representatives to the first Assembly were of that persuasion. Later, many of the Tories changed their views, and at the outbreak of the Revolution the two parties were about equally divided.

Field was chairman of the Revolutionary Committee of Safety, a delegate to the Provincial Constitutional Congress, and his store was a meeting place for the Patriots. In front of it they set up a Liberty Pole on July 29th 1774, as a boulder on the spot now commemorates. John Stebbins, the only man in Captain Lothrop's band who escaped unhurt from the Bloody Brook massacre, lived here earlier. His house was burned in 1704, and a number of his children carried off to Canada.

Four remained there when the others returned, and at least one daughter married a French Canadian. At the age of ten, her son was sent to Deerfield to visit his grandfather, and liked it so well that he remained. This boy's name, René de Noyon, was changed by the Deerfield inhabitants, whether purposely or because they found it too difficult to pronounce, to Aaron Denio, and as such he inherited his mother's share of Stebbins' property. That sturdy New Englander in his will stated that "those who will not live in New England shall have five shillings apiece, and no more."

Aaron is the ancestor of the Deerfield Stebbins family.

In the war of 1704, Brookfield, Middleborough and Dartmouth, Massachusetts, shared the fate of Deerfield, and were burned to the ground. Hadley was saved, although its inhabitants were taken by surprise, as they were observing Fast Day. They would probably have been routed, killed or made prisoners, had it not been for the sudden appearance among them of "a venerable stranger of commanding aspect, clothed in black apparel of unusual fashion, his hair white from age." [4]

The stranger rallied the frightened Hadleyites, formed them into something resembling military formation, and under his direction, so determined resistance was made that the Indians retreated, and Hadley was saved, whereupon the stranger disappeared. This was Edmund Goffe, the regicide judge, then in hiding in the town.

In 1744, Captain William Williams was directed by his uncle, Colonel Stoddard, in accordance with orders from Governor Shirley, to build a fort "near the brook," not far from the present town of Williamsburg. This was one of a chain of forts, and when completed was known as Fort Shirley. Fort Massachusetts, another of the same chain, was near the site of what is now North Adams.

Fort Shirley was a block house twelve feet high, and for its building "pine trees at least a foot and a half through," hand hewn, and smoothed to 14 by 6 inches were used. The fort was sixty feet square, and within its walls four great chimneys were built, and houses for officers, soldiers and their families.

It was ready none too soon. The attack came in 1746 and, as at Deerfield, many were taken prisoners, among them the chaplain, Parson Norton, who kept a diary. This was later published under the title: "Redeemed Captive," although that had already been used by the Reverend John Williams. It is said that of thirty-one in the fort,

[4] Edward Everett's Address at Bloody Brook, South Deerfield, Mass. 1835.

two were killed, the rest taken prisoners, and of the latter but fourteen returned from Quebec.

In 1750 there was a settlement not far away, known as West Hoosac, whose inhabitants then were all soldiers from the fort, with their families. This settlement is the present Williamstown. When the Indians attacked "Dutch Hoosac," now Hoosac Falls, some of those in West Hoosac repaired to Fort Massachusetts for shelter, the others scattering throughout Connecticut.

There are not many pre-Revolutionary houses in Williamstown. The Nehemiah Smedley house is one of them, although it was not finished until after war was over. Smedley had dug and finished his cellar with a kitchen in it, and had covered it with timbers, when the Revolution broke out. He thereupon stopped work on it, remarking: "We will wait now and see who is going to own it." Benedict Arnold is said to have lodged here. The cellar kitchen served the patriot cause, for in its great oven quantities of bread were baked, and sent to Bennington with Levi, eldest son of the Smedleys, for the Continental Army.

Mr. Arthur Latham Perry, in his "Origins of Williamstown," says that he never found any record of the existence of a single Tory in Williamstown, not true of Deerfield, as has been stated.

In his "Boyhood Reminiscences," published in 1895, Judge Danforth says that of five houses built before or shortly after the Revolution in that section of Williamstown known as Buxton, and which were called "regulation houses," not one remained standing.

Chapter X

ONE might expect to find many interesting old houses in New Bedford, that early fishing centre, but, oddly enough, this is not the case. Fine substantial dwellings line the old County Road, some of these much modernized, others but little changed, and a few survive on Water Street, down close to the harbor, but these are little more than a century old, and without special historic value. In the country outside of New Bedford, there are 18th century houses, some occupied, others fast tumbling to ruins, but here, too, there is little historic interest connected with them. Many old houses in town and country were burned by the British, during the Revolution.

As early as 1602, Bartholomew Gosnold " anchored in the bay of Cuttyhunkmoutermost, of the Elizabeth Islands," at which time these were covered with forests and thickets. New Bedford was largely settled by well-to-do Friends, and was not incorporated as a town until 1787. Union Street was first known as King, then Main, and the changes in name indicate the different epochs. Part of the present town was first used for village purposes in 1760. The first house east of the County Road, to-day a fine residential street, was built in 1761, by John Lowden, from Pembroke, Massachusetts. It was burned by the British in 1778.

Until 1812, New Bedford and Fairhaven, across the river, formed one town. When they were divided, the former was strongly Federal in politics, the latter equally Democratic, and this difference hastened the separation.

New Bedford was early prosperous, with " portly nabobs, who wore broadcloth and beaver hats, and jeweled watch fobs," although others were Quakers, and less finely clad. " New Bedford captains were the embodiment of affluence." [1]

When the British burned the town, Mr. Ricketson, another local historian, tells, a woman sat calmly knitting as the soldiers burst into her house, ate up her doughnuts, apple dumplings, etc. They then took coals from her hearth, and tried to set fire to the house, but she calmly extinguished the fire. Again they set fire and again she extinguished it. As they were about to make the third attempt, they warned her not to try again to interfere, threatening her with death. The intrepid woman was not obliged to face the alternative, for just then came orders from their commander for the soldiers to depart, so the house was saved. Its wealthy owner rewarded his brave tenant with a gift of five pounds of rice.

Whale fishing, long New Bedford's chief industry, began at an early date; shore fishing as early, it is said, as 1750.

One mile north of Central Village, part of Dartmouth, an old house built between 1660–77 stood until recently. This was the ancient home of Restcome Potter, but by 1905 it had sunk to usage as a pig sty and hen roost.

Another in this section, built in 1693 by Increase Allen, had been used in part as a chicken hatchery. In making some repairs and alterations not many years ago, a panel over an old mantel was accidentally touched in such a way that it moved, revealing a large compartment behind. This is thought to have been a hiding place for smuggled goods.

The house on Round Hill Farm, near Dartmouth, dating from 1727, was owned by Mrs. Hetty Green's grandfather. At his death, the heirs arranged its transfer to one of the sons, Mrs. Green's mother consenting. A picture shows a curious overhanging gambrel roof.

Mrs. Green as a girl spent much time in New Bedford with her aunt, Sylvia Ann Howland, whose first will left all her property to

---

[1] *Historic Bristol County, Mass.*, Frank Walcott Hull.

charities. A second will presented later, left everything to her niece, and after a lawsuit, a compromise was effected. The Howland house has been torn down, but its fine old doorway is preserved in New Bedford's Historical Museum, the gift of a former wealthy resident, the late Mr. Bourne.

James Arnold, a wealthy New Bedford man, gave Boston her Arboretum. His residence passed to William Rotch, who covered the fine old solid mahogany doors with black walnut veneer, in the style of his day, and added a mansard roof. The house is now a club.

The George East house, at the foot of Mill Street and Acushnet Avenue, stands, although it has not a look of age. The lot on which it was built was conveyed to East in 1780, and the house built about that time. It was at one period a tavern, popular with ministers. From its staircase, Jesse Lee preached the first Methodist sermon ever given in New Bedford. There is a remarkable tale to the effect that one minister's wife used to climb these stairs and, through a scuttle in the roof, shout announcements of services to the people of Oxford, across the river. As proof of this tale, one may see the scuttle.

Mr. Ricketson, in his early history of New Bedford, gives an interesting account of tea parties a century ago. He says:

" The front room parlour and other front 'keeping room' would be put in fine order, the Brussels carpets well swept, chairs, pier tables, large sofa studded with brass headed nails dusted." The alabaster urns and silver candlesticks, snuffers and tray, the brass andirons supporting burning logs must all be polished. The brass knocker announced the arrivals, and by four o'clock, the guests would proceed to the keeping room, and partake of " short biscuit rolls, quince marmalade and preserved plums, sponge and pound cakes." The women guests gossiped together, the men talked politics, and by nine-thirty, all had gone home.

The Dr. Tobey house in Acushnet, nearby, built about 1748, has a story connected with it. When the British troops visited it, they searched it for valuables, but the door leading down cellar when opened quite concealed that of the closet in which all the family treasures were hidden. This door escaped their notice, and so all were saved.

Fairhaven across the river, historic though it is, offers no old houses of interest, but claims the honor of the first naval capture in the Revolution — Providence makes the same claim — when Lieutenant Nathaniel Pope and Captain Daniel Egery captured two tenders of the British sloop, Falcon, on May 14th, 1775.

Canton has some old houses in the farming country near the town, but none of special historic interest, although the oldest, that of John Fenna, was built as early as 1704. An Isaac Royall lived here in the early days, probably a nephew of the Royall who built the Medford mansion, for the latter had two brothers.

Nantucket has long been qualified as " quaint." It was deeded in 1641 by Lord Stirling to Thomas Mayhew, who later deeded it to men known as the "ten original purchasers," including Mayhew himself. Each of these ten named another man to be associated in the company, Mayhew naming his son, and they two retained one tenth of the island. The terms of this transfer were £30 sterling and two beaver hats. Among these twenty men were four by the name of Coffin, Thomas Macy and two Starbucks.

Oldest standing on the island, preserved by the Nantucket Oldest House Association, which has opened it as a museum, is the Jethro Coffin house, built in 1686 for Mary Gardner, daughter of Captain John Gardner, who, in 1706, was Chief Justice of the Island. Mary was engaged to be married to Jethro Coffin, and one father gave the land, the other father built the house for the young couple.

It was substantial, with ships knees of oak fitted to floor beams, and uprights, with cedar laths, the original plaster made of ground up sea shells, later replaced by the modern kind. It is a story and a half in height, with an attic in the high-pitched roof, has two rooms on each floor, and a broad old door between the two front lower windows. The entire house was covered with shingles, but many of the original ones were torn off during the years when it was unoccupied, and even later others were ruthlessly removed for souvenirs. Now these have

The Hazard house, Newport, Rhode Island. Built before 1700, this is the oldest house surviving in that city.

"Old Vernon House," Clark Street, Newport, Rhode Island. This was the residence, during the Revolution, of General Rochambeau.

been replaced, and a new roof added. Double walls, with hand split cedar laths, hand made nails, all the usual marks of a very old house, may still be admired. The wide planks of the floors, too, are the originals.

On the second floor, in the larger of the two rooms a door opens into the " Indian closet."

One night Jethro was absent from home, and his young wife and their infant son were sleeping in this room. Suddenly a noise aroused the young mother. From the closet emerged an Indian, and seating himself, he began sharpening a knife. Her fright may be imagined, but catching up her sleeping child, she made a dash for the stairs, the Indian following. She reached the lower door, and escaped, running for help to her father's house. Help was forthcoming promptly, but when the men arrived at her house, they found the Indian in a drunken sleep. He had evidently hidden in the attic, and the noise which had awakened Mary was caused by his dropping down from the loose board floor of the attic into the closet.

Deciding that he had really intended no serious harm, the men aroused the Indian, " gave him a lesson that he would remember," and sent him off.

A bad fire on the island, in 1846, destroyed many of its old houses, but among those which recently were still standing are the Caleb and Joseph Gardner house — probably Mary's brothers — built in 1699, now known as the John C. Gardner house, and recently re-modeled, and Major Josiah Coffin's, built in 1724.

A house on Vestal Street was the birthplace in 1790 of the famous woman astronomer, Maria Mitchell, and it is now owned by the Maria Mitchell Memorial Association. Lucretia Mott was another celebrity born on Nantucket in 1793, and Walter Folger, astronomer and mathematician, lived here for a time. He invented and set in motion July 4th, 1790, a remarkable astronomical clock, which recently was reported as still going, but no longer keeping good time, and no one knew how to regulate it.

Still earlier in Nantucket history, Benjamin Franklin's mother,

Abiah Folger, was born here. Mary Starbuck, who married a Coffin, became the mother of the first white child born on the island. She was greatly loved by her neighbors and by the Indians as well, and, most unusual in those days, was a speaker who discoursed ably on public affairs. She died in 1719.

Another Coffin, Miriam, born on Nantucket in 1723, was an extensive ship owner, and transacted her own business, but was tried for smuggling, and apparently there was no doubt that smuggle she did, on a large scale.

One more Nantucket woman, Anna Gardner, born there in 1816, organized an anti-slavery meeting on the island, at which Fred Douglas made his first abolitionist speech.

Martha's Vineyard, deeded by Lord Stirling at the same time as Nantucket to Mayhew, has her share of old houses, some of which were standing a few years ago, and probably still are.

In April, 1603, Martin Pring or Prynne entered Edgartown harbor, and eight years later, Captain Harlow founded the first white settlement, consisting of four men.

The old Mayhew house, on what is now South Water Street, was built in 1698 by Governor Thomas Mayhew. His son Thomas, Junior, became a minister.

The Oliver Linton house has been said to date from 1615 merely because a brick with these figures on it was found in the chimney. It stands on East Chop.

At Vineyard Haven is the Nye house, built in 1801 by Captain Seth Daggett, who was active in defense of this coast in 1776. He was frequently captured by the British, because of his ability as a pilot. One night, when they came to take him he escaped from his bed, and left the house in such haste that when he paused at a safe distance to don the clothing which he had not had time to put on before, he discovered that he had brought his wife's garments instead of his own.

Then there is the " Great House," built in 1721 by Isaac Chase, son of Lieutenant Isaac Chase, of the Royal Navy.

At Huzzleton's Head is the home of the Tory Daggett, where two

British officers were captured when they went to say farewell to their host.

At Lambeth's Cove is Captain Nathan Smith's house. Once he saved his own and his neighbor's cattle from the British by a clever ruse. A small detachment of the enemy had collected the cattle on the beach near Captain Smith's house, until they were ready to drive them off. Smith hid in the bushes, and called out commands, as though at the head of a body of troops. The British ran off, leaving the cattle behind them.

The Herman Vincent house at Chilmark was the former home of Deacon Simon Mayhew, member of the Continental Congress, a tutor at Harvard, and, when he died in 1782 at Chilmark, Chief Justice of Dukes County Court. Chilmark formerly bore the ugly name of Beetle Bung Corners.

Martha's Vineyard has its mysterious tale of pirate gold. A store of this is supposed to have been buried off Wasque Bluff, near the blue rock of Chappaquaddick. Many have tried to find this gold, but none has succeeded. Always some strange occurrence frightens the searchers away. Either a mysterious ghostly ship appears, with plank already extended for luckless victims to tread, or, if the searchers do succeed in touching the pot of gold, as they try to raise it will come a blinding flash of light, a cave in of soil, and the treasure has once more vanished.[2]

On East Chop a substantial old house, in its early days a tavern, was later open for summer boarders. Built by an old sea captain, it had a secret passage from attic to cellar. The captain, like many of his neighbors, engaged in smuggling, but the revenue officers never succeeded in catching him, capturing any wares, or even getting evidence enough to convict him.

One morning they felt sure that they had him. They knew that smuggled goods were hidden in his house, and arrived early one morning to search it. The captain and his family were at breakfast.

" Come in and have a bite," he urged, and the revenue officers were nothing loth. They sat down, and their hostess must have been not only

[2] *Martha's Vineyard*, By C. C. Hine.

an excellent cook, but entertaining as well, for they lingered at table, and apparently did not notice when their host withdrew. When they finally rose, and proceeded to search the house, they found nothing. All of the goods had been lowered from attic to cellar, and carted off to a safe hiding place while they had been eating and talking. This house has been re-modeled, the great chimney and secret passage are gone.

When the Massachusetts Colony summoned Roger Williams to appear before the authorities, intending, as he well knew, to send him back to England " because he had drawn above twenty persons to his opinions, and they were intending to erect a plantation upon the Narragansett Bay, from whence the infection would easily spread into these churches," he sent word that it was not convenient for him to come, and fled from Salem through the forests, to an Indian lodge. There the chief, Massasoit, whom he had known in Plymouth, gave him shelter, and a grant of land, but finding it too near the Plymouth Colony for safety, he and four companions removed, as friendly Governor Winslow advised, " to the other side of the water," and settled where the city of Providence now stands. In 1648, one of his followers, William Coddington, the same who was obliged to leave his Quincy home, was elected President of the Rhode Island General Assembly.

Until 1900, there stood in Providence the Roger Mowry tavern, in which Williams is said often to have held prayer meetings. Williams' own house stood near the northeastern corner of North Main and Howland Streets, and here his eldest son was born in 1638, the first white boy born on Rhode Island soil. This house apparently was destroyed during some of the early Indian attacks. The homes of all Williams' children are also gone, but in Roger Williams Park, on land once owned by his youngest son, Joseph, is the Betsey Williams cottage, built by one of Joseph's descendants, Nathaniel, in 1773, for his son James, the father of Betsey. She lived here until her death in 1871, when the cottage and farm on which it stood passed by her will to the city of Providence for a public park. Joseph and others of the Williams family lie in their old burying lot on part of this property.

The houses built by two of the Brown brothers, and a third built by the son of the third brother, still stand in Providence.

John Brown took a leading part in the Gaspee plot and attack upon the British schooner of that name, in 1772. In 1786, he built the fine house on Power Street which stands to-day. John Quincy Adams called this " the most magnificent and elegant private mansion that I have ever seen on this continent."

In 1795–7, when the Duke de la Rochefoucauld-Liancourt was traveling in America, he wrote: " The richest merchant in Providence is John Brown, brother to Moses, the Quaker. In one part of the town he has accomplished things that, even in Europe, would appear considerable. At his own expense he has opened a passage through the hill to the river, and has there built wharves, houses, an extensive distillery, and even a bridge, by which the road from Newport to Providence is shortened at least a mile." At the end of this bridge Mr. Brown placed a statue of President Washington, " whom he greatly admired." [3]

The house is substantial, three stories in height, built of bricks brought from England in the builder's own ships, and finished with mahogany from San Domingo. His architect brother, Joseph, planned it. Set high above the street, with lawns shaded by great elms, and a terrace extending along one side, solid mahogany gates admit to the grounds, and the handsome main entrance with its portico is surmounted by a beautiful window on the second story. Still a private residence, although no longer owned in the family, it contains a remarkable collection of Chippendale furniture and Shakesperiana.

Many distinguished guests, including Washington, have been entertained in this old mansion, for in addition to being a very wealthy man, John Brown was prominent in all city affairs. He was interested also in Brown University, named after his brother Nicholas, who gave largely to it; he also sent the first ship, the George Washington, from Providence to the East Indies, and in the year 1789, appeared in public one day wearing a suit the cloth of which was made from the fleeces of his own sheep, as mentioned by William R. Staples, in his *Annals of the*

[3] *Old Providence*, The Merchants National Bank of Providence.

Town. Mr. Staples adds that "the yarn was spun by a woman eighty-eight years old," and Mr. Brown did this to encourage the home manufacture of clothing, duties on imported goods being then very high.

He served two years in Congress, and was largely instrumental in securing the ratification of the Constitution of the United States by Rhode Island. This small state had been so tardy in taking this step that Washington refused to visit it, when he made his first tour in 1789.

A. M. Eaton explains how Mr. Brown secured the ratification. "On the day when the final vote of the Convention was to be taken, he secured the loss of one vote by the party opposed to the adoption of the Constitution by kindly lending his horse and chaise to a member from the country and elder of a church, in order that he might drive out and preach that day."

Joseph Brown, the architect, built his house at No. 72 South Main Street in 1774, and it is now occupied by the Providence National Bank, of which John Brown was first President. At the time that the French troops under Rochambeau were camped in and near Providence, awaiting their return to France, some of the officers were quartered in this house, which Joseph Brown gave up to them. An old chronicler declares that one day "one of these gallant fellows, doubtless after a good dinner, and perhaps on a wager, rode his spirited charger up the flight of steps and into the spacious hall that leads through the house. The horse was unwilling to make the descent of the long, steep flight of steps, and was therefore taken through the great rear door of the hall into the grounds adjoining, where then stood a superb old pear tree, under which George Washington once sat, and regaled himself with the luscious fruit."[4]

In Count Segur's Memoirs, alluding to the period of French occupation, he says: "M. de Rochambeau gave several balls and assemblies at Providence, which were attended by all the neighborhood within ten leagues of that city. I do not recollect to have seen anywhere an assemblage in which a greater number of pretty women, and married people lived together happily — a greater proportion of beauty free

[4] *Old Providence.*

from coquetry; a more complex mixture of persons of all classes, whose conduct and manners presented an equal degree of decorum, which obliterated all appearance of unpleasant contrast of distinction."

In addition to being an architect, Joseph Brown was professor of experimental philosophy in Brown University.

Nicholas Brown did not build what is now known as the John Carter Brown house, opposite his brother's, on the corner of Power and Benefit Streets, but purchased it in 1814. It was built more than twenty years earlier by Joseph Nightingale. It, too, is a large three-story brick house, set well above the street, the entrance gate being reached by a flight of steps.

John Carter Brown inherited a large fortune from his father, Nicholas, and early in life began collecting books, sparing no time, money or journeys to accomplish his purposes. Soon after his father's death, he took into partnership Thomas Poynton Ives, who had married his sister, and the firm of Brown and Ives was known and respected all over the world. Mr. Brown's son, John Nicholas, succeeded to the house and collections, and on his death left the library, valued at over a million dollars, in charge of his executors, to be given to an educational institution, provided the books were kept together and open to the public. He also left $150,000 for a building to house them. They were given to Brown University, and now are contained in the John Carter Brown Library of that college, to which, during his life, Mr. Brown also gave two buildings: Hope College, named for his sister, Mrs. Ives, and Manning Hall, named for its first president.

Mr. Ives' house on Power Street, built early in the 19th century, resembling in general style the Brown houses, also survives.

Still standing, marked with a tablet, is the house in which lived Stephen Hopkins, the Signer, and where Washington was entertained. It is a plain frame building of two stories, and in its basement has been installed a shop.

Stephen Hopkins was born in Providence, in 1707; was a member of the Legislature, Chief Justice of the first Supreme Court of Rhode Island, a member of the Continental Congress of 1774, and several times Governor of his state. He was also the first Chancellor of Brown University. He built his house in 1742, down near the water, and it was moved to the present site in 1804.

Soon after Boston was evacuated, Washington came to Providence. He, his staff and General Gates " were invited to an elegant entertainment at Hacker's Hall, provided by the gentlemen of the town, where, after dinner, a number of patriotic toasts were drunk. The town authorities considered, and decided that no place of entertainment was so appropriate as Governor Hopkins' house. The master of the house was in Philadelphia, but his daughter, Ruth, was at home; and when the town representatives brought General Washington, Ruth calmly set herself to making her guest comfortable. Many were the suggestions, if tradition may be relied on, that were offered to Ruth Hopkins by her anxious neighbors. Silver was tendered, and linen, food and china, but to all these overtures Ruth turned a deaf ear, asserting, with all respect to her distinguished guest, that what was good enough for her father was good enough for General Washington. (' She adored her father,' a dear old soul added.) The room where Washington slept became from that day an historic place, and it was counted a great privilege to sleep in it." [5]

Washington visited the house again in 1781, when its host was at home. Moses Brown told of this visit: " I was with him (Hopkins) sitting, when General Washington by himself alone called to see him. I sat some time, viewing the simple, friendly and pleasant manner " in which " these two great men met and conversed with each other on various subjects." And again, when on another occasion Mr. Brown saw Washington, he spoke of the latter's easy, simple manner, " very like that of Stephen Hopkins." [6]

No likeness of Hopkins has come down to us. For Trumbull's group of the Signers, his face was sketched from that of his son. He went to Philadelphia to help draw up the Declaration of Independence, and when he signed it his hand shook with palsy, but he remarked: " My hand trembles, but my heart does not."

The home of Esek Hopkins, Stephen's brother, and the first Com-

[5] *Old Providence.*   [6] Quoted in *Old Providence.*

mander-in-chief of the American Navy, was given to the city of Providence in 1907. It is, like his brother's, unpretentious, a two-story frame house with a long, low wing.

Esek Hopkins, born in 1718, was appointed to naval command in 1775. Under him was Abraham Whipple, with the Columbus, another claimant for the honor of having fired the first cannon and taken the first naval prize in the American Revolution.

Hopkins sailed for Philadelphia soon after his appointment, on the Kay; captured a small craft, and took a few prisoners. He wrote from Philadelphia: "Our seamen arrived here day before yesterday. Those concerned in the naval department are highly pleased with them. Their arrival gives fresh spirit to the whole fleet."

The Commodore or Admiral (both titles were used in alluding to Hopkins), "received orders to locate and attack the enemy's ships in Chesapeake Bay. From there he was to proceed to Rhode Island to destroy the British fleet. . . . Disaster attended the expedition from first to last. Sickness spread among the crew, and there were many cases of smallpox. Heavy gales from the northeast began to blow. The harbors were occupied by the enemy. Commodore Hopkins used the discretion which his orders left to him, and sailed for New Providence in the Bahamas, where he seized cannon and some small stores of ammunition, loaded his ships, and started north again, capturing on the way two small vessels, loaded with arms and stores. The next morning he encountered the British frigate Glasgow. After a desperate encounter in which the American ships were partially disabled, the Glasgow escaped. No blame was attached to Commodore Hopkins for this episode." John Paul Jones highly praised his commander, and "John Hancock, on behalf of Congress sincerely congratulated Hopkins," but this was the beginning of nothing but trouble for him. His enemies did not rest until they had secured his dismissal in 1778 by Congress from the naval service of his country.[7]

In spite of this injustice, Hopkins declared: "I am determined to continue a friend of my country, neither do I intend to remain inactive."

He became a member of the Rhode Island Legislature, was ap-

[7] Old Providence

pointed to her Council of War, and won the title of " the inflexible patriot." He lived to be almost eighty-four years old.

This by no means exhausts the list of fine old houses in Providence, but gives the oldest survivors.

The exact age of the Hazard house, Newport, probably the oldest surviving, is not known. Some assert that the oldest part was built before 1700. The first recorded owner was Stephen Munford at the time that he transferred the house to " Richard Ward, Gentleman."

John Ward, an officer in Cromwell's Army, came to America after the Restoration, whither his son Thomas had already preceded him. The latter was General Treasurer of the Colony, and its Deputy-Governor. Richard was the son of this Thomas, and he was Colony Secretary, and from 1740 to 1743 Governor. It was before 1749 that Richard owned the house, for in that year it was the property of Samuel Marryatt, " taylor," chiefly distinguished in the annals of the town by the fact that his daughter, Betsey, lived to be one hundred and one years old.

After Marryatt, it was owned by several men; one, Martin Howard, Junior, a lawyer and member of Trinity Church, was a Tory, as was his wife, great-granddaughter of William Brenton, one of the original settlers here. In 1765, Martin Howard, Thomas Moffatt and Augustus Johnston were appointed Stamp Masters. Feeling at the time being what it was, this made the men very unpopular, and soon after their appointment a mob dragged their effigies, with ropes around their necks, in a cart through the town, hanged the effigies, and later tore them down and burned them. The following day, Howard's house was attacked. He took refuge on H.M.S. Cygnet, lying in Newport harbor, but the mob smashed his furniture and china, ruined valuable family portraits, tore out the woodwork, and even put ropes around the old chimney, and tried to pull it down. It was too stoutly built for them, and resisted their efforts. They also attacked the houses of the other two Stamp Masters.

Howard went to England, and was later awarded damages for his destroyed property. In 1770, he was appointed Chief Justice of North

Carolina, and again was the victim of a mob, but remained at his post until 1777, when he returned to England, and died there.

Before 1772, the old Newport house was sold, this time for £210 to John Wanton, who spent £60 in repairing it.

Wanton was the son of Governor Gideon Wanton, and there were four governors in this family in the Colonial period. They became Quakers after an ancestor, an officer, witnessed the execution of several members of that faith, and is said to have declared to his family that he believed them to be men of God.

John Wanton was a member of the General Assembly, and one of the incorporators of Rhode Island College at Warren, in 1764. The college was afterwards removed to Providence, and re-named Brown in honor of a lavish benefactor, Nicholas Brown.

The Hazard house stands on what was known as Bull's Gap, near the old Governor Bull house, burned to the ground twenty years ago. Originally this old survivor stood on a level with the street, from which it is now reached by a flight of steps. The oldest part probably consisted of two rooms on each of the two floors, and a kitchen in the rear. Here may be seen the massive hand hewn timbers, and the great fireplace in the solid chimney which the mob vainly tried to pull down. An attic and high-pitched roof top the house.

In 1782, additions were made in the rear by John Wanton, and the fine paneling in the front rooms was probably put in by him when he bought the house, which had been partly wrecked five or six years before.

On the steps of the renovated old house, his daughter, Polly, is said to have stood and watched the arrival of the French troops, escorted by Americans under General Heath. Among the American officers was young Daniel Lyman. The two exchanged glances and, according to the story, fell in love at first sight.

At all events, they had many occasions for meeting. The Wanton house hospitably entertained the French and American officers quartered in town, and was none the less popular for the fact that Mrs. Wanton had both a daughter and a beautiful niece. A diamond-written inscription on one of the window panes long survived: " Charming Polly Wanton." Years ago, Lyman's daughter Eliza wrote her " Reminiscences of Newport Before and During the Revolution, by a Lady," and remarks:

" I have heard Mrs. Wanton say she frequently had one of these young officers on each arm of her chair, and another hanging on the back; she had a pretty daughter and a niece living with her. ' Madame Wanton, you have one beautiful niece,' one of the French officers remarked, and then recollecting the daughter, added with true French politeness: ' And your daughter has a very cunning look.' "

" Charming Polly " with " the cunning look " married young Lyman, by that time a Major, in 1782.

The following year, John Wanton deeded the house to his daughter. Lyman made a number of improvements in it, changed the roof, added four rooms, two on each floor in the rear, bought additional land, and built an office, in which he practised law. The Lymans and the Wanton parents all lived in the old house, and here thirteen children were born to the young couple.

Daniel Lyman soon became prominent. He built a stone bridge which was three years in building, between Newport and the mainland. He became Chief Justice, and was a delegate to the Hartford Convention.

The Lyman's second daughter, Harriet, married a Hazard, and about this time her father deeded the Newport residence to her, and removed to Providence, where he purchased an estate known as The Hermitage, in Smithfield, and lived there until his death.

Harriet Hazard was the mother of nine children, and the widow of her son Benjamin, last of the name to occupy the house, lived there until her death in 1875.

The Newport Historical Society has been conducting an active campaign for the purchase and restoration of the old house, which at the time of writing seems practically certain of success, so doubtless within a few months, the historic dwelling will be opened to the public.

Until quite recently, several interesting old houses survived in

Pawtucket, but these have gradually yielded to modern demands, until now but one venerable survivor may be found. This, the Daggett house, is the property of the City, and the Pawtucket Chapter of the Daughters of the Revolution is its permanent custodian. Although it has not the romantic history of some houses already mentioned, it is of interest for several reasons, and especially because of the relics here preserved. Yet it has a history.

John Doggett, as the name was then written, who founded the family in America, probably came over with Governor John Winthrop in 1630. He first went to Salem, applied to be made a freeman, and this being granted the following year, participated in the " fourth Great Dividend " of lots, and acquired thirty acres in what is now Cambridge, later increasing this tract.

When, in 1641, the Earl of Stirling granted Nantucket, Martha's Vineyard and the Elizabeth Islands to Thomas Mayhew, Doggett was interested, and in 1642 began making plans to remove with his family to Martha's Vineyard. He changed his plans, and instead located in Rehoboth, Massachusetts, where the site of the present house was then situated. In 1648, as old records show, he was appointed surveyor of highroads here, and it is believed that he built his first house about that time. Soon afterwards, he left his son, John, installed in it, and moved to Martha's Vineyard. In 1652, he was laying out highways in Edgartown, but died in Plymouth.

The son John was born in England, but came to this country as a little child. He was always associated with Rehoboth's history, as he married there, filled his father's old office of surveyor of highways, and died there in 1707. It was in Martha's Vineyard that the name was first written Daggett.

During King Philip's War, the first house with others of the town were burned by the Indians, and the one now standing was built by the second John Daggett in 1685. Almost in sight of this spot Roger Williams and his companions had camped in 1635, believing themselves outside the jurisdiction of Massachusetts, but not until years later did Rehoboth become part of Pawtucket, Rhode Island.

In 1790, the Daggett house was re-modeled, and since the Daughters of the Revolution became its guardians, it has been repaired, restored, and is now filled with interesting and valuable collections; furniture, china, glass, portraits, historical documents, Revolutionary firearms, swords, utensils, etc. It has a great chimney, with big fireplaces, and in the attic is a secret chamber, whose existence, it is said, used to be made known to but one member of the family in each generation. Built between the walls, the entrance is concealed behind the great chimney, which was built of bricks brought as ballast in ships from Holland.

With the tearing down of several old houses, some of the relics here acquired additional value. For instance, on one of the four-post beds in an upper room is a counterpane owned by the first Mrs. Samuel Slater, and another owned by the second of that name. Here, too, are a clock and pieces of Royal Worcester china owned by Samuel Slater, so prominent in the history and development of Pawtucket, as well as a set of china owned by General Nathaniel Green of Revolutionary fame, whose home was at Coventry, Rhode Island.

Pawtucket should not be left without some reference to the man who founded it, Joseph Jenks, Junior. The old frame house of one of his sons, Nathaniel, was standing ten years ago on North Main Street. Unfortunately, it has gone, with other early houses belonging to this family.

Joseph Jenks, Senior, founded in Lynn, Massachusetts, the first important colonial iron works in 1642, setting up a foundry, under the supervision it is said of Governor Winthrop, with whom he came from England. His son Joseph came through the forests to Pawtucket Falls, and in 1655 set up a forge on the south side, building himself a house near what is now East Avenue. It was through his representations to Governor Cranston that one of the earliest bridges in the country was built near the Falls, in 1713. This bridge was for years a bone of contention between Massachusetts and Rhode Island, both colonies claiming the territory near the two ends. Once it was torn down, and William Jenks, who had assisted in this work, re-built it in 1735, receiving

£100 for his work. Not until 1860 did all of Pawtucket, including what had been Rehoboth, belong to Rhode Island, in exchange for her relinquishing other territory, including Fall River, to Massachusetts.

Joseph Junior's sons became distinguished. The third Joseph was Governor of Rhode Island from 1727 to 1742; Nathaniel was a major in the army; Ebenezer a preacher; William a judge. It was the Major who built the house which stood until recently. He took an active part in defending Pawtucket from Indian attacks, and many stories of his unusual strength have come down, such as that he " lifted a forge hammer weighing 500 pounds, together with seven men thereon," and " at another time he (on his hands and knees) lifted upon his back timber judged to weigh 3,000 pounds." [8]

In 1775, Captain Stephen Jenks patented and began the manufacture of muskets for the militia companies of the colony, and under the Jenks patents, others were made during the Revolution. Jenks also supplied 10,000 muskets to the American troops for the War of 1812.

Less than ten years ago, there stood on North Main Street the house occupied by Samuel Slater, Senior, who founded the first Sunday school in America. But he was also one of the first industrial men in Pawtucket, following Stephen Jenks and his foundry. His house has now been torn down.

Samuel Slater was apprenticed as a boy to the owner of a cotton mill in Belper, England, and after rising to be superintendent, emigrated to America at the age of twenty-one, believing that there he should find greater opportunities. First employed in New York, he there learned of Moses Brown, wealthy Providence merchant, and of the latter's recent establishment in Pawtucket of a mill, where he hoped to spin cotton. Slater wrote to Mr. Brown: " I flatter myself that I can give the greatest satisfaction in making machinery," and eventually an interview was arranged.

" Mr. Brown, in relating the first interview with Samuel Slater, said: " When Samuel saw the old machines, he felt downhearted with disappointment, and shook his head, and said: " These will not do;

[8] *Pawtucket, Past and Present*, The Slater Trust Co.

they are good for nothing in their present condition, nor can they be made to answer."

" 'Thee said,' urged Moses Brown, 'that thee could make machinery. Why not do it? ' "

The young Slater agreed to try to make machinery according to the Arkwright models which had been used in the English cotton mill, saying that " if I do not make as good yarn as they do in England I will have nothing for my services, but will throw the whole of what I have done over the bridge."

With only memory to aid, he began work in a shop near Joseph Jenks' original forge.

" His pay was a dollar a day. The windows of the small shop where he worked were shuttered and the doors barred, and every effort was made to keep the project secret. His patterns were made of wood, and the motive power was furnished by a wheel, laboriously turned by a negro, named Primus. Sylvanus Brown was employed as the wood-worker, and David Wilkinson furnished the iron-work. Every fore-noon, Moses Brown, in a carriage drawn by a span of horses and driven by a colored man, rode over from Providence to see how things were getting on. Hannah Wilkinson, daughter of Oziel Wilkinson, in whose house Slater boarded, later became Mrs. Slater, and it is recorded that she caught her first glimpse of the young mechanic by peering cautiously through the keyhole of his workshop, and that Samuel Slater, on turn-ing, found looking at him a pair of roguish eyes and at once loved their owner and vowed to win her."

He worked on, and when he finished the models, Moses Brown told him: " Samuel, thee has done well! "

An agreement of partnership to engage in " the spinning of cotton by water," was drawn up between Slater, William Almy and Smith Brown, the last two young men those who had previously been trying to spin cotton with the machinery which Slater had condemned. So much yarn was spun with the new machinery that in 1792 much remained unsold, and there occurred the first panic in the American Market over cotton yarns. Moses Brown was alarmed. " Thee must shut down thy wheels, Samuel, or thee will spin all my farms into cotton yarn," he declared.

Slater made a large fortune, but by working hard. He used to say: " Sixteen hours a day, Sundays excepted, for twenty years has been no more than fair exercise."

To his wife, Hannah, is due the beginning of the cotton thread industry in this country. She spun cotton yarn, and with the help of her sister, twisted it on her spinning wheel, making a good grade of thread. Trying this, the two women found it as strong and good as the linen thread which they had been using. In 1794, Samuel Slater began manufacturing cotton thread.[9]

The Wilkinson family, of which Hannah was a daughter, were inventors. Oziel at an early date made ship anchors, and by 1791 was making steel which Moses Brown pronounced equal to the English product. David Wilkinson made the engine for an early steamboat, and with Elijah Ormsbee, made a trip in this from Pawtucket to Providence and back. Lack of funds prevented the development of their idea, but this was ten years before Robert Fulton sailed his steamboat on the Hudson River. David invented a screw machine and a side lathe, which latter, when patented, brought him but ten dollars. After half a century, Congress voted him $10,000 as partial remuneration. Oziel's foundry turned out the machinery used for pressing out sperm oil in Nantucket and New Bedford, made many iron tools, and also the iron-work for a number of early bridges. David Wilkinson continued the business after his father, Oziel, died, and until 1829, since when it has continued under different firm names to the present day.

[9] *Pawtucket, Past and Present*, The Slater Trust Co.

Chapter XI

Other Old Massachusetts Coast Towns

A TRIP to Marblehead, quaintest of old towns, with its narrow crooked streets, will well repay one.

The place was given its name because of the " marble stone " on all sides of the harbor, as early as 1629. Two years later, Isaac Allerton came here from Plymouth, and established a fishing station. The fishermen soon acquired a reputation for hard drinking, and for a long time had no church, being " too remiss to found one," as the Plymouth colonists complained.

The first settlement was at Peach's Point, near Little Harbor, and here in a cove was built Marblehead's first ship, the Desire, third to be built in the Massachusetts Colony.

Many are the old houses of historic interest still standing in the old town, but they are not open to the general public.

Not far from the old burial ground is one known as the Old Brig. Built in 1650, this belonged to " Old Dimond," grandfather of Moll Pitcher, and in this house she is said to have spent her girlhood. Old Dimond was a skipper, and believed by his fellow townsmen to have the power of foretelling events, locating criminals, etc. " When the night was dark and stormy, and the wind gave evidence of blowing a gale, old Dimond would find his way to the burying hill, and there among the graves and tombstones, would ' beat about,' and give orders for the management of his vessels at sea in a voice loud and clear, distinctly to be heard above the roar of the tempest." He is said to have named the thieves when various goods were stolen, and to have given other evidences of his mystic powers.

Mary, his daughter, Moll's mother, had the reputation of being if not a witch, at least rather nearly one. She told fortunes, and eventually left for Lynn, where she practised her fortune telling. Local histories do not say that she took her daughter with her; on the contrary Moll seems to have spent her girlhood in the Old Brig, with her grandfather.

Although superstitious, like most fisherfolk, during the Danvers-Salem witchcraft delusion, Mammy Red was the only witch produced by Marblehead, nor, although they had long suspected her of witchcraft, did her fellow townsmen accuse her. It remained for the Salemites to do this, and hang her with the others, on Witch Hill.

On the grounds of a house a century and a half old, now owned by the Misses Scott, Captain Kidd is said to have had a shanty.

In Marblehead still stands the former home of Skipper Ireson, as does that of Azor Orne, who loaned the Continental Congress a barrel of silver dollars. That of " King " Hooper, noted for his magnificent entertainments, is now used by the Y.M.C.A. Over the front entrance used to hang Hooper's coat of arms, and the house was very fine, with a banquet hall in the upper story, and one room finished like a ship's cabin. Hooper's country place at Danvers was for a time used as headquarters by General Gage.

The beautiful old house on Washington Street, home of Colonel Jeremiah Lee, was at the time of its erection in 1768, considered one of the largest and most costly in New England. Built of bricks covered with clapboards, much of the material was brought from England. It had fifteen rooms, with hand carved cornices, and a remarkably beautiful staircase, so wide that four or five persons could walk abreast on it, and with finely carved bannisters and hand rail of mahogany. Mahogany was also used for wainscoting. On the walls of one room may still be seen one of the early wall papers, depicting the ruins of ancient Rome.

Colonel Lee, Elbridge Gerry, Senior, who was born in Marblehead, and Azor Orne, were all members of the Committee of Safety and Supplies. One night, the three met at the Black Horse Tavern, near Cambridge, and as their business occupied them until late, they decided to spend the night at the tavern. By doing so they had a narrow escape, for in some way the British troops, on their way to Lexington, learned of the proximity of the three patriots, and determined to capture them.

Fortunately for the Committee, news of this plan leaked out, and the sleeping men were awakened and warned. They escaped, but without time to dress, and hid in the bushes not far away, while the soldiers searched for them in vain. After the British departed, the three returned to the tavern, but Lee died three weeks later, as a result of the exposure. He left the sum of £5,000 to the American treasury, which must have been a welcome addition to the patriots' scanty funds.

Mrs. Lee occupied the house until her death, after which it was for a time the residence of Judge Sewall.

An old house with a single corner of the second story projecting oddly, is known as the Lafayette house because that general was twice entertained there. Parson Barnard's, built in 1716 still stands, but now divided into two separate dwellings.

Brigadier General Glover's large square residence not far from the street following the shore, is set aslant towards a narrow side street on which it faces. Glover had the honor of rowing Washington in the memorable crossing of the Delaware, and served with distinction at Valley Forge and on Long Island.

Washington visited Marblehead in 1789, to the delight of the inhabitants, their only regret being that because of poverty, they were unable to entertain their President as they felt he should be entertained. At the time, they had 459 widows and 865 orphans dependent on the town for support, so their poverty was very real, and later lotteries were held for the Marblehead poor.

Of course interest attaches to this town because it was the scene of the beginning of the romance of Agnes Surriage and Sir Harry Frankland; a romance which lasted to the death of that nobleman, long after he had married the woman who, at the risk of her own life, saved his during the Lisbon earthquake. No children survived, and at Frankland's death, he left his property to his wife, including a magnificent place not far from Boston. On her death, she willed this to her sister, Mrs. Swain, who in turn left it to her son. From him, it passed to Agnes' brother, Isaac, who sold it.

The birthplace of Elbridge Gerry is in excellent condition, a private residence. One of the framers of the Constitution, he later refused to sign that document as drawn up, declaring that it gave too much power to the Federal Government. Gerry was a Member of Congress, commissioner to France, Governor of Massachusetts and Vice-President of the United States.

Returning inland, at Topsfield is the Parson Capen house, carefully restored, with its interior of wooden sheathing, and huge fireplace. The Reverend Joseph Capen married one of the wealthy Appleton family of Ipswich, and it is said that the bride did not like the parsonage, so he built her this new house, with a studded door like Deerfield's " Indian door." The house is now a museum.

In Ipswich, several old houses claim attention. Most attractive is the Olde Burnham, now open as an inn, and already described in another work by this author.[1]

Close to the railway station is the Whipple house.

The Reverend Thomas Franklin Waters, who has made a study of old houses in Ipswich and elsewhere, doubts that any of the survivors were built before the middle of the 17th century.[2] The early settlers, he remarks, found this part of the country a wilderness, and built houses like all pioneers, of logs, or hand hewn timber, covered with clay. The first permit for a saw mill in Ipswich was not issued until 1649, and all locks, hinges and nails were hammered out by the local blacksmith.

John Whipple owned the lot, and there was a house on it in 1642, as the town records show, for he bought it in that year from John Fawn, who was removing to Haverhill. In 1669, Whipple's son, John, succeeded to the property, and Mr. Waters believes that the son built

[1] *Early American Inns and Taverns.*
[2] *Some Old Ipswich Houses*, Rev. Thomas Franklin Waters.

the present house either in 1669, or at least before 1683. The western portion is the oldest.

The first John Whipple was " admitted to be a freeman " in 1640, in Ipswich. In the same year, he was a deputy to the General Court, was one of the first Seven Men, as the selectmen were called, served on a committee appointed to further trade, and on another to promote the interests of the fishing business; was a deacon, and later a Ruling Elder.

The second John was a soldier, and in 1662 secured a license to " still strong water for a year, and to retail not less than a quart at a time, and none to be drunk in his house," an early application of the present Canadian liquor law in Massachusetts. He further built a malt house. In 1674, he served as representative to the General Court, in King Philip's war, went as lieutenant and later was made captain. As he became one of Ipswich's wealthiest men, he probably added the handsome eastern room, with massive carved summers, of the present house, doubling its size. The inventory of his possessions at his death shows him to have owned feather beds, " serge curtains, vallance and coverlid " for one or more beds, valued at £19 a set, leather and carved chairs, silver and pewter.

His son, Major John, added a leanto to the old house, and probably an attic above. He had two slaves, a negro man and woman, Tom and Flora, and there is mention of their marriage. The third John had no son to succeed him, but the three of his six daughters who grew to womanhood all married ministers, and one of these, Benjamin Crocker, the husband of Mary, with his wife succeeded to the old house.

In 1898, the Ipswich Historical Society purchased the old house, and also bought and removed some of the modern buildings near it. They tore off plaster, and brought to view the original sheathing; found the positions of the old casement windows, opened the old fireplaces, and have furnished the house with gifts of portraits, furniture, etc. of the proper period which have been sent by interested friends. A portion is now open as a museum to the public.

Another old Ipswich house, on the corner of Market and Central Streets, was built about 1707, by Colonel John Appleton. He was Chief

Justice of the Court of Common Pleas, for thirty-seven years a Judge of Probate, and a Deputy Councillor. This was one of the finest houses in town, distinguished for elegance and hospitality. In 1676, when Andover was in danger of attacks by Indians, Captain John Appleton hurried there with sixty men, thus causing much complaint, for Ipswich citizens felt that their own safety was thereby imperilled. In 1716, Governor Shute, on his way to New Hampshire, was entertained here. Colonel John's son, Daniel, was also a Colonel, Judge of the Court of Sessions, and Registered Probate Judge. Another Probate Judge, Daniel Noyes, succeeded to the ownership of the house, and finally the antiquarian, Abraham Hammatt, bought and re-modeled the old residence.

It contains a dark closet which for years was pointed out as the hiding place of one of the Regicides, but a later authority pronounces this preposterous.

Still another old Ipswich house is that built in 1728 by Nathaniel Wade, who served with honor in the Revolutionary Army. When Benedict Arnold turned traitor to the American cause, Wade was appointed to take command of West Point, Washington saying: "We can trust him." The Wade family possesses the original order giving this command to their ancestor.

Mr. Waters quotes in full a letter giving instructions for the building of a farmhouse at the same period that the early Whipple home was built, and practically the same kind of house. The owner, Deputy Governor Symonds, wrote in 1637: "I am indifferent whether it be 30 foote long, 16 or 18 foote broad. I would have wood chimneyes at each end, the frames of the chimneyes to be stronger than ordinary, to beare a good heavy load of clay for security against fire. You may let the chimneyes be all the breadth of the house if you thinke good — Be sure that all the doorwaies in every place be soe high that any man may goe vpright and under. The staires had best be placed close by the door. It makes no great matter though there be noe particion vpon the first floore, if there be, make one biger than the other. For windowes let them not be over large in any roome, and as far as conveniently may be I would have the house strong in timber though plaine and well brased." On the second story it was to have a " particion." He continues: " I think it best to have the walls without to be all clapboarded besides the clay walls." [3]

One gets a quaint picture of early Ipswich. " Working cattle were allowed to roam in the Commons at night, and on Sundays and wet days, when they were not in use," so in 1737, at a Town Meeting, it was voted that " a generall fence be built," to keep the cattle from damaging property.

Ipswich shared in the horrible witchcraft delusions. Elizabeth Howe was suspected of being in league with the devil, for Samuel Perkey's daughter, Hannah, was strangely affected, and had seen Mrs. Howe coming and going through a crack in the clapboards, and hiding in the oven! Although her pastor and teacher of the Rowley church pronounced her innocent of the awful charge, the Elders refused to admit her to the church. When the witchcraft trials began in 1692, she was arrested, tried, and sentenced to be hanged. Esther Rogers was another victim, sentenced by Judge Samuel Sewall.

On the principal business street of Gloucester in the very heart of the old fishing town, and enclosed by a high iron fence, is a large square house, painted in colonial yellow and white. This is known as the Sargent-Murray-Gilman house.

The interior is now little changed. One may still admire the fine staircase with hand carved spindles, the big fireplaces, set in paneled walls. At Mr. Sargent's death, his daughter Judith inherited it. She married first John Stevens, then John Murray. She must have been a remarkable woman, even as her portrait shows her to have been a beauty, for at that early period, when women seldom were conspicuous for other than domestic excellencies, she wrote books and plays, edited a magazine, and finished her husband's biography. After the Murrays, the house was purchased by Fred Gilman, who fell in love with and married Abigail Somes, daughter of a Gloucester tavern keeper. He made and lost a fortune, but during his occupancy of the house many

[3] *Some Old Ipswich Houses*, Rev. Thomas Franklin Waters.

The Maynards, Waban, Mass.

The Sargent-Murray-Gilman house, Gloucester, Massachusetts.

The Sargent room, Sargent-Murray-Gilman house, Gloucester, Massachusetts. In this room have been collected many portraits by the two artists of the Sargent family, and photographs of others.

distinguished guests were entertained in it, among them General and Molly Stark, who were great friends of the Gilmans.

Entering by an Ionic-pillared doorway, one comes into a wide hall, extending through the house. Two spacious rooms open on either side; of these four, one each is devoted to three prominent families whose names are associated with the house, while the fourth is a memorial to a beloved Gloucester teacher.

The Sargent room, with a very beautiful white mantel and paneling, contains a portrait by Copley of Judith Sargent, first mistress of the house, and a number of portraits, or photographs of portraits, of the long line of Sargents, including, of course, the two portrait painters of the family, Henry and John Singer Sargent.

There is the Murray room, the Reverend John Murray, Judith Sargent's second husband, having been known as the Father of Universalism in New England.

Finally comes the Gilman room, in honor of the family who made the old house a centre of entertainment.

From the fine hall, a flight of broad stairs, with hand wrought mahogany bannisters, white painted, like the rest of the woodwork, leads, with a landing, to the second story. A very beautiful Palladian window on this landing calls for admiration. On the second floor, several of the chambers have the little powder closets where wigs were dressed. In those days, people did not powder in public conveyances, or on the streets. The small fireplaces on this floor could hardly have warmed the bedrooms during cold New England winters.

As to the house's history, when Judith, daughter of Captain Winthrop Sargent, married her second husband, in 1768, her father built her this beautiful house.

After being left a widow the second time, Mrs. Murray sold the house to Frederick Gilman, a Gloucester business man, and major in its militia. When he died, leaving a widow and one son, Mrs. Gilman was unable to retain the house, and sold it. The son became the Reverend Samuel Gilman, for many years pastor of the Unitarian Church,

Charleston, South Carolina. He also wrote the words of " Fair Harvard."

Several people then owned the house, and finally it was threatened with demolition, the Metropolitan Museum of New York having been on the point of purchasing and removing the old woodwork. A descendant of Captain Winthrop Sargent interested others in forming the society which purchased the old house, now owns and cares for it, and has collected the interesting souvenirs and old furniture treasured within its walls.

Among members of the Sargent family who distinguished themselves, aside from the two painters, were Winthrop, son of its builder, a major in the Revolutionary Army, and Secretary of the Northwest Territory; Paul Dudley Sargent, aide de camp to Washington, and friend of Lafayette; Daniel, a prominent merchant of his day, whose wife, Mary Turner, was born in Salem's House of the Seven Gables, down to the modern Charles Sprague Sargent, of the Arnold Arboretum, and author of *Silva of North America*.

The greatest treasures of the house are modern; four early sketches done by its most renowned son, the child, John Singer Sargent. One of these was done at the age of four, a sketch of his father, but another, drawn four years later, the study of an old man, is remarkable, even were it not the work of a child.

There are other interesting old houses in Gloucester, not open to the public, but which charm those fortunate enough to be admitted. In one of these lives an old lady quite surrounded by interesting and beautiful furniture, ornaments, and other relics of the past. She has replaced the old leaded windows of the early period of her house with modern, large-paned sashes. A visitor remonstrated with her one day, but the old lady replied:

" Yes, I know they criticise me in this town, but I'm tired of looking through little bits of panes, so I've had the large ones put in. But after I'm gone the old ones can be put back by anyone who wishes, for they're all upstairs in the attic."

It would be useless now to look for the old house on Back Street, where lived one Peg Wesson, and which was in or near an old building called the Garrison. Shortly before troops left Gloucester on the Cape Breton expedition, in 1745, some of the men visited her, and incurred her displeasure. Already it had been hinted that she was a witch, so when she threatened the soldiers that she would be avenged on them at Louisburg, it made a disagreeable impression.

When they were in camp there, they noticed a black crow, which kept flying or hovering near them. They decided that the bird of ill omen must be Peg. Knowledge of witchcraft lore made them realize that only silver would serve to bring down a witch, and since they of course had no silver bullets, one of the men took a silver cuff link, loaded it into his musket, and fired. The crow fell with a broken leg, and was soon killed.

At the very time that the bird fell, Mistress Peg fell down in Gloucester, and broke her leg! Furthermore, when the wound was probed, the veritable silver cuff link fired in camp was extracted. Such was one of the amazing tales circulated and apparently believed in those days.

Cape Ann was discovered by Captain John Smith in 1614, and settlements were made there soon after the Massachusetts colonists landed in 1620. John Pool first settled in Rockport, which remained a part of Gloucester until 1840.

Pigeon Cove, a mile and a half beyond Rockport, and formerly known as The Gap, is a small village of summer homes, and all-the-year-round residents. Save for a small, sandy bathing beach, the shore is rocky. None the less, the rocky shore did not bar early settlers, and it boasts three very old and surviving houses. Another quite venerable one, although outwardly much transformed, is known to-day as Mammy's Old Tavern, and was an inn many years ago. This is said to occupy the site of the old John Babson house, which he built and occupied in 1695. The present may include a portion of the old building.

Samuel Gott, one of the first little group of settlers, built himself a gambrel-roofed house near Halibut Point. Other early settlers were

Jethro Wheeler and his son Jethro. These two built what is still called " The Castle," now but a few rods from the highroad, but then described as on " a wild and craggy site."

The fourth surviving old house of interest is always known as the Witch house.

First to be passed by the motorist from Gloucester will be the Castle.

Just how the house received its name is lost in oblivion. A few years ago, it seemed doomed to fall, and save for a few rooms, was unoccupied. Nor would a visitor last autumn have thought that many years of life remained to it, for the ceilings sagged, window panes had been replaced by boards, paper dangled from the walls. But the property had already been purchased by Mrs. Harry Rogers, and her brothers, the Messrs. Story. They intend to restore the house as much as possible to its original condition, and present it to the village as a memorial to their mother for community use. They have also purchased the house now standing between the Castle and the highroad, intend removing the building, and laying out a lawn on its site. This will greatly improve the appearance.

Of salt box type, the Castle has three large rooms on the first floor, and from a small entry, steep stairs mount to the second story. One room at the left of the entry downstairs has the old fireplace and cupboards beside it still remaining, but the ceiling in this room especially has sagged so much, with the massive beam crossing it, that only a short man could stand erect beneath the beam and he would have no difficulty in touching the rest of the ceiling with his hand.

The original part of the Witch house, believed to have been a garrison house, consisted of a front entry, and two or possibly three rooms. One of these had a big fireplace with cupboards set in one entirely paneled wall. Across the entry of this oldest part, which is now one side of the house, is a smaller room, whose broad plank-sheathed walls have been uncovered to their original state, all plaster and paint having been removed by the present interested owners. The big old rafters have also been bared, and, unusual for a room of this size, three cross the low ceiling. The original old fireplace here is, it is thought, concealed behind the newer, smaller one, which has a closet beside it. The owners intend searching for the old fireplace as soon as other and more pressing repairs and restorations are completed.

Behind this room is another, as to whose age there is doubt. That it is very old goes without saying, but it may or may not be part of the original building. The outer wall of this side of the house still shows the second story overhanging perhaps nine inches, and doubtless originally this overhang could be seen on all four sides, but has now disappeared with more modern additions. The present front entrance, hall, and rooms on the first and second story were added in 1750. Some modern owner had replaced the old front door with an ugly later one; had built an ugly, fan-like projection over the old side door, once the main entrance. Both of these have now disappeared, and a fine colonial door found in another town has been hung on the Witch house. A still later addition is used as the present kitchen.

In removing the plaster from the oldest portion, the inner planks were found to have the roughened, splintered surface first used to hold plaster on walls, before laths were substituted.

Upstairs, in the old part, is one large and beautifully paneled room, showing that the woodwork here is much later than the period of building. A smaller room across the entry has plainer paneling, mantel and cupboards, also later than the building of the house, but earlier than the woodwork in the larger room. It is thought that in this latter room the paneling and fireplace may mask a larger, older one. One board in the paneling is twenty-seven inches wide. Above all of these rooms is an attic, reached by quaint, steep old stairs.

The story goes that a woman was accused of witchcraft in Danvers or Salem Township, and that her two sons fled with her, walking all the long distance to Pigeon Cove, to seek safety. Here, according to one version, they took refuge in the garrison house, now the Witch house; according to another version, the sons built the house for their mother, and all three lived in it. Tradition also says that the woman's accuser was a clergyman. Later his own wife was accused, and since he *knew* that she was not a witch, he lost belief in their existence. There is no story of the mother and sons ever returning to their former home, and they seem to have spent the rest of their lives here in The Gap.

The house stands well back from the highroad, quite screened by trees, and last year was still wearing a coat of dingy yellow paint. A few years ago, the house was bought, and the new owner proceeded to make many changes to suit his taste. Among others, he directed the local house painter to paint the house this ugly color, with door and window trimmings of green. To his credit, the painter remonstrated.

" Why, it will not look like the Witch house if it is painted," he urged. " That house has never yet received a coat of paint. I'd almost sooner not take the job than paint it."

But the new owner was obdurate, and the deed was done. He did not long own the house, and when the present owners bought it, they at once set to work to remove the devastating changes. The green trim has disappeared, and presumably as soon as possible the yellow walls will be restored more nearly to the original weather-stained grey.

Gott house is a two-story building, with a very small ell, and a curious roof, hipped in front but not in the back, so that the second story is higher in the rear than in front, and gives a curious outline. The large kitchen has a fireplace in which a modern stove finds ample room, and a fireplace in the room across the hall also remains, with one old corner cupboard.

Very steep, narrow, winding stairs lead to the second story, with a cupboard opening off a small landing in front of the chimney. Its exact age seems unknown, but it is at least one hundred and fifty years old.

Oldest house on Cape Ann is the picturesque, charming old Riggs homestead, in Annisquam. Built in 1638, of logs, by Thomas Riggs, the first schoolmaster and second town clerk in this township, it has remained in the ownership of the Riggs family ever since, and is now used as a summer home by the eighth and ninth generations of that name. The original part consisted of the schoolroom and one or two

The Lee mansion, Marblehead, Massachusetts. At its building, it was considered one of the costliest in New England. Here lived an ardent patriot, who bequeathed $5,000 to the Patriot cause.

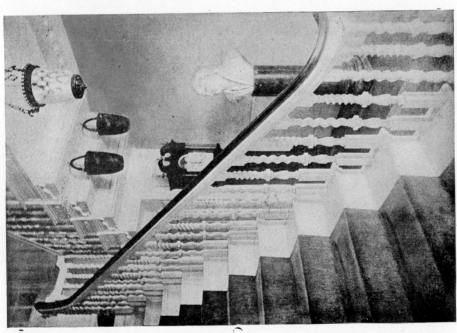

Part of the stairway, showing the beautiful hand carved spindles and mahogany handrail in the Sargent-Murray-Gilman house, Gloucester, Massachusetts.

The Witch house, Pigeon Cove, Massachusetts. A very old house with several additions, it is now being very carefully restored. Here, during the witchcraft delusions, an unfortunate woman took refuge with her sons. Some say that an earlier garrison house was standing here at that time; others that the woman's sons built it for her.

The Riggs house, said to be the oldest on Cape Ann. Ever since its building, for the first Cape Ann schoolmaster, it has been owned and occupied by the Riggs family.

rooms above, reached through the narrowest of doorways, by the narrowest, steepest of stairs. The *new* part of the house was added in 1660.

The former kitchen in this addition opens from the old schoolroom. It has a tremendous fireplace, eight feet across, large enough to contain as it does easily, a good-sized sofa, a spinning wheel, and a number of household utensils of early days. Among treasured possessions is a cannon ball, fired by a British sloop in Annisquam River at the village church, during the War of 1812. From this old room opens the present kitchen, where is a rare old soapstone stove, and at the side are two more low-ceiled rooms. An odd piece of furniture is a rush-bottomed chair, which the grandmother of the present younger generation used aptly to call the " wavering chair." It seems as though about to fall to pieces, for the legs twist back and forth at all sorts of angles, but it is in reality solid, and the grandmother says that it has been thus apparently unsteady ever since she can remember. Since one can rock in it, although the legs do not leave the floor, it would almost appear to have been made as it is.

The old mantels and wall cupboards are found in these rooms, and fine old furniture, including some Windsor chairs, all of which have been in the family for generations, add to the harmony of the interior. There is a second story over this part too, reached by a second narrow staircase, and the only modern addition is the broad porch overlooking the river. Otherwise, the grey old house has nothing new in appearance.

The narrow road or lane by which it is reached turns off from the highway, just beyond Annisquam's famous willows, which here border the road for some distance on both sides.

Returning to Gloucester, as one must to proceed in either direction, one may go north along the shore to picturesque old Newbury and Newburyport.

These two, which now practically are one town, have many fascinating old houses, some of which are not of actual historic interest, save for their age, dating from the 17th century. The Swett-Ilsley house, open as a museum, and cared for by the New England Association for the Preservation of Antiquities, is noteworthy.

It was built before 1670 — the exact date is not known — for Stephen Swett, who had previously kept the Blue Anchor Tavern nearby. He lived in it until 1691, when he sold it to Hugh March, who by that time had succeeded him as tavern keeper. Like most of the early innkeepers, March was something of a personage. He was a captain, had commanded a company in the expedition against Canada in 1690, and in 1697, commanded forces attacking the Indians at Damaris Cove, Maine. (The Indians attacked Newbury in 1696.) Still later, he bravely defended His Majesty's fort at Casco Bay against an attack by French and Indians, for which gallantry, as well as compensation for wounds received, he was awarded £50.

When Captain March died, in 1712, the old house was sold to Captain Henry Lyon, who also kept the Blue Anchor Tavern, but he soon moved away from Newbury, and the house was sold again and again. In 1772, it was owned by Dudley Colman, "town clerk and gentleman," who served in the Revolution, and became Lieutenant-Colonel of Colonel Wigglesworth's regiment. Colonel Colman participated in engagements along the Hudson River, and in the dreary winter spent by the Revolutionary Army under Washington, at Valley Forge. While he owned the house, at one time a " tobacconist business," and a chocolate mill were located in it. Another Revolutionary soldier, Nicholas Titcomb, then owned and installed a tavern in the old house, later selling it to Oliver Putnam, blacksmith and scythemaker, also of the Continental Army. He, too, kept the tavern open.

Oliver Putnam's son, Oliver, became wealthy, and in 1826 he bequeathed money for founding the Putnam Free School, in Newburyport.

In 1797, the house was owned by Isaiah Ilsley, a joiner, and remained in his family until, in 1911, it was purchased by the Society.

It now is, and has for many years been a long, low, two-story and attic building of the salt box type, with two front entrances on the street. The oldest part is at the left of the left entrance, and this is the part built for Stephen Swett before 1670; one room on the first floor, and a small entry, from which stairs lead to the chamber above. The original roof over this had a front gable and "peaked window," the front being what is now the eastern end of the present house. The second story overhung the first by several inches, which feature has now disappeared.

Perhaps ten years after its building, the house was enlarged, chimney and stairs at the western end removed, others built against the north wall, and the present middle rooms added, with the front then facing on the street, as now. The stairs built at that time are gone, but the present chimney is believed to be this second one, very large, and with enormous fireplace. The space occupied by the first chimney was used to make two small rooms, still existing in the rear of the house.

Several other additions were made; the last, with the second entrance on the street, and a second flight of stairs, has two rooms on each floor. It is beside this second door that the old tavern sign now hangs, luncheons and teas being served for the upkeep of the building.

The Society has removed the modern plaster from the oldest rooms, and the fine old sheathing now stands revealed. In the middle room, in the first addition, is the fireplace mentioned, one of the largest in New England, perhaps in the country, for it measures ten feet 2½ inches, lacks but an inch of being six feet high, and is a trifle over three feet deep.

Five rooms have thus far been carefully restored by the Society, which hopes, with added funds, eventually to restore the entire house. Of these five are the two earliest rooms, the chamber on the second floor, with beautifully paneled walls, untouched by paint, and two middle rooms, one with the enormous fireplace. In the newest part upstairs are rooms paneled and painted white, and here are some fine old H and HL hinges.

The Garrison house in Newburyport is worthy of mention because in addition to being 150 years old, it originally consisted of two four-story brick houses, just alike, adjoining, but with no connection inside.

These were the residences of two brothers, and when the property was bought for hotel purposes, one staircase throughout was removed and replaced by an elevator shaft, while connecting arches were opened in the halls on each floor. How thick the inner walls are may be seen now.

The Governor William Dummer house, built in 1715–16, is still used in connection with the school which, in 1762, he left money to establish. The school charter was signed by John Hancock in 1763.

Turning westward, away from the coast, it is not a long drive to Haverhill, where are a couple of houses of historic interest.

That in which John Greenleaf Whittier was born in 1807 is known as Fernside Farm. The present house stands on the site of a primitive one, doubtless of logs, built here by Thomas Whittier, whom Mr. Faris calls the poet's " three hundred pound ancestor." In 1668, Thomas wished a larger house, and built the present one, with massive hand hewn timbers, and a kitchen thirty feet long. Like the great kitchen in the Dorothy Q. house, Quincy, this served as general living room. Here the poet spent his childhood, and the house is now owned by a memorial association, and open to the public.

Another old house in Haverhill is of great interest, since it was the home of one of the most heroic of pioneer women. For those who have forgotten the story, it may be told that here, to a house built of imported brick, in 1677, Thomas Duston brought his bride, Hannah. He believed that it should not be necessary to import bricks, and began experimenting until he produced such excellent ones that Haverhill became noted for them. He then built a larger house of Haverhill bricks on the site of the former, with floors and roof of white oak, building it substantially, since it was to serve as a garrison house for refuge from the Indians. But on March 15th, 1697, when he was away from home, the Indians attacked the settlement, and dragged off with them his wife Hannah, with her week-old baby, the nurse, Mrs. Neffe, and a young boy. For a hundred and fifty miles, the little party journeyed with their savage captors, sometimes being told of the horrible fate that awaited them when the journey's end should be reached.

Courtesy of William F. McCurdy

The Swett-Isley house, Newburyport, Massachusetts. A very old house, with additions, it has frequently been a tavern, although now only teas and luncheons are served, to aid in maintaining it as a museum.

Fireplace Swett-Isley house.

King Hooper house, Marblehead, Massachusetts. Its owner received the nickname of
King because of the magnificent entertainments he gave. The house is now occupied by
the Y. M. C. A.

Then, one night, the Indians slept without leaving a guard. Probably they felt sure that the two women and boy could do nothing, out in the lonely forest, but they did not know the spirit of the pioneers.

Hannah incited her nurse and the boy to follow her example. Falling upon the sleeping Indians, they killed them all with hatchets before they could rouse to resist. The brave women and the boy, not forgetting the baby, sturdy infant, then started on the long homeward journey when Hannah remembered the bounty offered by the province for Indian scalps, and returning, she scalped the dead Indians, and took the bloody trophies with her.

How the two women, the boy and baby managed to get back to the settlement where they had long been given up as dead, seems a miracle, but they did so, paddling down the Merrimack River, eating what they could find in the forests.

The General Assembly of Massachusetts voted Hannah £25, and the same sum to be divided between Mrs. Neffe and the boy, Samuel Lennardson, thus recognizing that Hannah was the guiding spirit. The Governor of Maryland sent her a silver tankard, and one can imagine how that must have been treasured.

Chapter XII

⚔ The First American Baronet and His Home ⚔

From Newburyport, it is a delightful drive to Portsmouth, New Hampshire, where one will find not only beautiful old houses, but some which undoubtedly possess historic interest. Romance, too, is connected with some of these stately mansions.

Rockingham Hotel stands on the site of the mansion of the Hon. Woodbury Langdon, Governor, and member of the Continental Congress. The original house was burned in 1781, and re-built four years later. In 1830, it became a public house, but in 1884 all but one room, the colonial dining room, was destroyed by fire. The present hotel was built around this room, which is paneled in white and gold, with corner cupboards having very unusual and elaborate brass hinges. These cupboards are now filled with fine old china, and the room contains interesting curios. Decidedly a show room, the hotel people are glad to allow visitors.

The beautiful Winslow-Pierce mansion, still owned and occupied by members of the original family, is situated on Middle Street. Not open to the public, the occupants none the less are very kind in opening it for charitable entertainments, or special celebrations. Three stories in height, white, with green blinds, and charming colonial doorway, it is a fine specimen of its period, 1799.

The Aldrich house, home of Thomas Bailey Aldrich's grandparents, and where the author lived as a child, is extremely interesting because while not a mansion, merely a comfortable home, it contains the original furniture, many of the little everyday articles used by the family. The rooms have been arranged with loving attention, largely by the author's wife, to look as though the original occupants had but just stepped out for a moment. It is filled with fine pieces of Sheraton and Phyfe furniture, beautiful ladderback chairs, old china, silver and homespun linen.

A portrait of Thomas Bailey Aldrich's great-great-grandmother Adams, copied from the original by Copley, is among those hanging on the walls. The fire irons are of Bell metal, a mixture of brass, copper and tin. The custodian tells that Miss Abigail Bailey, a maiden relative, came to pay a visit in this hospitable home, and remained for seventeen years.

The room of Mrs. Aldrich, the author's mother, has some of her own belongings in the bureau drawers, night clothes laid out on the four-post bedstead, with its wonderful white counterpane in most elaborate hand-quilted pattern. Here are two rag dolls, a negro mother and baby, made by the same hands.

Mr. Aldrich's room, too, might have been left but a moment before by its occupant, while in " Grandfather " Aldrich's room are his large Bible, his spectacles in their case beside it on a small table, and his square old checkbook bound in stiff paper covers, lies on the bureau.

Thomas Bailey Aldrich's childhood room is a small one over the front lower hall. Here is the window out of which he climbed, here the small bed, covered with a quilt made by his mother.

One may mount to the big attic, " for all broken down things," and see some of these, including a large spinning wheel.

In the old garden has been built a fireproof room to house the author's interesting collections of manuscripts — some of these dating from the time when he was editor of the Atlantic Monthly — his autographed photographs of many poets and other authors; his autographed first editions, and the many beautiful and valuable gifts which he received from kings and queens, noble and commoner in Europe, as well as those from his own countrymen. The house is owned by the Thomas Bailey Aldrich Association, and is open to visitors.

The Moffet Ladd house, built in 1763, is owned and kept open by the Colonial Dames. It is a splendid example of a mansion of that period, although now in a rather shabby neighborhood. From a spacious, beautiful hall, rises a broad staircase with fine carved bannisters. The paper on halls and stairway walls here is the original French paper put on in 1820, showing scenes from various foreign countries, in *grisaille*. There are a number of double cross doors, and the woodwork throughout is beautiful, but none of the original furniture remains, although the Dames have filled the house with beautiful pieces loaned by different persons. Many doors have the old HL hinges.

The drawing room on the first floor, in the rear, looking out over the old garden, has a beautiful Gringling Gibbons mantel from an old English manor house. From this room, a secret passage used to lead to the sea, but this has now been bricked up, for it was haunted by rats, as well as somewhat dangerous as an entrance for thieves or tramps.

The mantel in the front dining room is framed with the original Dutch tiles, imported by the builder.

There is a beautiful bedroom above the drawing room, and one over the dining room has its powdering closet. All of the rooms have fireplaces, with broad panels above.

The Wentworth-Gardner house, built in 1760, is now a mere shell, for its fittings, fireplaces, mantels and doors, including the old front one, were purchased by the Boston Museum and practically nothing but the four walls remains of the old.

Two miles from the business centre of the town is the house built by Governor Benning Wentworth, in 1750. It is said that originally it contained fifty-two rooms. Many of these have been removed, but as it stands, the house is very large, although some of the rooms are small. It is a long, rambling structure.

In the great cellar, the Governor had room for stabling thirty horses. This was the Governor Wentworth who married the young maidservant, Martha Hilton, to the amazement of his guests and the officiating clergyman, as set forth in Longfellow's poem, "Lady Wentworth." This is the

"... pleasant mansion, an abode

" Near and yet hidden from the great highroad
" Sequestered among trees, a noble pile
" Baronial and colonial in style."

Here the Governor had invited " all his friends and peers, the Pepperel's, the Langdons and the Lears, the Sparhawks," . . . these names will recur in histories of New England towns — and after the feasting, he requested the clergyman to marry him to the young maid, and so " Martha was Lady Wentworth of the Hall."

After the Governor died, in 1770, the widow married another Wentworth, Michael, retired colonel of the British Army, who had come to Portsmouth three years before. Washington visited here after the second marriage. The couple had a daughter, Martha, who married Sir Jonathan Wentworth, of England.

The first Wentworth to come to America was of a noble English family. William Wentworth came over in 1638, and the following year settled in New Hampshire, became a preacher, and was known as Elder Wentworth. When eighty years old, he was sleeping in a garrison house one night, when he was awakened by the barking of a dog just as Indians were opening the door. Lying flat on his back, he pushed and held the door shut with his feet, while by his cries he aroused the other men. Although bullets fired at him pierced the door, they went over him as he lay there without touching him.

His son John became Lieutenant Governor, and Governor Benning was another son of the sturdy old Elder. Lieutenant Governor John's son was last of the royal governors.

Captain Archibald Macpheadies, in 1718 began to build himself a house which was not finished until five years later, and cost £6,000. He married a sister of Governor Benning, these being two of a family of sixteen children. Macpheadies took his bride to the new house, and later, their daughter married Jonathan Warner, and lived in it. Still standing, but modernized, a private residence, it is now always known as the Warner house, and to it Benjamin Franklin is said to have attached his first lightning rod.

Portsmouth's oldest existing, still occupied house is known as the

Jackson house, and was built, of salt box type, in 1664. It has a very high-pitched roof, with leanto of a later period, as can plainly be seen, since it blocks one of the earlier windows.

In the house now occupied by the Portsmouth Athletic Club, there still remains some wallpaper made in Alsace, in 1826. It shows views of the Hudson River, West Point, New York, Niagara Falls, Boston and its harbor, and the Natural Bridge, Virginia.

The house now owned and occupied by the Historical Association of Portsmouth, and open to the public, was built in 1758, by Captain Purcell. When he died, his widow found herself in reduced circumstances, so kept boarders to help make ends meet. In 1779, Paul Jones stayed here while the *Ranger* was fitted out in Portsmouth harbor, and again in 1782, while the *America* was undergoing the same process.

It is a large, square, two-story and attic house, now painted a colonial yellow, with fine white paneling and woodwork throughout, big old fireplaces, with closets in the walls beside them, etc. The front door opens on a square hall, with an archway at the rear, behind which the stairs mount, and a narrower hall leads to the dining room or library, with the old kitchen opposite. On each side of the front hall is a large square room. The present kitchen and the space above, which formerly was made into several rooms, but has now been thrown into one, is more modern. Interesting old furniture has been placed in some of the rooms.

The Historical Society has owned the property for six years. Shortly before the World War, it had been purchased by the Granite Insurance Company. During the war it was used for community purposes, and later, the Insurance Company planned to remove it, and erect a business building on its site. The Historical Society was anxious that the house should be preserved, and finally, through the generosity of the late Mr. Woodbury Langdon, a retired New York merchant, its purchase was made possible. In this house, Washington, Lafayette and Louis Philippe have been entertained.

Not far from Portsmouth is New Castle, and here the dwelling built by General Jaffray, and for seven years used as a Council House does stand, but would hardly be recognized as old. It remained in the Jaffray family until 1813, but eventually was bought by a wealthy man, who built a fine modern residence, reserving the old house merely as an ell.

Although New Hampshire was early visited with intent to colonize, the first attempts were not successful. Mason Hall, on Odiorne Point, the first frame house in the state, was built about 1623, but has disappeared. In 1631, Humphrey Chadbourne built the " Great house," three miles up the Piscataqua River above Mason Hall, on ground covered with wild strawberries, so that the place was sometimes known as Strawberry Hill. The old cellar and well are said still to be here, but the house was in ruins as early as 1685. Odiorne Point is the present Rye.

Another of the first four settlements, Portsmouth, Hampton, Exeter and Dover, which existed in 1641, offers a garrison house, almost as when built. This is Dover, in whose Woodman Institute the building, two hundred and fifty years old, is preserved. Presented by its last owner, Mrs. Rounce, to the Institute, it was removed to its present site, and, for better protection, has been surrounded by a high lattice, topped with a slate roof.

Originally it was surrounded, for the better protection of its inmates from Indian attacks, by a high stockade, with a wooden gate which could be barred.

The garrison house was built of hand hewn logs in 1672, by William Damme, and was known for more than a century as the Damme house. For eighty years it was then called the Drew garrison house, and later was for thirty-five years owned by the lady who gave it to the Institute.

The original windows were very small, unglazed, merely openings in the log walls. These logs rested closely on each other, the corners squared and fastened with oak pins. The roof timbers, of mortice and tenon construction, overhanging the walls were held in place by similar pins. In the centre is the big chimney built of large, soft bricks, imported from England, with fireplaces opening into the two rooms on the first floor. The second story was left unpartitioned, and was reached by a very narrow, steep staircase. A tiny entry, just the width of the chimney, admits to the two lower rooms.

It is especially interesting to be able to examine one of the old garrison houses which has been left so nearly in its original state. Usually when such have survived, they have been so modernized that it is difficult to picture them just as they stood when early settlers must often flee to them, there to defend themselves and their families as best they could from attacking savages. The Dover house has, too, been filled with interesting old relics and furniture of the early days.

The primitive " half house " in this part of the country was of logs, perhaps twenty feet square, with small windows, and a great chimney. The " double house," forty by twenty feet, indicated that its owner was wealthy. Furniture was usually made in the settlement, of pine, birch, cherry, walnut or curled maple. The first cattle here were imported from Denmark.

Almost as far south of Portsmouth as Dover is north, in old Exeter, is another of these log garrison houses, built by Councillor John Gilman, somewhere between 1650 and 1658. This is occupied as a dwelling by a family to-day, while an addition, built on by his grandson, Peter, at the time of a reception which he tendered to the Governor, is also a residence. The house is in good condition, but not open to visitors.

Peter evidently wished to make a good appearance when he entertained the Governor, and this for several reasons. The latter, last of the royal governors, was John Wentworth, young, popular, and fond of show and display. Furthermore, there had been much jealousy between Exeter and Portsmouth, so that until this Wentworth's governorship, the royal representatives had paid little attention to the former town. John Wentworth, however, visited it frequently.

At all events, Peter Gilman, about 1712-13, built on a front part to his house, with paneling, and elaborate woodwork, such as was then coming into fashion. The older part had sheathed walls, low ceilings, and no pretension to elegance.

Peter had seven daughters, but no son. He was Speaker of the Assembly, Councillor of the Province, Brigadier General in the French and Indian wars. After his death, the house was owned by Ebenezer Clifford, who came to Exeter from Kensington. He was fond of mechanics, invented a diving bell, and studied architecture. Daniel Webster at one time boarded with him in this house.

The Cincinnati Society occupies the Governor Gilman house here, the central part of which was built in 1721. This was the home of Governor John Taylor Gilman, and of the Honorable Nicholas Gilman, Treasurer of New Hampshire during the Revolution, when the house was used as State Treasury. The two sons of Governor Gilman both served in the Revolutionary Army, John enlisting the day after the Battle of Lexington.

The original part of the house was built of brick, by Nathaniel Ladd, and was bought about 1747 by Daniel, father of Nicholas, the State Treasurer. Two wings were added later, and it was then owned for many years by the Gilman family. As the Society has now furnished it with correct articles of the period of its building, it is most attractive.

What is still known in Exeter as the Nathaniel Gilman house, a two story, hipped roof dwelling, stood originally on the site of the present Town Hall. When the latter was re-built, the old house was moved to Franklin Street, changed, partly demolished, and is fast falling to ruin. Nathaniel Gilman was but sixteen when the Revolution broke out, so did not serve in the army.

Not far from the town, still another old garrison house, the Janvrin, stands, but has been greatly changed by recent owners.

Horace Greeley's birthplace in Amherst, and that of Daniel Webster in Franklin, forming the central part of a more modern house, are both still standing.

Further north in the state, on the Connecticut River, in the town of Haverhill, may still be seen the 17th century house of Governor Page, painted white, and with a modern piazza. It was occupied by a Page until a very few years ago.

Vermont offers few houses with histories. The grandfather of

President Hayes, who came to Brattleboro from New Haven, when just twenty-one years old, built himself a house there in 1784.

The Jenkins house, in Rutland, built in 1780, was for seven years used as a Court House, and within it the first Vermont Legislature sat. Here in Rutland lived Rufus Putnam, a cousin of General Israel. He served with distinction in the French and Indian wars, and during the Revolution in the engineering branch of the service. But Putnam was not born in the state, nor did he live in it long, coming to Rutland in 1780, and leaving it eight years later, at the head of a little band of pioneers, for Ohio, where they founded the town of Marietta. While in Rutland Putnam occupied a house built for the Tory Colonel, John Murray. This was confiscated by Congress during the Revolution, and bought by Putnam.

In Poultney is a house which was standing as early as 1800, but the date of its building cannot be established definitely, since the old town records were burned. There is a local tradition that Heber Allen, brother of Ethan, had some kind of a dwelling on the property, and he is buried in the East Poultney cemetery.

The present owner can trace the definite history of his residence no further back than when it was occupied by the Reverend Clark Kendrick, pastor of the East Poultney Baptist Church. The Kendricks were early prominent in New England, Kendrick being one of the first presidents of Harvard University. Several others of the family have been professors in prominent colleges.

The house was long known as the Pine Tree, because of an enormous pine close beside it. Several Kendrick children of a past generation used this as a means of entering and leaving their second story rooms unknown to their parents, and one of them told his daughter of this youthful prank. The tree no longer stands.

It has been asserted that the old house was once an inn, known as the Pine Tree, but there seems no ground for such statement. It once served as a Jewish synagogue. The present owner purchased it in 1913, when it had fallen into a most dilapidated condition, and has restored it to a comfortable modern home.

The old Jackson house, built in 1664, and probably the oldest now standing in Portsmouth, New Hampshire.

The Warner house, Portsmouth, New Hampshire, built by a Governor for his daughter. To this house Benjamin Franklin attached an early lightning rod.

Drawing room in the Moffet-Ladd house, Portsmouth, New Hampshire. The furniture here has been collected — gifts and loans — by the Colonial Dames, which organization now owns the house.

A mantel brought to Moffet-Ladd house, Portsmouth, New Hampshire, from an old English manor.

Almost a century old is a house in North Fairfax. Although a modern piazza has somewhat changed it outwardly, otherwise it is much as when built.

In 1805, Samuel Webster, brother of Peletiah, who helped frame the Constitution of the United States, came by ox sled from Bennington, Vermont, with his little family to North Fairfax, and built himself a house in what was practically a wilderness. This house was of logs, and although it has long since vanished, the old well and cellar were plainly discernible at least a year ago. Mr. Webster came here attracted by a beaver meadow nearby, which offered hay for his cattle, while the timber afforded possibilities for making potash.

Theron, a son of Samuel Webster, who was but a few months old when the family moved, grew to manhood and built himself the house at North Fairfax, doing much of the work himself. Staunch, square, two-storied, that its building was a labor of love with the youthful owner is shown by the very beautiful staircase which he installed. It is more than semicircular, beginning on the right hand wall, as one enters the big hall, making a circuit, and touching three walls, including the rear one, against which is the big chimney, on which the great fireplace in the rear kitchen opens. The staircase ends on the second story left hand wall, near the front, and one enters the left hand sitting room downstairs by passing beneath the stairs. Treads, spindles and hand rail are all of cherry, the latter two finely hand carved. The staircase has always been an object of admiration to neighbors and visitors.

As a young man, Theron became much interested in the new daguerreotype process for making likenesses. The house is no longer owned by the family, but a daguerreotype of it, with a likeness of himself, both taken by its builder, are treasured by his descendants.

If one follows the coast road north from Portsmouth into Maine, at Kittery Point will be found two interesting old houses, with romantic histories connected with them. Here is the home of the first American baronet.

Leaving the main highroad, and turning to the right from the park, it is not long before the house of Sir William Pepperell, is reached.

A private residence, it is not open to the public, but since it now stands close to the highroad, one may examine the exterior. Once it was set in extensive grounds, which sloped down to the water, with beautiful gardens, of which a portion remains.

There was a private burying ground here, where the first Sir William Pepperell, who doubtless fancied that he was to be the founder of a long titled line, was buried. Before examining this house, one should proceed a very little further along the same road, and look at an older building, also not open to the public, but unmistakable in its grey old appearance. This is the Bray house, built in 1662, the oldest in Kittery. Originally it was much larger than the part surviving and still occupied. The builder kept a tavern in it, but as his affairs prospered, this was discontinued. He was a pioneer shipbuilder, and laid the foundations for his son-in-law's future wealth.

Margery Bray came with her father from England, in 1660, to Kittery. William Pepperell came to this country when thirty years old, first on fishing expeditions, and later went into the fishing business with a partner on the Isles of Shoals. He then removed to Kittery Point, Maine, where the Brays had been living for some years, and Margery had grown to girlhood. In 1680 Pepperell and Margery were married. She was an heiress, but apparently her suitor had also prospered, and in 1682, on a lot given him by his father-in-law, William Pepperell built " one of the most magnificent of provincial residences."

Pepperell's house had a spacious hall and staircase, and originally was forty-five feet long. Both ends of the house were later removed, after the Pepperells were no more, and made into two small houses which now stand between it and the old Bray house. Yet even now what remains is a good sized dwelling. The fine old front door is at right angles to the street; on the water side is another of equal size, and a third is in the other end.

William Pepperell served in the fort on Great Island, or New Castle, and in 1700, when a garrison house was built on Kittery Point, it was called Pepperell. He died in 1734, the father of two sons and eight daughters. The elder son died, but William, Junior, became a partner in his father's business, which had greatly prospered. It was the second William who ordered from London the marble tomb which still marks the family burial place.

He also added extensively to the house built by his father, enlarged his holdings of land, and extended the grounds of the house to the water's edge. He married Mary Hirst, of Boston. Besides continuing the fishery business, ship-building, etc., he was a justice of the peace, a captain of cavalry, at thirty, a colonel, in command of all the Maine militia, and for thirty-five years commander of the fort close by. In 1745, with the rank of Lieutenant General, he headed the expedition to Louisburg, and his wealth at that time is shown by his contribution of £5,000 towards this expedition.

The fortress of Louisburg, which had been considered impregnable, surrendered after a short siege, and as a reward for his part, Pepperell was made a baronet of Great Britain, the first patent ever conferred upon a native born American. After this, he usually wore " a very showy and expensive coat of scarlet cloth, trimmed with gold lace."

He died in 1759, his only son to grow to manhood, Andrew, having died eight years before. A daughter, Elizabeth, survived. She had married Nathaniel Sparhawk, of Boston, and had one son, William Pepperell Sparhawk. To him his grandfather, Sir William, left the bulk of his estate, and his title, on condition that the child drop the name of Sparhawk. He did so, and became the second baronet. It was this Sir William who married Mary, daughter of Isaac Royall of Medford, and these two, with the second daughter, Penelope's Vassall kin, were probably largely responsible for enlisting Royall on the Loyalist instead of the Patriot side. The Pepperell estates were confiscated in 1778, three years after Sir William sailed for England, and as he left no son, the baronetcy became extinct.

The Mary Pepperell house not far away, with the date, 1760 prominent on its façade, was built by Mary, widow of the first Sir William, for her own home, after her grandson succeeded to the old house and estate.

The old Bray house became again a tavern after another daughter of the house, Margery's sister, Mary, married an Underhill. During the Revolution, it was used as barracks for soldiers.

At Brixham, York Corners, Maine, stands the old McIntyre garrison house, built of logs, the original portion never painted, but with a more modern addition at the left. The second story was built with a pronounced overhang. It has been greatly re-modeled, but is still occupied as a residence.

Maine is said to have had settlers in 1607, but nothing remains of such a settlement.

Gorges obtained a charter of the Province of Maine in 1639, and already had built a "mansion" at York, when, the following year, he sent his nephew Thomas out from England to act as deputy governor. The nephew organized a court at Saco, but this settlement was destroyed by the Indians.

Kennebunk has many old houses, some modernized, others almost as when built. Of the latter is the Crediford house, opposite the new Town Hall, and dating from 1784.

Kennebunk was originally part of Wells Township, from which it was divided only after many years. Although there was a settlement in the township by 1641–2, eleven years later, there were but twenty-five families here. One of the early settlers was William Wentworth, who came from Exeter, and had four acres assigned him. He was the ruling elder already referred to as ancestor of John, Lieutenant Governor of New Hampshire, Governor Benning, and Governor John Wentworth, of the same state.

The Storer mansion in Kennebunk, built in 1758, not far from the famous old Lafayette elm, still stands, although its glory has departed. One can see that the gardens must once have descended in terraces to what is now Kennebunk's main street, while the old elm stood on the estate. Beneath this tree, with its enormous spreading branches, luncheon was served the soldiers who escorted Lafayette on the occasion of his visit to the town. It was purchased not many years ago, by a tree lover, with sufficient land around it, and presented to the town, while props have been placed under the largest spreading limbs, to insure long life.

Although not in the best repair, the Storer dwelling is substantial looking. Once it entertained brilliantly many distinguished guests; among them Lafayette, although he had rooms in the tavern not far away. President Monroe stayed with the Storers in 1817. The host was then a prosperous business man, but even after much of the family wealth had been lost, the last of the name to occupy the old house was always called Madam Storer, and the town was proud of her, declaring that she was " a real aristocrat."

Through the roof of the barn there grows a very large elm, and no one could explain how this happened. Another house not far from the mansion was the original farm dwelling, and now serves as a residence for several families.

It seems probable that the larger one was the " mansion " built by Colonel Joseph Storer, who came from Wells to Kennebunk in 1757. He may or may not have been a descendant of Joseph, one of four Storers living in Wells between 1641 and 1687. That Joseph's house was the principal garrison house, built in 1690, and surrounded by a large palisade. In 1705, while four Storer children were playing outside it they were set upon by Indians, two killed, and the other two carried off.

This first Joseph Storer came to Wells in 1661, with his mother and stepfather, Austin. The latter kept a tavern, but Joseph, when he grew to manhood, engaged in the lumber business, and when he died, in 1730, was the wealthiest man in town, leaving an estate valued at $5,000, and *a half dozen silver spoons!* His two sons, John and Francis, were shipbuilders, building early coasters. John enlisted in a company to go on the Louisburg expedition, under William Pepperell's command, and set out for Boston from Wells by water.

This expedition tried the endurance of the Yankee troops, for every night in foggy weather, for fourteen days they had to drag their artillery and supplies over bogs and morasses, but after fifty days, Louisburg surrendered, and Storer reached home safely.

How primitive the early Maine dwellings were may be realized from a description given of the house of Edward Littlefield, the " richest man in town." It contained one large room, used as kitchen and for all ordinary purposes, with but two bedrooms, although at one time the family consisted of the parents and six children.

Tobias Lord of Kennebunk was with Captain Littlefield of the same town at Burgoyne's surrender. A ship builder, Lord had the misfortune to lose several of his ships, and this so crippled him financially that he was on the verge of bankruptcy, but William Gray, of Salem, told him to continue his business, as he would lend Lord money, having full confidence in his integrity. Lord did continue, and was soon able to repay the loan. In 1790, he built the fine three story house still standing on Kennebunk's main street. This is probably the one known as the Robert W. Lord house, set high above the present street level. It was originally of salt box type, but has been enlarged and modernized.

It was at one time the home of Jonas Clark, son of the Reverend Jonas who harbored John Adams and John Hancock on the eve of the Battle of Lexington, in the house in that town already described. Jonas, Junior, made voyages to the south and to the West Indies, and at one time was chased close to shore by British vessels. He stayed for some time in Portsmouth, Virginia, then went into business in Portland, Maine, and according to one chronicler, retired in 1790 to this house. There seems to be a slight confusion, for Tobias Lord was said to have built the house in that same year. Jonas Clark became Collector of the Port in this district in 1800, and built on the present front of the house.

In 1820, the grandfather of the gentleman now living next door, Mr. William E. Barry, bought the property. Mr. Barry, an enthusiastic antiquarian and retired architect, recently restored the old Jeffords Tavern at his own expense, simply because he could not bear to see it falling to pieces.

His own house is another fine example of those built by well-to-do Maine sea captains, in the palmy days of our merchant marine. In the spacious rooms on both floors are beautiful woodwork and mantels, apparently elaborately carved, but the graceful ornamentation, the artistic designs, are really fashioned of " London putty," fastened on so well that they still adhere tightly, showing no traces of where they are joined to the wood. The nature of the ornamentation was not suspected until, in overhauling the attic, a box full of unused ornaments was discovered.

This house is wonderfully well built, with twelve-foot ceilings, two-foot underpinnings, two feet high, and with an eight-inch thick brick wall with an airspace between it and the outer walls of wood, thus insuring protection against the bitter cold of winter. It has a beautiful winding staircase with two landings, the rail of mahogany. Retired sea captains usually had mahogany trim in the fine houses which they built for themselves along the New England coast, and it is in seaport towns, as a rule, that the handsomest old houses are found in New England.

Another Kennebunk house, almost a hundred and forty years old, is now the Snapdragon Inn, and interesting for two reasons. It is the first double house, or double tenement, built in this town. In a sitting room is an open fireplace of good size, but looking up into the chimney, one may still see the ancient crane of the original far larger fireplace. Another noteworthy feature is the wainscoting in the dining room. It is about three feet high, and running across the entire front of the room, is made from a single plank.

The city of Portland was burned by the British under Mowatt in 1775, but the Longfellow house is old, and since it is owned by the Maine Historical Society, is open to visitors.

This, the first brick dwelling in Portland, was built in 1785 by General Peleg Wadsworth, a distinguished Revolutionary soldier, on part of a tract of land granted him by Congress for his services. Save for the addition of a third story, and the removal of the original ell it is much as when he occupied it. Here the General lived for some years, several of his children being born in the fine new house. One of his sons, Henry Wadsworth, a lieutenant in the United States Navy, was killed during the Tripoli engagement in 1804, his commander being Commodore Preble. The Preble house, built in 1807, stood next door to that of the Wadsworths until quite recently, when it was torn down.

One of Commodore Preble's sons, Scammell, served on the ship, the Constitution, in the War of 1812.

Finally, General Wadsworth removed to Hiram, and gave the Portland house to his son-in-law, Stephen Longfellow. The poet was not born here but in another recently torn down. To the Wadsworth house, however, the poet came as a baby, and here his younger brothers and sisters were born, including his sister, Anne Longfellow Pierce, who at her death willed the property to the Historical Society. Stephen Longfellow added the third story in 1815, and also built on a small vestibule entrance to the large room at the right of the main hall, which he used as his law office.

The house stands almost on a level with the sidewalk, from which it is separated by an iron fence, with large brick pillars. On the first floor are four large rooms, and a hall running through to the rear. The front room at the left, the largest in Portland when the house was built, has been the scene of many festivities, weddings, etc., and also of many funerals. Behind it and connecting, is a smaller room, originally General Peleg's bedroom, and later used by the poet as a study. Here he is said to have written his poem, *The Rainy Day*.

Across the hall from this room is the kitchen, now fitted with old time utensils. It has the great fireplace of its period.

On the third story are seven good sized rooms. The front one on the left was Henry Wadsworth Longfellow's as a young man, and it is said that he always preferred to occupy this when he returned home on visits. The rear room on the same side was occupied by him and his two brothers when children, and in this he wrote his first poems. Across the hall is the apartment of Miss Lucia Wadsworth, a devoted maiden aunt to two generations of Longfellow children.

The house has fine old mantels, that in the second floor guest room set in the old time paneled wall. Many fine pieces of old furniture, pictures, coats-of-arms, china, etc., have been left in their places, or collected from members of the family, making of the house an interesting museum.

It came into the possession of the Historical Society in 1901, with

Stairway in the house now used by the Historical Association of Portsmouth, New Hampshire. In this house John Paul Jones stayed while one of his vessels was being fitted out, during the Revolution. At that time it was a boarding house.

The stairway, with beautifully carved spindles, and some of the old wall paper still on the walls of the Moffet-Ladd house, Portsmouth, New Hampshire.

Garrison house over 252 years old, at Dover, New Hampshire. This is practically as when built. The overhang is very distinct. The chief change was made when the windows were enlarged, some 75 years ago.

The Sir William Pepperell house, Kittery Point, Maine. This mansion — of which only a portion remains — was built by the first American baronet, Sir William.

Moffet-Ladd house from the Garden, Portsmouth.

the proviso that the main rooms on the first floor be preserved practically as they were, and this has been strictly adhered to. By removing the ell, sufficient space was made in the rear for the library building, another requirement of the will.

A curious story is told of a house still standing in Wiscasset.

Now known as the Marie Antoinette house, occupied during the summer months, it is said to have been destined as a refuge for that unhappy queen. Skeptics remark that a similar legend is told about an old house in Salem, Massachusetts, and of one in still another town.

The owner who fitted out his home for this purpose, as the tale is told in Wiscasset, was one Captain Stephen Clough. Mr. Stinson of this town has discovered the registry in the Custom House there of the Captain's ship, the Sally, in 1791, just previous to the voyage which Clough is alleged to have made to France. There is said to be another registry of the Sally's clearing for France, which he has not yet been able to discover.

On this tradition has been written a novel, by a late citizen of Wiscasset, which still circulates among summer visitors. It is entitled: *The Royal Tragedy*.

This is all of the story that can be learned. If Captain Clough really took the voyage, what happened to prevent the success of the plan to aid the hapless Queen to escape seems destined to remain unknown.

Chapter XIII

I F ONE enters Connecticut from the east, before reaching Willimantic the quaint, charming village of Brooklyn may be visited, full of associations with the patriot and hero, General Israel Putnam. Although he was born in Salem, Massachusetts, he came here as a young man, and here he died.

This old time village has its Green, through which the main highroad cuts diagonally, and fine old trees are plentiful. Here are some old houses, a few new ones, and the Town Hall, while on the Green itself stand two old churches, one, the Unitarian, a typical New England "meeting house," of wood, painted white, with a tall steeple. Here, too, is a village pump, even though a modern stone canopy now protects those who come for water.

Almost opposite the pump, on the far side of another highroad which skirts the lower end of the Green, is a boulder, to which is affixed a tablet. This sets forth that "In this field, behind this stone, after the close of the French and Indian war, Colonel Israel Putnam lived with his second wife, and dispensed hospitality in the Gen. Wolfe Tavern." In the field nearby, Putnam was plowing when he received news of the Battle of Lexington. Leaving the plow in the furrough, as the familiar old story tells, he and his son, Daniel, set out, and rode the hundred miles to Cambridge in eighteen hours. There the General planned and later commanded at the Battle of Bunker Hill. As a result of his services there, Washington commissioned him Major General, the first in the Revolutionary Army, and the only one confirmed unanimously. This appointment made him second to Washington himself.

No trace of the tavern remains, but three and a half miles from the village, now as then a private residence, is the big old-fashioned farmhouse wherein he died. For a time, this was Brooklyn's Poor Farm.

South from Willimantic is quaint old Lebanon. Extending over quite a large tract, the actual village consists of a church, a Town Hall, a couple of stores with the Post Office, and a dozen or more houses around the Green, or close to this centre.

Only a few hundred yards from the Green, on a road at the side of the church, stands the fine old Governor Trumbull house, a private residence now as always, occupied by a connection of the Trumbulls and descendant of another old Connecticut family, who loves and cares for the historic dwelling with appreciative interest.

Governor Trumbull was very decidedly the big man of this section. He built the first grist mill, which still stands, painted red, beside the pond at the foot of the hill as one continues past the Green. His house, built in 1740, originally stood on the corner near the Green, but was moved a number of years ago to the present site. It had passed out of the Trumbull family then, and this fine, substantial old house was actually sold for $100.

It is one of those square, two-storied white wooden dwellings so characteristic of old New England, with a sitting room on one, a formal parlor on the other side of the entry, with its staircase winding up to the second story. Behind the sitting room is the big kitchen, with great fireplace, large brick Dutch oven, and a cupboard, in whose doors are heart-shaped openings. Big fireplaces are in the other rooms as well, and H and HL hinges abound. On the massive front door, with its old brass knocker, is a pair of fine long strap hinges.

The parlor shutters are all hand made, joined with wooden pegs, and each has its circular peephole at the top. All the woodwork is hand hewn, and the doors, including the outer front one are unique, in that the lower half has one diagonal cross piece.

In the parlor are preserved Governor Trumbull's chair, high, straight backed, solid and substantial, and that of his wife, less massive, but equally straight backed. These chairs were used by the pair in their big square church pew, and were shown in the Connecticut house at the St. Louis Exposition.

The artist, son of Governor Trumbull, was born in the Lebanon home; in its sitting room he is said to have made his first drawings in the sand which then covered the floor, and now an engraving made in London of one of his historical paintings hangs on its wall. That he had great talent is shown by a photograph here of his self-painted portrait when he had then received no instruction.

Another photograph reproduces his portrait of his parents, the original in the State House at Hartford. The young artist, still untaught when he painted it, was deeply interested in the early Dutch artists, so instead of depicting his parents as the New Englanders that they were, he dressed them and painted them as a Dutch burgher and his wife. This portrait hung in the Connecticut house at the Chicago World's Fair, for which occasion a frame was made for it of boards from the old Trumbull attic.

John Trumbull, the artist, served his country with distinction, rose to the rank of colonel in the Continental Army, and afterwards held a number of diplomatic posts in Europe. He studied painting there under Benjamin West and others, and painted portraits of many prominent men. Four of his works are in the Rotunda of the Capitol in Washington, others hang in the Metropolitan Museum, New York City, the Hartford Athenaeum, etc.

If the artist has been mentioned first, it is not with any slight to his distinguished father. Governor Trumbull was very highly thought of by his fellow patriots. He was " Washington's right hand man during the northern campaigns, and when any perplexing question or pressing demand arose, he would say: 'Let us see what Brother Jonathan says.' " [1]

After wintering at Morristown, in the spring of 1780, Washington wrote to Governor Trumbull, imploring help, and sent the letter by

[1] *Tourists' Guide to Connecticut*, Rawson W. Haddon.

special courier from his headquarters. In a very short time, Governor Trumbull gave the courier a sealed answer to carry back to the Commander-in-chief, who after reading it remarked: " If the Lord would make windows in heaven might this thing be! " The letter stated that on a certain day and hour he, Washington, would receive at Newburgh by wagon train from Hartford 200 pounds of flour, 100 pounds of beef, and another 100 pounds of pork. The Governor requested that an armed guard be sent to meet the train.

Washington did not believe that this news could be possible, but sent the required guard, and at the appointed hour they saw the wagon train approaching, with the addition of a drove of cattle from Colonel Henry Champion, the Commissary General. Animals and supplies were then taken across the Hudson in small boats.

The whole village of Lebanon was intensely patriotic, and more than five hundred men from it alone at one time served in the Revolutionary Army. Delauzun's legion of five hundred horsemen camped here for one winter, a little west of the church, and according to Barber, Rochambeau stayed here for three weeks with five regiments which Washington reviewed, spending three days in Lebanon at that time, doubtless the guest of his friend, Governor Trumbull. He found the French troops " under the most perfect discipline."

An old building in Lebanon has had a varied history. Originally an office for a busy man, Trumbull, it became the War Office of the State during the Revolution, and more than eleven hundred meetings or councils were held within its walls, for Washington, Rochambeau, Lafayette, Jefferson, Franklin, and other prominent men of the day came to Lebanon, and were entertained in the Trumbull mansion.

After the Revolution, the old War Office was several times moved, and finally was owned by seven sisters, the oldest ninety years old, when it was purchased by the Sons of the Revolution, and restored as nearly as possible to its original state. During the summer months, it is open to the public on payment of a small fee.

Lebanon claims to be the birthplace of another American painter, Ralph Earle, born in 1751, and of Elkanah Tisdale, engraver, and " an excellent miniature painter, but he has lately taken to writing poetry, which is as great an hinderance to punctuality as taking to liquor," so an early local chronicle gravely assures one.

Hartford is too modernized now to offer historic houses of interest, but a few miles north, at Windsor, will be found several.

This, the oldest town in Connecticut, originally included what are now known as East Windsor and South Windsor. Here Roger and Oliver Wolcott, both Governors of Connecticut, and Oliver Ellsworth, one of her United States Senators, were born. The Ellsworth house, which was originally the Fyler, standing on land granted to Lieutenant Fyler for his services during the Pequot War, has been taken over by the Windsor Association, filled with old furniture and other relics, and a tearoom is now open in its quaint, low-ceiled ground floor rooms.

A short distance south of Hartford is Wethersfield, another of those quaint Connecticut villages, shaded by great elms, with a Green, and a number of square, white old-fashioned houses, lining the main street.

Here is the beautiful old Webb house, once known as Hospitality Hall, because of the lavish hospitality which its owner dispensed to many notable guests, among them Washington, Rochambeau and Lafayette.

The original building on this site is believed to have been one story high, of brick, and its roof line can be seen in the ell. The present front, consisting of four rooms on each of two floors, with an attic over all, was added much later. The early part dates from the 17th, the latter from the 18th century.

The newer rooms have high ceilings, the northeast apartment on the lower floor being especially beautiful, with white wood paneling, carved doorways and mantels, and its rare example of a " Christian door " with a double barred cross in the upper portion, a diagonal one in the lower. The most conspicuous other examples of this variety are the front doors of the Old North Church, Boston. Of course, such doors, with HL hinges, were supposed to be doubly efficacious in keeping off witches.

The Webb attic has a " Witch closet," where witches were to be locked safely, although how they were to be induced to enter it, and why lock and key might be relied on to keep them there, seems hard to understand.

The southeast room on the first floor is known as the Council Room, because it is told that Washington and Rochambeau here planned together the siege of Yorktown.

During the summer months, the Society of Colonial Dames, now owning the place, fill the house with loaned old furniture, serve tea in the old garden, and visitors are then admitted on payment of a fee. The Dames have furthermore re-papered the house with reproductions of old papers, save that in the northeast upper room, occupied not once but several times by Washington, the original has remained.

Still further south, in Meriden, is the interesting house built in 1711 by Samuel Goffe, and now an inn. The great cellar with massive walls, and the old kitchen with huge fireplace are especially interesting. The regicide judges, Goffe and Whaley are said to have been hidden for several days in " Pilgromes Harbor," a swamp about a mile east of Meriden.

Several other towns in another part of the State contain interesting old houses.

One is Washington, first town in the United States to be named after the First President. Originally part of Judea Parish, which included Woodbury, Litchfield, New Milford, and other towns, it was made a separate community, and named in 1779.

The Red House, always a private residence, still stands on the Green. Built about 1772, it was occupied at the outbreak of the Revolution by two brothers, Joel and Leman Stone. The former was an ardent Loyalist, his brother an equally ardent Patriot. To express their sentiments, each resorted to interior decoration. The Patriot, on the walls of one room had vines painted, forming oval spaces, in which were alternately a deer and an eagle. The eagle's head was surrounded by thirteen stars, and above were the words: Federal Union.

The west room was decorated by the Loyalist with pictures of British war ships and similar British objects. Not a trace of these decorations has remained, but those of the Patriot are still distinct.

Not far from Washington is Litchfield, with many old houses, some left as nearly as possible in the original form, others much modernized, and summer homes for city people. Litchfield has long been popular with the latter, nor can one wonder, for it is beautifully situated on a hill, with extensive views, its broad old streets are shaded by fine elms, and a general air of peace pervades it.

Almost all of the old houses have some historic associations. In its early days, the place was surrounded by a palisade to protect it from the Indians, who roamed and hunted near Bantam, named for the Indian tribe, and lying on the road between Waterbury and Litchfield. During the Revolution, Litchfield was an important military depot.

To the Governor Wolcott house, still standing in good condition on South Street, was brought the statue of King George III, when deposed from its pedestal on Bowling Green, New York City. This gilded statue when removed, was found to be made of lead.

Oliver Wolcott, Senior, was born and spent his boyhood in Windsor, represented it in the General Assembly, and was a member of the Council. He removed to Litchfield as soon as that town was made the county seat, became a judge, representative in Congress, and was present when the Declaration of Independence was read.

It was he who suggested bringing the king's statue to Litchfield, and his grandson later used to tell how, as a boy, he remembered when it arrived, and a shed was built in the orchard to hold it temporarily. The grandson's father, Oliver, Junior, broke it up with an axe.

Most of the statue, except a part now in the possession of the New York Historical Society, was duly melted and run into bullets by Mrs. Marvin, Mr. and Mrs. Wolcott, " and besides, the ladies made 42,000 cartridges."

After the war was over, Oliver Wolcott, Senior, went to Hartford, and in 1784, with Oliver Ellsworth, Senior, and William Samuel Johnson, helped adjust the claims of the State of Connecticut against the United States. He later became Lieutenant Governor of Connecticut.

The Deming house on North Street was built by William Spratts, said to have been Connecticut's first professional architect. He studied in London, and fought in the British Navy during the Revolution, but after peace was made, remained in America, and in 1790 began work on this house for Captain Julius Deming, Assistant Commissary General in the patriot army.

On Prospect Street, is the old Congregational parsonage. Here, while pastor from 1810 to 1826, lived Lyman Beecher, " father of more brains than any other man in America," and here Harriet Beecher Stowe and Henry Ward Beecher were born.

The beautiful old house on North Street, built in 1760 by Elisha Sheldon, was turned into a tavern by his son, and during that time Washington stayed there. Again a private residence, it has been re-modeled and enlarged, though in such a way as to preserve some of its old charm, and is now a handsome summer home.

Many more stately, handsome old houses here might be enumerated, but these are the most important historically.

If one enters Connecticut by a different route, just north of New London is the village of Uncasville. In 1681, the rather friendly Indian chief, Unchas, complained of " much damage to his corn by English horses." He died about 1682, and lies beneath a monument in Indian Cemetery, Norwich. But this village is named for a later Uncas.

The indefatigable John Winthrop, Junior, settled on Fisher's Island, building what is said to have been the first English dwelling in the Pequot country. In 1643, he established iron works at Lyme, Connecticut, and Braintree, Massachusetts, bringing implements, men and stock from England. Lyme was settled before this, for the Thomas Lee house still preserved there was presumably built in 1640, but at first the meadows along the river were cultivated under difficulties, the workers coming from Saybrook for the purpose, and arming themselves with guns and pikes. John Winthrop, Junior, built himself a stone house in New London, in 1648.

New London was burned in 1781, by the British under the traitor, Benedict Arnold, and only a very few houses survived. Of these, in the

"Ancientest Burial Ground" stands as a museum, open at certain hours to the public, the little story and a half building, now painted red, in which Nathan Hale taught school before joining the Army, which was to mean his early and tragic death.

Here, too, is the Hempstead house, said to have been built about 1646. Almost behind the Huguenot house, it is so hemmed in by modern residences that it is difficult to find, although its old roof and massive chimney are visible from several streets. Of it the story is told that at the time the British arrived in New London, the family had planned a reunion, the table was set out bravely, and when the soldiers appeared, the hostess offered to give them all the good things which she had prepared for her guests if they would spare her house. The men agreed, but after they had enjoyed the food, although they kept their word, they repaired to her cellar, and drained the bottles and barrels of wine and liquors which they found stored there.

The Huguenot house, now a gift shop and tearoom, with the customary big old fireplaces and cupboards, low-ceiled, is interesting not only because it is picturesque, with its brick walls almost entirely covered by vines, which enwreath the chimneys at both ends, but because of the reason for which it was spared. It is told that a British soldier had been ill and nursed here prior to the burning of New London. In return, he was able to save the house.

Down on Bank Street, once the actual bank of the river, but now some distance away, stands the fine old Shaw mansion, since 1907 the property of the New London County Historical Society. Of stone, with a basement, two stories and attic, with dormer windows, and having a large three story wing, this is interesting for many reasons.

On its site, on Shaw's Cove, as this part of New London was then called, was a stone quarry, owned by Nathaniel Shaw, who came to the town in 1733, as Commissioner of Lands. When a ship arrived with three hundred Acadians, and these were landed in town destitute, they begged for work. Shaw set them to work in the quarry, and with the stone they dug out, they built this spacious mansion.

Mounting a flight of steps, a narrow veranda runs across the front.

A hall goes directly through to the rear, where there is still a stretch of rising ground, terminating in a small hill. This and more land constituted the original beautiful garden, where many entertainments were given by Mr. Shaw. A large drawing room with three wide windows lies in front, at the right of the entrance, and behind is a smaller dining room, while across the hall are two more large parlors. The staircase ascends to a broad hall, with windows overlooking the garden. Known as the saloon this was a favorite sitting room with the Shaw family. Bannisters and handrail of the stairs are of solid mahogany. The story goes that one of the Acadian refugees was by trade a wood carver. He had no tools when he landed, but borrowed some, and from mahogany shipped into New London, made this fine bannister, rail and newel post.

There are five former bedrooms on this second floor, all but one now filled with the Society's interesting collections. The exception is the southeast chamber always occupied by Washington on his visits to this house. Here is a great fireplace, set in a paneled wall, but unfortunately the old mantel was replaced some ninety years ago by a black and white marble one. In this room are the original carved four-post bedstead in which Washington slept, with a little table, bureau, and several other old pieces of mahogany furniture which, if not always standing in this room, were at least part of the original furnishings of the house.

The Daughters of the American Revolution hold their meetings here, and have been active in securing old furniture, etc. for it. Portraits of the Shaw family and connections hang on the walls. Here are Nathaniel and his wife, Temperance, a stern visaged old lady. Here are the sons, Thomas " who never did anything," the second Nathaniel, who was Commissioner of Supplies for the American Army and Navy during the Revolution, and his wife, Lucretia, whose name the local Daughters of the American Revolution have chosen for their chapter. She was active in nursing and feeding the three hundred American prisoners of war, landed from the British ship, Jersey, in New London harbor. They were in a dreadful condition from illness, and through her kindness in visiting them, and helping to find them lodgings, Mrs. Shaw lost her life, for, as it proved, the unfortunates were ill with typhoid fever, she caught the disease and died, thus giving her life for her country as truly as did any soldier.

Among interesting articles that may be seen in the old house are one of the earliest American naval flags; the sword of Traitor Arnold, after its handle had been broken off, the sword itself twisted out of shape, and the barrel in which was brought the powder used for burning New London, under his directions.

Across the river from New London, and originally forming part of it, is Groton. Here still stands the Ebenezer Avery house, to which the British carried a large number of wounded Americans at the time of the surrender of Fort Trumbull. The house was set on fire, but they extinguished the flames, and, leaving the wounded behind, piled in heaps on the floor, after blowing up the fort, departed. In this house next day, the wives, mothers and sisters of the wounded men found them; often the particular man sought was not found until the searcher had bathed the blood and grime from the faces of a number of others.

Here, too, in Groton stands the house in which, during the War of 1812 lived " Mother Bailey." When flannel was much needed for gun wadding, this lady donated her red flannel petticoat, thus winning fame in later days.

Saybrook is filled with old houses, but these have little of special interest attached. Down by the ferry there still stands the old Hezekiah Whittlesey house, modernized, and a private residence. Aside from the fact that it is probably at least one hundred and fifty years old, it is interesting chiefly because Whittlesey was given permission to operate a ferry here at an early date.

The four oldest settlements in Connecticut are Wethersfield, Windsor, Hartford and Saybrook, and although the date of settlement for the oldest, Windsor, is given as 1633, it is probable that some kind of huts stood on the site even earlier.

The town of Guilford, on the old Boston Post Road, offers some fascinating old houses, most of them in excellent condition, and a group of these with decidedly interesting histories. First perhaps should be mentioned the Old Stone House, now a State museum.

Built of stone, set far back from the street, on a slight elevation, from which a well kept lawn now slopes gently down, the exterior of this venerable house looks older than the interior. Authorities seem pretty generally agreed that the north end, with its great chimney, the front, and the foundations are original, built about 1639, while the eastern end, at one time consisting of five small rooms, was added later, but still at an early period. The old timbered roof was replaced for fireproof reasons by one of slate, when the house was taken over by the State. But the interior has been the subject of much discussion.

Entering the front door — the house is open daily and free to the public — one finds himself in a spacious hall, the roof two stories above, with the old chimney at one end, and a more modern, but still large one at the other. A flight of stairs sufficiently broad, and with fine bannister, leads to the rooms on the second floor, not above the large hall, but over small rear rooms. Wainscoting extends to a height of three or four feet in the lower hall or room, with plaster above, and a modern plaster ceiling on wooden cross beams. Certainly one is tempted at first sight to pronounce hall and stairway distinctly modern in design and plan, even aside from the restoration admittedly done when the State acquired the property. It resembles rather the hall of a baronial home, than the dwelling of a pioneer minister. But its date may not be thus briefly determined, for tradition says that the front part of the house was built of such unusual size and height that it might serve as a church, until another building could be erected. Tradition further asserts that the house included this large hall, and three small additional rooms only, although Mr. Whitfield's family consisted of a wife and nine children. It adds as explanation that, not long before the Whitfields came over to America, " the eldest daughters even of country squires, slept with the serving maids, the boys with the men servants, in the common hall." The statement the " the large hall could be divided, when not in use for services, by movable partitions, resembling Venetian blinds," may be taken or left, as the reader pleases. There probably was an attic, even as now, in the steep roof above the entire building.

The Reverend Henry Whitfield was born in England in 1597, and educated at Oxford. Although Barber, in 1838, in his history of Connecticut, stated that Whitfield was never separated from the Church of England, but merely brought his little flock to the New World, and founded a new congregation, others say that like the Barnstable Lothrop, he did differ with the English church authorities, resigned his charge there, and escaped probable imprisonment by emigrating. At all events, in 1639 he came, and the little group settled on land purchased from the Indians, one condition being that the latter leave the vicinity at once.

This, the oldest stone house in New England, was probably begun in the autumn of the year of Whitfield's arrival. As to this date, too, authorities differ, but as Whitfield died in 1657, and two years later, there are records of the sale, by his son, of what had been the father's residence, it at least is venerable enough.

It is believed that at some time during the 18th century, the high front portion was divided into two stories, for when the building was restored, a fireplace in one end, of more modern construction than those below, was discovered at the second story floor level. The consensus of opinion, when the house was restored, led to the present arrangement, and the only reason for leaving plaster on the walls above the wainscoting and on the ceiling was the additional expense involved in removing it and replacing it with boards.

Whitfield returned to England in 1650, and offered to sell house and lands to the town, which was too poor to buy them. Mrs. Whitfield and her son, Nathaniel, remained behind to settle up affairs, and in 1657 Whitfield died. Two years later, the town, through Deputy Governor Leete, later Governor of the New Haven colony, offered to buy it, but the offer was not accepted. Finally, Nathaniel sold it to Major Robert Thompson of London, one of five brothers who came to this country, all the others settling in Virginia. His son-in-law, Sir William Ashurst, head of a missionary society, succeeded to the property, and entailed it. Later the entail was broken, and the property sold to Wyllys Eliot, a descendant of John, that early preacher to the Indians. Then it passed to Joseph Lynchon, a loyalist, and when he left the country, in 1776, he sold it to Joseph Griffing, a patriot refugee from Long Island. The State of Connecticut has owned it since 1900, and it is now filled with documents, rare pieces of furniture, a strange old clock which used to hang in Guilford meeting house steeple, a Guilford chest, and old communion silver, the property of the Congregational Church, Guilford, etc.

Next in interest, perhaps, is the cellar in which the two regicide judges, Goffe and Whalley, were sheltered for several days. Beneath the large barn belonging to the house at the end of Broad Street may be seen this cellar, only a portion of the present one. It belonged originally to a store used by Deputy Governor Leete, and his house was close by. The house is gone, but its probable site was not far from the present none too modern one near the barn.

When the High Court of Justice met to try King Charles I, twelve were relatives of Cromwell. Of the three who came to America, Edward Whalley was his cousin, and had fought with distinction in his army, especially distinguishing himself at Naseby, in 1645. The following year, Parliament made Whalley a colonel, in consequence, and later voted him thanks, and £100 with which to buy himself two horses. Cromwell committed the king's person to his care, and he was generally regarded as a man of unimpeachable integrity.

William Goffe, Whalley's son-in-law, was an Oxford honorary Master of Arts. As a boy apprenticed to a merchant, he entered the army later, and in time Cromwell gave him command of his own old regiment, the Ironsides. Goffe was a gifted public speaker, and was thought of as a possible successor to Cromwell.

John Dixwell, the third judge, was a wealthy gentleman of Kent, a colonel, and elected to Parliament.

When Cromwell divided England into eleven military districts, each with a major general in command, Goffe and Whalley were two of these.

After Charles II came to the throne, of the judges who had signed his father's death sentence, twenty-four were dead, sixteen had fled the country, and twenty-nine were sentenced to death, one of whom, through influence was pardoned. Whalley and Goffe left England before Charles II returned and, on July 27th, 1660, arrived in Boston under the names of Richardson and Stephenson.

The two called on Governor Endicott, who received them courteously. He had no reason to do otherwise, for news of Charles' accession had not arrived. They went to Cambridge to rest.

While they were there, a fencing master came to Boston, and one day in the streets, challenged anyone to meet him. Then appeared a man in rustic dress, with a broomstick for weapon, armed with a cheese for defense, and took up the challenge. The mirth of the fencing master and bystanders may be imagined. But soon the fencer found that he had more than met his match, and when he demanded that his opponent meet him with a real sword, the latter rebuked him, saying that the fencer knew very well that he was beaten, and turned to go.

" Who can you be? " cried the fencing master. " You are either Goffe, Whalley or the devil, for there was no other man in England who could beat me."

The Act of Indemnity did not, as perhaps they had hoped, include Goffe and Whalley. A royal proclamation denounced them as traitors, so when this news arrived in Boston, they started, February 26th, 1661, for New Haven. They stopped in Hartford and called on Governor Winthrop, who received them kindly, then arrived at Davenport's house, New Haven, on March 7th. Here they stayed for two or three weeks, when again news of the king's proclamation arrived, so they made a feint of starting for New York, but went only as far as Milford, showed themselves there, and that night returned to New Haven.

Then came an order for their arrest from Governor Endicott. Two royalists, Kellond and Kirk, set out from Boston with letters to Governor Winthrop, asking his assistance. By May 11th, Winthrop was dead, and Leete, the deputy, took his place. To him the royalists went with their papers, which Leete, for his own reasons, read aloud in stentorian tones, until they begged him to desist. He told the two men that he had not seen the judges in nine weeks.

A man named Scranton told the pursuers that Mr. Davenport of New Haven was known to have " put in ten pounds worth of fresh provisions at one time into his house," so the fugitives must be there. But Leete detained the royalists, who were anxious to set out at once for New Haven. It was the Sabbath (late Saturday afternoon), and nothing could be done on that day, even when another busybody, said to have been Leete's enemy, reported that one of the Indians was missing from the town, and that a man had been seen leaving on horseback, in the direction of New Haven. The man actually rode sixteen miles in one evening to warn Mr. Jones, to whose house in New Haven Whalley and Goffe had gone.

Meanwhile, it was decided that Mr. Jones' house was hardly a safe refuge, so the two men were again moved, this time to a mill about two miles away, owned by Mr. Jones. At one time, when pursuers were near, the two hid under a low bridge, crossing a small stream, and remained there while they were being hunted. After the party had gone, they returned to the mill.

Two hours later, Governor Leete arrived in New Haven. The two royalists indignantly accused him of being but lukewarm in aiding them, murmured of treason, etc. It is said that during this time, Mrs. Allerton, second wife of the Mayflower voyager, hid them in a closet in the wainscoting, very difficult to find, and to make its existence even less suspected, she hung over the door " brassery and elegant kitchen furniture."

She let them out of her back door to go a short distance, and then return, whereupon she concealed them in this closet, and when searchers arrived, justified herself to her New England conscience by telling them that the two men had indeed been there, but had gone out of her back door.

The royalists continued their search, going as far as the New York settlement, but in vain. On their return to Boston, they were each given a farm of 250 acres by the Massachusetts Committee.

Then the two judges hid in a cave, still pointed out as the " Judges' Cave," and marked with a tablet, at West Rock, New Haven. They are said to have taken to the woods, being driven from the cave from fear of wild beasts, for panthers, wolves and bears were common enough. Finally, they took refuge in Leete's cellar in Guilford. According to an old chronicle, the Governor " had a home on the east bank of the rivulet, and a store on the bank a few rods away from his house, and under it a cellar. Here they hid for three days and three nights, and the Governor afraid to see them." Their presence must have embarrassed him, and it is said that he never saw them officially, but sent them food from his own table by a trusted maid-servant, " who long after was wont to glory in it that she had fed these heavenly men."

Finally the two returned to New Haven, and then went to Hatchet Harbor, in the present town of Woodbridge, so called because of the tale that one of the two expressed a wish for a hatchet, and promptly found one. Here they built a cabin, about a mile west of a spring, and faithful Mr. Jones from time to time sent supplies.

Then they lived in Guilford. In time, they began going about here quite openly, and Goffe preached in their dwelling, but in 1664, a commission was sent from England to fix the boundaries, and was also charged to " look for persons attainted for high treason," so they started on another search for a safe hiding place, which they found in the home of one Russell, in Hadley, Massachusetts. A closet adjoining a large chimney in the north end of this house admitted by a trapdoor or a loose board in the floor, to a dark room from which there was access to a cellar, and this room became the " Judges' chamber." Here, and in other Hadley houses they lived for nearly twelve years, evidently feeling fairly safe.

Goffe had for some time then corresponded with his wife in England, under the name of Walter Goldsmith, she writing to him as her " dear son." In 1665, Colonel Dixwell, who had fled from England to Germany, arrived. He spent several weeks in Hadley, then went to

New Haven, and under the name of James Davids, lived unmolested. Only once does he appear to have run some risk. One Sunday morning, Sir Edmund Andross happened to be in New Haven, and attended church. After service, he asked who that tall man was, and when told that his name was Davids, remarked that he was certainly a soldier, as could be told from his military bearing. Davids thought it prudent to remain away from service that evening.

Whalley was first of the three to die, and was buried behind the Russell house, in Hadley. Some say that Goffe went to Hartford, and lived there for several years in the house of Captain Joseph Bull. Others say that he continued in Hadley until his death, in 1697, only once emerging from seclusion on the day when he rallied the Hadleyites to successful resistance to an Indian attack, as already mentioned.

Davids won the esteem of his New Haven neighbors, and when a certain Mr. Ling died, was asked by the dying man to take care of his wife. This he did by marrying her shortly afterwards; she died two weeks later, and he came into " a handsome property of £900," and later married Bathsheba Howe. They had children, and he lived to be eighty-two years old, dying in 1689. Before his death, he revealed his true name and identity to a few close friends.

Four gravestones used to stand in New Haven's public square, formerly the burial ground. These were supposed to mark the burial places of the three regicide judges, one of them apparently having two stones. But whether or not one of the three was buried here, it is doubtful if the second was, and certain that the third was not.

Guilford's present State Street was originally known as Crooked Lane; Fair Street was Petticoat Lane; St. Disbrow's Lane is now Water Street, and Hog or South Lane bears the appropriate name of Whitfield Street.

On State Street is the old Comfort Starr house, a square, two-story dwelling, still with the old wide planked floors, the big fireplaces. Comfort Starr was one of the early settlers, but the house has interest also because of the two tall walnut trees in front, near the old well still to be seen on the lawn. These trees were planted by a member of the family in 1814, to mark the end of the war with England. A bit further up the street is the Lee house, built in 1763, at one time belonging to one of the Starr family. Here at the time of the Revolution lived Captain Samuel Lee, and Agnes Dickinson Lee, his courageous wife. He was a lieutenant in the Coast Guards, very prompt and energetic in dealing with the Tories, who caused much trouble during those years by their illicit trading, and constant aggressions, without actual warfare. Captain Lee was also much given to engaging in discussions on Biblical subjects.

In front of the house was a small cannon. When the British landed in 1781, on Leete's Island nearby, Captain Lee was away from home, but Mrs. Lee fired the cannon to give the alarm.

Lee's house was constantly threatened, and at the time that the Tories burned Jared Bishop's house, they came here too. Lee was again away, but they were met at the door by his intrepid wife, who informed the men, who had come to search for confiscated goods stored in an upper room, that they could not enter. When they burst in the door, three times they blew out her candle, and three times she re-lighted it. She stood in front of the door of the room in which the goods were stored, and informed the invaders of her home that they should pass only over her body. Levi Lee, her husband's young brother, and a famous fifer, then came to her aid with his gun. She seized another, and assured him that she could load as fast as he could fire. The boy fired, the ball lodged in the side of a window, and the Tories withdrew. When voices were heard again outside, young Lee once more fired, and as the chronicler adds: " A North Guilford Tory was confined to his house with rheumatism for a long time thereafter."

When the Lees' daughter, Rebecca, married Timothy Seward, Tories in town cut the ladies' dresses, and put cords across the road to interfere with, or endanger the wedding party. At one time, when the Tories had set fire to another house, Mrs. Lee marched upstairs to her attic, which at the time was filled with ammunition, and calmly closed the window, that no sparks might enter. Lead was brought to the patriotic Lees' home, and bullets molded and run there. Deserv-

The Acadian house, Guilford, Connecticut. This was built in 1670 by Acadian refugees set ashore here from British ships.

The Captain Dayton house, Bethany, Connecticut. The scene of an attack by Tories, as described in *The Stolen Boy*.

The cellar on Governor Leete's place, in which two of the regicide judges hid. Now part of a barn on the property of one of Guilford's citizens.

edly the pair are commemorated by a tablet on the front of the house, placed there by the Colonial Dames.

The Hyland or Highland house — the name was written both ways — on the Boston Road, has been restored and opened as a museum. Of wood, with a slightly overhanging upper story, and more modern leanto, the oldest part was built about 1660, the rest sixty years later. It has the usual features of its period; the great fireplaces, low ceilings, and one of the unusual old stone sinks, with one end projecting through the wall as a drain, like one found in an old Plymouth house. Aside from its age, it has no special interest save that within it Ebenezer Parmelee, grandson of the builder, George Hyland, in 1727 built the old town clock, now shown in the Old Stone or Whitfield house.

One more old dwelling on Union Street, set aslant, and facing south, was for a time open as a tearoom, but when seen in the autumn of 1926, was deserted. It was built by Acadian peasants from Grand Pre, Nova Scotia, after they were driven from their homes, and put ashore here from British ships, in 1755. The town sheltered them, and they found work.

The old house, with its steep, sloping roof, is of salt box type; two stories and an attic in front, while at the rear, " shielding the house from the storms on the north," is a small hillock, which the old roof almost touches. There are traces of an old garden, the house is grey and unpainted. The rather narrow front door is made of great planks set crosswise, and there is a massive chimney in the centre. Known now solely as the Acadian house, there seems no other history connected with it.

New Haven, originally known as Quinnipiac, and settled in 1638, unfortunately now offers few old houses of interest. Washington, in his diary of 1789 found that " it occupies a good deal of ground, but is thinly, though regularly laid out and built." One house, the oldest part built in 1671, but with various later additions, has been filled with old furniture, and is open gratis to the public. This is known as Pardee's Old Morris house.

The Pierpont house, used by the British as a hospital in 1779, survives, as does the Jones house, built in 1755, occupying the site of Governor Theophilus Eaton's mansion, both of these on Elm Street. The Governor's mansion must have been very grand for those days, since it contained large, lofty rooms, and twenty-one fireplaces, but nothing of it remains in the newer house on the old site. New Haven imported bricks from England for early building, and is said by one historian to be the only New England colony which did so, save for the 10,000 bricks imported in 1628 by Massachusetts.

About ten miles from New Haven is Bethany, with an old house having a curious story. The hero figured as such in the book of an early writer, the Reverend Israel P. Warren, who published it under the title: "Chauncy Judd, or the Stolen Boy." This book is out of print, but a re-print was published not long ago.

Mr. Dayton, at the time of the Revolution, was living on Long Island. An ardent patriot, he was obliged to leave his home there because the neighborhood was largely Tory. He brought his wife and family, furniture, rare laces, wines and a considerable sum of money to Bethany, and settled in the house ever since known by his name.

One night he was absent on business, when a band of Loyalists of the neighborhood, under the leadership of an officer in the British Army, planned to rob his house. The only occupants at the time were Mrs. Dayton and a young child, so the marauders were able to carry out their plan very easily.

After binding and gagging Mrs. Dayton, "the band found 450 pounds in gold and silver which belonged to Mr. Dayton, besides other valuable articles. What they could not conveniently carry off, they wantonly destroyed, breaking in pieces all the crockery, furniture, etc. The robbers left about two o'clock, and went to a place in Middlebury (now Gunntown), where they were secreted in a cellar by a family who were friendly to the British cause."

On their way to Gunntown, they met a boy, Chauncy Judd, "who had been to see a young lady home from a quilting party." Some of them knew young Judd, and "fearing he might discover them, and betray them in time to lead to their capture, they forced him to come along with them."

Meanwhile, as soon as the robbery was discovered, the bell of the Congregational Church, which at that time stood opposite the Dayton house, was rung loudly, to give warning to the inhabitants of Bethany, and a party soon started in pursuit of the marauders.

The latter had a good start, however, and "were secreted in several different places, sometimes houses, barns and caves." From Waterbury they made for Stratford, "where they took a whale boat and crossed over to Long Island." In the meantime, Chauncy Judd had been missed, and his family joined in the search for him.

Several times during their flight, " the robbers had become almost exhausted with carrying their booty, and realizing that their captive was a dangerous burden, decided to put him out of the way — at one time in an open field near a pool, later on in the cellar of the Wooster house, Derby. People at Derby having received information of their passing through that place, two whale boats and crews pursued them to the Island, and were fortunate enough to catch all but one just within the British Newgate. They, however, broke prison, and fled to Nova Scotia."

Mr. Haddon states that " practically all of the houses, caves, and other places where this band was in hiding during their return to Long Island are in existence." [2]

When finally rescued from his captors, the boy, Chauncy Judd, was almost dead from exhaustion and fright. With the buoyancy of youth he recovered, and a great-great-nephew is now Town Clerk in Bethany, Mr. John E. Hinman. He has, of course, heard the story of his relative's adventures many, many times, and is authority for some of these facts related.

Continuing along the old Post Road, Milford is reached. This town was settled as early as 1639, for there is a town record of 1640, when it was voted that: " the earth is the Lord's and the fullness

---

[2] *Tourists' Guide to Connecticut*, compiled by Rawson W. Haddon.

thereof: Voted that the earth is given to the Saints; Voted, we are the Saints." Surely this is unique as a town record. However, Mr. Haddon adds: " It was not the Lord, but the Indians, who gave the town to the settlers, and they did so in consideration of six coats, ten blankets, one kettle, and a number of hoes, knives, hatchets and glasses." [3]

Milford is full of old houses, some of them apparently untouched by modernizing hands, and one of these has an interesting history.

The Stephen Stowe house, built about 1680, still stands on what used to be known as Wharf Street, running down to the wharf early owned by Peter Perit. Now the street has been re-named High, and the old house is decked out in fresh paint, a private residence, and with the interior entirely modernized. Gone are the wide old fireplaces, the old doors, but the story of it still lives, although the tablet placed on the old walls to Freelove Baldwin Stowe, 1751–1806, by the local chapter of the D.A.R. seems a bit one sided. Surely her husband, Captain Stephen, should be commemorated as well.

" Two hundred American Soldiers, in a destitute, sickly and dying condition, were brought from a British Prisonship, then lying near New York, and suddenly cast upon our shore, from a British cartel ship, on the first of January, 1777.

" The inhabitants of Milford made the most charitable efforts for the relief of these suffering strangers; yet, notwithstanding all their kind ministrations, in one month forty-six died, and were buried in one common grave," as the monument in the old burying ground of Milford to Captain Stephen Stowe sets forth.

Captain Stowe and Dr. Carrington, who lived opposite, in a house long since disappeared, conducted the American soldiers to the hospital where the forty-six died.

The Pequot War ended in 1637, in Fairfield, then covering the sites of the present Greenfield, Stratfield, Bridgeport and other towns. The " plantation " was originally called Uncoa. Ludlow, Deputy Governor of Connecticut, headed the first band of settlers, who immediately organized for religious services, and built a log meeting

[3] *Tourists' Guide to Connecticut.*

house, on the site of the present Congregational church; set up stocks and a whipping post, and were ready for business.

On the west side of the Green was a pond of sufficient depth to serve as a ducking pond for suspected witches, although it would seem that these had little chance of escape, for if they sank, that was supposed to prove their innocence, but records omit to state whether or not they were pulled out before drowning. On the other hand, if they floated, they were in league with the Evil One. Two suspected witches, Mercy Disbrow and Elizabeth Clawson, were ducked here, but at least one of them is reported to have survived the ordeal, so perhaps the pond was not so deep after all, or the bystanders more merciful than records show.

The house in which Dorothy Quincy and John Hancock were married is gone, but another, built almost immediately after the destruction of the first, still stands on the old site, and is a private residence.

It is said that Dorothy Quincy positively refused to obey the command of Governor Hancock, and leave her Quincy home for Boston, when the stirring times of Lexington and the Revolution came. Instead, she watched the Battle of Lexington from the window of her room. However, it grew too dangerous even for Dorothy, so she went to Fairfield, to stay with " Auntie Burr."

The Burr house stood back from the main street, and was large, with dormer windows on the second story; quite a " baronial structure," Mrs. Perry describes it, with " wide hall, heavy oaken staircase . . . chambers with their tiled fireplaces, and heavy oak panelings." [4]

The Burrs were wealthy and cultured people. The father of this Thaddeus, was the Reverend Aaron Burr, of New Haven. Andrew Burr, a cousin, led the Connecticut regiment against Louisburg, and the noted Aaron was a cousin of Thaddeus. Always the family and many in the town of Fairfield considered this Aaron a most unjustly treated man.

To the Burr house came Dorothy, in May 1775, and here Mrs.

[4] Kate E. Perry, in *Hurd's History of Fairfield County, Conn.*

Perry says, she " rode, she sang, she boated, she feasted with the young people at the beach; she flirted with the village youths; she wrote letters . . . and every fortnight the lumbering mailcoach brought her a packet from Philadelphia, addressed in the bold handwriting of John Hancock."

We are privileged now to read bits of the ardent lover and patriot's letters, a droll mingling of the formal style of the day with more impatient and modern phrases. Thus: " pray, my Dr. use not so much Ceremony and Reservedness. Why can't you use freedom in writing. Be not afraid of me. I want Long Letters."

One letter explains that he is sending and hopes they will suit, stockings of both silk and cotton, black satin shoes, a " very pretty light hat, a neat Airy Summer Cloak, 2 caps, 1 Fann." Philadelphia was the capital then, and evidently set the fashions.

Then an extract from the church records:

" Married at the residence of Thaddeus Burr, Esq., by the Reverend Andrew Eliot, the Hon. John Hancock, President of the Continental Congress, to Miss Dorothy Quincy, daughter of Edmund Quincy of Boston, September 28, 1775."

Governor Hancock and Samuel Adams also came to Fairfield for greater safety, and were lodged and had their meals at first in seclusion. Then one day they ventured to dine with the family, but hardly had they taken their places at the table, when a farmer of the neighborhood burst into the house, asking the loan of a horse and chaise to fetch his wife, as " the British are coming! " So again the two men had to return to their hiding place, although the alarm proved false.

Later, the British, under General Tryon did appear.

Mrs. Burr, when the first rabble of soldiers broke into her house, tried to save it, even as they shouted at her: " You d — d rebel, where is your husband? " as she wrote later, " at the same time stripping me of my buckles, tearing down the curtains of my bed, breaking the frame of my dressing glass, pulling out the drawers of my table and desk." General Tryon came in person, and demanded papers. When Mrs. Burr replied that she had none, except old ones relating to the estate, he declared that those were what he wanted. However, he departed, without burning the house.

Soon a second detachment arrived, more brutal than the others, and these actually dragged her out of her house and searched her, "pulling and tearing my clothes from me in a most barbarous manner," as she wrote. She then was forced to watch her home, with all its contents, burn to the ground.

The British did not long occupy the town. Soon the Continentals were in possession. Thaddeus Burr returned, and converted a store or warehouse into a dwelling for his family.

A few weeks later, Governor Hancock again visited him, and when the two gentlemen were looking over the ruins, Hancock told his host that he must re-build, and offered to furnish all the glass for the windows provided Burr would build his new house just like Hancock's Boston home. Burr agreed, and accordingly the second house was a replica of the Hancock house in Boston. But when, in the last century, it passed into strangers' hands, the new owner re-modeled and greatly changed its appearance.

It is said that Deacon Bulkley's house, one of the five in Fairfield which the British did not burn, was spared because the naval officer in charge of the British ships in the Sound was Mrs. Bulkley's brother, although that lady was none the less herself a patriot. However, General Tryon not only promised to spare her house, but also any others that she might point out to him which she was particularly anxious to have spared. Four houses opposite on the Green were accordingly pointed out by her and escaped burning.

This favor did not, however, prevent the British soldiers from plundering her house, stripping the buckles from her shoes — buckles seem to have had a marked fascination for these soldiers — and even when they were leaving, setting fire to the house in five different places. Mrs. Bulkley was able to extinguish the flames, and when, the following Sunday, the Green was occupied not by the British tents, but by those of the Continentals, the Reverend Andrew Eliot assembled his flock in the Bulkley house for services.

The house still stands on the Green, but has been considerably re-modeled. To-day, as always, it is a private residence.

Norwalk, settled in 1649, was made a town two years later, with the decree: " Norwauke shall bee a Towne."

Miss Patten Beard, the writer, has made a study of two interesting houses which formerly stood in Norwalk, one of which remains, and has written several articles about them. She vouches for the following:

On East Avenue, the wide street which was the original main road through the town of Norwalk, there stood before the Revolution, the homestead of Governor Fitch, one of Connecticut's first Colonial governors. During the Revolution, the house was partly burned by General Tryon, who landed at Fitch's Point, and burned all houses not under Tory protection. The long rear wing of the present house belonged to the old building, and this escaped. A modern front has been built on, and a direct descendant of Governor Fitch still occupies the house.

The Yankee Doodle house, which stood until a few years ago, when unfortunately it was torn down, was the home of Captain Thomas Fitch, son of the Governor. Miss Beard firmly maintains that he was the original Yankee Doodle, and gave rise to the doggerel verses composed on the Hudson River, by the English army surgeon, Dr. Shackburg, when troops from Connecticut had gone there to reënforce the British, in fighting the French and Indians.

After this engagement, Captain Fitch returned to his home in Norwalk, and married. His father, the Governor, bought the land on which the Yankee Doodle house was built for the Captain in 1763. Miss Beard states that it has proved impossible to establish whether the original house was burned at the time that Tryon and his men visited the town, and a new one later built on the original site, or whether the first one stood until it was torn down not long ago. In any case, the house so regrettably demolished still showed many of the original wide boards; it had the sloping roof of the salt box type, a Dutch porch beneath overhanging roof, the big fireplace and Dutch oven, and could not have been built much later than the close of the Revolution, even if it were not the actual house built in 1763. The old iron latch, and a number of old hand wrought iron nails are in Miss Beard's possession.

Continuing west on the Post Road, the town of Greenwich is reached, last of the Connecticut towns where we shall pause for an old house. This, the Knapp or Putnam house, owned by the Daughters of the American Revolution, is open gratis on Monday, Thursday, Friday and Saturday to the public. Two local Greenwich historians give no authority for stating that the house was ever a tavern, although it was occupied by the Knapps. One history of Connecticut further adds: "A family of Knapps here were Tories, and there were always a great many Tories in this town."

Since the family were Tories, it does seem strange that in 1779, General Putnam should have stayed here, whether or not it was a tavern. There are three distinct stories as to his ride down the precipitous hillside only a few rods from the house, and where a boulder now marks the start of the descent.

The house was built in 1721. On the left of the entry are two rooms, separated only by an archway, and probably originally but one. The stairs mount with two turns from the little entry; narrow, steep stairs, with roughly hand carved bannisters, fastened with wooden pegs. The rear part of the house is reserved for the caretaker, but in two large bedrooms, the Daughters have assembled some fine old furniture.

Now for the versions of Putnam's famous ride down the hill.

" On the approach of Gov. Tryon to this place with a force of about fifteen hundred men, Gen. Putnam planted two iron field pieces by the meeting house, without horses or drag ropes. Having fired his cannon several times, Putnam, perceiving the dragoons (supported by the infantry) about to charge, ordered his men, about two hundred and fifty in number, to provide for their safety, and secured his own by plunging down the precipice at full trot." The British cavalry sent a volley after him (one shot piercing his hat), "but dared not follow, although two or three dragoons of Lafayette's escort to the place in 1824 performed the feat safely." [5]

[5] *Tourists' Guide to Connecticut*, compiled by Rawson D. Haddon.

If this version be preferred, there are two old cannon mounted outside the house, and with a little imagination, they may be the two referred to. Or:

General Putnam was at Horseneck. (The part of Greenwich where the Putnam house stands was in early days called Horseneck.) He went to a ball at the house of Moses Husted at Pecksland, taking a lady, the daughter of David Bush, afterwards Mrs. Rogers, on his horse behind him, as was the custom. The dance lasted so late that when he took the lady to her father's house, he remained there. The following day, a group of Tories passing, saw the General spring on his horse in Captain John Hobby's barn, and dash down the road, whereupon they pursued him. When he reached what was later called Putnam's Hill, Putnam dashed down its steep sides, and escaped them, but could not resist calling back:

" God cuss ye! When I catch ye I'll hang ye to the next tree! "

Or: Putnam was staying in the Knapp tavern, and was shaving one morning, in the little room opening from the rear parlor, when in the mirror he saw the reflection of the British redcoats, rushed from the house to the barn, which then stood close to the house, mounted his horse, and dashed away, escaping them by the precipitous ride.

One old lady tells the story with more elaboration. Putnam was upstairs when he saw the British; ran down the stairs, descended by the trap door in the entry floor, (and still to be seen there), to the cellar, from thence escaping by a back door to the barn, etc.

Chapter XIV

❧ In Old New York ❧

The adventurous Madam Knight in 1704 wrote of New Rochelle: " This is a very pretty place, well compact, and good handsome houses, clean, good and passable roads." Unfortunately, the only very old houses in the historic city have little of special interest save age. The stone house of one of the Huguenot settlers does still survive precariously, as a garage; there is on Davenport's Neck a well preserved private residence, the oldest portion probably two hundred years old, but neither of these has other historic value.

On North Avenue, however, one sufficiently old house has been and, if possible, will be preserved for years to come. Known as the Thomas Paine house, although not on the original site, it does stand on part of the old farm, confiscated by the State of New York from its Tory owner, Frederick Davoue. Later, house and farm were presented by the State to Thomas Paine, in recognition of his services. Its preservation is due to the efforts of the New Rochelle Historical Association, which conducted a successful campaign to buy the house and its present site, when the farm was divided into building lots.

This society and the Huguenot Society of Westchester County now hold their meetings here, have filled the house with interesting souvenirs of Paine and other relics, and it is open to the public.

Paine lived here until shortly before his death, when he removed to the house in Grove Street, New York City, where he died. That house or site is marked by a tablet. A monument beside the New

315

Rochelle house does not mark his burial place. He was buried on the farm, but in 1819 his body was secretly removed, and taken to England.

The entire tract on which are the cities of New Rochelle, Mount Vernon, the Pelhams, Eastchester, etc., was owned by the Pell family, who received a large grant, and purchased additional acres. About 1680, John Pell, " Lord of the Manor," sold 6,000 acres of his holdings, part of a tract purchased by the Dutch East India Company from the Siwanoy Indians, to Jacob Leisler. The latter was acting as agent for a group of French Huguenots, who, after having been driven from France by the Revocation of the Edict of Nantes, had taken refuge in Holland, England and Germany, and now wished to come to the new country. Pell's terms of purchase were " Sixteen hundred twenty and five pounds *currant* silver money of this province," also to " John Pell, Lord of the Manor, every four and twentieth day of June yearly, and every year forever if demanded, one fat calf." In the years immediately following this purchase, when the calf was duly presented on demand, a feast usually followed, the day being the festival of St. John the Baptist.

Near the old Bartow mansion, in Pelham Bay Park, is the stump of the tree beneath which the first Pell proprietor, Thomas, is said to have ratified with the Indians his purchase of land from them. The original Pell house, long since gone, is thought to have stood nearby.

At one time, in and near the modern Pelhams, there stood three Pell residences. Two are gone, but it seems probable that the house just off from Carol Place, Pelham, overlooking the new Hutchinson Parkway, was the third. The solid stone basement is thought to be the original house built in 1750 by Philip Pell, and later occupied by his grandson, Colonel David I. Pell, until his death, in 1823. Here a messenger came with news that British troops had landed on Pell's Neck, whereupon David rushed down to the river, and rowed to Eastchester to warn the Americans there encamped.

The two upper stories are said to have been added by a Scotchman, James Hay, who bought the house from the Colonel's widow. He made the old front the rear, added double bay windows, and a circular vestibule, although leaving the staircase in its original position.

Within, some fine old doors and woodwork survive, and the rooms are large and lofty. It was purchased several years ago, when falling to ruin, and the present owner has carefully repaired and restored it.

Continuing into New York City, on the east side, at 86th Street and the River is a city park. In this, stands the Gracie mansion.

Archibald Gracie, a native of Dumfries, Scotland, came to this country at the close of the Revolution. He became one of the largest ship owners of the period, married Miss Esther Rogers, and either built or greatly altered a former house into the present residence.

In 1805 Josiah Quincy dined here, and wrote: " The mansion is elegant in the modern style, and the grounds laid out with taste in gardens."

Washington Irving, in 1813 wrote of the Gracie home:

" Their countryplace was one of my strongholds last summer. It is a charming warm hearted family, and the old gentleman has the soul of a prince."

Mr. Gracie's son married the daughter of Oliver Wolcott, Secretary of the Treasury under Washington, and a grand reception was given to the young couple in this house, but during the festivities, the bride dropped dead of heart disease.

One Gracie daughter, Hester, was married here to William Beach Laurence, afterwards Governor of Rhode Island. Another daughter married James Gore King, and a third, Charles King, later President of Columbia University.

As a result of the Berlin and Milan decrees, Mr. Gracie lost over a million dollars. He was one of the largest holders of claims against France. The French Government had certain claims against the United States at this time, which they agreed to relinquish, provided our Government paid our citizens' claims against France. Although this was agreed to, Congress persistently for generations refused to make the necessary appropriations.

During the Napoleonic wars, a French vessel, chased by a British frigate, took refuge in New York harbor. The English believed the enemy ship successfully bottled up, but the French captain slipped up the East River, through Hell Gate, then a difficult feat, and actually sailed so close to the shore that one of the sailors was swept from the rigging by the branches of a great elm at Gracie's Point, as the place was then known. To these branches he fortunately managed to cling, and climbed down safely to the ground. His ship sailed on, but Charles King set out with him in a rowboat, and landed him safely on the French ship, which escaped the chagrined British through Long Island Sound. The elm tree stood on Gracie's Point until 1880.

The property came into the ownership of the City of New York in 1891. In March, 1927 it was opened to the public by the Museum of the City, which association had put the old house in order, and filled it with loaned furniture and other articles.

It is a solid, square building, with a high stone basement. The hall is unusually broad; there is a spacious drawing room at the right, a sitting room and large dining room on the left, and six upper rooms. There are many windows, the ceilings are high, for this was a summer home.

From the lower hall, one passes through an alcove to the dining room, and the door has a fanlight, the only one of its kind in the house. A curious shaped chimney wall seems to show that this corner of the house may be the old portion, and that Mr. Gracie did build on to this.

On Sixty-first Street, close to the East River, but hemmed in by modern buildings, stands the Colonel Smith house.

Colonel William Smith married the only daughter of President John Adams, Abigail, familiarly known as " Nabby." Nabby went to Europe engaged to Royall Tyler, but after meeting the handsome Colonel there, sent Tyler back his ring and letters.

After their marriage, the Smiths first lived on Long Island, and when Colonel Smith built this house for his wife it bore the name of Smith's Folly. But the Colonel lost his money in real estate speculations. Had he remained prosperous it might not have been so named.

At the time of its building, extensive grounds surrounded the house and ran down to the river. Only a small portion of these remains. Grading has left the house set high above the street level, and one mounts a flight of steps inside the stone wall which now separates it from the street. The old stone edifice is now occupied by the Colonial Dames of America. A piazza runs across the front, from which two doors open, one possibly cut at the time that the house was a tavern. Within there are signs that the great square hall was once partitioned. A side hall leads to a third door which possibly was once the front entrance.

There are large rooms on two floors, with wide fireplaces, china cupboards with HL hinges, and a broad stairway mounts with a landing.

Colonel Smith purchased the property about 1795, but there are conflicting tales as to whether the house was then standing, and merely re-modeled by him, or whether he built a new one. It has also been said that the present is the re-modeled barn, and that the house itself was destroyed by fire, but this seems doubtful.

The Smiths had been married about nine years when the Colonel purchased this property. The wedding took place in London, with a bishop officiating. Colonel Smith had served his country with distinction in the Revolution, enlisting immediately after being graduated from Princeton, and was repeatedly promoted, becoming Adjutant General under Lafayette, and in the last year of the war, Washington's aide. Washington appointed him Secretary of the first American Legation in London.

Although the building at the corner of Broad and Pearl Streets is always now known as Fraunces' Tavern, and has been one for the greater part of its existence, it was originally a fine private residence. So was Claremont on Riverside Drive, but both of these have been described in an earlier book. [1]

Alexander Hamilton's residence, The Grange, stood on a tract of sixteen acres near Tenth Avenue and 142nd Street, but was moved to its present site on Convent Avenue, near 141st Street. Hamilton bought

[1] *Early American Inns and Taverns*, the Author.

the land in 1800, and built the house for his bride. Mr. Faris gives an interesting item of the building's costs; one laborer received $424.50 for three and a half years' work. [2]

From this house Hamilton set forth for the duel with Aaron Burr, believing that he should not return alive, since he had no intention of aiming at Burr, nor did he. A letter left for his wife explained this. He had his son sleep in the same room the night before, and in the dawn bade him a fond farewell. Another son had already fallen in a duel. Burr's bullet found its mark, and Hamilton died shortly after being brought home. After the fatal duel, one of his daughters went insane.

Since then the house has been a school, parish house, and recently has again changed hands. A square wooden structure, with high basement, and broad piazza across the front, it is occupied only by a caretaker, and no one is allowed to see it.

The familiar Jumel mansion at 161st Street and Kingsbridge Road stands on land originally conveyed by New Harlem to an early settler, Hendrik Kiersen, in 1691.

According to one story, James Carroll bought the farm from the Dyckmans in 1763, for £1,000, and two years later sold it to Robert Morris, who then built the present house. But the tablet placed here by the Daughters of the American Revolution states that Morris lived here in 1758, and that is the date usually given for its building by Morris, as home for his bride, Mary Philipse of Yonkers. Morris, with Washington, was aide to General Braddock on the latter's fatal expedition, and both men courted the fair Mary.

She is said to have persuaded her husband to remain loyal to the British, and in consequence, his estates were confiscated. Washington used this house as headquarters, in 1776, and here he first met Alexander Hamilton. The next year it was occupied by General Sir Henry Clinton, and was Hessian headquarters under Baron von Knyphausen. From 1779 to 1783 the British occupied it, and are said to have paid rent. The following year it was sold by the Commissioners of Forfeiture for £2,250 to John Berrian and Isaac Ledyard.

[2] *Historic Shrines of America,* John T. Faris.

In 1787 it was a tavern, known as Calumet or Landlord Talmadge Hall. In 1810, Stephen Jumel paid £10,000 for the building and thirty-six acres. He restored the house, and added the American Colonial doors on the front and east side.

Jumel was a very wealthy merchant, and of his wife many stories are told for which there is here no space. While the Jumels lived here many distinguished men were entertained, including Talleyrand and Jerome Bonaparte. In 1815, Jumel brought back from France some of the Egyptian cypresses set out near the Tuileries, and planted them near his home. Fourteen of these remained, at least recently, on the east side of St. Nicholas Avenue, near 159th Street.

In 1833, when nearly eighty years old, Aaron Burr persuaded the widowed Madame Jumel to marry him, but they quarreled bitterly. In the last years of her life she was a miser, and dying, left a fortune of about $2,000,000. The house was sold by her heirs, and owned later by several persons, including General Earl, who named it Earlcliff. In 1901 acquired by the City of New York, it was given into the care of the Daughters of the American Revolution, and is now open to the public.

The original approach was through what is now Sylvan Place. Here, when the American soldiers were quartered on the estate, wooden huts were built for them on each side of the driveway. In what is now Speedway Park, from behind rocks and trees, the Americans aimed and fired at the Scottish Highlanders, as in boats rowed by men of the Royal Navy, they came up the little creek whose mouth may still be seen at low tide, at 173rd Street.

In the broad hall hangs a full length portrait of Madame Jumel and her adopted son and daughter. Large front rooms open on either side of the hall, and in the rear is a small apartment known as the Guard room. Here, while repairing the great fireplace, wall closets of an early period were uncovered. In this room are samples of wall paper which in 1810 Stephen Jumel sent to Paris to have reproduced. When the City bought the house, the samples were again reproduced for the drawing room.

This is a beautiful apartment at the rear, with windows on three sides. It is also known as the Court Martial room, for at the time of Washington's occupancy, several courts were held in it.

The Van Cortlandt house, also owned by the city, stands in the park of that name, on part of a grant made to Adriaen Van der Donck, first lawyer in New Netherlands. Here he built a *bouwerie* or farm house. In 1699 he gave his son-in-law, Jacobus Van Cortlandt, the house and fifty acres, to which the latter added several hundred more. The Van Cortlandts had been granted a large tract themselves.

The first of the name here came from Holland in 1638, and was a soldier in the service of the Dutch West India Company, while William Kieft was its Director General in the North American Province. Olaf Van Cortlandt married a Belgian girl with a large dowry, who had come to America with her brother, Govert Loocker-man.

Their son Stephanus born in 1643, was the first American born Mayor of New York. He received a large grant of land, was a colonel in the Kings County militia, first Judge in the Admiralty, Chancellor, Collector of Revenues, Chief Justice of the Supreme Court, a prosperous merchant, and a warden of Trinity Church.

He sailed up the Hudson as far north as Anthony's Nose, where he landed, and sent Indians of his party " a day's journey into the wilderness," establishing what has remained the northern boundary of Westchester County, and was then the northern boundary of his estate. He owned 83,000 acres, applied for a royal charter for his manor, and in 1697 it was erected into a Lordship.

Jacobus Van Cortlandt built the present house near the old farm house, employing his own carpenters; dammed Tippett's brook to make a millpond, and set up a grist and a saw mill, which later were used by both the British and Continental Armies.

In 1777–8 a picket guard of Hessians were stationed here, and nearby Emmerick's chasseurs and Tarleton's legion attacked the Stockbridge Indians, faithful allies of the Americans, and owing to superior numbers, killed many of them.

The house has been owned by the city for fifty years.

Of stone, typically Dutch in style, it resembles many old houses in Pennsylvania. Square, substantial, the Dutch front door, and another large one at the side are not the originals, but are exact replicas of the old ones, which were too battered to repair. The beautiful brass knocker is original, and one of two door keys which are shown to those especially interested, but are guarded under lock and key, since one was carried off by some dishonest visitor.

At either side of the broad hall is a large square room, one now furnished as a dining room, although the old one was in the rear. The fireplace is framed with Dutch tiles, china cupboards with shallow, slightly carved shell tops are on either side. Across the hall is the drawing room, with an elaborately carved mantel set in a paneled wall, and this apartment contains a few pieces of furniture owned by the original family. The former dining room is now fitted with glass cases as a museum. A window on the east side of the house was brought here from the old Sugar House, a warehouse on Duane Street, used by the British during the Revolution, as a prison.

Downstairs in the old Dutch kitchen are the big open fireplace, the cranes, pots and kettles of the olden days, and here once a week, tea is served by the Colonial Dames.

Upstairs on the second floor, reached by a broad staircase, with low treads, are three more rooms, the large one at the left having the entire fireplace well paneled. The rear room, the old nursery, is charmingly fitted up with an old Dutch enclosed bed, such as one sees in parts of Holland to-day, a quaint cradle, and other interesting pieces. The high open fireplace is entirely lined with Dutch tiles and above this floor is an attic with other rooms.

In the museum is treasured the old Van Cortlandt family strong box, of massive oak, carved. In this important documents of the Revolution were placed, and when the British advanced, the box was buried on the hill nearby, and they did not find it. A white post now marks the spot where it was buried.

Still further up the old Albany Post Road, now Broadway, at 204th Street, stands the only true 18th century Dutch farmhouse remaining on Manhattan Island. Built about 1783, the same family owned it until some fifty years ago, but in 1915 it was presented to the city by two descendants of this family, who placed within much of the original furniture.

Near its site in early days was a large Indian village, and arrow heads and other Indian articles used to be found in the fields that once surrounded this house. It stands high above the street, on a terrace, and part of the old fashioned garden, with brick walks, and box-bordered flower beds, surrounds it. The builder, William Dyckman, planted orchards, but these have long disappeared beneath modern buildings. Adjoining the house but not connecting with it is a small two-story one, now occupied by the caretaker, which is said to be the first farmhouse, built fifty years before the larger one.

This consists of but two good sized rooms, the lower one, kitchen and living room, with dark beams crossing the ceiling, a great fireplace, with two Dutch ovens, filling one entire side wall, while the display of old brass and copper cooking utensils of all kinds adds to the attractive interior. This part is not usually shown to visitors.

The other house of two stories, with long curving sloping roof, and piazzas across front and back, is of wood, set on a stone basement.

The parlor or best room is kept in a state of twilight, and visitors are told that this is done to convey the exact appearance of the room when visitors were received there by Mr. and Mrs. Dyckman. The quaint old chintz curtains and rug must not be faded by sunlight, so the solid wooden outer shutters with peepholes are kept as then nearly closed. Unfortunately, this interferes with proper examination of the fine old furniture here assembled. The room has a large open fireplace, and built-in china cupboard in one corner. Behind and connecting, is a small room used by the first owner as an office.

Across the hall in front is the living room, also with big fireplace, and behind this room steep and winding stairs descend to the winter kitchen. The house was built on a ledge of rock, and part of this rock remains, a ridge beneath the stairs, never having been excavated or leveled completely.

The old Van Cortlandt house, now the property of the City of New York.

The Lady Deborah Moody house, Brooklyn. Home of a most unusual woman, who steadfastly maintained her right to liberty of belief.

Upstairs on the second floor are three bedrooms, and a windowless small room or closet, while a trap door gave access to an attic above.

This house was at one time occupied by the Continental Army, and a small hut, used by some of the officers, has been reconstructed on its supposed site in the yard.

In the 16th century, James Billop is said to have risked his life to save that of Queen Elizabeth. At all events, a descendant, Christopher, was educated for the Navy by command of Charles I. By the time he was a captain, he had already had thrilling adventures, including capture by Turkish pirates, who left him stranded on a lonely spot from which he fortunately was rescued. In 1667, he came to the New Netherlands, and won favor with the English Government and the Duke of York by circumnavigating Staten Island in twenty-four hours, thus winning it for the English in accordance with a previous agreement with the Dutch that any island in New York Bay which could thus be circumnavigated in that time should belong to the English. As reward, Billop was given 1163 acres on Staten Island.

Here he built himself a house; stones and timber being taken from his own land, while for cement he sent to England, and for bricks to Belgium. In 1700, he sailed for England on the Bentley, and was never heard of again. His only child, a daughter, had married a cousin, Thomas Farmer, who changed his name to Billop, that the name might not be extinct.

Christopher Billop, their son, was a firm Tory, as were many Staten Islanders, and became a colonel in the British Army. For some reason, his New Jersey neighbors were particularly bitter against him, and most anxious to capture him. Finally, some men stationed in St. Peter's steeple, Perth Amboy, spied him going into his house. A band was dispatched, and Billop was captured, sent to Burlington, New Jersey, and imprisoned in the jail there, his hands and feet chained to the floor. Later, exchanged for a captain in the Continental Army, he was a second time taken prisoner, but released by Washington at the special request of Lord Howe. After the Battle of Long Island, Lord Howe dispatched General Sullivan, then a prisoner, to request that a committee be sent to discuss peace terms with him. This committee consisted of Benjamin Franklin, John Adams and Edward Rutledge. Lord Howe had been considered friendly towards the colonists, had met Franklin when the latter was in England representing the thirteen colonies, and had been go-between in efforts of the British Ministry to win Franklin by means of a bribe, not only of money at once, but with the promise of future rewards if that patriot would persuade the colonists to accept the terms offered. Howe believed that there would not be great difficulty in thus persuading them after the disastrous Battle of Long Island.

Morris' Memorial History of Staten Island tells that: " along the sloping lawn in front of the house, long lines of troops that formed the very flower of the British Army were drawn up, between which the distinguished commander escorted his no less distinguished guests."

The troops appear not to have in the least impressed John Adams, who described them as " looking fierce and furious and making all the grimaces and gestures and motions of the muskets."

Howe reminded the three delegates that the fact that there was a Continental Congress must not be considered, but that they three must look upon themselves as merely private individuals.

Franklin thought that it might be a conversation between friends. Adams did not care what he was considered " so long as he was not regarded as a British subject." Rutledge reminded Lord Howe that the delegates' official position was determined by the Colonies, not the Congress.

The conference ended without peace results, but at least it showed the determination of the colonists to be independent of the mother country. When the preliminary peace treaty was signed six years later, at Versailles, Franklin and Adams were again delegates.

During this conference in the Billop, now often known as the Conference House, Benjamin Franklin and John Adams were lodged in the same bedroom. Franklin opened the window as he was about to get into bed, and this brought loud protests from his roommate, but as Adams later explained, Franklin thereupon advanced so many arguments and at such length, in favor of admitting the " night air," that Adams in despair dropped off to sleep.

After the war was over, Billop removed to New Brunswick.

He is described as very tall, haughty, but also extremely kind hearted. He had slaves, and once a year always held a harvest home on his lawn, to which all the neighbors were bidden, and well entertained. He was an expert shot and horseman, and before the Revolution, Billop House was noted for hospitality.

Very strongly built, the walls and foundations are of stone, several feet thick. In the basement is the old kitchen, with a huge fireplace, before which the slaves used to gather. Two very large rooms are on the first floor, and two large and two small ones above. In the high-pitched, sloping roof is an attic with two sets of windows, one above the other, and there are great chimneys at either end.

The owner of the house at the time that it was ransacked and plundered by both Hessians and Americans was the great-grandson of the original Captain Billop.

There is a ghost room in which a murder was committed, leaving the usual indelible stains, and, furthermore, a dungeon in the cellar, with a massive iron gate bearing the marks where both American and British prisoners tried to escape. An underground passage is said to have connected this dungeon with the river.

Fenimore Cooper is thought to have laid one scene of his " Water Witch " in the Billop house.

House and twenty-five acres of land are now owned by the Borough of Richmond, an aim towards which the Staten Island Historical Society has been working for years. Memberships in the Association are being sold towards raising funds to put the old house in thorough repair, furnish it with suitable articles of the period of its palmy days, and as soon as possible, open it to the public. The grounds around will be converted into a park.

Brooklyn, the name probably derived from Breuckelen or Brocklandia, meaning moist meadows, was settled several years after New York, or New Amsterdam.

In 1614, Adrian Block in his ship, the Restless, built the year before on Manhattan, explored the East River and Long Island Sound, discovering the Connecticut, Thames and Housatonic Rivers, but returned to Holland shortly afterwards. An island in the Sound commemorates him. By 1636, white settlers established themselves in a few cabins at Gowanus. The early houses were of bark and saplings, but soon more substantial buildings replaced these; by 1656, there were already some of stone, while in 1660 brick was the fashionable building material.

The pioneers made their own tables, stools, chests and " *slaap bancke*," or sleeping benches, instead of bedsteads, on which were placed the big Dutch featherbeds. The floors for many years were sanded, and the "best" room contained a bed for guests, a round table for tea, as part of the regular furnishing.

In 1636, William Adriaense Bennet or Benet, and Jacques Bentyn bought 930 acres of land from the Indians, Bennet's being near the present Third Avenue and 28th Street, Brooklyn. Here before 1642 he built a house which was burned during the Indian fighting. When he died, his widow married Paulus Van der Beeck, "surgeon and farmer," but the son, Adrian Bennett inherited his father's farm, and lived there in a house which may have been re-built then or earlier. It was taken down some years ago, but to a house now standing on East 22nd Street, a descendant of this Adrian Bennett moved about a century ago. The exact date of its erection is not known, but it was before the American Revolution. A massive old beam in the barn, bearing deeply cut into its surface the date, 1766, is thought evidence that this was the year when it was built. Descendants in the eighth and ninth generations of the original Adrian Bennett still occupy it.

A typical old Dutch farmhouse, a story and a half high, with dormer windows enlarged by later owners, the original massive Dutch doors are still in place at each end of the big hall through the centre. A fine old knocker instead of bell announces visitors. The front door still retains the two original bull's-eyes of thick bluish glass, and enormous strap hinges are on both doors.

A long ell at the side contained the large Dutch kitchen, with great fireplace now closed, but the old thick, square beams are still uncovered, hand hewn, and with rests for firearms. Adjoining was originally a milk room, now converted into a dining room, and above is a wonderful attic, where many interesting old pieces of furniture, arms, foot-warmers, wafer irons, one bearing the name, Wynant Bennett, and date, 1780, and a drum used by another Bennett in the War of 1812, may be examined.

The main part of the house has the customary two large rooms on either side of a hall, and although they are closed now, one may still admire the size of the old fireplaces. The front room on the right, probably the " best room," has its fireplace set in a fine hand carved, paneled wall, with china cupboards on each side, and in one are still the old shelves, their fronts cut out in a pattern of curves. A charming old Grandfather clock has ticked here for a hundred years or more, and still keeps excellent time.

By some happy chance, panes of glass on which several names had been scratched with a diamond, remained until the present mistress of the house came there as a bride. She was interested in them, and asked questions. One of these inscriptions read: " Capt. Ernst Töpfer, de Diffurth, Nov. 3, 1780," but none of the family knew who he might have been. Mrs. Bennett hunted, until in old records in the City Library, of Hessian soldiers who fought with the British against us she found this and other names. In the case of Töpfer, he had been educated in France, which accounts for the use of " de," and all of the names scratched on the panes were those of officers, who might well have owned the diamonds which made the inscriptions. The panes have now been removed for safe keeping.

There is even a secret chamber, an unlighted room, opening by a small door into the attic, but if ever there was a secret staircase from it, or other means of exit, no trace now remains. Many of the long wooden pegs which hold the old roof in place may still be seen, and the rafters are good for many years yet.

What is thought to be the oldest house now standing in Greater

New York is the Schenck homestead, on what was Mill Island, although the creek which made it such has now been filled in.

Jan Martinus Schenck Van Wydeck, of a noble Holland family, came to America in 1656, and, probably in the same year, built this house still quite isolated, surrounded by trees and grass. Although but a story and a half high, unpainted and weather beaten, it contains more rooms than would be expected from the exterior. The beams for it were taken from a ship which was wrecked nearby, and their origin is evident in the ceiling of the living room, at the right of the entrance hall. Nearby used to be an old mill, and flour ground there was sold by the thrifty Dutch to the British for $1 a pound.

In this house, Captain William Marriner, of the Continental Army, captured the British Major Moncrief. Captain Schenck, although a Loyalist, contributed $15,000 to the Revolutionary cause, which makes one suspect that he was but apparently a Tory for reasons of policy. Dutch patriots on Long Island had a hard time of it then, for most of Brooklyn was in the hands of the British for the greater part of the War.

Captain Marriner had been taken prisoner by the British, and was living nearby. He frequented the same tavern as did the British officers, and when later he was exchanged, formed a plan to capture some of these officers, among them Moncrief, one of the best engineers in the British Army. Marriner with some other Americans attacked four houses in this neighborhood at once, and captured Moncrief and four or five others in the Schenck house. Another old Schenck homestead, built in 1705, stands to-day in Highland Park, Brooklyn.

In October, 1687, Captain Coert Stevens and Marities, his wife, conveyed for £385 to Johannes Lott of Jamaica, property near what is now Avenue U and 36th Street. In 1719, Johannes Lott built a small house, consisting of the present kitchen and two small rooms on the first floor, with an attic above, which may or may not then have been divided into rooms. This house was removed a hundred feet south, and added to in 1800, since when it has been little changed except for modern improvements, including some larger windows. A few of the old windows, with their quaint old glass panes, still remain.

It is a charming old place, with lawns and a big old fashioned garden, and its preservation is due to the present owner, a descendant's love for it, for she bought her brothers' and sisters' shares in the acre of land when the rest of the estate was sold for building lots. The fifth and sixth generations of Hendrik Lott's descendants now occupy it. Here are old Dutch doors with fine hinges, and several of the hand wrought iron latches. A new roof was a necessity not many years ago, so the old one, with its great wooden pegs attaching it, and broad shingles hard almost as iron, has disappeared, but the owner treasures a few of the pegs.

Hendrik I. Lott in 1792 married Mary, the daughter of Dr. John Brown, of this section, the window weights of whose house furnished bullets for the Revolutionary Army. Another old Lott homestead, considerably modernized, also survives not far away, on Avenue P.

Ten years ago, a number of the old Dutch farmhouses in New Lotts, New Utrecht and Flatlands, as different villages came to be called, might still be found, but they are rapidly disappearing. One of these, when threatened with demolition, was purchased by the city, and removed to Prospect Park. This, the old Lefferts homestead, stood at 563 Flatbush Avenue. It is now open to the public on Wednesday and Saturday afternoons, and is in charge of the Fort Greene Chapter, Daughters of the American Revolution, whose members have furnished it with fine pieces of maple and mahogany, early hooked rugs, samplers, etc.

A grant of land was made in 1660 to Lefferts Pietersen Van Hagewont, or Leffert Pieterse, as the name appears in different records. He came to New Netherlands and built a house in that year. His son Jacobus settled Bedford Corners. John, grandson of the first settler, a judge and member of the Provincial Congress, lived in the old house, which was burned by the British in 1776. He seems to have re-built it immediately, for it became headquarters for British officers, and at one time Major André was quartered here. With true French politeness, one day when two women members of the family were talking freely in his presence, believing themselves safe in doing so since they were speaking in Dutch, he interrupted to tell them that he understood what they were saying.

An old Dutch door, with massive knocker admits to a fairly broad hall, from which stairs mount with a landing, on which is a small, high window. The spindles of the bannisters though plain are very delicate.

Large double drawing rooms, connecting by a broad archway, are at the right side of the hall, and two other rooms, one furnished as a bedroom at the left. Above are four chambers with sloping ceilings, all containing old furniture, chiefly maple, with one four-post bed which belonged to the Lefferts family. A valuable possession is an autograph letter from Washington to Lord Fairfax, written during the reign of King George II.

In the vicinity of Avenue U, Van Sicklen Street and Neck Road, is a group of dwellings, several with modern additions, but none the less unmistakably old. One of these, the Stillwell house, was originally owned by the Van Sicklens. Ferdinandes, head of the family, a widower, one long past day, spied the maiden, Katrina Stillwell, milking a cow, and was instantly attracted, doubtless thinking that the strong, rosy cheeked girl would be a good worker. He proposed at once, and after taking one day to think it over, she accepted him. Later, the house passed to the Stillwells. An early member of this family, Nicholas, was known as "The Tobacco Planter." Another old Van Sicklen house stands near the corner of Avenue U and Van Sicklen Street, but its days are probably numbered.

The most venerable house in this section, as well as one of the oldest in New York, is the Lady Deborah Moody's, and even although it has been partially re-modeled, much of the original remains. Seen in spring or summer it is especially lovely, almost covered with ivy and wistaria.

It stands in a charming garden, with old fashioned flowers, fruit-bearing trees and bushes of many kinds, screened from the street by a tall hedge. A typical old story and a half Dutch dwelling, with sloping

Walt Whitman's birthplace, Huntington, Long Island.

Washington's Headquarters, Newburgh, N. Y.

The Hamilton room, Schuyler Mansion, Albany. In this room, Elizabeth Schuyler was married to Alexander Hamilton.

The Schuyler Mansion, Albany, New York.

roof extending beyond the front and rear walls, the original front wall of stone has been covered with cement, but the other three of shingles remain as they were long ago. Thirty years ago it was found necessary to make extensive repairs, and in addition to the cement covering, a cellar was dug underneath the entire house. The inner partitions on the lower floor were probably removed then, throwing the two front rooms and passage into one, most attractive, with the massive old beams, although painted, still supporting the upper story; the marks of the axe which hewed them still visible; the ceiling of broad old planks forming the floor above. Dormer windows upstairs were enlarged, modern improvements installed, but the old stairs are little changed, and the side partition wall against which they rise was left, with the old plaster, made of ground up shells, earth and straw. There are plenty of old strap hinges to delight the lover of antiques, the two big fireplaces remain, and the old woodwork is now as hard as iron, and still held in place by hand wrought iron nails or wooden pegs.

All of the old Dutch doors survive, and although the front windows are larger than originally, and it was necessary to set new frames, panes of the old glass, with its rosy and bluish coloring, were used. The cellar now beneath the house has unfortunately closed one entrance of a secret passage, which led from the small old cellar up behind one of the big chimneys to a closet on the second floor, where that end may still be seen.

Lady Deborah Moody, who is believed to have built and certainly occupied the house, was a character. Her father, Walter Dunch, Member of Parliament during the reign of Queen Elizabeth, was a sturdy champion of liberty and the rights of man. She married Sir Henry Moody of Garsden, Wiltshire, who was created a baronet by King James I in 1622. Left a widow, she went up to London, and becoming interested in new religious teachings, overstayed her leave, for at that time English subjects were allowed to be absent from their domiciles for a specified period only. Her conduct was even investigated by the Star Chamber. Five years later, she left England for America, going first to Lynn, Massachusetts, then to Salem. Here she became interested in the preachings of Roger Williams, and so fell out of favor with the Massachusetts Colony. Governor Winthrop mentions in his journal: " the Ladye Moody, a wise and anciently religious woman, being taken with the error of denying baptism to infants, was dealt with by many of the Elders and others, but, persisting still, to avoid further trouble, she removed to the Dutch."

This removal took place about 1643, and Governor Kieft of the Dutch West India Company, gave her a grant of land which, it is said, included all of Coney Island, and much of Gravesend and Sheepshead Bay. Lady Deborah, most unusual for a woman, headed the list of patentees who settled in this part of present Brooklyn. The settlement consisted of a square, surrounded by a palisade for protection against the Indians, this square being subdivided into four others, of eight lots each, with the present Neck Road, an old Indian trail, dividing them in one direction, the present Van Sicklen Street in the other. Lady Deborah received two lots inside this palisade, and on the central one of three fronting on Neck Road, built her house. Each small square had an inner yard in common for all householders, where cattle might be kept at night for greater security.

Attacks from Indians came, and since Lady Deborah's house seems to have been the most strongly built, it was used as a refuge by other settlers, forty men at one time being therein engaged in warding off the attacking Indians.

Lady Deborah soon became a personage in her new home. She was a woman of education and refinement as well as wisdom, and her advice was sought in matters of public welfare by Governor Kieft and Peter Stuyvesant, both of whom were often guests in her house. At one time, she contemplated returning to Salem, whereupon Deputy Governor Endicott wrote to Governor Winthrop, urging him not to let her return unless she retracted all her obnoxious views. Her son Henry removed to Virginia, and some chroniclers declare that she went with him, but it is believed that she is buried in the old graveyard, neglected and forlorn, almost opposite the house.

It was in this part of Brooklyn that, when Washington sent word of the approach of British troops, a boy watched for them, perched on one of the steep Dutch roofs, and in the early dawn, spied the line of red advancing, and gave the alarm. When the Battle of Long Island was fought, wounded patriots were brought to the Moody house, which was converted into a hospital, the women of the neighborhood nursing them. It is told that the occupant of the house then was as determined as Lady Deborah herself, for when a British flag was raised here at another time, she promptly hauled it down. In 1789, Washington was entertained here.

By an odd coincidence, the present owner, who has occupied the old house for five years and loves it, was born in England, not five miles from where Lady Deborah was raised. She has a collection of interesting old copper, brass and iron utensils, a kettle which once belonged to Lady Deborah, a waffle iron, branding iron, tongs, etc., all hand made, and furniture. It is thought that the place may be bought by the city or some patriotic organization for a museum, and certainly it will be a pity if it is not preserved.

Although the present owner has never seen it, there is a ghost, and she admits having heard odd sounds. Stairs sometimes creak late at night, as though beneath an invisible tread, and once, when she and her son had lingered late beside the open fire, a strange moaning was heard. The son asked what it was, but rejected possible causes proffered by his mother, and finally announced that it was the swinging back and forth of a certain upper window shutter. The next day he removed that shutter — but the sound persisted.

For a long time, the house was known around Flatbush as the Hicks homestead. Cornelia Van Sicklen married Thomas Hicks, came to it, and lived here, while the Hicks family owned it for almost all of the last century.

At 1752 — 84th Street the old Van Brunt house stands, but can hardly long survive. A story and a half high, of plastered stone, the upper part of wood, one corner has already been removed to make room for a street. Within are rather small rooms, with big old fireplaces, and there is a large high attic reached by steep, narrow stairs.

When Mrs. Van Brunt saw the British troops drawing near, her slaves crowded weeping around her. Calmly she directed them to harness horses to a cart, in which she packed them, her children, and such of her belongings as could be added, and departed for the Hendrik Lott home, one of the children losing a sunbonnet on the way, as later, an old woman, she delighted to tell. Arrived safely, Mrs. Van Brunt decided that she had made a foolish move, so packed up and returned home again. Finding her house occupied by British officers, nothing daunted, she entered, remarked that the house was hers, and since she showed her intention of remaining, the British assigned part of it to her use. (One suspects that the original was larger than what has survived.) A short time later, the lady appeared again, and demanded " my cows."

" Madam," one of the officers is said to have replied, " the cows have been requisitioned by us."

She was not to be rebuffed, and persisted in her demands until one cow was returned to her, which she is said to have kept in the cellar, lest it be again taken from her.

Long Island outside of Brooklyn was early settled, Southold and Southampton in 1640, and Easthampton eight years later. In the latter town the John Howard Payne home stands, filled with old furniture. In 1653 a party of ten families located at Oyster Bay, already known for some years by that name. All over the Island old houses of more or less historic interest survive, and among these is Walt Whitman's birthplace, at Huntington.

This house, still a private residence, was built by the poet's father in 1810. The old Dutch door still leads into the dining room, and in the attic some of the wooden pegs holding the old roof in place may still be seen, while cupboards beside the chimney are in several of the lower rooms.

In one of these first floor rooms, which has a great fireplace, it is said that the poet was born, and he lived in the house for some years. His father was a carpenter, and did his work well, for the building is in excellent preservation.

The upper hall, Schuyler Mansion, Albany. Here in old times the young people used to dance.

The lower hall.

The Memorial house, New Paltz, New York. This, the home of one of the little group of French Huguenots who settled here, is now preserved as a museum.

Wing of the very old Schenck house, Mill Island, Brooklyn. This is probably the oldest house in that Borough.

At Roslyn the house in which William Cullen Bryant lived for years, and which was built in the early days of the last century, still stands, although more modernized than the Whitman house, and in Jamaica may be seen the old home of Rufus King, one of the framers of our Constitution, twice our Minister to Great Britain, and three times United States Senator.

Since 1639, Gardiner's Island has been known by the name of the family which then acquired it. Lion Gardiner purchased it from the native Indians, his title being confirmed by James Farret, who three years earlier had been empowered by William, Earl of Stirling, " Secretary of the Kingdom of Scotland," to sell lands for him on the whole of Long Island, although at that time the Dutch were in possession there.

In a series of leaflets compiled by Morton Pennypacker, and issued in 1919 by the North Shore Bank, Oyster Bay, the following pretty story is told:

" Wyandanch, Sachem of all the Long Island tribes, had a son and daughter who were the idols of his heart. One day a party of Narragansett Indians came across (to Long Island) in their long canoes, and taking advantage of a favorable opportunity, killed the braves who happened to come within their reach, and carried away the Sachem's daughter. Fortunately, Lion Gardiner met them and rescued the maiden. Gardiner made little account of this, and it would soon have been forgotten but for the appreciation and thoughtfulness of Wyandanch. Appearing before the authorities on July 14th, 1659, he recorded a deed to a tract of land running from Huntington town across the Island, including the present village of Smithtown, and in it he declares that he gives it to Lion Gardiner in appreciation of his kindness in rescuing his daughter from the Narragansetts. Gardiner later sold a part of this property to Richard Smith, and it became known as Smithtown."

Shelter Island received its name because it served as shelter for Quakers and others, persecuted because they did not hold the same doctrines as their accusers. A house known as Sylvester Manor, well over 130 years old, stands to-day on the site of the much older home of

Nathaniel Sylvester. Bricks for the early house were shipped from Holland. Mr. Sylvester was a sugar trader with the West Indies. When Quakers came begging for a safe harbor he gave it, and it is told that George Fox preached to the Indians from the doorsteps of the manor house.

Other refugees here were Lawrence and Cassandra Southwick, after they had been imprisoned, whipped, and banished from Boston because they did not believe as the Puritans. Their son and daughter had been ordered sold into slavery, but to his everlasting credit, the captain who was directed to take them on his ship to the Virginia slave markets positively refused to do so. The parents died in the Manor. Mr. Sylvester's rent for their home is said to have been " one lamb annually if demanded."

Along the east bank of the Hudson, so many are the towns and houses with historic associations that an entire volume might be devoted to them alone. In the city of Yonkers is a house preserved now as a museum, which was built on one of the early land grants in the old Dutch days.

Adriaen Van der Donck, whose daughter married into the old Dutch Van Cortlandt family, came to New Netherlands in 1641, and was sheriff of Rensselaerwyck. He received a valuable grant of land from the Dutch West India Company for his services as peacemaker between Director Kieft and the Indians. He was a *Yoncker*, and from this title Yonkers derived its name.

Van der Donck built a mill on his grant, and in 1672, Frederick Philipse acquired a third interest in the grant, and built Manor Hall.

Philipse came to America when about twenty-seven years old, before 1653, and was Peter Stuyvesant's carpenter, probably more of a builder, and had a number of workmen under him. He lived in New Amsterdam, was a highly successful trader, and is even said to have had dealings with pirates, landing their goods in a small creek, and conveying them by an underground passage to the cellar of his Yonkers home, where he entertained lavishly.

He died in 1702, his son, Frederick, predeceased him, so it was the grandson who became known as the second Frederick Philipse. But seven years old at his grandfather's death, he was left in charge of his grandmother, and for his share of the estate received that on which stood the Manor House. He and his grandmother lived in state in New York, with seven servants to wait upon them. Later, he went to England to be educated, and there, when he grew to manhood, married Joana, daughter of Lieutenant Governor Anthony Brockholls.

This Frederick Philipse is identified with the beginning of New York's park system. In 1745, he enlarged the Manor House to three times its original size, put in wainscotings, ceilings with plaster arabesques, then coming into fashion, a broad staircase with mahogany rail, and made other improvements. In the enlarged residence, he entertained Governor Clinton, when for the first time Neperhan Harbor was used for embarking troops.

In 1750, Philipse came into ownership of the other part of the estate on which had been built the Castle, but the Manor remained the residence. He kept fifty servants, thirty of whom were white, and on his two annual rent days, feasted his tenants in feudal style. Susannah, his daughter, was married about this time to Beverly Robinson, and went to live opposite West Point.

In 1751, Frederick's son, Frederick, succeeded him. He built St. John's Church, Tarrytown. His sister Mary was courted by Washington, but preferred Roger Morris, and the young couple used to ride together, fifty miles at a time, over the estate and adjoining country. They were married in Manor Hall on January 19th, 1758, her brother giving the bride away, wearing the gold chain and jeweled badge of his ancestral office, Keeper of the Deer of the forests of Bohemia. During the festivities, according to an old tale, an Indian, wrapped in a red blanket, appeared among the guests, and addressing the bride, remarked: " Your possessions shall pass from you when the Eagle shall despoil the Lion of his mane."

Mary Philipse Morris is said to have pondered this saying often, wondering what it could mean. It certainly came true, for after the Revolution, the Morrises, like the Robinsons, Philipses, and others, being Tories, their estates were confiscated. Morris and his wife went to England, Philipse was arrested, sent a prisoner to New Rochelle, then to Hartford, Connecticut, and finally, given his parole, was allowed to live in Middletown until after the war, when he, too, went to England.

Although Tryon burned many American houses, when the Americans had an opportunity to burn Philipse Manor they spared it. At one time, it was Sir Henry Clinton's headquarters.

In 1885, the confiscated estate was bought by Cornelius P. Low, but re-sold. In 1868, the town of Yonkers bought the manor house and some adjoining land, using the house for a Town Hall, and later a City Hall until 1911. It is now a museum, open to the public.

Built of red bricks brought from Holland, and laid in Flemish bond style, the oldest part, dating from 1682, contained the south hall and staircase, the room behind this, a large and small room on the second floor, with attic above, and probably a leanto kitchen, long since removed. The old rooms are large, lofty, and have great fireplaces framed in Dutch tiles, those in the upper room with designs of Biblical subjects, chapter and verse duly given.

The early front door has a quaint, flawed, glass bull's-eye, and the stairs, mounting with a landing, although far less ornate than the newer front staircase, are unusually fine for the period. On the walls of the lower old room hang part of the collection of seventy-one portraits of prominent Americans, including three of Washington, and one of every president since, owned by the Association now in charge of the house. This lower room has the old paneled fireplace wall with cupboards on each side, and the floor planks are very broad. Deep window seats testify to the thickness of walls.

At the time when the manor house was built, the only interruption to the view southward, towards Manhattan, was old St. John's Church, near the present Geddes Square.

When the addition was made, the entrance was changed to the east side. Two great doors with massive strap hinges open here, one into the kitchen, an enormous room, possibly originally divided. The adjoining dining room is at the right of the other door, and on the other side of the wide hall, from which broad stairs with fine bannisters ascend, is the drawing room, in which Mary Philipse was married. It has a highly ornate plaster ceiling, elaborate and beautiful hand carved woodwork, the doors on either side of the beautiful paneled mantel surmounted by elaborate broken pediments. The walls here, as in the older portion, are enormously thick.

One room above, its fireplace framed by Dutch tiles, is as when built, but some years ago, rooms on the other side of the hall were thrown into one, to include the attic as well, making a large hall. This is now used as a Chapter Room by the Daughters of the American Revolution, and is decorated with replicas of early American flags, including that of Hendrik Hudson.

The Manor House at Tarrytown, formerly known as the Castle, which for the past twelve years has belonged to Miss Elsie Janis, had a life of vicissitudes. After passing to Frederick Philipse, Third, it was used as a tenant house, then after the estate was confiscated, was sold again and again, and had been empty for a year when the present owner bought it.

Here, too, one part of the house is older than the other. The first faced at right angles to the present, and comprised the rear hall and staircase, one room on either side, with perhaps part of the present library and dining room. The large drawing room, wide hall and staircase, with rooms above these, are additions, although not recent. But although different owners have made changes, they seldom undertook to break through the massive walls of plastered stone. When Miss Janis added a window to the dining room, it was a long job to remove the solid wall. The old beams supporting the ceiling of this room are left exposed, very large and square, hand hewn.

The house is charmingly placed, back from the highroad, while the brook which flows beneath the Headless Horseman's bridge runs through these grounds, where once stood an old mill, now vanished.

Near Katonah, is the old estate of John Jay, first Chief Justice of the United States Supreme Court, first Governor of the State of New

York, and our first Minister to England. Built in 1782, the house has been occupied ever since by his descendants, the present owner being his great-granddaughter. About a year ago, it was seriously damaged by fire, and valuable papers destroyed. From here, Jay went to Paris to sign the Treaty of Peace after the Revolution. The estate is part of 85,000 acres, originally owned by Madame Brett.

Fishkill is a historic old town, which in Revolutionary days extended from Fishkill landing, including the present Beacon, and back to the Connecticut border.

Although no battle was fought here, there were skirmishes, and furthermore, the Fishkill patriots rendered valuable services by preventing the union of two British forces which might have meant a different result in our struggle for independence. Night after night, watch fires burned on these mountain tops, from which Beacon Mountain takes its name.

Fenimore Cooper's story, *The Spy*, is laid in this section, and Harvey Birch is said to be an actual person, who was imprisoned in the old Dutch Reformed Church at Fishkill, taken for trial to the Wharton house, from which he escaped, and hid in a cave in the mountains.

The Wharton house, although long occupied by those of other names, has historic interest besides, for Washington often came here to confer with the patriots. Until a few years ago, a great oak tree opposite the house, to which he is said often to have tied his horse, stood, but was blown down in a severe storm. Its picture, framed in its own wood, is cherished in the Wharton house.

This stands on the outskirts of the town, on the Albany Post Road, a lawn shaded by fine trees stretching between house and highroad. It has been modernized, but the beautiful staircase at the rear of the broad hall survives, and so do a couple of the big old fireplaces. A curious iron ring which once encircled the old tree is preserved. Some say that it was used not merely for tying horses, but that runaway soldiers were fastened to it and then flogged.

For six weeks, Lafayette lay ill with typhoid fever in Fishkill.

In 1683, the Province of New York was divided into twelve counties, Dutchess being immediately north of Westchester. At this time there probably were no white settlers in this territory, but they came soon after. The first grant was to Robert Livingston, who acquired his " Manor " Rombout; then came Schuyler, who received two tracts, one of these Red Hook; the third was the Poughkeepsie grant, in 1697; the fourth that same year, to Adolphe Philipse, and another, known as the Great Partners'; in 1703 the Rhinebeck and Beekman grants followed, and in 1806 the " Little Nine Partners' ", given under the colonial Governor Bellomont.

In 1701, the statement was made by the Colonial Governor to the Lords of Trade, London, that: " Mr. Livingston has on his grant of 16 miles long and 24 miles broad, but four or five cottages, as I am told, men that live in vassalage under him, and work for him, and are too poor to be farmers, having not wherewithal to buy cattle or stock a farm. Old Frederick Philipse is said to have about 20 families of those poor people who work for him on his grant. I do not hear that Frederick Philipse's son, Colonel Schuyler, or Colonel Beekman have any tenants on their grants."

At this time, class distinctions were very sharply drawn. In the first, were the large land owners. Lawyers were in the second class, since it was considered that members of this profession often rose to high office. Merchants were in a third class, and of these it was gravely said that " many rose suddenly from the lowest ranks of the people to considerable fortunes, and chiefly in the last war, (the French and Indian War), by illicit trade." Lieutenant Governor Cadwallader Colder made this statement in 1765.

One of the original eight men to receive the " Little Nine Partners' " grant was Augustine Graham, son of James, Attorney General of the Province. He came of a very old and eminent Scottish family, claiming descent from the ancient Kings of Briton, of the third century.

In 1125, William de Graham was one of the witnesses to Holy Rood House foundation charter, and his son received a grant of lands. The older line finally became extinct, the succession passing to a younger branch, then known as lords of Montrose. James, Baron Graham, later known as the " Great Marquis," was descended from the two lines.

Born in 1612, he married Magdalene, daughter of Lord Carnegie, and a portrait of him by Van Dyck is said to hang in Warwick Castle. He espoused the cause of Charles II, but when the latter's forces were defeated, wandered through the country for three days without food, finally giving himself up to one McLeod, whom he believed his friend. The man betrayed him for " 400 bolls of meal," and Montrose was executed, bearing himself on the scaffold with such dignity that those who came to jeer averted their faces.

He left two sons, John and James. James succeeded to his father's estates, John's son, James, was the Attorney General, father of Augustine previously mentioned.

Augustine, great-grandson of the Marquis, was a major in the Westchester militia, and one of the patentees in both the Great and Little Partners' grants. His son, James, married his cousin, Arabella Morris, but neither they nor their son, Augustine, settled on the Little Nine Partners' grant. It remained for the latter's son James to do so. In what is now Pine Plains, on Lot 27, he built " the stone house under the mountains "; was the last of his name to occupy it, and dying in 1855, left no sons. A sister married a Thomas, and their descendants still occupy the old house.

Morris Graham came here in 1767, after his father's death (he was a son of Augustine, the Major), and remained for five years. He took for his share a tract two miles from Pine Plains, on the road to Poughkeepsie, and from rough stone quarried on the place, built a house 24 by 34 feet. When the Revolution broke out, he and two other Graham brothers joined the American Army, Morris becoming Colonel, and no member of the Graham family has occupied this house for over a century.

The younger James Graham's brother, Morris, built on Lot 29 a stone house in early colonial style, the first and only stone house in the town near Halcyon Lake. In 1859, this was purchased by Mr. Eno, and both he and his son used it for a tenant house. It is the only surviving house associated with the name of Graham in this locality. Morris seems to have been the most prominent of the Graham brothers, and while living here engaged extensively in cattle breeding.

Lewis, another brother, in 1773-4, built in the village of Pine Plains what was known as the Brush house. It consisted of a large hall with one room on either side, and was of oak logs, hewn square.

Of the six sons of Augustine, three of whom were early settlers in Pine Plains, Lewis was a member of the first Provincial Congress, and Morris was a delegate to the second one.

Rhinebeck and Spencer grants were settled fifteen or twenty years before Pine Plains, their settlers coming from the Palatinate. During the Revolution lead was mined here.

The Livingston grant has been mentioned. In 1673, Robert came to this country, going first to Charlestown, Massachusetts, where he remained but a year, removing to Albany, where he married Alida Schuyler, daughter of Philip and his wife, Margaret Van Schlotterbeck. In 1686 he received a grant of 160,000 acres, and built a manor house near Linlithgow on the Hudson. His son Philip succeeded him, and when the latter died in 1728 he was given a grand funeral at the manor, and also at his city residence on Broad Street, New York. " A pipe of wine was spiced for the occasion, and to each of the bearers a pair of gloves and mourning scarf and handkerchief, with a monkey spoon was given." Tenants on the manor were also given a pair of black gloves each. These monkey spoons had unusually broad flat bowls, the handle with a monkey carved on the end. The origin of this curious gift seems unknown.

Philip's son, Robert, inherited the southwestern part of the estate, and in 1730 built himself Clermont, close to the Hudson, standing on a cliff. This house, of brick and stone, was burned by the British in 1777, but re-built the following year, on exactly the same plan, and is still owned and occupied by the family. It is now the oldest Livingston house in existence, for the original manor house is gone.

Both Philip and his son Robert were deeply interested in the welfare of the Indians, and Philip built many churches. These he always painted red, and the successor to one, the old Dutch Reformed Church in Dutchess County, near the manor line, is still known as the Red Church.

The third Lord of the Manor placed iron mines and a foundry at the disposal of the Committee of Safety during the Revolution, and his five sons served in the Continental Army. Of these, four built residences on the manor estate. Oak Hill, built in 1795, belonged to Robert's son, John. The Revolution broke the entail in which until then the estate had been held.

In a biography of Francis J. Morgan, Mrs. Delafield tells that, in the autumn of 1773, Robert was talking with his son, Judge Robert, his grandson, later Chancellor Livingston, and Montgomery, husband of his granddaughter. He remarked: " This country will be independent, but I shall not live to see it, neither will you, Robert, (to his son). You, (turning to his grandson) will, and Montgomery may." Judge Robert and his father died before our independence was declared, Montgomery was killed at Quebec, but the future Chancellor did live to see the day, as his grandfather had predicted.

The Chancellor built for himself Arryl House, on the manorial estate, but now in ruins. Later, he inherited Clermont. He had made experiments with boats propelled by steam, and, while living in Paris, returned to his apartment one day and remarked to his family that he thought he had found a man who could help him with his schemes. This man was Robert Fulton, and the first steamboat to sail up the Hudson was named Clermont.

It is the Chancellor's great-grandson who now occupies this large two story and a half house, Clermont, on the Hudson.

In 1615, the Dutch re-built on Castle Island, the " chateau " or fortified trading post built at an earlier date by the French. By 1624, there were huts there, covered with bark, and a log hut, Fort Orange. Sixty odd years later, there was a " city " of one hundred houses on the site of Albany.

The first Van Rensselaer came to this country from Holland in

1660, and a village near Wykerk is still known by their name. But this man was not the original grantee.

The Amsterdam Chamber at the time of the Dutch occupation of New York, made a Patroon of any member of the company who would found a colony, and conferred on him baronial honors. He might appoint his own civil, military and judicial officers, import slaves, etc. The Patroon retained one tenth of all grain, fruits, etc., his tenant receiving a certain amount of free pasturage, but must pay one guilder for swine that ranged the woods.

Kilian Van Rensselaer was a wealthy pearl and diamond merchant of Holland, and while his patent was pending, sent three of his own ships over in 1630, and purchased from the Indians a tract of land 48 by 24 miles, extending on both sides of the Hudson. Then he died.

His son's guardian, Van Schlectenhorst, waged fierce combats for his ward's rights with Peter Stuyvesant. His estate, Beverwyck, now Albany, became separated from the rest, but Governor Andross never executed the order, and under English rule it was restored. The Patroon was authorized to levy a tax of three beavers on each house on his domain for thirty years, and afterwards to come to an agreement with the occupants. Andross' successor purchased feudal rights over the settlement, Albany, from the Patroon in 1685, and the next year the town of Albany was incorporated.

The third Van Rensselaer Patroon, Johannes, succeeded to the title in 1685, but never came to this country. His half brother, Jan Baptist, succeeded as director.

Only bronze tablets now mark the site of the first manor house, and its successor, built in 1765 by Stephen, seventh Van Rensselaer Patroon, and to which he brought his young wife, Catherine, daughter of Philip Livingston. This stood outside the present city until 1893, when it was torn down, stones and timbers being shipped to Williamstown, Massachusetts, where it was set up again for a college fraternity house.

Fort Crailo, a large red brick house of most irregular shape in the rear, stands close to the river in what is now Rensselaer, but which was known to the Dutch as Greene Bosch, because, when they sailed up the Hudson, they found this spot covered with pine trees. It was long known as Greenbush, and lands here formed part of the Van Rensselaer grant. The house was built for a member of that family, very stout and staunch, that it might serve as a fort. Holes for muskets still pierce the front wall.

It was occupied as headquarters by General Abercrombie at the time of the French and Indian wars, and here, so the story goes, while sitting on the well kerb, an English army surgeon, watching the arrival of the raw colonial troops coming to reinforce the British regulars, wrote the doggerel lines of Yankee Doodle, struck with their uncouth appearance. A secret passage was said to lead from the old well to the cellar of the house.

For a number of years, no member of the Van Rensselaer family ever lived here, and the last owner, a descendant, Mrs. Susan De Lancey Van Rensselaer, not long ago offered it to the State of New York. The offer was accepted, but as yet nothing has been done to restore it, or open it to the public. The windows and doors are boarded up, and the place looks forlorn, although the walls are solid.

Meanwhile, the Daughters of the American Revolution, with more enthusiasm than accuracy, have placed a tablet on the façade stating that it is " supposed to be the oldest building in the United States. 1642." This is the year of its erection, but of course it is by no means the oldest building.

Still surrounded by extensive, even though diminished grounds, is the old Schuyler mansion, Albany, open daily to the public. Built in 1761-2 by Philip Schuyler, Major General and member of the Confederacy Congress before the Revolution ended, it was a noted home of a noted man. The grounds originally sloped down to the Hudson River.

One enters a small circular vestibule, and then passes into a very broad hall, from which rise wide stairs, the bannisters having hand carved spindles of three different designs to each tread. The single upper window of the rear façade is on one of the two landings. Downstairs are a handsome dining room, a beautifully paneled drawing room, in which, in 1780, Elizabeth Schuyler was married to Alexander Hamilton, the room being now known as the Hamilton room. Behind is General Schuyler's office, and there are wide fireplaces, some still framed by their original Dutch tiles.

Upstairs is a very large central hall, which was used as a reception room, and here, in its gala days, the young people used to dance. Doors and woodwork throughout this mansion are very beautiful. The very large bedroom over the Hamilton room was Mrs. Schuyler's, and opposite was that occupied by General Burgoyne, while a prisoner here. So well treated was he during his captivity that afterwards he spoke of it before the British Parliament, while for souvenirs, when leaving, he presented two of the Schuyler children with his handsome paste shoe buckles. These came down as treasured relics in the family until presented to the museum, which is installed in another of the upper rooms, the fourth being the old nursery. Above all is the great attic, and on one window frame two boats were long ago cut by childish fingers, with the names: " Peter Schuyler, Jr.", and " Hannah B. Latham."

The house is filled with fine colonial furniture, and the gay paper which covers the walls of the upper hall was made from the original French blocks, 1800 pieces being required.

Philip Schuyler, builder of this mansion, was a descendant in the fourth generation from that Philip who emigrated to this country from Holland before 1650. It was the latter who took four Mohawk chiefs back to London, where they were presented by the Earl of Shrewsbury to Queen Anne.

His descendant had an adventurous life. Once, while walking in his extensive grounds, a bullet whistled close by. Stepping behind a tree, Schuyler fired in the direction from which the bullet had come, heard an Indian yell, but although he pursued him and found his tracks, the man escaped.

In 1781, there was a plot to capture him, and take him to Canada. Tories, Canadians and Indians for several days surrounded the house, and finally forced an entrance, whereupon the family took refuge in the upper rooms. In the confusion, the youngest member of the family, a baby, was left behind downstairs, and the elder sister went down to get her. She was chased by Indians, and fled upstairs again, presumably with the baby. An Indian threw his tomahawk at her, but it missed, lodging instead in the bannister rail, near the newel post, where its mark may be seen to this day.

At the time that he was plotting treason, Benedict Arnold, then a trusted officer in the Continental Army, visited Schuyler, and tried to sound him out for information which might be valuable to the British, also thinking that he might win Schuyler over, but he failed, for Schuyler was an inflexible patriot.

From the roof of this house the family listened to the guns of the Battle of Saratoga, and here they were cheered with news of the victory. At one time, Mrs. Schuyler is said to have set fire with her own hands to their wheat fields, that the British might not secure the grain.

Schuyler had a very fine library which Aaron Burr often consulted. Alexander Hamilton came to the house one day to consult Schuyler, and it is said that then he met his future wife, Schuyler's daughter Elizabeth. Her father approved the match, so they were married in the drawing room.

Washington, Lafayette, Kosciusko, Baron Steuben, Hamilton, Generals Greene and Knox were entertained in this hospitable home, when they were making a military tour of inspection.

When Burgoyne came here a prisoner, he may have anticipated harsh treatment, for he had done all possible injury to American property, burning and destroying, and had burned one of his host's own houses. With him came the Baroness Riedesel and her family, which so crowded the house that some of the General's men were compelled to sleep on mattresses on the floor, but so courteously were they treated that when he took leave, Burgoyne is said to have been quite overcome, as he expressed his thanks to his host.

The western side of the Hudson River is no less historic.

Kingston was almost entirely burned by the British, and of the five or six houses left standing, only one, the Van Steenburg house on Wall Street, was entirely undamaged. Now an attractive private residence, although modernized, it still has many of the quaint old features. A story and a half building, with the old dormer windows on the upper floor, the sloping Dutch roof, and original Dutch door, with its great brass knocker, are still in place. A hall runs through the middle of the front and old portion, which probably originally, as now, consisted of a room on either side, but an addition has been built on in the rear.

What is known as the Senate House, on Clinton Avenue, withstood British attacks, although it may have been damaged. As a tablet beside the door states: " Col. Wessel Ten Broeck, born at Westphalia in 1633, built this stone house about 1676. The Senate of the State of New York met here in 1777, and until October 16, 1777, when the British burned Kingston."

In 1775, the house was occupied by the Van der Lyns, and in it the artist was born that year. The large room at the left of the entrance is now called by his name, and contains a number of his paintings and personal belongings. He was educated at Kingston Academy, and showed such talent, that under the patronage of Aaron Burr, he went to Paris to continue his art studies.

Across the hall is another square room, filled with old furniture, utensils, documents, etc., and beyond this what is known as the Colonial dining room.

The old Dutch kitchen, with big fireplace and Dutch oven has been little altered, but many changes, not improvements, have been made in the house since it came into State ownership seventy-five years ago. The Senate Chamber occupies the entire depth of the house, with Dutch doors at the front and back. Although strap hinges, Dutch doors, hand wrought latches and locks, old glass bull's-eyes, etc., abound, and are genuine, most of them have been brought from other old houses in this section.

Upstairs are five rooms with small windows and sloping ceilings beneath the high-pitched roof.

The State will shortly build a fireproof museum behind the old house, which will then be furnished throughout as a colonial dwelling.

It is open daily and gratis to the public.

From Kingston, a couple of trains run daily, or one may travel by a fine motor road up through beautiful country to the old town of New Paltz, less visited than it merits.

On its Huguenot Street, down by the Wallkill River, a placid stream, are the oldest houses, the original settlement of what was then Paltz. Where Huguenot Street meets the River road, is a small grassed triangle, setting for a large boulder, with the following inscription:

> To the memory and in honor of
> Louis Du Bois
> Christian Deyo
> Abraham Hasbrouck
> Andre Lefevre
> Jean Hasbrouck
> Pierre Deyo
> Louis Bevier
> Anthoine Crespel
> Abraham Du Bois
> Hugo Frere
> Isaac Du Bois
> Simon Lefevre

" The New Paltz Palatinates, who driven by religious persecution from their native France, exiled for conscience' sake came to America after a sojourn in the Rhine Palatinate near Nauheim here established their homes on the banks of the Wallkill, settled the country purchased from the Indians, and granted by patent issued by Governor Edmund Andross on the 27th day of September, 1677, and nobly bore their part in the creation of our free government. The Huguenot Patriotic Historical and Monumental Association of New Paltz erects this monument the 29th day of September, 1908."

The old Bevier house, New Paltz, New York.

Photo by Patten Beard

One of the old houses at Old Hurley, New York. This town was settled before New Paltz, and to the latter the Huguenots removed.

The Abraham Hasbrouck house, New Paltz, New York. Residence of another of the twelve French Huguenots who settled here.

Home of Louis Du Bois, leader of the Huguenots who settled New Paltz.

Much history is briefly summarized in this inscription. These names are those of the twelve men associated with their leader, Louis Du Bois. There is a tradition that Abraham Hasbrouck served in the English army, and there met Andross, which accounted for the latter, when Governor, giving the little group such a large and well located tract of land. Abraham Hasbrouck's house still stands, opposite the church. Long, low, of stone, with high-pitched roof and dormer windows, it is explained that when each of his sons married, Hasbrouck built on an addition for him, and within are several floor levels. A tablet on this house gives the date of its building as 1719.

The widow of Abraham's son, Daniel, had a number of boys, and " Wyntje's kitchen " was a favorite place for holding cock fights.

Close by is the Frere house, built about 1720, and in 1732 known as the Louw house, having passed to Frere's son-in-law, Johannis Louw or Low. When the *new* stone church, long since gone, replaced one of logs, the Freres gave more than one fourth of the money needed.

The Bevier house, owned by that family from 1697 to 1735, when it passed to the Eltings, has been vacant for several years. Its old roof projects at one side over a porch, with floor perhaps once flagged, or merely of hard packed dirt. Here the old people used to sit until the bell summoned them to church opposite. A massive Dutch door opens on the porch. There was a very deep subcellar to the house, which, like the others, is built solidly of stone, the mortar of lime, loam and chopped straw.

All of these are on the right side of the street as one comes from the monument. On the left stands the Du Bois house, built in 1735, and still occupied by descendants of that name. In spite of modern changes, the original stone building with loopholes is easily distinguished, but although built to serve as a fort, it is pleasant to know that it was never needed for that purpose. The settlers bought their land from the Indians, and lived peaceably with them, although occasionally some of the nearby settlements had trouble. Some of the original settlers in Paltz first located in Old Hurley, not far away, where there are also a number of old stone houses, smaller and less pretentious than these of New Paltz. The Esopus Indians attacked Hurley in 1663, and carried off Catherine Du Bois and three children, but later they were rescued.

Ye Paltz lived in peace with the Red Men, and the old fort was the home of the leader of the community, and a social meeting place for all.

The Manorial House, behind the monument, is the only one of this group, save the Library, on the main street, located in another old house, which is open to the public. The former was the home of Jean Hasbrouck, built in 1712, quite the mansion. In 1899 it was purchased for a memorial museum, and is open every day.

The Dutch front door unfortunately is a replica, but one will instantly notice the great beam extending the entire length of the hall, running through the house. Two large rooms are on either side, and in all but one, the great beams supporting the ceiling are uncovered. Stairs in the rear are broad, but unmistakably old, their treads deeply worn; the narrow flight near the entrance was probably built in when the house was later occupied by several families. Upstairs is a great attic.

Jean Hasbrouck's large family and his slaves lived here, and the lower room at the right was a store. The Eltings also kept a store, and there was a great rivalry between the two.

The Paltz community had a unique system of government, and it is said that none other similar existed save in one South African colony, likewise founded by the French Huguenots. The results of all labor, crops, etc., went into a common store, and for fifty years, the heads of the twelve original families met in executive and legislative session, to administer affairs, make necessary regulations, appoint the building of fences, fines for stray cattle, etc. This body, known as The Dusine, had broad powers, and continued in authority until 1820. The first outsider to own property in Paltz was Jean Cottin, schoolmaster, who came in 1689, stayed seven years, then removed to Kingston, and married Catherine, widow of Louis Du Bois.

Few frame houses were built here until after the Revolution, and the oldest of these stood on Huguenot Street.

Horse racing on the meadows was popular, especially after town meeting. On the brook which empties into the Wallkill were three mills, their wheels turned by its waters, but only traces of them now remain.

Pierre Deyo, one of the original patentees, had a son, Abraham, rather a weakling. Not so his wife, Elizabeth, daughter of Isaac Du Bois. So strong was she that she was nicknamed " Captain Batche." One day when a slave was impudent, she gave him such a blow that she broke his arm, whereupon, since there was no doctor in Paltz, she sent him to Kingston to have the arm set. She stood in the mow and pitched hay the day before her son was born.

In Newburgh, the house known as Washington's Headquarters, now the property of the State, stands in a park in the heart of the city. Tradition says that a log house, built about 1709, stood on this site, but nothing definite is known of it, although the first settlement in what is now Newburgh, dates from that year.

The oldest part of the present large stone house was built not later than 1727, and some say twelve years earlier. This was the southeast corner, consisting possibly of but two rooms on the river side; that known as the room with seven doors and one window — actually there are eight doors — and the adjoining apartment which was the dining room when Washington occupied the house as headquarters, from March 31, 1782, to August 18, 1783. The hall, two rooms on the south and one on the north of it, with a broad new staircase were added in 1770. The first staircase, now closed to the public, is beside the old door, now the rear entrance.

Old Dutch doors, strap and H hinges are plentiful. An odd feature is that three great fireplaces in the oldest portion of the house, as well as one in the newer kitchen, have their hearth entirely unenclosed by chimney walls, save one at the rear.

In 1609, Hendrik Hudson sailed into Newburgh Bay, but the earliest settlers here came from the Newburg Palatinate, Germany, on a German patent, about 1708, although the patent was dated 1719.

Among these first settlers were Michael Weigand or Weigant,

Andreas Valch, Mynders and Webber. They laid out two streets, one the present South Street, south of the Glebe, the other on the western boundary of the patent, which became the Newburgh-Cohocton Turnpike.

Elsje Hasbrouck, a widow, bought a considerable amount of property in the 1750's, at " a place called Quassaick," the old name for Newburgh, and in 1754, transferred it to her son Jonathan. The land on which the Headquarters House stands was part of the original Michael Weigant grant. The Hasbroucks held it until 1850, when it was acquired by the State of New York.

They had been in this country since 1660; Abraham, as has been mentioned, being one of the original twelve families which founded New Paltz. He seems to have previously been associated with Louis Du Bois in founding Esopus, second settlement in this part of the Province, Haverstraw being the first, on a tract bought from the Indians by Balthazar De Hart, an early emigrant from Holland. De Hart took the oath of allegiance to the Duke of York, and his brother, Jacob, first settled in New Amsterdam, where he became a prosperous merchant. The Palatine settlement of Quassaick was fourth in this section, and was not known as Newburgh until 1762, when Highlands was divided into Newburgh and New Windsor.

Jonathan Hasbrouck, owner of the stone house, was a supervisor, and built a grist mill. When a Revolutionary meeting was held at Paltz, he represented Newburgh there.

It is not true that Alexander Hamilton stayed in the old house, nor did any of the Hasbrouck family occupy it while Washington lived in it. At that time, the northwest room was the parlor, the room across the hall had been a store, kept by Mrs. Hasbrouck, and the adjoining room remained the kitchen. The two small northeast rooms were Washington's bedroom and private office. These newer rooms have hand carved mantels, and more modern fireplaces than the others.

It was in this part of the State that the Tory Colonel Ettrick lived. He invited Washington to dinner at his place, Ettrick Grove, and planned treacherously to take him prisoner on that occasion. But Washington was warned. He kept his dinner engagement, but during the meal several horsemen were seen approaching. The Colonel too hastily taking them for his men, cried: " General, you are my prisoner."

But they were American, not British soldiers, and Washington calmly replied:

" I believe not, sir, but you are mine! "

Ettrick's life was spared, and he was allowed to go to Nova Scotia.

In 1858, a very old gentleman, James Donnelly, of Newburgh, wrote or dictated some reminiscences, " looking back almost eighty years." He tells that he often saw Washington, and that he " seemed different from anyone else. Mrs. Washington was short and stout. I thought she was homely, and that she never could have been a handsome woman." General Wayne he " saw almost every day. He was short and heavy set, and had red eyes," as Mr. Donnelly remembered, because as a child, he " had a cross dog that had red eyes, and the soldiers said he had Mad Anthony's eyes." He also recalls the store kept by Mrs. Hasbrouck in the room mentioned, but does not remember ever to have seen Mr. Hasbrouck. Mrs. Hasbrouck always waited on customers herself. " She was tall, thin, and dark, and laced herself up in stays. She always carried a great bunch of keys by her side, and held all her conversation with her servants in Dutch."

In 1779, Washington was at New Windsor, where huts were built for the army, and a building " to serve for public worship on Lord's day," for lodge meetings, and public assemblies. Washington's headquarters then were in the house of William Ellison, but that house is gone.

Chapter XV

⟡ New Jersey and Pennsylvania's
Historic Old Houses ⟡

THE first settlements in New Jersey were made as early as 1615, by the Dutch, and although many Swedes followed, the Dutch retained possession until 1664, when the Province passed to the Duke of York, who divided it between Lord Berkeley and Sir George Carteret.

The town of Elizabeth is very old, the first settlement having been made in the year when the English obtained control.

In August, 1665, the ship Philip brought Captain Philip Carteret, a young man of twenty-six, with a Governor's commission from Lord Berkeley and Sir George Carteret. He brought with him, beside several other English gentlemen and laborers, " sondry ffrench men that know the making of salt in ffrance."

The house still known as Carteret Arms stands on the site of a long, low tavern, built before 1728. Officers stayed there, and it is said that Lafayette once danced at an entertainment held on its lawn. Nearby was a wharf, on the south side of the river, while on the north bank stood an old mill, built by John Ogden, one of the earliest settlers here. Philip Carteret was granted the land on which the present house stands in 1675, and it was built in 1795.

After the Carterets, the Thomases owned it, then it was an orphan asylum, the Public Library, and in 1913 became the property of the Elizabeth Historical Civic Association. Before they acquired it, there had been many changes made. Four rooms and the hall between on the first floor had been thrown into one, the old stairs replaced by a modern flight in one corner. Upstairs there were less marked changes. The club is now making others, building a needed addition in the rear, but hopes soon to restore the lower floor to its original appearance, and install a replica of the old staircase.

St. John's Parsonage, now called St. John's Home, stands on Pearl Street, set well back, with a garden in front. It was built at an early date not determined, but was enlarged in 1765, and largely re-modeled in 1817, which accounts for the fairly modern appearance.

According to tradition, it was built by Andrew Hampton or Hamton, who eloped from Scotland with Lady Margaret Cummins, and a stone above the front door used to bear the initials: A.M.H. (Andrew and Margaret Hampton), and the date: 1696–7.

In 1749 it was purchased for £162 for St John's Parsonage, and in 1902 became St. John's Home.

On Rahway Avenue still stands the " old chateau," on what was the estate of Cavalier Jouet, descended from Daniel Jouet, Mayor of Angers, and Marie Cavalier, sister of Jean, the " Camisard " hero of the war of Cevennes, during the reign of Louis XIV. Camisard was, it will be recalled, the title given the Protestants in Cevennes, when they rose after the Revocation of the Edict of Nantes, because they wore shirts over their ordinary dress, as a kind of disguise. Cavalier was their chief leader, and was so successful that some concessions were granted by the French Government. He, however, went to England, and later became Governor of the Isle of Jersey.

Cavalier Jouet remained loyal to England during our Revolution, because that country had afforded his ancestors a refuge when they were compelled to leave France. His property here was therefore confiscated. His grandfather's house opposite, built before 1750, has been torn down, and modern houses built on that part of the estate, but although lots have been sold on three sides, a large tract of land still remains to the survivor.

Set well back from the street, with a lawn shaded by fine old trees, the Chateau, built in 1759, is a long brick house, with a central portion three stories in height, and large two-storied wings on either end, each with its own entrance, practically separate seven-roomed houses. The central portion has a wide hall, with a great Dutch door, its planks arranged in V's. Front and rear doors both have fan- and side-lights. The stairs run around a well directly to the third floor.

On the northwest corner of Rahway Avenue and Cherry Street, little changed outwardly, save that a filling station has been installed in what probably was a front garden, is the De Hart house, built in 1766, either by Colonel Jacob De Hart, or his son John. The latter was Member of Congress, and an early Mayor of Elizabeth. During the Revolution, the house was occupied by British soldiers. It is a typical two story stone dwelling, still with the old wooden shutters, is in good preservation, and a private residence.

On East Jersey Street are three fine old specimens. At No. 1073 stands the Boudinot house, which for fifty years has been a home for aged women. Save that the old high gambrel roof has been replaced by two modern stories, to give additional rooms, there is little changed. The unusually broad door admits to a wide hall, from which stairs with broad, low treads, fine bannisters and handrail mount in the rear. There are, as usual, the two large, high-ceiled rooms on either side, those on the left being separated merely by ornate pillars and railings. The woodwork is elaborately hand carved, with Corinthian columns in half relief, cornices, and mantels, and there are several of the plain variety of Christian doors. In the hall, the wainscot panels are very broad.

This house was built between 1750 and 1763 for Mayor Samuel Woodruff, but during the Revolution, the Hon. Elias Boudinot, Member of the Continental Congress, lived here. In 1781, the body of the Reverend James Caldwell, who was shot and killed by British soldiers, was placed on this doorstep. Boudinot, as President of the Continental Congress, signed the treaty with Great Britain which ended the Revolution, and Washington stopped here on the way to his first inauguration, when he was given a luncheon lasting over two hours. The Boudinot china, made to order in Europe, and silver specially for the family in New York, were used on this occasion. The house was sometimes known as Boxwood Hall, was occupied at one time by the Hon. James Dayton, and later was a girls' boarding school.

On the same side of the street is the Scott house, square, of brick with small front porch surmounted by a charming Palladian window. It is for sale, and since it is in the heart of the city, will probably soon be replaced by a modern apartment building. Dr. William Barnet, surgeon in the Revolutionary Army, lived here from 1763 to 1790. In 1781 it was plundered by British soldiers. After Dr. Barnet, Colonel John May, who married General Winfield Scott's daughter, lived here for many years.

On the opposite side of the street is the fine old Belcher mansion, on a lot originally owned by John Ogden, built in 1742 for Jonathan Belcher, Royal Governor of the Province from 1751 to 1757, and a patron of the College of New Jersey. Jonathan Edwards visited here. Later, William Peartree Smith, a Revolutionary patriot occupied it, and entertained Washington and Alexander Hamilton. His daughter was married here in 1778 to Elias Boudinot. While Smith occupied it, it was raided by the British. Still later, the residence of Governor Ogden, he entertained Lafayette, and in 1901, the Frenchman's grandson, Count Lafayette was a guest in the house.

Still another old house on this street is the Bonnell, built by Nathaniel Bonnell or Bunnell, one of the early settlers. For more than sixty years, it has been owned and occupied by the Barber family, descended from another early settler. A fine old brass knocker, although not originally on the door yet is rightly in place. It is one of the spread-eagle knockers designed for members of the Society of the Cincinnati, and Colonel Francis Barber, ancestor of the present residents, was one of the original members of that Society.

As first built, the house had two rooms on each side of the passage on both of its two floors, and although some changes and additions have been made, the early, plainly molded mantels remain, the staircase is the original, and outwardly the house seems little changed. The story and a half type, with dormer windows, frequently found in dwellings of its period all over the country, it is not unlike the Governor Page house in Williamsburg, Virginia.

The present occupants treasure the original deed to the land given Nathaniel Bunnell. This is the second oldest house in Elizabeth.

Oldest is Hetfield house, at the foot of Pearl Street, but in 1927 unoccupied and dilapidated. It was built in 1667, slaves doing most of the work, and living on the land. Hetfield was a weaver, and gave the land for the Presbyterian church and burial ground.

Outside the city, on the Salem road, stands the old Livingston mansion, built in 1773 for New Jersey's Revolutionary Governor. Known as Liberty Hall, it has been modernized and altered, but the marks made by angry Hessians may still be seen on the stairs.

To Liberty Hall, fifteen year old Alexander Hamilton came from the West Indies, and following Livingston's advice, attended school in Elizabeth.

The Governor's hobby was fruit growing, and he planted trees of many varieties. A shade tree planted by his daughter Susan was standing at least recently. It was she who prevented her father's correspondence with Washington and the Continental Congress from falling into the hands of the British.

Her sister Kitty probably inadvertently saved the house from destruction. One evening, a band of drunken British soldiers came and knocked. Kitty fearlessly opened the door, intending to ask what they wanted. She was dressed all in white, and at sight of her, the foremost soldier started back in terror, exclaiming:

" Good God! It is Mrs. Caldwell, whom we killed to-day."

He had evidently been of the party, if not the actual wretch who, as the murdered parson's wife spoke to them, took deliberate aim, fired, and killed her instantly, the bullet piercing her heart.

At all events, they departed, leaving Liberty Hall unharmed.

Mrs. Washington stayed here in 1789, her husband joining her the next day.

In 1790, after eloping with the schoolgirl daughter of Baron Hompasch, and leaving a wife behind him in England, Lord Bolingbroke came here and bought the place, which later returned to the original family through its purchase by the daughter of Governor Livingston's brother.

The Ford House, Morristown, preserved by the Daughters of the

American Revolution, who have filled it with old furniture, and many other articles of historic value, is open to the public. It was Washington's headquarters for a longer period than any of the other houses thus distinguished.

It was begun in 1776 by Colonel Jacob Ford, Junior, who made a compact with the Provincial Congress of New Jersey to "erect a powder mill for the making of gunpowder, an article so necessary at the present time." Congress agreed to "lend him $12,000 of the public money for one year, without interest, on his giving satisfactory security for the same to be repaid within the time of one year in good merchantable powder." This mill served through the Revolution, but Ford died in 1777.

At the time that Washington lived here, Mrs. Ford and her son Timothy lived in one side, and Washington's party, which sometimes comprised eighteen persons, were crowded into the rest of the house. Crowded they must have been, for except for the kitchen wing, there are but four rooms on each of the two floors of the house, with an attic above. The east room on the second floor was General and Mrs. Washington's bedroom, and in January, Washington complained that there was "no kitchen to cook dinner in, and almost no room for servants, for 18 of his family," (as he called the young officers of his staff) were crowded together in what had been the kitchen, "and scarce one of them able to speak for the colds they have." A log house to serve as kitchen was finally built in answer to Washington's plea.

Young Timothy Ford was ill for months in the house, from a gunshot wound, and Washington used to stop at his door every morning, on his way downstairs to breakfast, to inquire for him.

In April there arrived the Chevalier de la Luzern, Minister from France, and Don Juan de Miralles, Spanish representative, for whom, on April 24th, 1780, a grand ball was given. De Miralles, however, was so ill that at first it was proposed to cancel the ball, and although this was decided against, the Spanish gentleman died soon afterwards.

Alexander Hamilton and Tench Tilghman were members of Washington's staff here, and both courted Elizabeth Schuyler, when she came to live with her parents in the Campfield house nearby.

On the Cherry Hill Road, just outside of Princeton, is Tusculum, where lived from 1768 to 1794 Dr. John Witherspoon, President of Princeton University, and during his term of office, many students, later distinguished patriots, were graduated. Tusculum has been restored and furnished according to that period by the present owners.

Dr. Witherspoon was a member of the convention which framed the Constitution of the State of New Jersey; helped to overthrow Governor William Franklin; with Benjamin Rush and Richard Stockton signed the Declaration of Independence, and urged the President and Secretary of the Colonial Congress to do the same; he was furthermore a member of the secret committee of Congress which helped to raise money and supplies for the Continental Army, served on boards of war and finance, and in November, 1776, was chosen to confer with Washington, and together with Richard Henry Lee and John Adams was appointed on a committee the following winter, to encourage the patriots when their cause looked gloomy, and Congress was driven from Philadelphia to Baltimore.

Princeton students had early shown their patriotic feelings when, in 1774, they gathered " all the steward's winter store of tea, and having made a fire on the campus, we there burnt near a dozen pounds, tolled the bell, and made many spirited resolves."

In Princeton is charming old Morven, taking its name from a quotation from Ossian: " Sons of Morven, spread the feast, send the night away in song." Shaded by fine old trees, it once stood in a far more extensive tract, and was built by slave labor, in 1701, for John Stockton, since when it has been occupied by his descendants. Its timbers and woodwork all hand hewn, the rooms are large, and high-ceiled, the mantels, door and window frames, and paneling made from great planks, all from timber cut on the estate. There is little attempt at ornamentation, save for a curious molding with small parallel horizontal lines cut with a rasp, which molding is found around doors and windows, at the top of wainscoting, etc. The house has a square central portion with a long wing on either side, the old kitchen was in the slave quarters, a two-story building separated from the left wing by a brick paved court, across which food was carried to be served. The quarters were in two distinct parts, unconnected, one for the men, the other for the women, and still stand.

In 1844, some rather unfortunate alterations were made by Commodore Stockton. He tore out the old woodwork in the library wing, replaced the wooden mantels with modern marble ones, raised the roof, etc. The main part of the house is practically unchanged. Seven rounded archways are an unusual feature of the first floor, with its hall running through the middle, a massive door, topped by a fanlight at each end. The old window shutters are lined with iron, to help ward off Indian attacks, for the house stood on an Indian trail.

From its builder, Morven descended to his son Richard, the Signer, who married Annis, daughter of Elias Boudinot, whose house in Elizabeth has been mentioned. The present Mrs. Stockton is descended from Samuel Woodruff, for whom that house was built.

Almost every room in Morven is distinguished. On September 15th, 1789, Mrs. Annis Stockton wrote:

" I had the honour of seeing the President and Mrs. Washington. They partook of a Collation of fruit and cake, and wine and some sweetmeats which I had in readiness." This was served in the drawing room. Across the hall, in the dining room, ten Presidents and all the Governors of New Jersey except the last have been entertained. In the morning room, in the right wing, to which one descends by three steps, Dr. Benjamin Rush was married to Julia, eldest daughter of the Signer, in January, 1776, by Dr. Witherspoon. " Julia was between 16 and 17 years of age, and I was between 30 and 31," as the groom noted in his " Commonplace Book."

Dr. Witherspoon at first declined to come to Princeton, his wife refusing her consent, but Mr. Stockton went to Scotland, and succeeded in overcoming the lady's objections, so her husband came, and lent distinguished aid to American independence.

In the library, re-built in 1781, Daniel Webster wrote one of his famous speeches. The bedroom above was originally connected with the library by a secret staircase.

On the landing of the fine old staircase, Susannah Stockton stood to attract the attention of the last " royal Governor of the Jersies," (the minx!). Her twin sister Mary, handsomer, as the portraits of both show, was evidently popular with students, and not long ago a pane of glass was found in Nassau Hall on which was scratched: " Pretty Polly Stockton." " Sukey " was witty, sharp-tongued, and somewhat of a termagant. She did not marry until she was twenty-five, and then into a Canadian Tory family, the Cuthberts. Since her sympathies were all with the American patriots, it is not strange perhaps that her husband's father alluded to her as " Alexander's devil wife," while she wrote her family that the birthnight ball in her new home did not compare with a similar entertainment in Philadelphia.

The bedroom, opening on the stair landing contains an earlier Susannah's own four-post bed, recently brought back after long absence. It is beautifully carved in pineapples, pomegranates, sunflowers and Prince of Wales feathers, and bears a signed, hand woven, embroidered counterpane, for in the border is worked: " A. B. & S. S." (Annis Boudinot and Susannah Stockton, the makers).

The large bedroom above the drawing room was that of the Signer, and later occupied by Cornwallis, when he made Morven his headquarters.

Portraits of many members of the family hang on Morven's walls; of the Signer and his wife, the latter wearing appropriately a sprig of white myrtle, which she was the only one ever to grow in the old garden; in the hall hangs a full length portrait by Waugh of the Commodore, showing the gun, Peacemaker, which, fired in peace times, for a woman's whim, exploded, killing two and wounding several persons; here, too, is a painting of the Commodore and his three daughters on horseback, showing the old Arabian which lived to good old age, but broke his neck coming from the stable one day. The Commodore's old naval flag, with its slightly different red from modern ones, is also pictured with its owner, and the flag itself is treasured here, having been brought out on three recent occasions: President Cleveland's visit to Princeton, Armistice Day, and President Harding's visit.

The garden must not be passed by. Its first history recorded dates from a letter written in 1766–7, by the Signer, from London to his wife at home: " I am making you a charming collection of bulbous roots, which shall be sent as soon as the prospect of freezing on your coast is over. The last of April, I believe, will be time enough for you to put them in your sweet little flower garden, which you so fondly cultivate." He goes on to say that he intends visiting Mr. Pope's garden at Twickenham, and that he shall take with him " a gentleman who draws well to lay down the exact plan of the whole."

The garden was, it is believed, laid out in accordance with this plan, which was treasured, but presumably perished when the Hessians burned the library wing.

Some time before 1770, two young French Huguenot *emigrés* came courting Abigail and Susannah, sisters of the Signer, and brought with them chestnuts from a famous tree in the courtyard of the old fortress chateau of Loche-sur-Inde, Touraine. The great tree on the north side of Morven, and others bordering a walk sprang from these nuts.

In 1776, news of the approach of the Hessians came to Morven. Plate and valuables were hurriedly packed and buried, so well that only one box fell into enemy hands, and Mrs. Stockton and the children were sent for safety to Monmouth, Mr. Stockton escaping barely in time. The Hessians occupied the house, doing much damage, and among other things, cutting the throat of the portrait of its master. When they left, they set fire to the house, but young Richard, later known as the Duke, because of his elegant manner, was hiding with a slave in the woods, and saw this. Returning as soon as the soldiers were gone, he gave the alarm, and the flames were extinguished after damaging seriously the library wing. The boy later became a renowned lawyer.

Richard Stockton eventually was captured, put in irons, and sent to a British prison ship in New York. When finally released, he was already ill with the disease of which he died three months later. His wife, a poet, of decided literary tastes, proved herself a good manager, overseeing the estate, selling farm produce, and in time was thus able to restore the burned wing. She also maintained the reputation for hospitality.

The present mistress of Morven succeeded in obtaining a copy of Pope's original plan, and has restored the old garden accordingly, with many varieties of flowers and shrubs, some from historic European estates. Morven's 200th anniversary was celebrated by setting up in the garden a sun dial, for which Dr. Van Dyke wrote an inscription.

The 225th anniversary was charmingly celebrated indoors, with family movies, recording the best-known incidents of its early history, the actors being children, descendants of the first Stocktons, dressed in their ancestors' costumes.

Trenton was first known as Ye Falles of Ye De La Ware, and one of the first emigrants to come here was Mahlon Stacy, a Friend, from Hull, England. He built a grist mill in 1680, and called his place Ballifield, which his son Mahlon sold to William Trent. The latter came from Inverness, settled in Philadelphia, became wealthy, and removed to New Jersey. He either built or altered an early house at Ballifield, importing bricks from England, adding a tenant or lodge house, and named the place Bloomsbury. The lodge stood where now is the corner of Union and Market Streets. Later, Chief Justice Lettis Hooper owned it, and during the Revolution, Dr. William Bryant, then Colonel John Cox, Assistant Quartermaster under General Greene. Cox, another Philadelphian, owned an iron foundry which furnished ordinance for the Revolutionary Army.

Bloomsbury, on the main stage route between Philadelphia and New York, was always a favorite stop. William Penn was entertained here in the early days, and Mrs. Cox, daughter of Sir Francis Bowes, was a brilliant hostess, and the mother of six lovely daughters. Martha Washington and her distinguished husband, the Duke de la Rochefoucauld, Lafayette, and his aide, Jean Fersen, were some other guests.

Fersen was said personally to have driven Marie Antoinette from Paris to Varennes during the days immediately preceding the French Revolution. Mrs. Cox was on the reception committee when Washington visited Trenton in 1789, and two of her daughters were among the young girls who strewed his pathway with flowers as he entered the city.

The original Bloomsbury was a square brick house with large, lofty rooms, only three on each of the two stories, with a wide hall through the middle. There are large fireplaces set in paneling, mahogany doors, massive old shutters, and a graceful staircase with mahogany handrail. Many years ago, a large two-story addition was built, now occupied by the caretaker, while the rest of the house is closed, and almost all of the furniture removed, the owner not caring to live here. On the walls of the hall may still be seen the handpainted wall paper, scenes from El Dorado, unique in this country, presented by Joseph Bonaparte to a French family then occupying the house.

Some years ago, the owner tried to have it copied, but since it was impossible to reproduce the old coloring, a workman with great care, taking over a year for the task, removed it, and transferred it to canvas, which now hangs on the walls.

The place was later known as Woodland.

The Battle of Trenton raged along North Warren, then King Street, and especially near old St. Michael's, on the site of the present church. Until very recently, although so re-modeled as hardly to be recognizable, the former dwelling of Pontius Delare Stille stood on the corner, next the church, but it has now been razed, and the site is to be a community park. When in 1884 the old roof was removed, many bullets were found imbedded in it.

This house was headquarters and watch guard house for the Hessians before the battle, Colonel Rall or Rahl making his headquarters in the Stacy Potts residence opposite, home of Trenton's first City Treasurer. This disappeared more than half a century ago.

The old Douglass house, where on January 2nd, 1777, Washington met with a number of his officers, and laid plans for the battle which resulted in victory next day, still stands, but removed from its original site to the Mahlon Stacy Park. Bow Hill, residence for a time of Joseph Bonaparte, and the Hermitage, another old Trenton home, are both standing, but the latter has been greatly modernized.

Visitors to Philadelphia's Sesqui-Centennial will remember the High Street exhibit. Of the buildings carefully and accurately reproduced there none is now standing, but Philadelphia is fortunate in the number of historic houses in her midst which have been preserved.

The old home of Mordecai Lewis, later of the Fisher and Wharton families, survives on Spruce Street, but as a shabby rooming house, only the fine old classic doorway suggesting its period of distinction.

On Eighth Street, the Morris house, built in 1787, is not only in excellent condition, set in a large garden, but is still occupied by the Morris family. Its handsome paneled rooms are filled with beautiful old furniture, and it is still distinguished, although now in a street devoted to business.

The American Flag House and Betsy Ross Association, formed to raise money to preserve the building at 239 Arch Street, has accomplished this, and offered the house to the City of Philadelphia. The only difficulty now is to decide whether or not the city shall be permitted to remove it to a park site.

The old number and street were 89 Mulberry, and to this house Betsy, eighth of seventeen children, came as the twenty-one year old bride of John Ross, upholsterer, she being a good seamstress. The front room in which Betsy kept a shop is now used, somewhat altered, for displaying souvenirs, the little hall which led to the rear rooms has been removed. Behind the shop is an entry from which enclosed stairs lead to two upper floors, and another flight descends to what was a basement kitchen and dining room, now, through changes in the street level, a cellar. The doors have fine old latches and hinges. Behind this entry is the room in which Betsy made our first flag, 150 years ago, and here is a big old fireplace framed in the original blue and white Dutch tiles, with their Biblical subjects.

When the Revolution broke out, Ross went as guard for ammunition stores in Philadelphia, and was killed by an explosion when the couple had been married less than three years. Then the Continental Congress appointed a committee, Robert Morris, General Washington and George Ross, the Signer, uncle of Betsy's husband, to confer on a design for the flag. They met at Betsy's, and favored the six-pointed star, but she pointed out that that was an English star, and suggested those with five points instead, to which they agreed, and on June 14th, 1777, she made our first flag.

In her old home, the story that Betsy really sewed this first flag not in her Philadelphia home, but while visiting relatives on a farm called Success, in Cecil County, Maryland, is treated with scorn.

Soon after making the flag, Betsy married Captain Joshua Ashburn, who fought in the Continental Army, was taken prisoner to England, and died there before the war ended. The Ashburns had two children. A young fellow prisoner and friend, John Claypoole, after his release came to Philadelphia, bringing Betsy some of her husband's effects, fell in love with and married her. They had four daughters, all of whom married and lived to old age. Claypoole had been wounded in the Battle of Germantown, and when but forty-five years old was paralyzed as the result. Betsy cared for him faithfully until his death.

By marrying her second husband, an Episcopalian, Betsy, a Quaker, lost her church membership, but as Claypoole was a Friend she regained it, and was buried in the Friends' cemetery at Mount Moriah.

In Fairmount Park are six old houses, four standing on their original sites. Of the others, the Penn house, believed to be the first one of bricks in Philadelphia, built in 1682, was removed here from Letitia Street two centuries later. Only the front room into which the door opens may be seen, with no furnishings save a few old prints, and a copy of the original land grant to Penn. His house, "Solitude," now used for office purposes, is in the Zoölogical Gardens.

The other transplanted house is a large two-story and attic stone building, the Frankford country home of the Quaker Morris family. When completed, a descendant, Miss Lydia Morris, who is bearing the expense, will fill it with old furnishings, as many as possible the originals, and it will then be a city museum.

Samuel Breck built " Sweetbrier on the banks of the Schuylkill " in 1797. " It is a fine stone house, rough cast, fifty-three feet long, thirty-eight broad, and three stories high, having outbuildings of every kind suitable for elegance and comfort. The prospect consists of the river, animated by the great trade, carried on in boats of about thirty tons, drawn by horses; of a beautiful sloping lawn, terminating at the river, and nearly four hundred yards wide opposite the porticoes.

" In my family, consisting of nine or ten persons, the greatest abundance is provided; commonly seventy pounds of fresh butcher meat, poultry, and fish a week, and when I have company, nearly twice as much; the best and kindest treatment is given the servants; they are seldom visited by Mrs. Breck, and then always in a spirit of courtesy; their wages are the highest going, and are freely paid them when asked for; yet during the last twelve months we have had seven different cooks and five different waitresses. . . . I pay, for instance, to my cook one dollar and twenty-five cents a week; to my gardener, eleven dollars per month; to the waiter, ten dollars, to the farm servants, ten dollars, etc., etc. Now if they remain steady (with meat three times a day) for three or four years, they can lay by enough to purchase two or three hundred acres of land." Thus Mr. Breck wrote to a friend soon after occupying his new residence, now owned by the city, but not open to the public.

Very beautiful is what is known as the Benedict Arnold house.

Built in 1761, by John Macpherson, in the period of Philadelphia's greatest cabinet makers, John Adams, when he dined here in 1775, described it as " the most elegant seat in Pennsylvania — upon the banks of the Schuylkill."

Macpherson, a brave sailor, made a fortune by privateering in the French wars, and according to Adams, having had " an arm twice shot off," as well as having been " shot through the leg," retired to live on his fortune. These injuries did not keep him from volunteering for service with the American Navy when the Revolution came, and

Morven, home for many generations of the Stockton family, at Princeton, New Jersey.

Waynesborough, near Paoli, home of the Waynes for generations, and the birthplace of "Mad Anthony." It is still owned by the Wayne family.

his son, Captain John Macpherson, died fighting in the American assault on Quebec.

The services of the father were not accepted, and he found his means insufficient to maintain the handsome house that he had built. In 1770 he leased it for the summer for £70, including the furniture, which was a large rental in those days, the usual sum paid for houses in Philadelphia for the entire year being £100. Later, it was rented to Don Juan de Miralles, the Spanish envoy who died in the Ford house at Morristown, and in 1779 was sold to Major General Benedict Arnold, then commanding the American troops in Philadelphia, and who had been Captain John Macpherson's commander at Quebec.

Arnold, retaining a life interest, settled it as his wedding gift on lovely Peggy Shippen. Dr. Shippen, her father, had for some time refused his consent to this marriage, considering her suitor far too extravagant. He was appalled by the amount which Arnold spent in maintaining his household. Arnold took his bride to a house in town, and de Miralles had possession of Mount Pleasant as this house was called, until the death of the envoy, when the widow relinquished her lease. As Arnold's treason was discovered in the following September, while he was in command at West Point, and his wife and child were taken to the British lines in New York during that November, it will be seen how improbable it is that any of the Arnold family ever lived in Mount Pleasant.

Arnold's property was confiscated, including his life interest in Mount Pleasant, which was sold to Blair McClenachan. Edward Shippen, to protect his daughter's interests, finally purchased it the following year. During this period, the house had been leased to Major General Baron von Steuben. This brave soldier was so horrified at the discovery of Arnold's treason, that with true German peremptoriness, he forthwith announced that any and every man in his command who bore the name of Arnold must change it immediately. Later he discovered one soldier named Arnold who had not obeyed this dictum. Demanding to know what he meant by this, the soldier replied that he would be more than willing to give up the name of

Arnold if he might take that of a brave hero and soldier. Asked what that name was, the soldier replied: " Von Steuben." The Baron gave his consent, and the soldier adopted the name. After the war was over, he kept a tavern under his adopted name for years in New England. The Baron received a pension of $2,000 a year from the State of New York, for his services in aid of our independence.

Whether Von Steuben lived in the house is uncertain, for about the time that he leased it, he left for Yorktown. Mrs. Arnold and her children returned to America in 1785, to visit her family, and possibly then occupied the house which her father had purchased. She did not find life in America comfortable, for people had neither forgotten nor forgiven her husband's treachery, so she returned to England, the house was sold in 1792 to General Jonathan Williams, and remained in his family until 1853.

Fairmount Park included the house in its boundaries in 1868, and for a time it was known as the " Dairy."

In 1923 restoration was begun by the park commissioners. As far as possible to discover, the original colors of paint have been used, a garden has been re-planted, and the entire house put in perfect condition, while valuable furniture of the period of its building has been loaned and placed in the old rooms.

It is of brick, with hipped roof, two stories in height, with basement and attic. A wide hall runs through the house, opening on a porch from which there is a charming view of the river. Downstairs is a large drawing room occupying an entire side of the house, with two big fireplaces, the mantels surmounted by immense panels cut from a single plank, the framework elaborately carved. Across the hall is the dining room, and behind this are the stairs, and a passage leading to the basement.

These stairs lead to a wide upper hall, lighted by beautiful Palladian windows at front and rear, and there are three large bedrooms. Over the dining room, the guest chamber, with fine old cupboards on either side of the great fireplace, was once occupied by Benjamin Franklin, and a table with his initials now stands here. From the walls of this room when the house was being restored, it was necessary to remove thirty-seven coats of paint before what seemed the first one was discovered, and copied for the present color scheme of ashes of roses and cream.

There are here none of the rooms paneled from floor to ceiling found in some old mansions. An unusual feature is supplied for harmony; namely, false doors in the hall, directly opposite the two real ones opening into the drawing room, and again in the upper hall.

One could spend a long time examining the beautiful furniture, silver and china assembled here, much of it with personal as well as historic interest. The house was fitted throughout with Venetian blinds, which must have been comparatively a new fashion, and an engraved card of the London tradesman who supplied them is still preserved.

On the opposite side of the river in Fairmount Park, owned by the city, but leased, stands the fine old Belmont mansion. It has had a varied career, and for many years has been a restaurant, road house, eating stand, etc. In the autumn of 1926, a new tenant took possession, made extensive repairs, planning to open it as a first class restaurant, while the theatre already standing was restored for dances, summer concerts, plays, etc.

The original part of the house, little changed save for the removal of some partitions, was built in 1745 by a member of the Peters family, probably William. He was an early colonist, and his brother Richard was Secretary of the Land Office under William Penn.

In old Belmont, Richard, William's son, was born, and here in 1828 he died. William and his son took different sides when the Revolution broke out, and the Loyalist father returned to England, where he lived for the rest of his life. Richard, the son, devoted himself heart and soul to the patriot cause. He was Secretary of the War Board, later Member of Congress, and for nearly forty years, Judge of the United States District Court. A close friend of Washington, until a few years ago, a chestnut tree stood on the lawn and was always said to have been planted by the President, Judge Peters' cane having been used to dig the hole for the roots. In 1824, Lafayette planted a white walnut tree, and this survives.

The old portion of the house contains the present restaurant kitchen. Judge Peters was a wit, a most agreeable host, an eminent lawyer, and also took much interest in agriculture, and the restoration of the state farm lands. He was the first President of the Pennsylvania Agricultural Society. Among guests entertained in his beautiful home were, besides Washington and gallant Lafayette, Benjamin Franklin, Chevalier de la Luzerne, Baron von Steuben, Talleyrand, Louis Philippe, John Penn, John Adams and Thomas Jefferson.

In the old part, the narrow stairs, uneven floors and sagging ceiling, strong though it is, testify to the age. This wing connects with what was apparently a new house in itself, complete save that the old kitchen was used. This newer building has the spacious, high-ceiled rooms, the winding staircase, with broad low treads, of the later period.

Laurel Hill, now in Fairmount Park, was known as the Randolph Mansion, but was built about 1748 by Joseph Shute. In 1760, Francis Rawles and his brother-in-law, Joshua Howell, bought it, Rawles taking the house, while Howell built himself one on part of the estate, and this stood until the city bought it for park purposes.

When Rawles died, he left Laurel Hill to his widow, who married Samuel Shoemaker, a great friend of her late husband. She and the children of her first marriage were Friends, but Shoemaker was a member of the Church of England. Twice Mayor of Philadelphia, Judge of the County Courts, and Justice of the Peace, he did sign the Non Importation Act, but when the time came for the choice, adhered to the Loyalists. When the British occupied Philadelphia, he and Joseph Galloway were asked to take charge of civil affairs for them.

In 1778 he was pronounced by the Americans guilty of treason, and when the British evacuated Philadelphia, Shoemaker and his stepson, William Rawles, sailed for New York with the British fleet. All of his property, and even that belonging to his wife and stepchildren was sold, including Laurel Hill. Mrs. Shoemaker vainly applied for leave to go to New York and visit her husband and son, but two months later, was told to go, under promise that she would not return to Philadelphia without permission. She went, and remained a year, doing much to relieve the sufferings there of Americans imprisoned by the British, and even securing for some their liberty.

Meanwhile, General Joseph Read, President of the State of Pennsylvania, occupied Laurel Hill. In October, 1781, while only Mrs. Shoemaker's daughters and other women were in the house, it was attacked by an angry mob, who broke the shutters, smashed the windows, but fortunately did not harm the occupants.

The house was then sold to James Parr, for £5,000, and he leased it to the Chevalier de la Luzerne, French Minister to the United States. In 1784 Parr offered to sell it back to Mrs. Shoemaker for £400, but she declined this as excessive, and it was finally re-conveyed to her for £300. Two years later, in 1786, Mr. Shoemaker returned with their son. In 1828, it was sold by William Rawles to Dr. Philip Syng Physick, an eminent surgeon, and from him it passed to his descendants, the Randolphs, remaining in their ownership until purchased by the city in 1869.

The Germantown road is the result of a "peticon" in 1719 from freeholders having "Plantacons lying very remote in the country." It was signed by fourteen of these, five of whom made their marks. They complained that a dirt road here in bad weather became mire, "horses were sprained and weakened." In 1793 another petition was sent in, this time for a turnpike, and in 1801 a company was incorporated to build "an artificial road from Philadelphia to Germantown to the 10 mile stone on Chestnut Hill, and from thence to the new stone bridge on Perkiomen Creek."

Near the 19th milestone, on Lincoln Drive, a small house with the original stairs and floors still stands, near the site of the first paper mill in America, on the Germantown road. Here David Rittenhouse was born. Benjamin Franklin was a frequent visitor, and he and Rittenhouse together watched the transit of Venus in June, 1769.

In the heart of Germantown, with its gable end on Main Street, now Germantown Avenue, and surrounded on the other three sides by charming lawns and gardens, stands Wyck, oldest surviving house here. The present residence originally consisted of two separate houses, the rear one, the older, built by Hans Milan, about 1690. His daughter married Dirck Jansen from Holland, and from this couple the Germantown Johnsons descend.

One of their daughters, Margaret, married Reuben Haines the Elder, in 1760, while Catherine married Caspar Wistar, as the name was then written. Reuben Haines visited England, and the home of Sir Richard Haines, Wyck, near Bath. He believed that Sir Richard was his ancestor, and returning to America in 1814, named his home for the English house. Although it was later learned that the two were not related, the name was retained.

Just when the front house was built is not known, but before the Revolution, a covered passageway lay between the two, and was used as an operating room during the Battle of Germantown, when the British occupied the house. The Americans are said to have attacked it vigorously from a house opposite. In 1824, this passage became a room, part of the one house then formed, the line where they were joined being easily discerned on front and rear façades. About this time, the front house was altered to make the present large drawing room and bedroom above, instead of the original smaller rooms. A broader staircase was installed, the old one in the rear portion still remaining, with its curious, irregular treads, set in the outer stone wall, and following the irregularities of the supporting stones.

The same owner threw the old kitchen and an adjoining room into the present dining room, tearing out the old chimney and Dutch oven, using the bricks to build a garden wall.

The present long, two-storied stone house, with an attic and dormer windows is charming. Great hinges, paneling, all the interesting features of its day are here, and it is filled with old furniture. Here is a beautiful chair made especially large for Richard, son of Caspar Wistar, who was of such size that a carriage had to be built specially for his use. Here is one of two chairs, the other in the Wister house, said to have been brought from France by Benjamin Franklin, and in it

Lafayette sat when he visited Wyck. He breakfasted on that hot July day in 1825 in the Chew house, in the afternoon came to Wyck, and in the covered passageway, then as now a room, with French windows at either end, " received visits from ladies and gentlemen of respectability," presented to him by Charles J. Wister, brother of Sally the diarist. " The chair was placed on the right side of the passageway nearest the street, and the guests filed through into the garden at the rear. Here (they) were ' embraced by the General with his usual politeness and courtesy. ' " [1]

A tall, vine-wreathed stump in the garden is what remains of a fine chestnut tree, a seedling from the one planted by Washington at Belmont.

One enters the Wister house directly from Germantown Avenue, but in the rear the old gardens extend for a long distance. In 1800 the original stone front of the house was unfortunately covered with pebbledash, but the interior is little changed, and still owned by the Wisters. Much of the old furniture remains, and on shelves rising from floor to ceiling in the library may be found interesting volumes, although some of the rarest have been given to the Historical Society. Here is a large old clock, which used to announce the hour with a tune. Here are the paneled rooms, hand wrought latches and hinges, those on the heavy front double doors having additional curved pieces almost encircling the upper edge of the doors. Much of the furniture was made for early owners from timber cut on their estate.

In the charming garden is the summerhouse in which Sally used to sit and meditate, and here are the ruins of the old observatory where the present owner's grandfather used daily to take the sun time with his friend, Isaiah Lukens, reporting it to Washington. The two also made the first observations in this country of a transit of Venus. The observatory was intact until a year or so ago, when it, with the mounted instruments, crashed down during a severe storm.

Known as Grumblethorp, this house was built about 1744. In 1776 the Wisters left it for the Foulke house, where Sally wrote most of her

[1] *Sketch of Wyck*, Charles F. Jenkins.

journal. The British then occupied it, and into the drawing room General Agnew was brought to die. His old tattered headquarters flag is treasured here, as is the painted wooden figure of a British grenadier, believed to be the work of Major Andre.

The fine old Johnson house, of hand cut native stone, was begun in 1763 by John, son of Dirck Jansen, for his son, John, and not finished until 1768. It is now occupied by the Woman's Club of Germantown, and twice a week may be visited.

The Club has carefully restored it, the only marked change consisting in throwing two rooms into one, on the right side of the hall. Those on the other side on both floors have old fireplaces set in paneled walls, with cupboards on either side, and many old hinges and latches are in place. An ornamental archway divides the lower hall, and this ornamentation brought severe condemnation to the builder from his Quaker brethren. Some fine old furniture has been collected and installed, notably a set of maple in a room furnished as a bedroom.

Fierce fighting occurred near the house, and the marks of several bullets may still be seen. One pierced the shutter of the front left hand room, went through the heavy door, crossed the hall, and finally embedded itself in the opposite door. Here it remained for years, until pried out and carried off by a thoughtful visitor. Another bullet mark may be seen in the outer molding, while part of the fence riddled with bullets, once standing between this and the next house, is preserved by the Site and Relic Society, installed in another old Wister house.

Two blocks away, set in an entire square, is the old stone Chew mansion, with many marks of bullets on its walls, while a mutilated statue also testifies to the fierce fighting which raged here.

It was built in 1760 by Benjamin Chew, Attorney General of the Province, member of the Provincial Council, and later Chief Justice. The kitchen and servants' quarters are in separate buildings. In the old coach house may be seen the high-swung family coach, its door handles of solid silver. Washington rode in this coach.

During the Battle of Germantown, the family was absent. The British installed themselves in the house, and under Colonel Musgrave,

A view of the reconstructed Old High Street, Philadelphia, as seen at the Sesqui-Centennial, 1926. The houses were built in exact accordance with the originals — all of which are gone — save that they were one third larger.

The hall and stairs of the so-called Benedict Arnold house, Fairmount Park.

defended it against the Americans, who had placed their cannon opposite, where stands another Johnson house, not built until after the war. Musgrave placed a few soldiers at each outer door and window, others upstairs, even on the roof, and although the Americans battered in the front door with a tree trunk, the house was never taken. Five carpenters are said to have been kept busy all the following winter, repairing it.

On this same avenue stands the stone Morris house, built in 1772, and occupied by Washington during the yellow fever epidemic in 1793-4. Watson's *Annals* state that he was "a frequent walker abroad up the Main Street, and daily rode out on horseback or in his phaeton."

This does not exhaust the list of interesting old houses here, merely mentions the most important.

Beautiful Stenton, in the custody of the Pennsylvania Society of the Colonial Dames of America, standing at 18th and Courtland Streets, more than repays a visit.

A large square brick house, with a long wing, it has been carefully restored, even to an old fashioned flower garden, with pump and well. Within the Dames have placed some fine old furniture.

There are a beautiful staircase, big fireplaces, paneled walls, and many cupboards, all with old latches and hinges, those on the front door enormous. Downstairs are the usual four large rooms in the main portion, and in the wall near the stairs in the rear is what might pass for a bit of ornamental woodwork, high up near the ceiling, but in reality it is a listening wall. Within the adjoining room is a closet, and in the top a panel, which when pushed back reveals a compartment large enough for a listener. This was designed for use during Indian councils here, when many Indian delegations visited Stenton. Upstairs in a closet in the eaves, a secret passage begins, leading from attic to cellar.

The house was built in 1728 by James Logan, Secretary of the Province, President of the Council, and for many years Chief Justice of the Supreme Court of Pennsylvania. An enormous apartment now divided, which extended across the entire second story front, was his library. Before the Battle of Germantown, Sir William Howe chose

Stenton for his headquarters; later it was occupied by Washington and his staff, and still later Washington was entertained here by Deborah Norris Logan. Other distinguished guests were Franklin, Lafayette, Dickinson, Jefferson, Madison, Monroe, and John Randolph of Roanoke. Until acquired recently by the city, the place had always remained in the Logan family.

On the Valley Forge Reservation, the Headquarters House is one of a group of old farmhouses, all of which were occupied when the Revolutionary Army was entrenched here. Among these is Mount Joy Manor Farm, then headquarters of General Varnum, home now of William Moore Stephens, oldest male descendant of the Stephens who purchased the estate from William Penn, in 1686. Not far away is the old Stephens homestead, in which eight generations of that name were born.

Headquarters House, a two-storied and attic stone farmhouse, with a separate kitchen connected by a covered passageway, is daily open to the public, and has been furnished appropriately, although nothing is actually of Washington's use. The attic chamber, with its sloping ceiling, is the room used by him, and in the rafter of the sloping roof directly over the stairs a section has been cut out, so that one of moderate height may pass beneath without stooping, but the tall Washington could not have done so.

Front and rear doors are Dutch, and there are a number of old hinges.

This is the " little stone house near the house of Isaac Potts," where the Washingtons spent the dreadful winter of 1777–8. Mrs. Washington wrote: " The apartment for business is only about sixteen feet square, and has a large fireplace. The house is built of stone. The walls are very thick and below a deep east window out of which the General can look out upon the encampment, he had a box made which appears as part of the casement, with a blind trapdoor at the top, in which he keeps his valuable papers."

A log cabin built to serve as dining room has gone.

Near Paoli, still occupied by Waynes, is Waynesborough. Captain

Isaac, first of the family in America, was like his descendants, a brave soldier. He fought in the Battle of the Boyne, then came to the new country, and in 1724 built himself this house. His son, Captain Isaac, who fought in the French and Indian wars, enlarged it in 1765, a wing was added in 1802, and to-day the building is as solid as ever.

Here the child later known as " Mad Anthony " was born. His father was a member of the Provincial Assembly.

A large box bush near the house is said to have served " Mad Anthony " for hiding place while the British searched the house for him. Two miles away, near Malvern, he met with one of his greatest disasters, when the British surprised him and his men, killing eighty. This, the Paoli Massacre, occurred on September 20th, 1777. At his own request, Wayne was court-martialed, but was honorably acquitted.

Dawesfield, where this court-martial was held, stands near Blue-Bell, its owner in the fifth generation of continuous ownership by inheritance. Her ancestor, Abraham Dawes, purchased four hundred acres here in 1726, and the house stands on part of this tract. Washington made it his headquarters in 1777.

Near Swarthmore, at Leiperville is a house built by the present owner's grandfather. Incidentally, Swarthmore, originally known as Westville, was the birthplace of the artist, Benjamin West; the house which his father occupied is still standing.

The Leiper house, set well back from the road, on the side of a hill, has a beautiful old Ionic doorway. The house is plastered, painted yellow, with white trimmings. Over the door is a charming fanlight, and within some of the old doors are still in place.

The builder had a stone quarry, still in operation, and planned a small railroad to haul the stone, but when he explained his plans to some Philadelphia friends, they ridiculed his belief that steam could haul loads on rails as rapidly as horses over roads. He built the railroad none the less, and the tracks remain, although motor trucks are now used for bringing stone from the quarry.

Mr. Leiper also invented a stone sawing machine, something unheard of then, but was unable to perfect it, for the neighbors complained bitterly of the noise. Many years later, a group of men visited the house and examined the old model and designs with interest.

Thomas Leiper was a dictatorial old gentleman. Frequently chosen as presiding officer by various meetings, he none the less had the habit if interested in the affirmative, of *forgetting* to put the negative vote. He had planned to build a canal in connection with the quarry, but this was pronounced far too visionary. In 1828, his son built the canal. Beside the quarry, Mr. Leiper owned cotton and grist mills, and engaged in the tobacco business.

Not far away from Willow Grove, the old residence known as Graeme Park, built in 1721, still stands, now owned by the Penroses. In 1722 it was reached by the Keith Road, through forests. Sir William Keith, appointed by Queen Anne Surveyor General of royal customs for the American colonies, at a salary of £500 a year, became involved deeply in debt, and under George II lost his office, and went to Philadelphia. Friends asked Hannah Penn to appoint him Deputy Governor of Pennsylvania, he borrowed money, brought his family from England, and built this house, of which part of the old slave quarters also remain. Near the farmhouse stands a large boulder which Keith used as a test for the strength of applicants for work. If they could lift it, they were engaged.

Keith returned to England in 1729, and twenty years later, died in the Old Bailey, London, imprisoned for debt.

In 1739, the place was bought by Dr. Greene, whose daughter secretly married Henry Hugh Ferguson, since her father did not approve of the match. Her husband urged her to confess, and one day it is said she had determined to do so, but before she spoke, her father dropped dead. His objections were apparently well founded, for Ferguson wasted his wife's property, and during the Revolution was accused of treason, his wife's estate confiscated. In 1777, this was restored to her, since it was proved that she was loyal, and in 1791 she entertained Washington here, and then sold the property to the present owner's family.

One of the most beautiful examples in this country of a Georgian

Photo by Charles R. Pancoast

The stairway at Stenton.

Courtesy of the Penna. Society of Colonial Dames of America

Stenton, a beautiful example of its period.

The "Flag House," Philadelphia, home of Betsey Ross, and here she is said to have made the first American flag.

house is Hope Lodge, almost opposite Fortside Inn, and built between 1721 and 1723 as a manor house on his estate of 500 acres, by Samuel Morris, a Friend. To it he hoped to bring his bride, but she did not marry him after all, and he died a bachelor.

All of the beautiful interior paneling and other woodwork, with the bricks for the front of the house were imported from England. Entering the wide hall extending through the house, one is impressed by the size of the rooms, their high ceilings, and general air of spaciousness. The fireplaces are six feet broad, two with blue marble facings, and four others with the original blue and white Delft tiles. Here, too, are many old HL hinges.

The house stands on a terrace, and behind the main portion is a lower two-storied ell, which used to be known as the cook house, for in Pennsylvania, as in the southern states, at the time when this was built, it was not customary to have cooking done in the actual house. The rooms in the upper story of this ell were for the servants, leaving the main part of the mansion for the family exclusively.

Samuel Morris was taken suddenly ill here at three o'clock one morning in 1770, and instructed those with him at the time to bring him his will. In their excitement, they failed to find it, so he gave verbal instructions to his physician, and to Peter Adam, keeper of the old inn at the nearby crossroads, as to its substance, and what he wished done. After his death, upon their testimony before Benjamin Chew, then Registrar for the Crown, the unsigned will, which later had been found, was accepted and probated, a rare legal occurrence.

The brother of Samuel Morris inherited Hope Lodge, and it then passed to William West, who owned it at the time that General Washington and his army occupied the surrounding hills, and fortified one on the adjacent farm, Fort Hill. It has been said that West was a Loyalist, but his descendants treasure a letter from Washington to the master of the house, stating that his soldiers had orders not to destroy Mr. West's timber. One of Washington's officers, Alexander Anderson, married Mr. West's niece Susanna.

While occupying this part of Pennsylvania, Washington made the attack on the British which resulted in the Battle of Germantown, a defeat for the American troops. The Manor house was then used as a hospital for the American wounded. It is here, too, that Washington received the information from Lydia Darragh of the surprise attack which the British were planning, and in consequence of this news there was no surprise.

After Mr. West, the property passed to James Horatio Walmough, and at this time first received the name of Hope Lodge, because of the reconciliation of the owner to Henry Hope. It then passed to the Wentz family, who owned it for ninety years, and then to the present owner, Mr. William L. Deyn.

In Carlisle is the Watts house, on Hanover Street, built by Colonel Ephraim Blaine, great-grandfather of James G. Blaine, an officer of distinction, and Commissary General of the northern department of the army during the last four years of the Revolution. Landscape paper on the walls displayed scenes from Paul and Virginia. The house is still used as a dwelling, altered to install an ice cream parlor, but the rooms used as his law offices by Judge R. M. Henderson, one of the residents after Colonel Blaine, are now storerooms.

In early days, Carlisle assemblies were quite noted. Only men subscribed, $8 for eight evenings, and then invited the ladies. The Marquis de Chastellux recounts that on one occasion, when a young lady was chatting with a friend, and forgot her turn in the square dance then in progress, the manager of ceremonies thus addressed her:

" Give over, Miss, take care what you are about. Do you think that you are here for your pleasure? "

Chapter XVI

C✷ HOMES OF THE PIONEERS ✷

Into Kentucky, then part of the great state of Virginia, at an early date there journeyed from the more settled, civilized eastern portions, those seeking adventures, or anxious for pioneer life. Pioneers were encouraged by Virginia, desirous of having a settled country on her western boundaries, as protection from Indian attacks, and as early as 1705, she passed an act encouraging settlements west of the Blue Ridge Mountains. Before this, Gabriel Arthur, an early explorer in 1674, had been taken prisoner by Indians in what is now Kentucky, and wrote an account of the country which has only recently come to light. Dr. Thomas Walker, mentioned in the Charlottesville section, explored the Cumberland Mountains and Gap in 1750, and built a settler's cabin near what is now Barbourville, Kentucky.

Among early explorers and settlers was Colonel James Harrod, who, with a party, journeyed in canoes down the Monongahela and Ohio rivers to the mouth of the Kentucky, up that stream to Landing Run Creek, then overland to a spring, where they camped, and in 1774 founded Harrodsburg. Although the site of Louisville was surveyed before this, Harrodsburg claims to be not merely the first, but the only colonial settlement in Kentucky, and three years later was made county seat of the new Kentucky County, then a part of Virginia. This settlement was a stockaded fort, within its enclosing walls the cabins of the early settlers, all near the spring which later became historic, when Fort Harrod was attacked by Indians. Fort Harrod is further interesting because here George Rogers Clark planned his journey into the Northwest, and Daniel Boone helped survey the town, the cave where he spent the winter of 1774–5 is still shown. Although no old cabin of the first settlement survives, it is hoped before long to reproduce the fort and cabins as a national monument.

Twenty miles from Harrodsburg, on a farm in Washington County, close to Beech Fort Creek, there stood at an early date a log cabin which has become of national interest, and is still standing. In this cabin, on June 10th, 1806, were married the parents of Abraham Lincoln, and in it for several years the young people lived. In 1910, the cabin became the property of the Harrodsburg Historical Society, has been carefully taken down, removed to that town, and set up in the Kentucky State Pioneer Memorial Park, on Old Fort Harrod Hill, and on land given by its owner, Miss Irene Moore. Visitors may now see and enter this primitive home.

James Haggin's ancestors were pioneer settlers, and the Haggin race track, the first in Kentucky, existing at least as early as 1784, was laid out here.

Lexington, founded and named for the distinguished old Massachusetts town on the day when news arrived of the victorious encounter of American patriots with the British troops, has much of historic interest, and houses with histories, even if younger than some of the eastern dwellings.

It is said that beneath the site of this town there once was an Aztec village, and that in 1776, a party of hunters discovered ancient catacombs, mounds containing pottery, copper utensils, weapons and ornaments which were not Indian relics. In the exciting war times, these discoveries were lost.

A blockhouse was built here in 1779, which has disappeared, but a dwelling built before 1787 on Mill Street, Lexington, still stands, known as the Thomas Hart house. Colonel Thomas Hart was an early and wealthy settler here, and built himself a mansion designed by a well-known architect, Benjamin Latrobe. The latter's own home with a rotunda, fine staircase, elaborate carved woodwork, and marble mantels, also stands, but re-modeled into an apartment house. In its drawing room President Monroe, General Jackson and Governor Isaac Shelby were elaborately entertained in 1819.

Isaac Shelby was Kentucky's first Governor, and when, in 1790, he went to Lexington to take office, he rode on horseback from his home, Travellers' Rest, escorted by the infantry company organized the preceding year, its members having served against the Indians under " Mad Anthony " Wayne.

In the Hart home, Henry Clay was married to Lucretia Hart, and in a house nearby, built for them by the bride's father, the young couple lived until, in 1806, Clay purchased Ashland, on the outskirts of the town. John Bradford, who, after serving in the Revolutionary Army, came to Lexington from his native Fauquier County, Virginia, and established the *Kentucky Gazette* in 1787, died in this Hart house. Later, it was the home of the distinguished General John Hunt Morgan.

Furthermore, the ell of this house is one of the three sites on Mill Street in which differing historians have located the Great Commoner's law office, although this is not the site favored by the Clay descendants.

Another of many interesting houses in this town which should be mentioned is that of Robert S. Todd, father of Abraham Lincoln's wife. It stands at 574 West Main Street. Here Mary Todd was living just before her marriage, in 1842, to the obscure young lawyer in Springfield, Illinois. The couple frequently visited this Lexington residence, which remains much as at that time, except that two rooms on the corner of the lower floor have been turned into a grocery store.

A fine old Lexington residence, that of the Gratz family, has remained in their ownership for more than a century.

The Gratzes were distinguished Philadelphians, who came to this part of the country about the beginning of the 19th century. Gratz Park, Lexington, was formerly part of Benjamin Gratz's estate. He aided in building up Transylvania College, the first college west of the Alleghenies.

The Lexington house was not built by Mr. Gratz. In 1795, Thomas January built one on this site for General John McCalla, but this was removed or destroyed, and January replaced it by the present building in 1806. Mr. Gratz bought it in 1824, and made extensive additions and alterations, but save for modern piazzas the house has since been little changed.

What is now a garage was once the old kitchen, said to be the first brick building in Lexington, the bricks having come from a house in the present Gratz Park, once occupied by John Breckenridge, Attorney General under Thomas Jefferson. In the old garden is a bed of cane, carefully preserved, part of the old canebrake which originally covered the present site of the town. The house has one of the handsomest doorways in the state. The hall is sixty feet long, and the cornices, carved woodwork and mantels throughout are lovely. Among cherished possessions are a pair of sofas on one of which Lafayette sat when he called at this house on the widow of his friend, General Scott, but since the two are exactly alike, no one can identify the particular sofa thus honored.

The family originally owned all of the property beneath which lies the famous Mammoth Cave, and it was from this that they obtained the nitre used in manufacturing black powder, supplied for the Battle of New Orleans. They were great friends with Washington Irving, and according to one of the cherished family traditions, this author described Miss Rebecca Gratz to Sir Walter Scott, who used the description for Rebecca in his *Ivanhoe*.

The present house at Ashland is not the one purchased by Henry Clay, for soon after his death, the foundations of the original one were pronounced unsafe, and it was torn down. His son, however, re-built it on the same site, on practically the same plan, and some of the old materials were used in its construction. The square, ivy-covered building with two long, low wings presents the same general aspect, and within is much of the original furniture, and many interesting relics of Henry Clay. The ivy-bordered walk beneath the pine trees, the slave cabins, and some of the catalpa trees which he planted remain as during the lifetime of the great owner. Part of the estate is now included in Woodland Park.

Henry Clay came to Lexington from Virginia in 1797, and at Ashland he entertained lavishly; it was from Ashland that he went to Congress in 1811, and while living here he made his unsuccessful fight for the Presidency, his third and last defeat being due, it is said, to the personal animosity and great popularity of General Jackson. While living at Ashland, in spite of his disapproval of the practise, Clay fought three duels.

He loved his estate, took an active interest in agriculture, as well as in breeding various kinds of cattle. From Spain he imported asses, from Portugal pigs, and cattle and sheep from England. The Kentucky Agricultural Association, founded in 1814, awarded him a silver cup for "the best Saxon ram," and his horses were noted even in that state of fine horses. Many were the distinguished guests entertained here; President Monroe, the Governors of various states, Lafayette and other eminent foreigners among them.

After the death of Henry Clay, on the portion of the estate which his son John inherited, he laid out one of the first private race courses in Kentucky, and made his place famous for its horses. When John Clay died, to the surprise of many, in a day when such things were practically unheard of for a woman, his widow carried on her husband's affairs successfully, and became one of the first woman horse breeders in the country. Day Star and Riley, winners in the Kentucky Derby, and Maggie B., mother of Iroquois, winner of the English Derby, are some of the horses which made these Ashland stables renowned.

The house at Ashland was inherited by James Clay, another son, and at his death, passed to Kentucky University. It was later purchased by Major Henry Clay McDowell, who, in spite of his name, was no kin, but married Henry Clay's granddaughter. Major McDowell is dead, and a movement is now on foot, headed by prominent citizens of Lexington, to purchase Ashland, and make it a national monument.

Three miles from Lexington is Ellerslie, home of Levi Todd, first clerk of Fayette County, grandfather of Mary Lincoln. The Todds were pioneer settlers, and the original brick house here, built by John Todd, Governor of the Territory of Kentucky, still stands, containing a big square hall and rooms, while an addition is of later but not modern construction. The exact age of the house could not be learned, but a map of Kentucky drawn in 1784 has the name: "Col. Todd," and a cross to indicate a dwelling. Behind this house is a small stone building in which the county records were kept, and it replaces a former one, burned in 1803. The present occupants say that in stage-coach days this house was a noted inn, the only one between Lexington and Richmond.

Keeneland Farm, not far from Lexington, is another old place. Here, in 1825, Lafayette spent a night before going on to Lexington. The bed, its coverings, and the furniture of the room he occupied have been treasured by the family ever since.

Situated on the top of a hill, from which there is a wide view of the beautiful Blue Grass Country, and south of Lexington, is the brick house known as Chaumiere. Although almost a hundred years old, it includes the sole surviving room of an older, more magnificent house. The latter, built in the last years of the 18th century by Colonel David Meade, was the handsome residence of the first large estate west of the Alleghenies.

Colonel Meade was one of two brothers born in Tidewater Virginia, and, as was the custom with wealthy Virginians of the 18th century, they were sent to England to be educated. While students at Harrow, one of their professors was Dr. Thackeray, grandfather of the eminent novelist, and it is said that they served as models for the two leading characters in *The Virginians*.

When David Meade returned from England, he married, and for a time lived in eastern Virginia, later buying land near Lexington, Kentucky. Here he built his house and laid out extensive grounds. The gardens were enclosed by a hedge of roses and clipped box; there was an artificial lake, in the centre of which was an island, reached by a rustic bridge, and on the island was a fountain. Through a thicket of plum from lake to house was cut a path, known as "Birdcage Walk." A troop of slaves was kept busy maintaining the estate in the fine order upon which Meade insisted.

A grove of sugar maples surrounded the house, and a few of these

The McClure Studio

Ashland, home of Henry Clay.

Chaumiere, near Lexington, Kentucky. One room of the original house, which was a remarkably fine residence in early Kentucky days, is standing; the one-storied wing shown above.

Photo by Shores

The Harrison house, built in pioneer days, Vincennes, Indiana. Here General Harrison met and signed a treaty with the Indians.

trees survive. So does the lake, although reduced in size, and also the cave which always interested early visitors.

Here Meade entertained lavishly, and from the first it was one of the show places of the country. Meade even affected annoyance if guests notified him in advance of their arrival, and it was not unusual for eighteen to sit down to table. Four Presidents, Thomas Jefferson, James Monroe, Andrew Jackson and Zachary Taylor were guests here; Aaron Burr and his ally or dupe, Blennerhasset, attended the wedding of Colonel Meade's daughter, and a descendant of the Colonel still treasures the mirror which Burr used while dressing his hair. He and Meade are said to have been school fellows. Henry Clay was also an intimate friend.

The original house, the "cluster of rustic cottages," or as others styled it, "the thatched cottage on the prairie," was a rambling structure, built of different kinds of materials, but any outward deficiencies were more than made up for by the gardens with their statuary, and the magnificence of the interior. The drawing room, the only part of the old house which survives, octagonal in shape, had a high, domed ceiling lofty windows, and fine walnut paneling. Once four gilt framed mirrors hung between the windows, and the curtains were of purple brocade. On both sides of the entrance to the drawing room were small, triangular powder closets.

After Colonel Meade died, his slaves used to insist that they often saw "Ole Marster" come up the lawn, and enter the house at five o'clock of an afternoon, the hour for serving tea.

The Colonel and his wife rest in a small burial ground on the estate, but their death marked the beginning of Chaumiere's decadence. The property was sold to someone unable to appreciate its beauty, and he cut down many of the fine old trees, destroyed or removed much of the house, and even turned his hogs loose on the beautiful old lawn.

Later, the property again changed hands, and the new owner built the present substantial house beside the fragment of the old one remaining. Much of the fine old furniture is cherished elsewhere by Colonel Meade's descendants.

Cynthiana, one of Kentucky's oldest towns, has been in existence since 1793. Robert Harrison, a landowner in this section, gave the town site, and it was named after his two daughters, Cynthia and Anna, the county being named for him, Harrison.

Cynthiana's first court house was older than the town. A log cabin built in 1790, used as a residence, court house, law office, printing office, it was standing at least in 1925, behind the present fairly old but substantial court house.

In the old low, two-story log building, in 1806, Henry Clay held court, and many celebrated lawyers prosecuted or defended cases.

Nashville, Tennessee, cherishes the home of Andrew Jackson, now owned by the Hermitage Association, under a charter taken out in 1889.

The first house on the estate which Jackson acquired here was built in 1804 of logs, and a year later Aaron Burr was entertained in it. To this Jackson returned after the Battle of New Orleans, but four years later he built on the present site, not far from the log house, one of bricks made on the place, and it was in the new home that Lafayette was entertained in 1825. Nine years later, it burned to the ground, but was re-built on the same foundations, and even some of the old walls used. This is the house now owned by the Ladies' Hermitage Association, and preserved by them as a national monument. The General's adopted son, his wife's nephew, Andrew Jackson, Junior, succeeded to the estate, and his son, Andrew III., a colonel in the Confederate Army, was the last of the name to occupy the house.

It is of brick, in colonial style, with broad verandas at front and back, supported by pillars extending to the roof, and with a low wing on either end. A wide hall runs through the centre, from which open large, high-ceiled rooms.

On the walls of the hall may still be seen the paper ordered by General Jackson from Paris, when the house was re-built in 1835. This paper represents the story of the travels of Telemachus. Several old family portraits, including one of the first great owner, by Earl, hang on the walls, and Jackson's umbrella stand and hatrack are in their old places.

In the front drawing room is another portrait by Earl, showing Jackson on his horse, Sam Patch, while in the rear parlor are portraits of four staff officers, General Coffee, General Bronagh, Colonel Gadsden, and Lieutenant Eastland, who were known as "General Jackson's military family." In this room, too, is preserved a mahogany table, sole remnant of a set of furniture presented to General and Mrs. Jackson when they visited New Orleans after the battle.

General Jackson's bedroom remains as when he died, with the same furniture, curtains, drapery and pictures. The room which until Mrs. Jackson's death was the couple's bedroom has many of its original furnishings. After his beloved wife died, this room was used by their adopted son. Here the wall paper is a reproduction, made from a small piece of the original, but all of the other papers are the originals.

The great hall, with its fine winding staircase, is two stories high. The library on the lower floor, adjoining General Jackson's bedroom, has five bookcases filled with more than four hundred of the General's books, and the Association has spared no pains in assembling these interesting souvenirs. Then there is the dining room, and the old kitchen should not be omitted, for it has been restored to its former state.

Upstairs, one of the rooms was always known as "Earl's room." The painter married a niece of Mrs. Jackson, but she soon died, and he then spent much of his time at the Hermitage, with the Jacksons, and here he painted a number of portraits of the General, in addition to the two already mentioned. Another bedroom is that occupied by Lafayette, and all over the house are interesting small souvenirs of the Jacksons, preserved in glass cases.

Here at the Hermitage, Mrs. Jackson had a fine flower garden, which she tended with loving care. Furthermore, in the old coach house may be seen the identical coach used by Jackson at the White House, and on several trips from there to the Hermitage.

When Jackson died, the house was surrounded by a farm of 1200 acres, and there were a hundred negro slaves, the entire estate being estimated at $150,000. When Colonel Andrew Jackson, third of the name to live here, moved in 1893, he took with him all of the furnishings, but the Association has been able to restore a surprising amount of them.

There is a ghost connected with the house, for two ladies who spent the night here to investigate the story for themselves, reported the sounds as of dishes falling down, chains clanking, and " a war horse tread."

General Jackson, his wife, their adopted son and his wife, with other members of the family, and their friend Earl are buried in the private plot on the grounds of the Hermitage.

The Francis Vigo Chapter of the Daughters of the American Revolution owns the house in Vincennes, Indiana, which was occupied by Governor William Henry Harrison, and where, in 1810, councils with Tecumseh, the Indian chief, and several hundred of his braves, were held.

Local tradition says that a family by the name of Thompson came here in 1803, established a brick kiln, and that their first order came from Harrison. The deed given them in payment for the bricks is still in existence. Probably the house which cost $26,000, was the first to be built of bricks in this section. Glass for the first windows was imported from England, carried from the east to the mouth of the Ohio River on the backs of horses, then by boat to what is now Evansville, and thence up the Wabash to Vincennes.

The basement walls of the house are two feet thick, the upper ones eighteen inches. Doors, stairs, and other interior woodwork are of black walnut, hand carved. In the cellar is the entrance to a tunnel leading to the Wabash River, six hundred feet away, the tunnel designed to serve as a refuge or means of escape from Indians, should occasion arise. In the basement are the large kitchen, with big open fireplace, store rooms for arms and ammunition, and four bedrooms for servants. Upstairs on the main floor are the dining and other rooms, among them the great apartment used for councils, and for early meetings of the Legislature. In this, one year after the house was built, the Reverend Thomas Clelland preached the first Presbyterian sermon ever delivered in what is now the State of Indiana.

Here, too, Harrison held the council with Tecumseh and his Indian warriors. The story goes that at one point in the discussion, the Indian chief became so angry that he rose from his seat threateningly, whereupon his braves did the same. Harrison, standing alone, calmly drew his sword, and faced them so determinedly that either intimidated, or in admiration of his courage, Tecumseh resumed negotiations, and they were peaceably concluded.

A room in this house was also for a time used as a schoolroom, and in one of the inner shutters may still be seen the hole from a bullet aimed at Harrison, as he walked the floor one night with a sick child.

The Daughters have filled the house with articles of the period of its erection, a few pieces of furniture, including his desk, having been used by the illustrious first owner. One room is further set apart in honor of Francis Vigo, and contains his bed. The memorial tablet near the house is inscribed to this " Patriot whose devotion to the cause of American liberty made possible the capture of Fort Sackville, Feb. 25, 1776," and who died in Vincennes.

Chapter XVII

CAESAR RODNEY, THE RIDER

Traveling in Delaware, one will hear the names: Broadkill Hundred, Indian River Hundred, etc. Into thirty-three hundreds her three counties are divided, an old term dating, it is said, from the time of Alfred the Great, and Delaware alone of the States has kept it. But Delaware's earliest settlements were made by Swedes and Dutch, and the English did not obtain possession of the territory until 1664, notwithstanding that the State is named for Lord De La Ware, Governor of Virginia, who, in 1610, explored Delaware Bay. Of her three counties, only one, New Castle, bears the original name, the other two, Kent and Sussex, having formerly been known as St. Jones, and Hoorne Kill, or Deale.

Wilmington, a natural first stop in entering the State from the north, is by no means the oldest town, nor does it contain the most interesting old houses, but one prominent object, the equestrian statue in front of the Du Pont Hotel, commemorates one of Delaware's distinguished sons whose exploit is less well-known than it deserves. This is Caesar Rodney, hero of a ride which, if not so important as Revere's, yet had importance, and was made under a serious physical handicap.

Caesar Rodney lived at Poplar Grove, St. John's Neck, Kent County, Delaware. His grandfather, William Rodney, came to this country with William Penn, in 1682. He was of an honorable family in Bristol, England, and took an active part in organizing the government in his new home. His son William, Caesar's father, was chosen in 1701 Speaker of the Assembly organized by the Delaware counties, then part of Pennsylvania. This William's mother was Alice, daughter of Sir Thomas Caesar, so when he married, to his youngest son he gave the family name of Caesar. Although he left eight children, it was to Caesar that his estate finally came. Denbigh, in Sussex County, was part of this second William's holdings. It was sold to Benjamin Chew, then to Vincent Loockerman, who sold it to the Bradfords, and they finally sold it out of their family in 1852.

Left an orphan at seventeen, Caesar chose for his guardian William Ridgely of Dover, and with this family and town his history was then closely connected. Mr. Ridgely saw to it that his ward received a classical education, was taught dancing, fencing, and all the accomplishments suited to a gentleman of that day. Caesar Rodney has been described by his contemporaries as vivacious, active and brave. About five feet ten inches in height, one of them remarks: " his person was very elegant and genteel, his manners graceful, easy and polite. He had a good fund of humor, and the happiest talent in the world of making his wit agreeable, however sparkling and severe."

While a minor, he made his home with his guardian at Eden Hill Farm, the Ridgely home, situated about a mile from Dover, and still owned by the Ridgely family.

At thirty, Caesar was Sheriff of Kent County, then a prized office; became Justice of the Peace, Judge of the " lower counties," as what are now Delaware's counties were then called, member of the Assembly, and in 1762, when only thirty-four years old, was chosen by the Assembly, together with his close friend and associate, Thomas McKean, to revise and print the laws of Delaware. In 1765, he attended the Stamp Act Congress in New York City, where met delegates from nine states, four sending their written agreements to whatever the others should decide.

He served with distinction in the Continental Army, was made a Brigadier General of the Delaware militia, and later Washington appointed him a Major General. During the early days of the Revolution, Rodney wrote daily to Haslet, urging him to enlist troops, and when the Declaration of Independence was passed, sent a mounted messenger to him with the news. John Haslet, who is buried in the old Presbyterian churchyard at Dover, was killed at Princeton.

In 1774, Rodney, McKean and George Read, the latter two men of New Castle, were chosen deputies to the Continental Congress. Four years later came the famous ride.

Caesar Rodney, leaving the Convention in Philadelphia, had gone to Lewes, Delaware, because of reports of Tory activities in that neighborhood. The story goes that in Lewes he became infatuated with beautiful young Sarah Rowland, daughter of the postmaster, and an ardent Tory, although either Rodney did not know this, or fancied that she could do no harm to him or the patriot cause. He underestimated the young lady's ability. The time for ratifying the articles of Confederacy then before the Convention drew near. Without Rodney, Delaware's vote was tied, since Read, although no less patriotic than the others, believed the adoption of these articles premature. McKean wrote urgently to Rodney to return, and sent letters to him by a sailing packet bound for Lewes. Sarah Rowland intercepted the letters, and Delaware's ratification would have been withheld, and the patriot cause seriously hampered, had it not been for her patriotic maid. She told Rodney of the trick, and without delay, he set out for Philadelphia, eighty miles away, on horseback. This was on the evening of July 2nd, and the vote on ratification was to be taken by Congress on the 4th.

He succeeded in reaching Philadelphia in time to cast his vote with McKean, thus insuring Delaware's ratification. There are few details of this story obtainable. Some historians do not even mention it, but the Colonial Dames of Delaware give a longer account than others in a pamphlet issued by their society.

At the time that he took this ride, in fierce summer heat, Rodney was already suffering from the dreadful malady which later killed him, cancer of the nose, and it is said that he rode with his face swathed in bandages. In 1778, and for three years afterwards, he was President or, as it would now be called, Governor of Delaware, and in 1782 was re-elected to Congress, but owing to his illness did not take his seat. Two years later, after submitting to several operations, he died, and is buried in old Christ Church graveyard, Dover, where a plain granite monument, with only his name inscribed, now marks the spot.

When elected President of Delaware, he took a house at 606 Market Street, Wilmington, the site of which is now included in that of a department store. His cousin, beautiful Mary Vining, presided with grace over the household, for Rodney never married. Here many prominent persons were entertained, and in its cellar, Lafayette hid the little casks of gold which he used in paying his men.

Mary Vining, a famous beauty and belle of Revolutionary days, was wooed by many suitors. She and " Mad Anthony " Wayne fell in love with each other although, or because, they were of very opposed types, became engaged, and their wedding day was near when he was killed. She never recovered from his death, withdrew almost entirely from society, and would not hear of marrying. It is told that she could never bring herself to use a set of china which Wayne had given her for their future home. Through some inexplicable act of vandalism, more than fifty years ago, many of the tombstones of the Vining family were stolen from the churchyard, pounded to fragments, and used in making mortar.

Mary Vining later lived at The Willows, on Brandywine Walk, Wilmington, and one is free to select a site for her home along the present charming Brandywine Drive, while doubtless its gardens sloped gently down to the pretty stream, whose banks are now for some distance a park. She must have been not only a beauty but a clever and interesting woman as well, for Lafayette corresponded with her for a third of a century; Marie Antoinette had heard so much about her that she expressed a wish to see her at the Tuileries, and the Duke de Liancourt and Louis Philippe were among her distinguished visitors. She is buried in Old Swedes' churchyard, Wilmington, her grave unmarked.

After her death, her nephew, Henry Ridgely, took charge of all her papers, and for safe keeping stored them in the attic of his aunt, Mrs. Ogden's house. The house burned to the ground, and all were destroyed, including a manuscript history written by Mary Vining.

Cool Springs, an estate near Wilmington, was the country seat of

Rodney's nephew and namesake. This second Caesar Rodney was the last of six Attorneys General in Jefferson's cabinet, was sent to Argentina as our minister, and died there, his illness being indirectly caused, it was reported, by the abominable treatment of the captain on whose ship he made the voyage.

In Dover, on the Green, there stands a three-story brick house which at one time was owned by Caesar Rodney, although it is believed that he never lived in it, merely held it for three days and then sold it, having taken it in exchange for other property. Outside of Dover, at Byefield, standing on a tract of 900 acres, is the house which Caesar Rodney the rider inherited from his father, and to which he returned after making his ride. Those now visiting the place will be disappointed, for although part of the house, originally a long, low building with dormer windows, remains, the dormer windows have disappeared, replaced by a full story with ordinary ones, and the beautiful old staircase has been removed as well, either sold, or because it was too dilapidated.

Other Rodney relatives buried in old St. Peter's churchyard, Lewes, include two governors of Delaware, Daniel and Caleb, and John, a Judge under the Colonial government, member of the Council of Safety, and Military General of Delaware in 1772. Near the old church still stands the home of Governor Daniel Rodney, built about 1766, a few years ago and perhaps still occupied by the Mayor of the town. It will be seen that the rider was of distinguished and patriotic lineage.

His brother Thomas left a diary which gives an interesting picture of early Delaware days. He says in part:

"The manners and customs of the white people when I first remember were very simple, plain and social. Very few foreign articles were used in this part of the country for eating and drinking and clothing. Almost every family manufactured their own clothes, and beef, pork, poultry, milk, butter and cheese, wheat and Indian corn were raised by themselves, and served them with the fruits of the country, and wild game for food; and cider, small beer, and peach and apple brandy for drink. The best families in the country but seldom used tea, coffee, chocolate or sugar, for honey was their sweetening . . . they constantly associated together at one house or another to play and frolic, at which times the young people would dance, and the elder ones wrestle, run, leap, jump, or throw the disc, or play at some rustic and manly exercise. This manner of life continued until the war commenced, in 1755, but this occasioned a sudden and universal change in the country."

Returning to Wilmington, the real founder of the town was William Shipley, but it was his wife who inspired him to do so. They were both Friends, and Elizabeth was a noted preacher of that denomination. One night she dreamed that she was on horseback, traveling through the country, and came to a turbulent stream. A guide seemed with her, and told her that he was conducting her to " a new and fruitful land, and it is the design of Providence that thou shouldst enter." Some time later she took a long trip to preach, and after traveling eighteen miles, came to and recognized the river of her dream. She persuaded her husband to come and settle on its banks in 1730, and the city of Wilmington is the result. Their house at Shipley and 4th Streets, built in 1736, stood until about 1880.

After the Battle of Brandywine in 1777, while stricken with her last illness, Elizabeth Shipley suddenly exclaimed that she " saw in the sight of the Lord that the invader of our land shall be driven back," and urged those around her to remain " firm in the faith that this nation will secure its independence." This made " a stupendous impression," not only because she was a well-known preacher, but also because the Quakers have always opposed war. Her words were re-printed in all the newspapers devoted to the cause of Liberty, for they were " a voice from the grave " of " one who had long been considered an extraordinary person," while the Tory papers derided them as an attempt on the part of the adherents to a losing cause to bolster up their courage.

For more than a block above Wilmington's Market Street bridge, on the left hand side, a row of fine old square stone houses has survived. The second house above 18th Street is the old Tatnall house, built in 1770 by Joseph Tatnall, who owned the first flour mills here on the Brandywine. A third story has replaced the old attic, and a large addition has been built on in the rear, but otherwise the house is not greatly changed outwardly. This was Anthony Wayne's headquarters at one time, and here Washington came daily to confer with him and with Lafayette and other officers before the Battle of Brandywine. After that, it was occupied by British officers. Almost opposite is a still older surviving house, the usual two story and attic building of its period, with a solitary front dormer window in the attic, but this is now a gas filling station.

Thomas West's house on the corner of 5th and West Streets has been torn down, but a tablet high up on the present building on its site commemorates it. West was a distant relative of Lord De La Warre or Ware, whose name was also Thomas West. He was furthermore the uncle of Benjamin West, the artist. The youngest son of this Thomas, Joseph, owned one of the first tanneries in Wilmington. The family were Friends.

Tusculum, a fine old square brick house, not beautiful but comfortable, survives, but is the contagious disease department of the hospital. Set high in the midst of still extensive grounds, at the corner of Chestnut and Broome Streets, it was built by James Broome about the beginning of the 19th century. Early in that century Mr. Broome's father-in-law, Dr. Thomas Read, and his wife made their home with the Broomes, and here Lafayette was entertained.

At the time of the Battle of Brandywine, Dr. Read was pastor of the old Drawyers Presbyterian church, just outside of Odessa. Washington was encamped near Stanton, six miles below Wilmington. He knew that the British were near, but was unfamiliar with the country. One of his officers told him that he knew a man who was thoroughly acquainted with it, and Washington directed him to go in search of him. The officer rode to Read's parsonage, and arrived there at midnight. He roused the parson, and in ten minutes the latter was dressed, his horse saddled, and the two set out for the camp, riding over bad roads at such a pace that they reached the camp in half an hour. Read was taken at once to Washington's tent, and there so thoroughly mapped out and described the country that the information was invaluable to the commander in the ensuing battle and retreat.

New Castle across the river, and six miles south of Wilmington, is one of the oldest towns in America. On the way here one may pass the house once occupied by the Jacquette family, in which Washington and Lafayette were entertained, but it has been modernized and is not now interesting. It stands on the tract owned by Jean Paul Jacquette or Johan Paul Jacquet, whichever spelling is preferred, the first Governor of Delaware under the Dutch, and here he lived in 1684.

New Castle was settled by the Swedes in 1638, and has been known by at least eight different names from the first, Quinnimacook, to the present, given it by Sir Robert Carr, when, in 1644 the British won it from the Dutch. Even the modern railroad does not detract from New Castle's quaint old world appearance, for the station is distant from the heart of the town, the old Green, given by Peter Stuyvesant. Many of the old buildings around the Green remain, yet it was the terminus of one of the first railroads in the country, the New Castle and Frenchtown. In 1682, William Penn was given a grant which included New Castle and land within a twelve mile radius.

There are many interesting old houses here, and the visitor is tempted to linger admiringly almost at every turn. The oldest house in New Castle, built about 1665, stands as the wing to a larger one. The old portion is a typical Dutch cottage, a story and a half high, with one window on each side of the broad old door, and a steep roof above. Oldest of the most interesting group is the Amstel House, a modern name for a residence built before 1730, since in that year it was advertised at a sheriff's sale. The first known occupant was Governor Nicholas Van Dyke, and tradition says that Washington was a guest at the wedding of Ann, daughter of the house, to Kensey Johns. Nicholas Van Dyke was major of Delaware militia during the Revolution, member of the Committee of Correspondence in 1774, a deputy to the Convention of 1776, and from 1777 to 1783, member of the Continental Congress. He was also Governor of Delaware before it became a State in 1789, in which year he died.

This house is a fine example of the colonial period, with paneled walls, beautiful woodwork and staircase, large rooms, and old doors with their original HL hinges. Its name, given not many years ago, is most appropriate, since New Amstel was one of New Castle's early names.

Opposite is the house built by Kensey Johns, Junior, son of Ann Van Dyke Johns. Although only a bit over a century old, it is interesting not merely as a fine example of an early 19th century residence, but also for the family portraits, old furniture and silver contained in it. Among the portraits are Gilbert Stuart's of George Read, and Benjamin West's of George Ross, both Signers, with others by Sully and Alexander. Treasured here is a "spider" which belonged to Caesar Rodney, and has come down to this family through a cousin of the Rider's. Among some examples of woman's handiwork is a tiny shirt, one of twelve made by the present owner's grandmother, for Tom Thumb, who visited Wilmington as a seventeen year old lad in 1848, announcing that he "had kissed 1,000,000 ladies, and had a few more kisses left for Delaware lasses." At Third and Delaware Streets is the square brick house with a long wing, built in 1781 by Chief Justice Kensey Johns, who married Ann Van Dyke. It has a fine old staircase, mantels, and paneling, while the keyplates and doorknobs are duplicates of those in Mt. Vernon. When the house was inherited by a descendant of Governor Stockton, she sent one of these doorknobs to replace one stolen by some visitor from Washington's home.

This house has the great old-fashioned kitchen, with Dutch oven, and has recently been sold to a great-great-granddaughter of Governor Van Dyke. Her husband, a physician, now uses the old law offices. Wall paper made in 1804 in France, with the design of the lily, remained on the walls until 1910.

Opposite Amstel house is one built in 1797 by Senator Nicholas Van Dyke, and opposite the first Kensey Johns house is another Van Dyke home, with massive old shutters. In the latter, Dorcas Van Dyke was married in 1824 to Charles Irenée Du Pont, son of Victor Marie Du Pont de Nemours, who came to this country in the French diplomatic service. Charles was born in Charleston, South Carolina. This wedding was one of the most brilliant social events ever known in New Castle, the bride given away by Lafayette, who claimed the privilege of kissing her.

Opposite the Court House, oldest in America, is another very old dwelling, built early in the 18th century, and enlarged in 1790 by the senior Chief Justice James Booth, when he owned and occupied it. Here, too, are beautiful mantels and panels, a fine staircase with mahogany rail, and from the upper rear windows there is a charming view out over the river. In May, 1927, the house was empty and for sale.

Down on the Strand, laid out with Benjamin Franklin's aid, is another group of interesting old houses. At the foot of Delaware Street, William Penn first landed in America, on October 28th, 1682. At the Court House he was presented with " Turf, Twig, Water and Soyle," as tokens of his proprietorship. On the corner of Delaware and the Strand is a house which, although enlarged and modernized, has a rear portion, easily distinguished, built in 1732. To it came the messenger with news of the Battle of Bunker Hill, and here his letter was franked and sent on south by the occupant, Zachariah Van Leuvenigh. Nearby is one of the oldest houses in New Castle.

Most beautiful of all the houses here is the George Read house, with charming gardens extending back to the Green.

John Read came to this country in its early days, because his English fiancée died. He lived in both Maryland and Delaware, and long remained a bachelor, but finally married and had three sons, George, James and Thomas. George was the author of the first Delaware Constitution, and for twelve years a member of the Assembly. He came to New Castle about 1754, and his house stood on what is now a part of the gardens of the later house. Eleven years before the Declaration of Independence, he warned the British Government that unless the attitude towards the Colonies was changed, these would become independent, and eventually would surpass England in her staple manufactures. Of his brothers, James, a Colonel, was at the head of the American Navy Department during the Revolution, and died in Philadelphia, while Thomas was the first Commodore in the American Navy, and lived at Bordentown, New Jersey.

George Read was one of the Signers, even though he hesitated to ratify the Articles of Confederacy for Delaware.

In his New Castle home he entertained Washington and many other Revolutionary Generals, but in a disastrous fire which visited New Castle in 1824, the house was entirely destroyed.

The present house here had already been built in 1801, by his son George. In 1844, the fourth George Read sold it to William Couper, and the beautiful garden dates from him. Here is a " Captain's walk," and above the front door, with its fan- and side-lights, a Palladian window is admirable. Doorknobs within are of silver, and the woodwork is very handsome. Drawing room and library are separated by a doorway with beautiful fanlight above, while the carving in the former apartment is supplemented by delicate ornamentations in London putty, showing a man at arms, in a chariot drawn by lions, classic figures, arabesques, etc. Across from the drawing room is the dining room, its walls covered with paintings showing old New Castle, the landing of Penn, the old Court House, first Read house, etc.

The house is filled with choice furniture and ornaments, among others a curious water clock, made in 1685.

Acrelius, an early Swedish pastor, amused himself by cataloguing popular Delaware beverages, and among them are Madeira, punch, home brewed cherry and currant wines; the punch, chiefly drunk before dinner, was called a " meridian." Then there was " Manatham," made of small beer, rum and sugar, like the New England flip, while hot rum punch was always served at funerals.

Edmund Cantwell, Sheriff of New Castle County under William Penn, built himself a house three miles from what is now Odessa, which was standing at least recently. In 1731, Richard Cantwell was granted permission to establish a toll bridge here. The land had originally been patented to Abraham Coffin, in 1671, but was re-surveyed in 1686 to Jonathan De Haes and Ephraim Herman. De Haes was a member of the first Legislature, in 1683, under Penn. Part of this tract afterwards came to Thomas Noxon, and on these fields Caesar Rodney camped with his Delaware militia, while General Howe marched to the Brandywine on a road to Middletown. Thomas Noxon was a member of old St. Anne's church near Middletown.

Adjoining Richard Cantwell's land was a tract owned by William Corbit, descendant of a Scotch Quaker, who started an early tannery. Another Corbit, Daniel, occupied a fine old brick house still standing in Odessa, and his daughter married David Wilson in 1769, who built a house for her next door to her father's in that same year. It was left in 1847, by a descendant, Mrs. Mary Corbit Warner, with a sufficient endowment to maintain it, to the town for a library and museum.

The house is finely paneled throughout, and has one of the beautiful staircases usual in handsome dwellings of its period. The main portion consists of but one room on each side of the hall on the two floors, but there is an ell containing a dining room, kitchen, and bedrooms. The library is on the first floor; above is a room furnished as an old time bedroom, and opposite is the museum, with collections and relics of former days.

Not far from Odessa, the old home of Commodore McDonough, distinguished in the War of 1812, was formerly the home of Kirkwood, who fought in thirty-two battles of the Revolution, enlisting under Rodney's friend, Haslet, in the first year of that war. At the end of it, Kirkwood was a major, removed to Ohio, and was killed in the Battle of Miami in 1791.

Closely connected with Delaware history from its early days is the name of Ridgely. The first to come to this country was Henry, from Devonshire, England. He settled in Annapolis in 1659, was a colonel of militia, one of the commissioners appointed to survey and oversee the building of the Annapolis court house, and member of the Assembly and Council. His son Henry died when but thirty years old, leaving several children. Nicholas, third of these, came to Delaware in 1732, and lived first at Duck Creek, then removed to Dover. He was Treasurer of Kent County, and Judge of Delaware's Supreme Court.

A mile outside of Dover, reached by a long, grassy avenue, is Eden

Hill Farm, where he lived. Of brick, painted white, two stories high, with a long, low wing, it is in excellent condition, occupied by the tenant who farms the land. There is a large old Dutch porch in the rear; massive old shutters with hand wrought latches, and doors with hand wrought hinges may be admired.

This is the house mentioned as for a time the home of Caesar Rodney.

Nicholas Ridgely's son Charles studied medicine, and for him his father bought the house occupied ever since by Ridgelys, in Dover. It faces the old Green, laid out in 1717 by William Penn's orders, at which time the town consisted of some three hundred persons. On this Green markets and fairs were held; here the Declaration of Independence was read, the Revolutionary soldiers formed to march away, as later did those in the last war. A tablet on the Green to the memory of the earlier patriots mentions that but few ever returned.

What has always been known as the Ridgely house since the first of the family came to occupy it in 1760, is the oldest house now standing on the Green, and was built in 1728. Outwardly, save for a new addition in the rear, it is practically unchanged, and the interior has been carefully treated.

The old office used by Dr. Charles has since been the law office of several Ridgelys, was for a short time used by John M. Clayton, who from 1824 to 1842 lived in a fine old house on the other side of the Green, and by Chief Justice Comegys, a connection of the Ridgely family. The Clayton house, built in 1730, and shortly after its erection the home of Samuel Chew, was torn down to build a wing of the State House, its old garden destroyed.

Charles Ridgely was a member of state assemblies, and of the Constitutional Convention in Delaware, in 1776. His father married three times, and Charles was the son of the first wife, Mary Wynkoop. The second wife, Mary Vining, was a widow, daughter of Judge Hugh Middleton, of Salem, New Jersey. Her first husband, Captain Benjamin Vining, on his deathbed said to her:

"I know that you will marry again, but will you promise me to make over to *our* children all of your estate which you have inherited from your father?" She gave the promise, married Nicholas Ridgely, but none of her own property descended to her Ridgely children.

Her second son by her first marriage, John, married her stepdaughter, Rachel Ridgely, and it was their daughter Mary, beauty and belle, who loved Anthony Wayne, and remained ever true to his memory. The first Mary Vining's daughter, Mary, married the Reverend Charles Inglis, rector of Christ Church, Dover, and later of Old Trinity, New York. Inglis, a Tory, was a man of spirit, for when threatened by American soldiers should he persist in praying for King George, he boldly faced them the following Sunday, in spite of the bayonets they carried and made the prayer as usual. His property was confiscated, and he was obliged to leave the country, later becoming the first Colonial Bishop of Nova Scotia, and marrying a New York woman. His first wife had no children.

Charles Ridgely married twice. Of his sons by his first wife, Dr. Abraham was Secretary of State, Charles died young, and Nicholas became known as the "Father of Chancery," Chancellor of Delaware. The second wife's son, Henry, studied law, was President of the Farmers' Bank, Dover, from the time of its incorporation, and for forty years; a Representative in Congress for his State, and twice Secretary of the State. He also married twice; Sarah Banning, by whom he had fifteen children, and Sarah, daughter of Governor Cornelius Comegys, but they had none.

He was severely wounded in a duel which was practically forced upon him. Mr. Barrett, of Dover, had been insulted by a man from Wilmington, named Shields. Barrett asked Mr. Ridgely to act as his second, and take a challenge to Shields. The latter then refused to meet Barrett, but challenged Ridgely.

This Henry Moore Ridgely's daughter, Ann, married Charles Du Pont, of Wilmington, Delaware, and now treasures in her possession the pearl pin, always worn by a Ridgely bride, down to the most recent one, who was the twenty-fifth so to wear it.

Charles Ridgely's second wife's family deserves mention, for it was noted on both sides. Her father was William Moore, of Moore Hall, which he built on the estate given him by his father, who came to Pennsylvania from South Carolina. Near Phoenixville, Pennsylvania, this house is still standing, but has long since passed out of the family.

Moore was a Tory, but would not take up arms against his fellow countrymen. While Washington was at Valley Forge, a number of Continental officers were quartered here, and courteously treated, but any mention of the right of the Colonies to revolt was liable to bring on violent arguments, and almost drive the old Judge into a stroke of apoplexy.

One day when Moore was laid up with an attack of gout, some American soldiers visited Moore Hall for plunder. Among other things which they seized under the helpless owner's eyes was a fine sword, with beautifully jeweled hilt. Controlling himself, and it must have been with a great effort, Mr. Moore requested permission to hold this treasured sword for the last time. The soldier unsuspectingly surrendered it, whereupon the old gentleman broke from its hilt the blade, and throwing this at the feet of the astonished man, while retaining the hilt, cried out:

" There, take that if you want to fight for it, but you shall not rob me of my plate! "

His wife was Lady Wiliamina Wemyss, who, with her brother James, came to America, driven from Scotland when the Pretender's cause was lost, because their father had espoused it.

Henry Moore Ridgely's first wife, Sarah Banning, also came of a distinguished family, but on the patriot side. Her father married Elizabeth Alford, who had a curious story connected with her family. Her grandmother was almost buried alive. Had it not been that, one daughter being absent from home in another state, they waited for her return to hold the funeral, she might really have been buried. But fortunately for her, when the undertaker came to make the final arrangements, she showed signs of life, and regained consciousness. After that, on each anniversary of her supposed death, and she lived for a number of years, Mrs. Alford used to take her children to the churchyard, and there among the tombstones, the hapless children were made to eat their supper, while the mother discoursed on death and immortality.

John Banning gave liberally to the patriot cause, and at the close of the war, stood on the steps of the old Dover Academy, and offered sound currency to the soldiers in exchange for their depreciated paper notes.

One more anecdote of the family must be told. When Chancellor Nicholas Ridgely was living in the old Dover house, shortly before his death, he entertained there the well known abolitionist, Lucretia Mott. The announcement of her coming to the town had called forth ugly threats of what would be done to her should she persist in coming. Chancellor Ridgely, who was not at all in harmony with her views, then promptly invited her to stay in his home. When remonstrated with, he replied that it was not because he "liked the abolitionists, but I will not see any woman ill-treated in Dover."

He chivalrously escorted his guest to the hall in which she was to give her lecture, when instead of urging the abolitionist views, she gave a graceful lecture on art. Escorted home by her host, they were followed by an ugly mob, but the Chancellor refused either to have the shutters of the front windows closed, or the front door barred, but standing with his back to the fire, in full view of the crowd which had assembled outside, he calmly conversed with his guest until the crowd dispersed.

After this digression, returning to the old house, it stands, close to the street, but in the rear is a large garden, which will soon be even larger. Next to the old house, on the corner, stood the old Biddle Tavern. Later, the Capitol Hotel succeeded it, and not long ago, when the property was again for sale, the Ridgelys bought it, tore down the old house, and have kept enough land to make an addition to the garden, and insure the privacy of their home.

This is very substantial. The old shutters still shield the windows, as in the days when the Chancellor refused to have them closed; within are old locks and hinges, Dutch doors give entrance, the one at the rear, opening into the garden, built of great planks, with a curious hand wrought iron latch.

One enters a square hall, from which the early staircase led, steep and narrow. Originally there was a room on either side on both of the two floors, but later another room behind each of these was added, with hall between, from which a broad new flight of stairs — no longer new however — mounts.

The house is furnished throughout with wonderful old pieces, most of them heirlooms in the Ridgely family, a few brought here by the present Mrs. Ridgely's grandfather, who was a Lloyd, related to the Wye, Maryland, family, although he settled at Elkton. Here is a fine old table which belonged to Commander Jones, of the Wasp, a chair which belonged to Penn's secretary, etc. Here is a portrait of Mary Vining, wife of the first Nicholas Ridgely, a fine three-quarter length by Peale, with another believed to be of the daughter-in-law, Wiliamina, wife of Dr. Charles. A pair of French vases given to the latter as wedding present by General Cadwallader, who married a sister of the bride, shows on one, Hector, and the emblems of war, on the other, Venus, and emblems of love, which some one has remarked constituted a most appropriate wedding gift. Here is Chancellor Ridgely's wedding china, is one of the old glass-doored cupboards beside the fireplace in the drawing room, and here, too, is a large facsimile of the signatures of those who ratified the Constitution, Nicholas Ridgely's among them.

The Court House opposite stands on the site of the old George Tavern. Here Thomas McKean's mounted messenger met Caesar Rodney, on his ride, with urgent request for his return to Philadelphia, and from here, after an hour's rest, Rodney set out again. On the west side of the Green, modernized, but the old walls little changed, are the house first owned by John Banning, then by Caesar Rodney, and later, among others, by the Claytons; the home of John Vining, and his beautiful daughter, Mary; and The Green, built in 1791 by John Fisher, and partly re-built by Joseph P. Comegys, Senator from Delaware and Chief Justice. He lived here for many years, until his death.

On State Street, just beyond the Green, stands the house built in

1742 by Vincent Loockerman, descended from Govert, who came to this country from Holland in 1633, with Van Twiller, and whose sister married Olaf Van Cortlandt.

Oldest is the large square portion, the long wing on the street having been added by a later member of the family to give room for his five children, since, like other of these fine, large houses, there were but three rooms on each of the two floors.

The original knocker hangs on the original old Dutch door. The house is beautifully finished; there are the paneled walls in which are set big old fireplaces, and fascinating cupboards; elaborately hand carved woodwork framing doors and windows, columns in half relief; great spacious, lofty rooms, filled with marvelous old furniture, brought by the family from Holland or England, or later imported from these countries. Ships brought goods almost to Dover, up a creek to what was known as Ship Yards, nearby. The beautiful staircase has delicately carved spindles, and of course a mahogany rail. Shutters and doors are of broad hand hewn planks, there are great rimlockers, latches and hinges. A three-quarter length portrait of the first owner, dressed all in scarlet, hangs in the lovely old drawing room, looking out upon the beautiful garden, where are many varieties of trees, including the rare Irish yew, the tulip poplar, holly, with more familiar kinds, and shrubs and flowers in bewildering number.

One bedroom upstairs must be mentioned, with its fireplace framed in beautiful old Dutch tiles, and needless to say, in the old cupboards, with their shell tops and curved shelves, are collections of china to drive the antique lover wild with envy.

Another fine old house in Dover on King Street is Woodburne, built about 1790. It, too, has an extensive garden in the rear, and fine old shade trees. Built of brick, a later owner added brick terraces on three sides, and replaced an incongruous bow window by French doors. There are but two rooms and a hall on the lower floor, in the main portion, a rear wing containing the kitchen and servants' rooms above, but the hall runs across the entire front of the house, is forty-one feet long, and proportionately broad, with an old Dutch door opening at either end on the terraces, while drawing and dining rooms are almost twenty-one feet square. On the Dutch doors are huge latches, and very long strap hinges, with locks whose keys no one would wish to carry. It is said that these keys would not open the doors from outside, and served merely to lock them, but in any case, a rear door opening from the dining room is provided with a modern lock.

The truly exquisite woodwork and paneling, all hand work, was paid for by the builder with a farm. The present owner, Dr. Hall, who loves his beautiful home, has furnished it throughout with antique furniture, hangings and ornaments, all in keeping. Both drawing and dining room have the paneled fireplace wall, with cupboards on either side.

In one of the two Dutch doors a piece of wood has been fitted in to fill a hole. About this the following tale has been related in an old story, The Entailed Hat, part of which is laid in Woodburne.

The owner at that time was a cruel man, who delighted in tormenting his own children. One of his favorite amusements was to order them to stand on tiptoe in the great hall, and when, tired, they sank to the soles of their feet, he would then lash their ankles. One day, infuriated by this treatment, a son snatched a rifle from the wall, and fired at his father, but the bullet missed, and pierced the door instead.

It has a ghost, although the owner says that he has never seen it. Lorenzo Dow thus described it years ago:

He was a guest here, and as he was going up the beautiful stairs to his room, met a little elderly gentleman, dressed in knee breeches, long-tailed coat, powdered wig and queue. He drew aside with a bow to allow the old gentleman to pass, which the latter did, bowing in turn, but saying nothing. When the family assembled at table that evening, Mr. Dow noticed that the old gentleman was not there.

" Are you not waiting for your other guest? " he asked.

" What other guest? " was the surprised query.

" Why, the little old gentleman in knee breeches," replied Dow. To his surprise, his hostess seemed greatly embarrassed, and made no answer. Afterwards he was told that this was an apparition often seen.

Eden Farm near Dover, Delaware, home of Nicholas Ridgely, and of his ward, Caesar Rodney, the Rider. It is still owned by the Ridgelys.

Amstel house, built 1730, New Castle, Delaware.

The Ridgely home and its beautiful garden in the heart of old Dover, Delaware.

On the outskirts of Dover, Foxall Farm was bought and named by Nicholas Ridgely, and is now owned by his great-great-granddaughter, Mrs. Charles Du Pont, of Wilmington. Near, too, is Pleasanton Abbey, now a farmhouse, built by Henry Stevens, a devoted Tory, and here he several times during the Revolution concealed British soldiers.

About eight miles from Dover, on the Bay Road, is part of the Logan tract, on which are a number of old brick houses. Largest is Towne Point, in which the first courts were held in Kent County. There are spacious rooms in this mansion, its broad staircase has low treads, mahogany handrail and delicately wrought spindles. The stairs mount to a great open attic, where wooden pegs still hold the roof in place. The bricks of the house are laid in Flemish bond. It faces away from the road, and in the distance is a grove of trees marking an old slave burying ground, where several hundred are said to have been laid to rest.

Some distance further, at least a mile from the highroad, is another brick house, with a very old appearing stone wing. This seems to be Kingston-upon-Hull, residence of Samuel Dickinson, and which originally had a front of about eighty feet, but is in a rather dilapidated condition now. The old names are unknown here now, and one has difficulty in locating the residences where others have long since occupied them.

The first Dickinsons to come to America settled in Talbot County, Maryland, where the head of the family built a home. His son John, born in 1732, was Governor of Maryland and the founder of Dickenson College at Carlisle, Pennsylvania. His brother Samuel is said to have removed to Kent County, Delaware, with his son John, and it was probably this man who built the old brick house just mentioned. Thomas Parke built the large one that stands in so much better condition now, and owned a house in Dover as well, leaving the country house to his wife as a dower house, when he died.

This by no means exhausts the list of fine old houses, or those once fine, in the vicinity of Dover. One can scarcely drive a mile without seeing red brick, solid, substantial houses, typical of Delaware even as the big stone farm houses are typical in Pennsylvania.

Chapter XVIII

Many are the charming old houses to be found in Maryland. Unlike Virginia, Maryland in the early days imported very few bricks, for suitable clay with which to make them was available in many localities. The highly glazed red or brown bricks found in old walls were usually made on the estates, and clay pits are often found near the houses.

In 1634, a band of colonists led by Leonard Calvert, landed at what became St. Mary's, Maryland. This town, once capital of the Province, has, like old Jamestown, Virginia, practically disappeared, but St. Mary's Female Seminary was built on its site.

It was Governor Francis Nicholson who removed Maryland's capital from St. Mary's to Annapolis, despite the petitions of inhabitants of the former town. St. Mary's was Roman Catholic, and in 1654 Maryland's Governor, Richard Preston, was a Quaker. The Preston mansion became the seat of the Provincial Court, and here the Assembly met, and official records were kept until 1660, when Lord Baltimore again regained power.

The citizens of St. Mary's petitioned that their city be once more the capital, and offered to provide "a coach or caravan or both to go at all times of public meetings of Assemblies and Provincial Courts every day daily between St. Mary's and Patuxent River, and at all other times once a week, and also to keep constantly on hand one dozen horses at least with suitable furniture for any person or persons having occasion to ride, post, or otherwise with or without a guide to any part of the province on the Western Shore." But in 1694, the capital was permanently established at Annapolis.

Lord Baltimore, while at the head of the government, had maintained feudal state, and lived in a " palace," but Richard Bennett, who later was Governor of Virginia, Edward Lloyd, Richard Preston, William Berry and William Burgess, with others who were to become prominent in the new city, were Puritan refugees from Virginia.

Annapolis, however, was never a Puritan city. By 1752, it had its theatre, and eight years later another was opened with a performance of " The Orphans."

When the city plan was made, two adjoining circles were mapped out; one for the Province, with the Capitol to stand upon it, the other for the church, and on this second one St. Anne's was built. Another circle was laid out for trade, another for " gentlemen's houses." In the heart of the latter was built the Chase house.

Annapolis is filled with fine old houses, and from its early days was noted for them.

In the hotel, Carvel Hall, may be found almost intact the splendid mansion built for himself in 1703, by William Paca, already described in an earlier book. [1] Of Italian origin, a distinguished citizen, he married Mary Chew, of the Philadelphia and Germantown family. Her brother Benjamin built beautiful Cliveden in Germantown, Pennsylvania.

Paca was Chief Justice, twice Governor of Maryland, Judge of the United States District Court, appointed by Washington himself, who, when some of Paca's enemies remonstrated at this appointment is said to have replied:

" Without him and others like him there would have been no United States."

An annex now to the hotel, the Brice house was considered one of the most magnificent in Annapolis. Built about 1740, it was the gift of Thomas Jenings, a cousin of Sarah, first Duchess of Marlborough, to Juliana, his daughter, who married Colonel James Brice. It has now

[1] *Early American Inns and Taverns*, the Author.

been converted into suites of apartments, but the large rear room on the first floor has been practically unaltered. Every one of the fifteen or more rooms in the house has its fireplace, each, with its carved mantel, different. Elaborate carving and plaster work, and many varieties of rare woods are found within its walls. The stairway is of mahogany. The rear room already mentioned has an especially elaborate carved mantel, for it was the state drawing room.

Colonel Brice fought in the Revolutionary Army. His eldest son, Thomas Jenings Brice, had made provision in his will for all of his servants, and was found dead from a blow on the head, but the murderer was never discovered. Whether with reason or not, it was supposed that the provisions of the will had in some way become known, and that one of the servants had thus hastened his inheritance.

Another magnificent residence in the heart of the fashionable section was the Samuel Chase house.

Two years were required to build its outside walls alone, and it was finished in 1769. It has a very broad hall, with stairs at the rear which divide half way up into two flights. The doors throughout are of solid mahogany, the latches and hinges of wrought silver. There is much fine woodwork, elaborately carved window shutters, and beside the dining room, there was an ornate breakfast room.

Two miles south of Princess Anne still stands the house in which Samuel Chase was born, built in 1713. He received his earliest education from his father, then studied law in Annapolis. He joined the Sons of Liberty, and was involved in the destruction of the property of Zachariah Hood, Stamp Collector for the Province of Maryland. Later he was elected to the Assembly, was a member of the Continental Congress from 1774 to 1776; went with Benjamin Franklin and Charles Carroll on a special mission to Canada in 1774, was one of the Signers, and in 1786 moved to Baltimore, when he was appointed judge of the court there. Once during a riot in the streets of that city, Chase alone, and with his hands, captured two of the ringleaders, and marched them off before a justice. He had also been a member of the committee appointed in 1774 in Annapolis to "effect such association as will secure American liberty," fellow members being John Hall, Charles Carroll, Thomas Johnson, Jr., William Paca and Matthias Hammond.

Chase was Chief Justice of the Courts of Maryland, then Assistant Justice of the Supreme Court of the United States, appointed by Washington.

In 1805, he was tried for impeachment, the case creating great excitement, but he was acquitted by a tremendous majority of any conduct justifying impeachment. He was accused, and it is said justly, with " mingling diatribes against current political conditions with his judicial utterances."

After his death, the house was owned by Edward Lloyd, the fourth of that name in this country, and he was succeeded by the fifth Edward Lloyd, Governor of Maryland. After him it was left for a home for Aged Women, which it is to-day.

Opposite the Chase house is the Hammond residence, built by Matthias Hammond at the time that the former was owned by Edward Lloyd. It is said that at the latter's request instead of the three-storied building which Hammond had planned, he agreed to erect a central portion of but two stories, with low wings on either side, so as not to cut off Lloyd's view, provided Lloyd would defray the cost of the wings. This was agreed upon, but since the house had already been begun, the five foot foundations for the central portion are much thicker than would have been the case if the original plans had been followed.

Hammond, so the story goes, built his house in 1774, for his bride, but before the wedding day the lady jilted him, declaring that he cared more for his house than for her. He died a bachelor.

After his death, the house came into the possession of Jonathan Pinkney, a Tory. His son William, however, was Senator, another son, Ninian, United States Minister to Great Britain and to Russia, and Attorney General of the United States. William, Ninian's son, was the fifth Episcopal Bishop of Maryland. In 1811, the house was sold to Chief Justice Jeremiah Townley Chase as a home for his daughter, who married Richard Lockerman, descendant of an old Knickerbocker family. Their daughter inherited the house, and married Judge William Harwood. After the Civil War, he refused to take the oath of allegiance to the Federal Government, so could not travel on a train. Accordingly he walked once a week thirty miles to and from Baltimore to his law office there.

Last owner of the house was Miss Anne Harwood, and in the early autumn of 1926 it was sold at auction to old St. John's school, and is to be preserved as a museum. During the autumn, workmen were already busy tearing out bricks from the old filled-in fireplaces that they might resume their original appearance. It was also planned to remove the modern partitions dividing large rooms into small ones, and in short to restore the old house, which had passed through many vicissitudes, in so far as possible to its original state.

Entering a broad hall, there is a rather small room on either side, and a large one in the rear, the old dining room, which once overlooked a very beautiful and extensive garden. Although some of this has been sold, enough remains to make a pretty garden.

Stairs ascend in an alcove at one side of the hall, and from this side a narrow passage connects with the right wing. The other wing was not open at the time of the writer's visit.

Above the dining room is the ballroom, still beautiful, although its exquisite carved woodwork is blackened, window and door frames painted an ugly brown. Heavy old shutters still screen the windows, and there is a handsome cornice; the doors have curious old brass latches.

The Peggy Stewart Inn, an attractive old house down by the Navy Yard, must not be confused with the residence a few doors away, a colonial house, former home of Alexander and Peggy Stuart.

Alexander arrived from England on his ship, the Peggy, with a cargo consisting of tea, consigned to Thomas and Charles Williams and Company. Stewart paid the duty and tried to land it, but tea had by that time been banned by all patriotic colonists, and so great was popular indignation in Annapolis that in spite of Stewart's explanations that he ought not to be held responsible for goods ordered by others, it was actually proposed to tar and feather him. Only by apologizing humbly and offering with his own hands to burn and sink his ship, with the offending cargo, did he escape with his liberty, perhaps his life. From an upper window in their house, his wife watched her husband ground and then burn his ship, and Annapolis had her Tea Party.

In 1783 his son Anthony was one of fifty-one men in New York who petitioned for a grant of land in Nova Scotia, and left the United States.

The Scott house in Annapolis, built in 1760, was owned by a great-uncle of the author of the Star Spangled Banner, and Francis Scott Key often stayed here as a boy. Key's father, John Ross Key, lived in a brick house, now gone, in Middleburg District, Carroll County.

Carrollton, one of the many houses owned by the Carrolls of Carrollton, is now occupied by a body of Redemptionist priests. Here Charles Carroll of Carrollton wrote four letters to the Maryland Gazette in 1773, defending the rights of the people, and signed them: " First Citizen." It is said that the Assembly adjourned in a body after the publication of these letters, and went to Carroll's house to express their thanks to him.

Wherever one goes in this part of Maryland, whatever of history one reads, the name of Carroll will be frequently met.

Daniel Carroll of O'Neill, Ireland, is said to have had twenty sons, "whom he presented in one troop of horse, well acoutred in habiliments of war, to the Earl of Ormond, for the service of Charles I." Most of the twenty died in foreign service, but from them all of the Carrolls in this country are by some historians said to descend. Others maintain that there were two distinct families, not connected.

The eldest of the twenty sons, Daniel, had two sons, Charles and John.

Dr. Charles Carroll " chyrurgeon," son of the other Charles mentioned, came from Ireland at an early date, settled in Annapolis, and later bought a tract of land in Georgia, which was rich in iron ore. Educated a Catholic, after coming to this country he became a Protestant. He prospered, and before long, the iron on his estate was paying for silver, glass, furniture, carriages, etc., as well as for the building of several houses. He owned a number of states, Mount Clare, now within the city limits of Baltimore, The Plains, near Annapolis, Claremont and The Caves being some of these. He claimed descent from Daniel and his wife, Dorothy, of Ely and O'Neill, Ireland.

Dr. Carroll's eldest son, Charles, was sent to Eton and to Cambridge University to be educated, and became a student at Inns of Court, The Temple, London.

While Charles Carroll was living " at the Middle Temple, Garden Library, Staircase No. 2, London," his brother died, and Charles, returning from England in 1757, arrived only a short time before the father's death.

He had a home on Shipwright Street, Baltimore, which has been replaced by a modern school building.

In Carroll Park, far above the street level, high enough to look over and beyond the factories and other buildings between street and river, stands the beautiful old house built in 1768 by The Barrister. The street, Columbia Avenue, was the Indian trail running north and south, so it requires no vivid imagination to picture the travelers who once passed here.

Originally the grounds of Mount Clare extended to the river, but enough of them remain as a park to make a charming setting.

Entering the gate, one mounts a series of terraces which were part of the original grounds. John Adams, who was entertained by the owner, thus described them: " There is a very beautiful garden and then a fall, another flat garden and then a fall, and so on down to the river."

" Fall " is still the name given in Maryland to terraces.

Close beside the old front door, the Maryland Society of Colonial Dames of America affixed a tablet, stating that the house was built by Charles Carroll, the Barrister.

The fine old house had fallen into a sad state when the Park Board of Baltimore purchased it, carefully restored it, and leased it to the Colonial Dames for a museum. To this society much credit is due, for they have succeeded in acquiring through gift or loans much of the original furniture, some of the pictures, and other interesting articles, so that the house is now practically as it was in the days of its great owner.

Entering the square hall, almost opposite the entrance is the large drawing room, with view over the garden down to the river, while at the left hand is a small breakfast room or office. This has a fine carved mantel, and on the walls now hang the arms of Maryland and those of some of her most distinguished families.

The drawing room is beautiful. Here is a set of six chairs in gold and white wood, upholstered in gold brocade, the color still unfaded, although these were the property of the Barrister. On the wall hangs a copy of the original portrait of him by Peale, copied by his great-granddaughter.

The title, the Barrister, was added to his name for a very definite reason. After his return from England, he wrote to his friends: " There are so many of my name in this town that some particular direction is necessary to prevent mistakes. Please, therefore, direct to me either ' Counsellor ' or ' Barrister-at-Law,' and when you write to my correspondents, be pleased to mention me with that addition."

The dining room has a charming carved mantel, flanked by arched-topped china closets, on the shelves of which have been assembled some fine examples of old glass and china. One set of the latter was actually used by Mr. Carroll. An unusual table, with a Gothic window design beneath the top, and hanging acorn drops will arouse the admiration of any lover of old furniture, as will a beautiful pie crust table.

The stairs leading to both second story and attic have delicate hand carved spindles, and the mahogany handrail usual in fine old houses of the period. In one of the spacious bedrooms, with two powder closets opening from it, Lafayette slept when on a visit here, and the mahogany bed and chest of drawers are those which he used.

One of those subterranean passages so often found in old houses led from this house to the Patapsco River, and it is said that this passage was used by the people of Baltimore when, after Braddock's defeat, the authorities ordered all the women and children placed on board ships in the harbor for safety. The Indians at that time came within thirty miles of the town. The passage, and a small room into which it opened near the house have now been walled up, so the eager visitor may not explore them.

Charles Carroll married Margaret, daughter of Matthew Tilghman, of the distinguished Talbot County family. His wife long survived him, and her will, which hangs in the old office here, naming as her executors Henry Brice and Tench Tilghman, requests that they free and provide for her slaves, and leaves the negro boy, Tom, to Henry Brice until he shall be thirty-one, when he is to be set free.

Like the other Charles Carroll, in spite of his English education, and his close friendship with Governor Sir Robert Eden, the Barrister threw himself heart and soul into the patriot's cause, and lived to see it victorious.

After his father's death, he was elected a member of Maryland's lower house, and was a member of the Committee of Correspondence, together with Matthew Tilghman, John Hall, Samuel Chase, Thomas Johnson, Jr., William Paca and Charles Carroll of Carrollton. He was also elected to the first State Senate of Maryland, and re-elected. He died in 1781, a few months after another Charles Carroll, of Cole's Harbor. That he was related to Sir Daniel O'Carroll, who owned estates at Ely, O'Carroll, Mallebrit, Leap and Castletown, Ireland, is proved by letters exchanged between Sir Daniel and Dr. Carroll.

The Colonial Dames have some interesting invoices of Carroll's purchases for Mount Clare after his wedding. For instance: " one four-wheeled Post chariot made light and fashionable without a box, but strong and neat, with plain simple strong springs, lined with green cloth, painted and ornamented fashionably with the enclosed coat-of-arms, and strong good harness, not for travelling into the country, but for town use, as they answer much better than heavy chariots, as our horses are but small, and the ground deep and sandy." He also orders clothes for himself and his wife:

" One suit of blue cloth for an undress suit, a coat, waistcoat and breeches made in French fashion, lined with narrow double gold lace, about ten guineas. One rich flowered brocade for a dress. (They were fashionable when I was in England.) which has a light gold sprigg or flower woven into the silk which should cost about eight guineas a yard; a lady's watch with coat-of-arms quartered with the Tilghman coat-of-arms," etc.

Homewood, beautifully situated on a hill in the suburbs of Baltimore, was built by Charles Carroll of Carrollton as a home for his son, outside the town, that this son, who was given to dissipation, might be further from temptations, and perhaps reform. The latter did live here, but died before his father. He married Harriet Chew.

This house, practically unchanged, is now the Johns Hopkins Club. A two-story brick building, with a wing at each end, one enters a broad hall, terminating in a room reached through a wide archway. Two rooms open on either side of the hall, and narrow passages lead to the wings, where are a number of small rooms. The great mahogany doors have no hinges, but turn on pivots. There are beautifully carved mantels and woodwork throughout the house.

Many are the fine old estates in the vicinity of Baltimore. Among the most famous is Doughregan Manor, home of Charles Carroll of Carrollton, longest lived Signer. The Carrolls were distinguished patriots and citizens, as well as among the wealthiest of colonial families.

This house is three hundred feet long and but thirty deep, and contains a private chapel, where every Sunday for more than a century mass was said. The family were devout Roman Catholics, and here was an apartment known as the Cardinal's room, decorated in scarlet and gold, in which any high dignitary of the church when visiting the mansion was lodged.

Charles Carroll, grandfather of the Signer, and founder of this branch of the family in America, was a claimant of estates of the O'Carrolls, princes of Ely, in Kings and Tipperary counties, Ireland. Petitioning for these estates, he was given instead a grant of 60,000 acres in Maryland, and later, 10,000 more. He first chose a tract on the site of Frederick, Maryland, but later changed, and the manor house stands on land finally accepted by him. Appointed Attorney General by Lord Baltimore, he became involved in political quarrels, was imprisoned, but later liberated, and appointed Judge and Register of the Land Office, both important posts. When the second Lord Baltimore died, he was attorney for the widow. Like later Carrolls, he was educated at Douai, France. He was twice married, and the father of ten children.

His son Charles built the Carroll mansion in Annapolis, on two lots of ground which he is said to have purchased from a widow, paying her much more than they were worth. In this Annapolis house Washington was often a guest, and it, too, had a private chapel.

The second Charles had but one son, the Signer of the Declaration of Independence. The latter was born in 1735, sent to France to be educated, but absence in a foreign country did not lessen his love of his native land, and on his return, in 1765, he threw himself heart and soul into the patriot's cause. Mr. Hammond quotes the following story.

" 'Will you sign? ' said Hancock to Charles Carroll.

" ' Most willingly.'

" ' There goes two millions with the dash of a pen,' says one of those standing by.

" ' Oh, Carroll, you will get off; there are so many Charles Carrolls.' " [2]

When this third Charles Carroll died, he owned more than 80,000 acres in Maryland, and over 27,000 in Pennsylvania. His son died before him, and Doughregan passed to the grandson, Charles, born at Homewood. The latter's son, the sixth Charles, married a descendant of Washington's grandfather Ball, but had no children, and after his death the place was purchased by his brother, John Lee Carroll, one of Maryland's governors. Folly Quarter, willed to his granddaughter, was another of the third Charles' estates.

Dr. Charles Carroll, a kinsman of the first Charles Carroll of

[2] *Colonial Mansions of Maryland and Delaware*, John Martin Hammond.

Carrollton, married Dorothy Blake, a granddaughter of Madame Henrietta Maria Lloyd, a person of importance. When she married Philemon Lloyd of Wye, she was the widow of Richard Bennett. She was the daughter of Captain James Neale and his wife, born Anne Gill. The Neales went to England, where Mrs. Neale was maid of honor to Queen Henrietta Maria, and when her daughter was born, the Queen is said to have stood godmother for the baby. Captain Neale was one of seven gentlemen who stood beside Charles I on the scaffold, to each of whom he gave a ring, which, on a spring being pressed, opened to reveal a tiny portrait of the monarch, with " Jan. 30, 1648 ", the date, old style, of the execution. The ring has been handed down in the Lloyd family ever since.

This Dr. Charles was the father of still another Charles Carroll, author of the Declaration of Rights.

At Mattapany, the old brick house built by Governor Charles Calvert, later Lord Baltimore, still stands, on part of a tract of land said to have been given by Pantheon, King of the Indians, to the Jesuits. They established a store and mission here at an early date, for in 1641 they gave the land to Lord Baltimore. In 1663, the Hon. Henry Sewall, Secretary of the Province and member of the Council, received a grant of 1200 acres of this tract, which his widow, Jane, inherited two years later. She married Charles Calvert. Maryland deputies, driven from St. Mary's City, took refuge here, and it became a garrison house for them.

William, son of the first Calvert, had a home on Calvert's Bay. He was Deputy Governor.

Mt. Airy, near Croome, Prince George's County, is the Calvert mansion, built by Benedict, son of Lord Baltimore's fifth son, Charles. There is a mystery about Benedict's parentage. No one knows who was his mother, nor where he was born. In 1748 he married a distant cousin, Elizabeth Calvert, and began building this house.

The Calverts had wished to found a Maryland landed aristocracy, but failed in the attempt. In 1636 it was decreed that every estate of 2,000 acres should constitute a manor. Large houses were built, as has been seen, usually with spacious rooms grouped around a central hall. As in many old Virginia homes, the walls were usually wainscoted from floor to ceiling, the woodwork often finely hand carved. Portraits of six or seven generations frequently hung on the walls, for by the middle period of the colony, there were wealth and luxury in these homes. Sideboards in the dining rooms were covered with decanters, glasses and silver adorned with the family crest, which had all been in the family for several generations, or brought with the first settlers from England.

An early English writer remarks: " Their furniture is of the most costly wood, and rarest marbles, enriched by skillful and artistic work. Their elegant and light carriages are drawn by finely bred horses, and driven by richly apparelled slaves."

Mt. Airy is said to have been a hunting lodge, built by Lord Baltimore. One wing, long, low, with dormer windows and hipped roof, built of bricks laid endwise, forming walls almost two feet thick, is pointed out as the original building. The main house, two stories high, was added to this wing. The cellar of the newer portion connects with that under the old wing, and through the five-foot walls of the latter runs a secret passage, long unexplored. The gardens are said to have been laid out by Major L'Enfant, planner of the city of Washington.

The land on which fine old Belmont stands was sold in 1735 to Caleb Dorsey, of Annapolis, who gave it to his son Caleb. The latter built the house in 1738. Inheriting a large fortune, he greatly increased it by developing iron ores in this section. With his brother, he built a foundry, and later alone two more. Caleb Dorsey was an ardent patriot, and many cannon used by the American forces in the Revolution were cast in the Dorsey foundries.

His son Edward inherited the place, which then passed to Edward's daughter, who, when her guardians refused their consent, eloped with Alexander Contee Hanson. His father as a youth was Washington's second secretary, the first being Hanson's cousin. In 1784, Alexander was called upon with Samuel Chase to make a digest of Maryland's laws, and later was United States Senator. A man of strong convictions, he edited the Federal Republic of Baltimore, and once, for some of his views therein expressed, was attacked by an angry mob and almost killed.

Four Hansons, wards of the Queen, came to New Sweden in 1642, with Lieutenant Colonel John Printz, the Governor. Later, all four came to Kent Island, Maryland. Equality, Mulberry Grove, Harwood and Oxon Hill were all Hanson places. Samuel Hanson was one of the first to come to the Upper Potomac section, after 1650. John, his grandson, and father of Alexander, signed the Non Importation Act, was chairman of a committee appointed to stop importations from Great Britain and the West Indies, President of the Continental Congress, and welcomed Washington officially, after the surrender of Cornwallis.

Belmont, like other Maryland mansions of its period, consists of a central building, with two wings. A hall runs through the middle from front to rear, and rooms on both sides are beautifully paneled in oak, from floor to ceiling, as is the ballroom in one wing, the other containing the kitchen. Half a mile from the house is the family burying ground.

It has its ghost, a strange one. There comes first the sound of horses' hoofs, with the jangle of harness. Then feet are heard going down the hall to the front door, which opens, and other feet come in, while the horses, apparently drawing a heavy coach or carriage, pass around the house towards the stables.

Whitehall, nine miles from Baltimore, was the home of Governor Horatio Sharpe. It is a Georgian house of bricks, said to have been made on the place by slaves. Finished with beautifully carved woodwork, this was executed by a young redemptioner from England, to whom the Governor, becoming interested in his carvings, offered freedom if he did good work for the new house. The young man died soon after it was finished, without ever having revealed any particulars of himself or his early history.

Governor Sharpe is said to have been responsible for the Stamp Act, final piece of tyranny which caused the Revolution. In a letter to Lord Baltimore he suggested " a duty on all spirituous liquors and wines," or that money might be raised " by a Duty or something similar on Deeds and writings."

Sharpe left Whitehall to John Ridout, whose fortune he early made by recognizing his ability, making him his secretary and eventually admitting him to close friendship. In Belmont, Ridout's sister, Mary, is said to have danced with Washington, then a young officer with the Provincial militia, while Benjamin Franklin played a tune for them on the musical glasses.

The present owners are singularly averse to allowing anyone to see the place.

This is not the case with the charming family living in Hampton, the old Ridgely house, near Towson, some thirteen miles from Baltimore, and said to be the largest colonial mansion in Maryland. The first house on this estate was a story and a half farmhouse, built in 1729, later and still used by the overseer.

Charles Ridgely, a sea captain, great-grandson of Robert, first of the family to come to this country, built the beautiful old house still occupied by his descendants of the name. It was seven years in building, the carpenter-builder occupying the eastern side, first to be finished, until the entire house was completed in 1783. Captain Ridgely himself laid out the beautiful gardens. The eastern portion is the handsomer, containing finer paneling, but the whole house calls for superlatives.

Two stories and a half in height, one enters an unusually broad hall running through the middle, from front to back, the windows paned with stained glass, while over the great front and back doors are the Ridgely coat-of-arms, also in colored glass. The walls of this hall and of the lower rooms are literally lined with family portraits, including a lovely one of Eliza Ridgely — of whom more later — taken with her harp, at the age of fifteen, a full length painting by Sully.

The stairs are in a smaller hall between library and dining room, while a rear staircase, with housekeeper's room on the landing, were added *only* seventy years ago, as testified to in a diary kept by a daughter of the house: " The back stair was finished to-day, and my squirrel died."

Courtesy of the Maryland Chapter, Colonial Dames of America

Mt. Clare, Carroll Park, Baltimore, Maryland.

Dining room, Mt. Clare, Carroll Park, Baltimore, Maryland.

The George Read house, built in 1801, and originally standing in the gardens of the older house, built by the senior Read, and which burned to the ground.

The drawing room, a very large apartment, filled with old furniture, has but one door, that opening from the hall. When it was once suggested that another be cut into the room behind, the owner of the house objected that a "withdrawing room" should be one in fact as well as in name, an apartment into which one could withdraw without being annoyed by too much passing in and out.

One wing contains the kitchen, laundry, etc., the other a room which was really the first bathroom, at a time when modern plumbing was unknown, for the grandfather of the present owner installed two tin tubs therein. Above, reached by its own staircase, is the old schoolroom. Each generation since has introduced improvements; thus, the father of Captain Ridgely added gas, the present owner installed heating apparatus and the telephone, as well as modern bathrooms.

At front and rear of the main part of the house is a great portico, its columns rising to the roof, while a balcony is built in on the second floor level. When seen in May, the rear one was a mass of wistaria in full bloom, and the gardens were charming, stretching away in the rear. Eliza Ridgely loved these gardens, and planted many flowers and shrubs which are still blooming.

In 1790, when Captain Ridgely was building Hampton, workmen quit at four o'clock daily, not because of union regulations for an eight hour day, but because wolves so infested the country between there and Baltimore after dark. When Hampton was finished, Mrs. Ridgely, who was Rebecca Dorsey, and a devout Methodist, wished to have a religious service as house warming. The Captain agreed provided the opening address be delivered by the Reverend John Cole, an Episcopal clergyman, after which, he declared, "she might have all the praying and shouting that she pleased."

Governor Eden's act of November 26th, 1770, regulating the fees of public officers, was thought to usurp the rights of the citizens, and Charles Ridgely, Thomas Cockey Deye, Aquila Hall, and Walter Tolley, Junior, were instructed to "testify their thanks to the 'First Citizen' (Charles Carroll of Carrollton), " for his spirited, eloquent

and patriotic opposition to the proclamation in the controversy with
' Antillon'." (Daniel Dulany).

Captain Ridgely left Hampton to his nephew Charles, who changed
his name from Carnan to Ridgely to inherit it. He became Governor
of Maryland, Brigadier General, appointed by Governor Stone, and
United States Senator. His wife was a Puritan, and would not consent
that her portrait should be painted to add to the family collection, so
the husband brought an artist into the house under the pretext of decorating the ceilings. The artist worked secretly behind closed doors,
and produced a portrait of the lady, which now hangs with the others.

The Governor and his wife had eleven children, and Hampton
passed to the second, John, the eldest having died before his father.

John married Eliza, daughter of Nicholas Ridgely of Delaware,
thus allying the two families of the name. He owned a famous race
horse, Post Boy, which after winning many races, finally broke his leg
during a race, gamely finished victor on his three sound legs, but his
owner was forced to have him shot.

In the bedroom above the drawing room, although supporting
beams have been pronounced perfectly sound, the floor sags perceptibly
towards the centre. This, known as the White Room, is very lovely
when the old white hangings are brought out for special occasions. It
is the " haunted room." Mrs. Swan, a beauty and close friend of the
mistress of the house at the time, occupied it while on a visit. One morning she remarked at the breakfast table that she had repeatedly dreamed
the same dream during the night. She was walking on the shore in a
storm, and saw a distorted little man in a boat, vainly trying to reach
her. He then cried out: " Never mind, I'm coming for you in a week."
Within a week she died, in the white room, and now is seen there,
putting on her bonnet.

John Ridgely left Hampton to his son Charles, the latter to his
son John, the present owner, who has a son and grandson, both named
John, to whom to bequeath it, for although not entailed by law, of
course, yet family tradition has always willed the estate to the eldest
son.

Cross Manor stands near Grayson's Wharf, St. Inigoes Creek. Sir Thomas Cornwaleys came to this country in 1634 with Leonard Calvert, on the Ark, was a Member of the Council, and when Lord Baltimore put down Claiborne's rebellion, he commanded in the first naval battle ever fought off our shores. He built Cross Manor in 1642, but since one historian states that his Protestant servants burned down his house and fences soon after this date, possibly the house that still stands here was the first one repaired, or was newly built on the old foundations. He was one of the richest manorial lords who came with Calvert, and was Deputy Governor.

The house has been much changed, and re-built, but is thought the oldest brick house in the state. There are fine old trees here, one of box being forty-five feet in circumference, and there is a charming old garden as well.

Various stories are told concerning the origin of the name. One is that a great friend of Cornwaleys was killed near here by Indians, and that when Cornwaleys later built his manor house, he placed a cross on one wall, in honor of his friend.

The Eastern Shore, Maryland, has many interesting, picturesque old houses. At Secretary is one of these, Warwick Fort Manor, built in 1740 by Colonel Henry Hooper. He was a Brigadier General of militia for the lower half of the Eastern Shore peninsula. Its very thick walls are thought to have been built as protection against Indians, at the time when the Choptanks roamed through the nearby forests. Some of the old hinges are four feet long, and inside were iron bars which could be pushed across, still further to strengthen them.

The rooms were paneled and finished in rosewood and mahogany, the fireplaces had carved mantels, while the winding stairs had rail and bannisters of mahogany. It, too, has its haunted room, and traditions of buried treasure.

The Point, the oldest house in Cambridge, was built between 1706 and 1710 by Colonel John Kirk, Lord Baltimore's agent for Dorchester County. Two rooms were added in 1770 by Robert Goldsborough, and two more with a hall, by James Steele in 1796. Colonel Kirk's daughter inherited the place from her father, and married the Reverend Thomas Howell, first rector of the first Episcopal Church in Cambridge at Church Creek. He planted a double row of cedars around the two acres in which the house was set, and also a cross of cedars, which grew to great size, three feet in diameter, but finally were struck by lightning, only the stumps remaining.

The town of Easton, near which are a number of fine old places, stands on part of a large tract surveyed in 1664 for three men, one of whom, Phill Armstrong, later sold to the judges two acres of his tract " whereon to build a courthouse." The tract was originally known as London-derry, but the house built by Armstrong in 1650 has long since disappeared, although a modern residence was built near the old site after the Civil War.

Beautiful Hope stands on the original land grant given by Lord Baltimore in 1666. The house, built in 1740, had finally fallen into a sad state, its gardens overgrown with grass and weeds, when it was purchased by Mr. William J. Starr. He labored lovingly from 1906 to 1910 to restore it, while his wife, who admits that when she first saw her husband's purchase she was in despair at its condition, laid out with loving skill and care the present gardens, both working " not for an age, but for all time," as a tablet affixed near the front doors states. Flowers of all kinds now bloom here, in the " heart garden," its beds bordered with box, of which Mrs. Starr has planted quantities. The trees, too, in addition to those already on the estate, have been planted with care and discrimination, and the owner is the proud possessor of a testimonial from the Maryland Tree Association as to their rank. She has a " Field of States," with trees from every state in the Union; there is a remarkable old English yew, which experts have pronounced 250 years old, English lindens, and many rare species.

The red brick house, partially veiled by ivy and creepers, is very beautiful. From the terrace in the rear, a charming view may be had of the winding Miles River, on which boats used in the old days to bring guests to Hope. Within is a great hall, and handsome old stairs, their treads and rail of mahogany, lead to the upper stories. On either side of the hall are finely paneled rooms, with exquisite hand carved wood-work, all now restored to the original beauty, and suitably filled with furniture and ornaments of the proper period. The two wings, with their unusual ogee roofs, contain one a large library, which tempts the book-lover to linger, the other a dining and a breakfast room.

Approaching Hope by one road, the Anchorage will be passed, lying directly on the Miles River. The original house here was built in 1732. During the Revolution, the British fleet sailed up, and attacked the town of St. Michael's, but did little damage, for the inhabitants had put lights in the upper stories only of their houses, so the shots were aimed too high. At that time the place was the home of the Reverend John Gordon, Episcopal clergyman in charge of Miles Church, a Revolutionary parish, now standing, a ruin, on the opposite side of the high-road from the house. He built a residence here, apparently to replace the old one, two stories high, and Governor Lloyd added wings on either side, connected by passages with the main portion. The present handsome residence now standing here is this one modernized.

In this section of Maryland is a group of old estates once belonging to the Goldsborough family, several still remaining in that ownership. The first of the name came from England in 1668, and went to Barbadoes, but remained only a short time, going then to New England. Nor did he long tarry there, but removed again, this time to Kent Island, Maryland, where he died within a few months. He had left two sons and a daughter behind him in England, but his wife accompanied him, and within a year of his death married George Robins. The two sons came to Maryland a few years later. The elder, Robert, settled at Ashby, and married Elizabeth Greenbury, daughter of a Deputy Governor of Maryland. By grant and purchase, he acquired an estate of 20,000 acres. He was the great-grandfather of the Honorable Robert, of Cambridge.

The younger son, Nicholas, married Ann Powell, and settled at Otwell. This is now the oldest of all the houses belonging to the Goldsboroughs.

It stands aloof from the highroad, reached by its own long drive, and almost surrounded by the waters of Goldsborough and Trippe's creeks, and the Tredavon River.

The original portion, built in 1663, probably consisted of two rooms, with two more on an upper half story. Here the walls are very thick, the mantels plain and hand hewn, while the great front door of massive hand hewn planks, has old hinges, hand wrought latch, and heavy old key. Frequently added to, the house is now a long, low, irregular brick building. One addition was the broad hallway, with door at each end, and fine staircase, with hand carved bannisters. Opposite the old rooms is another, added at an early date. In this, the present dining room, is a powder closet, not the kind in which wigs were powdered, but a small compartment set high up in the old chimney, and in which powder could be kept dry.

From the early added broad hall, a narrower one runs across the rest of the front, connecting the various additions, and the entire interior contains enough strap, H and HL hinges to delight lovers of the antique.

Pleasant Valley, another Goldsborough place, but no longer in the family, was built in 1734 for Howes, son of the Honorable Robert of Cambridge. It, too, is far off the highroad, a fine old brick house, with beautiful paneling and woodwork, and large, high-ceiled rooms.

The Honorable Robert, always so known to distinguish him from the other Roberts in the family, was a great-great-grandson of the original " emigrant." He was a delegate to the Continental Congress, and would have been a Signer, had he not been prevented from this by a bad attack of gout.

Although Ashby was the first home of the elder son of the first Goldsborough, Myrtle Grove, " next door," meaning several miles by road, has the older house, for the original Ashby house was destroyed long ago. Both places are still owned by Goldsboroughs.

A long, low wing, built of wide boards, is the original Myrtle Grove dwelling, built in or about 1699. The large, square, high-ceiled addition, now the main part of the house, was built a hundred years later. A fine old avenue bordered with trees leads to its front door, but it is now seldom visited by the family, and only the wing is occupied by the tenant farmer. When George Robins Goldsborough married Eleanor Rogers, daughter of Lloyd Rogers of Tulip Hill, near Washington, and great-granddaughter of Martha Washington, a wedding reception was given the young couple in Myrtle Grove, and they went to spend their summers at Ashby, their winters being usually passed in Washington.

The present house at Ashby had already been built then, indeed it is probably not more than seventy-five years old, a substantial frame house, with large rooms, and high ceilings, now unoccupied. It is open to the passing stranger, but so far its unshuttered windows are practically intact, and although a party of youths not long ago wantonly tore out a couple of the mantels, and did some other damage, as yet but little expense would be necessary to put it in condition.

Beautifully situated, the lawn, shaded by fine old trees, runs down on two sides to the winding Miles River. The Goldsborough burying ground close to the house is in good condition, enclosed by an ivy-grown brick wall, whose single iron gate is wisely kept locked against lawless intruders.

Wye, although cared for, is another old place seldom occupied by the owner, but is still in the possession of the Lloyds.

This family is of Welsh origin, and one of the name had come to Virginia as early as 1623. The Maryland Edward Lloyd, a Puritan, came to the state about 1645, and at an early date owned large tracts of land on the Wye River. In 1668, he went to England on business, leaving his son, probably Philemon, in charge, and there is no record of his return. Philemon and his brother Edward are said both to have fallen in love with a pretty Quaker, Sarah Covington, and she married Edward.

Philemon was a business associate of Governor Bennett, and after his death, married his daughter Henrietta Maria. She was a devout Roman Catholic, and is credited with having built the first chapel for that denomination in the county, at Doncaster, or Wye town. It and the town have long since disappeared.

Edward Lloyd is believed to have built the first house at Wye before returning to England, but it may have been built by his son. The original house was burned in 1776, by the British, and all the family records perished with it, all the family silver was also carried off, although later a portion of this was recovered. Of the old buildings the orangery, and probably the smoke house and a couple of brick slave dwellings remain. The present residence was built before the close of the Revolution by the Reverend Edward Lloyd, fourth of his name in Maryland, where there have been seven, all holding prominent offices, including burgesses, members of the Assembly, councillors, captains and colonels in the army, and three governors. The Reverend Edward was a member of the Provincial Convention, delegate to the lower house of the Assembly, and later a State Senator.

The present long frame house, with its two wings, was tightly closed, the windows shuttered when visited, but the beautiful circular lawn shaded by fine old trees could be admired. Behind the house is a broad stretch of lawn, bordered on the sides by great hedges of lilacs, white, pale and deep purple, and at the end by the old orangery, of stucco-covered bricks. Its windows are broken, there is no longer a vestige in it of orange trees or shrubs of any kind; it is used merely as a storehouse for farm and garden tools. Behind this is the old family burying ground, overgrown with violets and myrtle, containing tombstones of many early and recent Lloyds, including Henrietta Maria and Philemon, with their children.

One of their daughters married Matthews Tilghman Ward, who owned another great estate not far away. Until he was eight years old, Fred Douglas lived on Wye estate, the son of a mulatto woman owned by one of Governor Lloyd's sailing masters, and as a little boy played with the Governor's small son.

Old Rich Neck estate at Claiborne was sold in the spring of 1927 to a New Yorker. This tract was first surveyed in 1649, was owned by several men, and in 1684, upon payment of £104, and 23,000 pounds of tobacco, 2,000 acres became the property of Captain James Murphy. He was captain of militia, justice of the peace, was commissioned with

Dining room, Hope, Easton, Maryland.

Hope, Easton, Maryland.

Edward Lloyd, Richard Tilghman and William Hemsley Gentlemen of the Quorum, to hold provincial courts, and perform other duties, and shortly before his death, was President of this Quorum.

He married Mabel Dawson, a belle and beauty of the Colony, and at his death left his large fortune entirely to her. She married Matthews Tilghman Ward; they had one daughter, who died young and unmarried, and when Mrs. Ward died, her husband married Margaret Lloyd of Wye. They had no children, and when Ward died, he left his large fortune to his widow for her lifetime, then it was to go to his cousin, Matthew Tilghman, who made his home with the Wards. Tilghman came into ownership of this property in 1790, and lived on it until his death.

Matthews Tilghman Ward had for twenty years held many important posts; Speaker of the Assembly, member of the Council, Lieutenant General of the Colony's militia, etc. Matthew Tilghman played an even more important role in the affairs of the Colony.

He, too, was Speaker of the Assembly, and delegates were appointed under his leadership to the Continental Congress in Philadelphia which signed the Declaration of Independence. Tilghman attended this Convention, but was absent, detained in Annapolis, when the Declaration was signed.

Throughout the Revolution he played an important part. He was Chairman of the Committee of Safety for the Eastern Shore; a member of the committee which drew up Maryland's protest against the Stamp Act, and until the colony became a state, was President of the Provincial Assembly. Since this body was in harmony with the patriots, and the Governor, Robert Eden, was not, Tilghman was practically the acting governor, and his estate, Rich Neck, the seat of government.

The old residence is in good condition, and the new owner intends to make all necessary repairs, and live in it.

Hermitage, in Queen Anne's County, the birthplace of Matthew Tilghman, is still a show place, a large house, approached by a mile-long drive, with views of the Chester River. Land here was taken up in 1659 by the first Tilghman of this branch to come to America.

Another branch, descended from Richard Tilghman, a surgeon who came from England in 1622, furnished a Revolutionary rider, whose mission was to carry good news instead of warnings.

Richard was a commissioner of the Province of Pennsylvania, appointed by William Penn to settle the boundaries with the Indians at Fort Stanwix, in 1658. He was a member of the Governor's Council, and later private secretary to Juliana, widow of the Proprietor. James, his son, married the daughter of Tench Francis, who came as a boy from Ireland to Talbot County, Maryland, there married a Miss Otwell, and later removed to Philadelphia.

James Tilghman had a plantation at Fansley, Maryland, and here his son Tench was born, in 1744.

Tench was one of twelve children, and attended school in Easton, Maryland, then went into business in Philadelphia with his uncle, Tench Francis. He was a volunteer in what the Tories jeeringly called the "Ladies' Light Infantry," or the "Silk Stockings," a military organization commanded by Captain Sharpe Dulany, while young Tilghman was a lieutenant. But although Tench's father was a Tory, his brother Philemon in the British Navy, Tench was an ardent patriot, member of Washington's staff, with that commander when he crossed the Delaware, and for a great part of his military career refused to accept any pay for his services.

He married a Tilghman cousin, daughter of Matthew, but the wedding was postponed for several months, because of the serious illness of Barrister Charles Carroll, who married a sister of Tilghman's bride.

Colonel Tench Tilghman's ride has been less sung than that of Paul Revere, but while in one sense it may have been less important, since his mission was to carry good news, instead of to arouse the patriots, it is none the less noteworthy. He rode from Yorktown to Philadelphia with news of the surrender of Cornwallis, and certainly it was most important that this news should reach that city without delay.

Tench Tilghman's home at this time was Plinhimmon, on Town

Creek, Talbot County, but he was visiting his married daughter at Hope.

He rode through the night at full speed, now and again stopping at a farmhouse on the way, knocking at the door, and arousing the inmates from sleep. When they demanded in alarm what was the matter, he re-assured them: " Cornwallis is taken! A fresh horse for the Congress." When this was supplied, on he dashed.

He " lost one whole night's run by the stupidity of the skipper, who got over Tangier shoals, and was a whole day crossing in a calm from Annapolis to Rock Hill," as his report states.

According to the familiar story, he arrived in Philadelphia in the night of October 27th, 1781, and went directly to the house of Thomas McKean, President of the Convention. Here he knocked repeatedly on the door, and so vehemently that the watchman was about to arrest him as a disturber of the peace when Tilghman told him the news. Then McKean appeared, and the watchman proclaimed the glad news throughout the city, by calling out, with the usual: " All's well! " the additional " And Cornwallis is taken! " The sleeping city awakened, there were impromptu illuminations and great rejoicings.

A boy who since he was fourteen years old had been riding back and forth along the Lancaster Road with dispatches, and had cleverly evaded many British traps set for him, was in Philadelphia that night. As this youth, Christopher Wolf, sped away to carry the good news to his townspeople, he must have felt rewarded for the long, lonely and dangerous rides that he had taken. He arrived in Lancaster at a very early hour in the morning, and aroused the residents, as Tilghman had aroused the Philadelphia watchman and McKean.

The fatigue of Tilghman's journey in an open boat from Yorktown to Rock Hill, followed by the long horseback ride, at a time when he was suffering from malarial fever, confined him to his bed for several days, but one fancies that he did not greatly complain, having been privileged to bear such vitally important good news to the Congress.

Many more old mansions of Maryland, even as many in other

States, might be included did space permit. Of those whose omission may surprise, several, such as Rose Hill Manor, outside of Frederick, Maryland, the old Robinson house, near Wilmington, Delaware, the Franklin Palace, at Perth Amboy, New Jersey, have been mentioned in *Early American Inns and Taverns*, since they were not only historic mansions, but became inns, restaurants or taverns later in their histories.

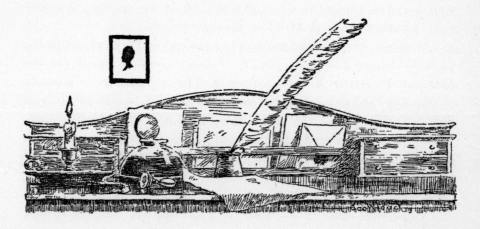

ALBEMARLE COUNTY IN VIRGINIA — Rev. Edgar Woods. Charlottesville, Va., The Michie Press, 1901

ALBEMARLE OF OTHER DAYS, THE — Mary Rawlings. Charlottesville, Va., The Michie Press, 1925

ANECDOTES OF THE AMERICAN REVOLUTION — Alexander Garden. Charleston, S. C., A. E. Miller, 1828

ASHLAND, ARTICLE BY LORINE L. BUTLER — *New York Times*, November 14, 1926

BLUE GRASS REGION OF KENTUCKY, THE — James Lane Allen. New York, Harper & Bros., 1902

BOYHOOD REMINISCENCES — Judge Keyes Danforth. New York, Gazlay Bros., 1895.

BRIEF SKETCH OF THE FIRST SETTLEMENT OF DEERFIELD, MASSACHUSETTS — By one of the Descendants of the First Settlers. Greenfield, Mass., 1833.

CARLYLE FAMILY, THE — Richard Henry Spence. Richmond, Va., Whittet & Shepperson, 1910

CHARLESTON, THE PLACE AND THE PEOPLE — Mrs. St. Julien Ravenel. New York, The Macmillan Co., 1906

CHESAPEAKE BAY COUNTRY, THE — Swepson Earle. Baltimore, Thomson Ellis Co., 1923

CHRONICLES OF BALTIMORE — J. Thomas Scharf. Philadelphia, Louis H. Evarts Co., 1881

COLONIAL MANSIONS OF MARYLAND AND DELAWARE — John Martin Hammond. Philadelphia, J. B. Lippincott Co., 1914

COLONIAL VIRGINIA — Samuel H. Young. Richmond, The Hermitage Press, 1907

COLONIAL WALKS IN THE HEART OF PHILADELPHIA — Historical Committee, Women's Division, Sesqui-Centennial, Philadelphia, 1926

CONCORD, A PILGRIMAGE TO THE HISTORIC AND LITERARY CENTER OF
AMERICA — Boston, Mass., Perry Ealton, 1925

CORNERS AND CHARACTERS OF RHODE ISLAND — Geo. C. Laswell. Providence, R. I., The Author, 1924

DAGGETT HOUSE, THE — Compiled by the *Pawtucket Magazine*, 1923

DISTINGUISHED FAMILIES IN AMERICA DESCENDED FROM WILHELMUS BEEK-
MAN AND JAN THOMASSE VAN DYKE — Wm. B. Aitken. New York,
G. P. Putnam's Sons, 1912

DWELLING HOUSES OF CHARLESTON, THE — Alice R. & D. E. Huger Smith.
Philadelphia, J. B. Lippincott Co., 1917

EARLY CONNECTICUT HOUSES — Isham & Brown. Providence, R. I., The
Preston & Rounds Co., 1900

EASTON STAR DEMOCRAT, Easton, Md.

EVOLUTIONARY HISTORY OF A NEW ENGLAND HOMESTEAD — J. M. Arms
Sheldon. Deerfield, Mass., 1925

FAIRFIELD ANCIENT AND MODERN — Frank Samuel Child. Fairfield Historical Society, Conn., 1909

FORTY OF BOSTON'S HISTORICAL HOUSES — Boston, State Trust Co., 1912

FREDERICKSBURG, VIRGINIA — J. Willard Adams, Fredericksburg, Va., 1898

FREDERICKSBURG, VIRGINIA — Edited by L. J. Houston, Jr. Fredericksburg,
1924

FREDERICKSBURG, PAST, PRESENT AND FUTURE — Robert Reid Howison.
Fredericksburg, J. Willard Adams, 1898

GENEALOGY OF THE PAGE FAMILY IN VIRGINIA — Richard Channing Moore
Page. New York, The Author, 1923

GUIDE BOOK TO HISTORIC GERMANTOWN — Chas. F. Jenkins. Germantown,
Pa., Site & Relic Society, 1902

GUIDE TO FREDERICKSBURG — Mrs. Vivien Minor Fleming. Fredericksburg,
Va., Chamber of Commerce

HERMITAGE, THE — Mary C. Dorris. Nashville, Tenn., The Hermitage Association, 1915

HERMITAGE, THE — Mrs. Reau E. Folk. Nashville, Tenn., 1925

HISTORIC ELIZABETH — Frank Bergen Kelley. Elizabeth, N. J., The Daily
Journal Press, 1914

HISTORIC FREDERICKSBURG — John J. Goolrick. Richmond, Va., Whittet &
Shepperson, 1922

HISTORIC GUIDE TO ALBEMARLE COUNTY — Colonial Dames & D.A.R. Charlottesville, Va., 1924

HISTORIC HOMES OF THE SOUTH WEST MOUNTAINS OF VIRGINIA — Edward C. Mead. Philadelphia, J. B. Lippincott Co., 1899

HISTORIC HOUSES OF NEW JERSEY — W. Gay Mills. Philadelphia, J. B. Lippincott Co., 1902

HISTORIC HOUSES OF SOUTH CAROLINA — Harriette Kershaw Leiding. Philadelphia, J. B. Lippincott Co., 1921

HISTORIC MEMORIES OF THE OLD SCHUYLER MANSION — L. B. Proctor

HISTORIC PERIODS OF FREDERICKSBURG — Mrs. Vivien Minor Fleming. Fredericksburg, Va.

HISTORIC AND PRESENT DAY GUIDE TO OLD DEERFIELD — Emma Lewis Coleman. R. A. Kishpaugh Print, 1925

HISTORIC SHRINES OF AMERICA — John T. Faris. New York, Geo. H. Doran Co., 1918

HISTORIC TOWNS OF THE MIDDLE STATES — Edited by Lyman P. Powell. New York, G. P. Putnam's Sons, 1899

HISTORIC TOWNS OF NEW ENGLAND — Edited by Lyman P. Powell. New York, G. P. Putnam's Sons, 1898

HISTORIC TOWNS OF THE WESTERN STATES — Edited by Lyman P. Powell. New York, G. P. Putnam's Sons, 1901

HISTORIC TRENTON — Louise Hewitt. Trenton, 1916

HISTORIC VIRGINIA HOMES AND CHURCHES — Robert A. Lancaster, Jr. Philadelphia, J. B. Lippincott Co., 1915

HISTORY OF BALTIMORE CITY AND COUNTY — J. Thos. Scharf. Philadelphia, Louis H. Evarts, 1881

HISTORY OF BILLERICA, MASSACHUSETTS — Rev. Henry A. Hazen. Boston, A. Williams & Co., 1883

HISTORY OF BROOKLYN, NEW YORK — Henry R. Stiles. Albany, J. Munsell, 1869

HISTORY OF THE CITY OF FREDERICKSBURG, VIRGINIA — Richmond, The Hermitage Press, 1908

HISTORY OF THE COUNTIES OF GLOUCESTER, SALEM AND CUMBERLAND, NEW JERSEY — Cushing & Sheppard. Philadelphia, Evarts & Peck, 1883

HISTORY OF THE COUNTY OF ORANGE, AND OF THE TOWN AND CITY OF NEWBURGH — E. M. Ruttenber. Newburgh, The Author, 1875

HISTORY OF DELAWARE — J. Thos. Scharf. Philadelphia, L. J. Richards & Co., 1888

HISTORY OF ELIZABETH, NEW JERSEY — Rev. Edwin F. Hatfield. New York, Carlton & Lanahan, 1868

HISTORY OF EXETER, NEW HAMPSHIRE — Chas. H. Bell, Exeter, The Author, 1888

HISTORY OF FAIRFIELD, CONNECTICUT — Hurd

HISTORY OF GLOUCESTER, MASSACHUSETTS — J. J. Babson. Gloucester, Proctor Bros., 1860

HISTORY OF KINGS COUNTY, NEW YORK — Harry R. Stiles. New York, W. W. Munsell, 1884

HISTORY OF LITCHFIELD, CONNECTICUT — Alain C. White. Litchfield, 1920

HISTORY OF LITTLE NINE PARTNERS OF NORTH EAST PRECINCT AND PINE PLAINS — Isaac Hunting. Amenia, N. Y., The Author, 1897

HISTORY OF MARBLEHEAD, MASSACHUSETTS — S. J. Roads, Jr. Marblehead, N. A. Lindsay & Co., 1897

HISTORY OF MARYLAND — Wm. Hand Browne. Boston, Houghton, Mifflin & Co., 1903

HISTORY OF NEW BEDFORD, MASSACHUSETTS — Ricketson. Boston, Houghton, Mifflin & Co., 1903

HISTORY OF NEW HAMPSHIRE — Edwin D. Sanborn. Manchester, N. H., John B. Clarke, 1875

HISTORY OF NEW LONDON, CONNECTICUT — Francis M. Caulkins. New London, The Author, 1860

HISTORY OF NEW PALTZ, NEW YORK — Ralph Le Fevre. Albany, 1909

HISTORY OF OLD BRAINTREE AND QUINCY — Wm. S. Pattee. Quincy, Mass., Green & Prescott, 1878

HISTORY OF THE PLANTATION OF MINUNKATUCK AND OF THE ORIGINAL TOWN OF GUILFORD — Bernard Christian Steiner. Baltimore, The Author, 1917

HISTORY OF SOUTH CAROLINA — Edited by Yates Snowden. Chicago, Lewis Pub. Co., 1920

HISTORY OF TALBOT COUNTY, MARYLAND — Oswald Tilghman. Baltimore, Williams & Wilkins, 1915

HISTORY OF WILMINGTON, DELAWARE — Compiled by " Every Evening." Wilmington, 1894

HISTORY OF WELLS AND KENNEBUNK — E. E. Bourne. Portland, Me., B. Thurston & Co., 1875

HISTORY OF YE OLDE BURNHAM HOUSE — Ipswich, Mass.

HOMES OF OUR FOREFATHERS — Edwin Whitefield. Reading, Mass., The Author, 1886

IN OLD PENNSYLVANIA TOWNS — Anne Wharton Hollingsworth. Philadelphia, J. B. Lippincott Co., 1920

IN TIDEWATER VIRGINIA — Dora Chinn Jett. Richmond, Whittet & Shepperson, 1924

JOHNSON'S ANECDOTES OF THE REVOLUTION

LANDMARKS OF NEW YORK — A. Everett Peterson. New York City Historical Club, 1923

LAUREL HILL AND SOME COLONIAL DAMES WHO LIVED THERE — William Brooke Rawle. Philadelphia, J. B. Lippincott Co., 1911

LEADING EVENTS OF MARYLAND HISTORY — J. Montgomery Gambrill. Boston & New York, Ginn & Co., 1917

LETTERS FROM AMERICA — Wm. Eddis. London, The Author, 1792

LIFE OF GENERAL HUGH MERCER — John T. Goodrick, New York, Neale Pub. Co., 1906

LITTLE TOURS AMONG HISTORIC SHRINES — Bessie Taul Conkwright. Lexington, Ky., The Author, 1923

LIVINGSTON MANOR — John Henry Livingston

MANORS AND HISTORIC HOMES OF THE HUDSON VALLEY — Harold Donaldson Eberlein. Philadelphia, J. B. Lippincott Co., 1924

MANORS OF VIRGINIA, THEIR HOMES AND THEIR CHURCHES — Charleston, S. C., 1861

MARYLAND'S COLONIAL EASTERN SHORE — Swepson Earle. Baltimore, 1916

MARYLAND PILGRIMAGE, A — Gilbert Grosvenor. *Geographical Magazine*, Washington, D. C., February, 1927

MOUNT CLARE, AN HISTORICAL SKETCH — Maryland Society of Colonial Dames. Baltimore, 1926

NEW YORK OLD AND NEW — Rufus Rockwell Wilson. Philadelphia, J. B. Lippincott Co., 1909

OLD BUILDINGS IN NEW YORK CITY — New York, Brentano's, 1907

OLD CHURCHES, MINISTERS AND FAMILIES OF VIRGINIA — Bishop Wm. Meade. Philadelphia, J. B. Lippincott Co., 1878

OLD HAZARD HOUSE, THE — Maud Lyman Stevens. Newport, R. I., Historical Papers, 1920

OLD MARYLAND MANORS — John Johnson, A. B. Baltimore, Johns Hopkins University, 1883

OLD PROVIDENCE — Compiled and published by the Walton Advertising Co., for the Merchants' National Bank, Providence, R. I., 1918

OLD ROADS OUT OF PHILADELPHIA — John T. Faris. Philadelphia, J. B. Lippincott Co., 1917

OLD SANTA FE — Ralph Emerson Twitchell. Santa Fe Pub. Co., 1925

OLD WASHINGTON MANSION, AN — Maud Burr Morris. Columbia Historical Society, 1918

OLDEST HOUSE IN THE UNITED STATES — Chas. B. Reynolds. New York, The Foster & Reynolds Co., 1921

OLDEST HOUSE ON NANTUCKET ISLAND, THE — Ida G. Coffin. New York, Chas. Francis Press, 1905

ORIGINS OF WILLIAMSTOWN — Arthur Latham Perry. The Author, 1894

OUR FOREFATHERS, THEIR HOMES AND THEIR CHURCHES — Charleston, S. C., 1861

PALACE OF THE GOVERNORS OF THE CITY OF SANTA FE — Ralph Emerson Twitchell. Santa Fe, N. M., The Author, 1924

PAWTUCKET PAST AND PRESENT — Compiled for the Slater Trust Co., Pawtucket, R. I., 1917

PEPPERELLS IN AMERICA, THE — Cecil Hampden Cutts Howard. Essex Institute Historical Collections

PETERSBURG GUIDE BOOK, THE — Richmond, Va. Central Pub. Co., Inc., 1925

PHILIPSE MANOR HALL — Edward Hagaman Hall. American Scenic and Historical Preservation Society, Yonkers, N. Y., 1912

PIGEON COVE AND ITS VICINITY — Henry C. Leonard. (out of print)

POTOMAC LANDINGS — Paul Wilstach. New York, Doubleday, Page & Co., 1921

PROCEEDINGS ON UNVEILING THE MONUMENT TO CAESAR RODNEY — Thomas F. Bayard. Wilmington, Del., The Delaware Printing Co., 1887

RAMBLES ABOUT HISTORIC BROOKLYN — Brooklyn Trust Co., 1916

RAVENEL RECORDS — Henry Edmund Ravenel. Atlanta, Ga., Franklin Printing & Publishing Co., 1898

REMINISCENCES AND MEMOIRS OF NORTH CAROLINA — John H. Wheeler. Columbus, O., 1884

ROMANCE OF FORGOTTEN TOWNS, THE — John T. Faris. New York, Harper & Bros., 1924

SEEING THE SUNNY SOUTH — John T. Faris. Philadelphia, J. B. Lippincott & Co., 1921

SHADOWS OF THE PAST — The Ancient Lady. Charleston, S. C., Wm. C. Mazyck, 1870

SIDE LIGHTS ON MARYLAND HISTORY — Hester Dorsey Richardson. Baltimore, Williams & Wilkins Co., 1913

SITE OF OLD JAMES TOWNE, THE — Samuel H. Young. Richmond, The Hermitage Press, 1907

SIXTY YEARS RECOLLECTIONS OF MILFORD — Nathan Stowe. Milford, Conn., Village Improvement Association, 1917

SOME COLONIAL HOMESTEADS — Marion Harland, New York, G. P. Putnam's Sons, 1897

SOME COLONIAL MANSIONS — Thomas Alden Glenn. Philadelphia, Coates & Co., 1898

SOME HISTORIC FAMILIES OF SOUTH CAROLINA — Frampton Erroll Ellis. Atlanta, Ga., Foote & Davis Co., 1905

SOME OLD IPSWICH HOUSES — Rev. Thos Franklin Waters. The Salem Press, 1898

STORY OF AN INTERESTING AND HISTORIC HOUSE IN GLOUCESTER, MASSACHUSETTS

STORY OF MONTICELLO — Mrs. Martin W. Littleton

STORY OF REMEMBRANCE SHELDON — Transcribed from the original manuscript by Matilda S. Hyde. Deerfield, Mass., 1920

SWETT-ILSLEY HOUSE IN THE ANTIENT TOWN OF NEWBURY — Society for the Preservation of New England Antiquities

THREE JUDGES, THE — Israel P. Warren. New York, Warren & Wyman, 1873

TROY AND RENSSELAER COUNTY, NEW YORK — Rutherford Hayner. Lewis Historical Pub. Co., New York & Chicago, 1925

UNPUBLISHED HISTORY OF DARTMOUTH OLD HOMES — Compiled by Henry C. Worth and Emma C. Austin

VASSALLS OF NEW ENGLAND, THE — Edward Doubleday Harris. Albany, J. Munsell, 1862

WHAT TO SEE IN MARBLEHEAD — Sara S. Bartlett. Salem Press Co., 1907

YE OLD FAYERBANKS HOUSE — Alvin Lincoln Jones. Boston, 1894

Alphabetically under States are listed the houses mentioned in the text, those which are open to the public marked with an asterisk.

CONNECTICUT

Bethany
    Dayton
Brooklyn
    Putnam
Fairfield
    Deacon Bulkley
    Thaddeus Burr
Greenwich
    *Knapp or Putnam
Groton
    Ebenezer Avery
    Mother Bailey
Guilford
    Acadian
    *Hyland
    Lee
    *Old Stone or Whitfield
    Regicide cellar
    Comfort Starr
Lebanon
    Gov. Trumbull
    *War Office
Litchfield
    Deming

Litchfield (*continued*)
    Parsonage
    Sheldon
    Gov. Wolcott
Lyme
    Thomas Lee
Meriden
    *Goffe
Milford
    Stephen Stowe
New Haven
    Jones
    *Purdee's Old Morris
    Pierpont
New London
    Hempstead
    *Huguenot
    *Shaw
Norwalk
    Gov. Fitch
Saybrook
    Hezekiah Whittlesey
Washington
    Red House

Wethersfield
   *Webb

Windsor
   *Ellsworth — Tyler

DELAWARE

Dover
   Eden Hill Farm
   Green, The
   Loockerman
   Ridgely
   Rodney
   Vining
   Woodburne
(near)
   Foxhall Farm
   Kingston-upon-Hull
   Pleasanton Abbey
   Towne Point
New Castle
   Amstel House
   Booth
   Dutch cottage
   Jacquette (near)
   Kensey Johns houses

New Castle (*continued*)
   McIntire
   Read
   Van Dyke houses
Odessa
   Cantwell (near)
   Corbit
   McDonough — The Trap
     (near)
   *Warner
Port Penn
   Oldest
   Stewart
Wilmington
   Cool Springs (near)
   Tatnall
   Tusculum
   West (site)

DISTRICT OF COLUMBIA

Georgetown
   Tudor Place
Washington
   Decatur

Washington (*continued*)
   *Granger — Arts Club
   *Octagon
   *White House

FLORIDA

St. Augustine
   Governor's House — *P. O.
   St. Francis Convent — Geronimo Alvarez—*Oldest House

St. Augustine (*continued*)
   Treasury Building (private residence)

INDIANA

Vincennes   *Harrison

KENTUCKY

Bardstown (near)
   Louis Philippe
Cynthiana
   Oldest house
Harrodsburg
   *Lincoln cabin
Lexington
   Ashland

Lexington (continued)
   Chaumiere (near)
   Ellerslie (near)
   Gratz
   Thomas Hart
   Keeneland Farm (near)
   Latrobe
   Robert S. Todd

MAINE

Brixham, York Corners
   McIntyre garrison house
Kennebunk
   Barry
   Crediford
   Lord
   *Snapdragon Inn
   Storer

Kittery Point
   Bray
   Lady Mary Pepperell
   Sir William Pepperell
Portland
   *Longfellow
Wiscasset
   Marie Antoinette refuge

MARYLAND

Annapolis
   *Brice
   Carrollton
   *Carvel Hall — Gov. Paca's
   *Chase
   *Hammond
   Scott
   Stewart
Baltimore
   Carroll town house
   *Homewood
   *Mount Clare

Baltimore (continued)
near
   Belmont
   Doughregan Manor
   Hampton
   Whitehall
Cambridge
   The Point
Claiborne
   Rich Neck
Croome (near)
   Mt. Airy

Easton (near)
    Anchorage
    *Ashby
    Hope
    Myrtle Grove
    Otwell
    Pleasant Valley
    Wye
Mattapany
    Calvert

Princess Anne
    Samuel Chase
Queen Anne's County, in
    Hermitage
Secretary
    Warwick Fort Manor
Town Creek, on
    Plinhimmon

MASSACHUSETTS

Acushnet
    Dr. Tobey
Annisquam
    Riggs
Barnstable
    Lothrop — *Sturgis Library
Beverly
    Balch
    *Cabot (Beverly Historical Society)
    Andrew Cabot (site)
    Elizabeth Cabot (site)
    George Cabot (site)
Billerica
    *Manning
Boston
    John Quincy Adams (site) Hotel Touraine
    Capen
    Clark — Frankland (site)
    Ebenezer Hancock (site)
    Cotton Mather (site)
    Josiah Quincy
    *Paul Revere
    Leonard Vassall

Cambridge
    Elmwood (Lowell)
    *Longfellow
Canton
    John Fenna
Central Village
    Restcome Potter
Chatham
    Oldest house (Historical Society)
Concord
    *Art Association
    *Antiquarian Society (Reuben Brown)
    Blockhouse (site)
    D.A.R. House
    R. W. Emerson
    Jones
    Old Manse
    Orchard
    Wayside
Dartmouth (near)
    Increase Allen's
    Round Hill Farm
Dedham
    *Fayerbanks

Deerfield
  Barnard — Dickinson
  Bartholomew — Belding —
    Stebbins
  Beaman — Bunker — Allen
  Carter — Allen — Barnard —
    Willard — The Manse
  Henry Dickinson
  Frary
  Nims
  Pink House
  Sheldon — Hoyt
  Ensign Sheldon (doorway)
  *Williams
Dorchester
  Pierce
Duxbury
  *Alden
Gloucester
  *Sargent — Murray — Gilman
Green Harbor
  *Winslow
Haverhill
  Hannah Dustin
  *Whittier
Hingham
  Garrison
  Gen. Lincoln
  Rev. Daniel Shute
  Wampatuck Club
  *Willard
Hyannis
  *Library
Ipswich
  Appleton
  Nathaniel Wade

Ipswich (continued)
  *Whipple
  *Ye Olde Burnham — Harte —
    Lord
Kingston
  *Gov. Bradford
  Gen. John Thomas
  Willett
Lexington
  *Hancock — Clark
  Jonathan Harrington (two)
  Munro
Marblehead
  Parson Barnard
  Elbridge Gerry
  Gen. Glover
  Skipper Ireson
  *King Hooper
  Lafayette
  Col. Jeremiah Lee
  Old Brig
  Azor Orne
  Scott
Marshfield
  Webster office
Martha's Vineyard
  Daggett —Nye
  *East Chop Inn
  Great House
  Oliver Linton
  Mayhew — Vincent
  Capt. Nathan Smith
Medford
  Craddock (The Fort)
  Garrison
  Isaac Hall

Medford (*continued*)
  *Royall Mansion
Nantucket
  *Jethro Coffin
  Josiah Coffin
  Caleb & Joseph Gardner
  *Maria Mitchell
New Bedford
  Arnold
  East
  *Howland (doorway)
Newbury
  Gov. Dummer
  *Swett-Ilsley
Newburyport
  *Garrison
North Plymouth
  William Cross
North Truro
  Highland Light farmhouse
Pigeon Cove
  *The Castle
  Gott
  *Mammy's Old Tavern (Babson)
  Witch
Plymouth
  *Antiquarian
  *Harlow
  *Howland
  *Tabitha Plaskett
  Edward Winslow
  John Winslow
Provincetown
  *Hooked Rug
  Lothrop — Hall
  *Snug Harbor

Quincy
  *Dorothy Q.
  Leonard Vassall — Adams
Quincy-Adams
  *Adams houses (two)
Salem
  Andrew — Safford
  Assembly
  Cabot — Endicott
  Cook — Oliver
  Benj. Crowninshield (Home for Aged & Destitute Women)
  Derby
  Downing (site) Essex Museum
  Gardner — White
  *Dr. Grimshaw (doorway)
  *Hathaway
  Hawthorne's birthplace
  *House of the Seven Gables
  Pickering
  *Peirce — Nichols
  *Retire Becket
  Ruck (site)
  *Ward
  Josiah Ward (site)
  *Witch
South Duxbury
  Myles Standish
Topsfield
  *Parson Capen
Upper Medford
  Gov. Brooks
Williamstown
  Nehemiah Smedley
Woburn
  Baldwin

NEW HAMPSHIRE

Amherst
  Horace Greeley birthplace
Dover
  *Damme garrison
Exeter
  Councillor Gilman
  *Gov. Gilman (Cincinnati Society)
  Nathaniel Gilman
  Janvrin garrison house (near)
Franklin
  Daniel Webster birthplace
Haverhill
  Gov. Page

New Castle
  Gen. Jaffray
Portsmouth
  *Aldrich
  Jackson
  *Hon. Woodbury Langdon (Hotel Rockingham)
  *Moffet — Ladd
  Portsmouth Athletic Club
  *Purcell — Historical Association
  Warner
  Winslow — Pierce
  Gov. Benning Wentworth

NEW JERSEY

Belcher — Elizabeth
  Bonnell
  Boudinot
  *Carteret Arms
  Chateau
  De Hart
  Hetfield
  Liberty Hall
  St. John's Parsonage
  Scott
Morristown
  *Ford

Princeton
  Morven
  Tusculum
Trenton
  Bloomsbury
  Bow Hill
  Douglass
  Hermitage
  Stille (site)

NEW MEXICO

Santa Fe
  *First Apartment House in the U. S.

Santa Fe (continued)
  *Governors' Palace
  Tiguez

NEW YORK

Albany
  *Schuyler Mansion
  Van Rensselaer manor
Brooklyn
  Bennett
  *Lefferts
  Lott houses
  Lady Deborah Moody
  Schenck houses
  Van Brunt
  Van Sicklen
Easthampton
  Payne
Fishkill
  Wharton
Gardiner's Island
  Lion Gardiner
Huntington, L. I.
  Walt Whitman
Jamaica
  Rufus King
Katonah (near)
  John Jay
Kingston
  *Senate
  Van Steenberg
Newburgh
  *Headquarters
New Paltz
  Du Bois
  Frere

New Paltz (*continued*)
  A. Hasbrouck
  *J. Hasbrouck — Memorial
  *Library
New York City
  *Claremont
  *De Lancey — Fraunces Tavern
  *Gracie
  Grange
  *Jumel
  *Smith
  *Van Cortlandt
Pelham
  Pell
Pine Plains
  Graham houses
Rensselaer
  Fort Crailo
Roslyn, L. I.
  Wm. Cullen Bryant
Shelter Island
  Sylvester
Staten Island
  Billop — Conference
Tarrytown
  Philipse Manor
Tivoli (near)
  Arryl (ruins)
  Clermont
Yonkers
  *Manor Hall

PENNSYLVANIA

Blue Bell (near)
  Dawesfield

Carlisle
  Watts

Fortside
    Hope Lodge
Germantown
    Grumblethorp
    *Johnson (Woman's Club)
    Morris
    Rittenhouse
    Wyck
Paoli (near)
    Waynesborough
Philadelphia
    *Belmont
    *Laurel Hill
    Lewis
    Morris
    *Morris in Fairmount Park
    *Mount Pleasant
    *Penn

Philadelphia (continued)
    *Ross
    *Solitude
    Sweet Brier
Phoenixville
    Moore Hall
Stenton
    *Stenton Mansion
Swarthmore
    West
Valley Forge
    *Headquarters
    Mad Anthony Wayne's Headquarters
    Mount Joy
Willow Grove (near)
    Graeme Park

RHODE ISLAND

Newport
    *Hazard — Wanton — Ward — Howard
Pawtucket
    *Daggett
Providence
    John Brown
    John Carter Brown — Night-

Providence (continued)
    ingale — Nicholas Brown
    Joseph Brown (Providence Nat'l Bank)
    *Esek Hopkins
    Stephen Hopkins
    Thomas P. Ives
    *Betsey Williams

SOUTH CAROLINA

Beaufort
    Old fortified
    Tuscarora Jack's
Charleston
    Alston
    Bennett

Charleston (continued)
    *Miles Brewton
    Robert Brewton
    Dale
    Judge Thomas Heyward
    Horry

Charleston (*continued*)
    Wm. E. Huger
    Izard
    Manigault
    Jacob Motte
    Nicholson
    *The Patio, site of 1st Miles Brewton
    Charles Pinckney
    Pringle
    Col. William Rhett
    Dictator Rutledge (Mayor Rhett)
    Tidyman
    Tradd (site)
    Washington
    Williams
near
    Belvidere
    Comingtee
    Crowfield
    Drayton Hall
    Elms, The
    Exeter
    Fairfield

Charleston (*continued*)
    Fairlawn
    *Fenwick Castle
    Hampton
    Lewisfield
    Medway
    *Middleton Gardens
    Mulberry Castle
    Oaks, The
    Otranto
    Yeamans Hall
Clarendon (near)
    Manning's Folly
Columbia (near)
    Fort Granby
Parris Island
    Charlesfort
Sheldon
    Gen. Bull's
Stateburg (near)
    Ruins, The
Wedgefield (near)
    Home Place (site)
    Melrose
    Midway (site)

TENNESSEE

Nashville
    *Hermitage

VERMONT

Fairfax
    Webster
Poultney
    Pine Tree

Rutland
    Jenkins
    John Murray — Putnam

VIRGINIA

Alexandria
  *Carlyle — Braddock
  Ramsay
Charlotte County
  Red Hill
Charlottesville
  The Farm
  Jowett's "Swan Tavern" — Red Lands Club

near
  Belvoir
  Castalia
  Castle Hill
  Cismont
  Clover Fields
  Cobham Park
  Cuckoo Tavern — (private residence)
  Edgehill
  Maxfield
  *Monticello
  Shadwell
Clark County
  Carter Hall
Culpepper (near)
  Salubria
Ditchley (on Chesapeake Bay)
Fredericksburg
  Charles Dick
  Federal Hill
  Glassel
  Hazel Hill
  *Kenmore
  Matthew Fontaine **Maury**

Fredericksburg (*continued*)
  Mercer's apothecary shop
  *President Monroe
  Paul
  *Rising Sun
  Sentry Box
  Stevenson
  *Mary Washington
near
  Belmont
  Brompton
  Chatham
  Ferry Farm
  Sabine Hall
  Travellers' Rest
  Willis Hill
Gray's Creek (near)
  Smith Fort Farm
Ivy (near)
  Locust Hill
Jamestown
  Philip Ludwell's (foundations)
near
  Green Springs (ruins)
King George County
  Marmion
Orange County
  Montpelier
Petersburg
  Col. John Bannister
  Bollingbroke
  Center Hill
  Dunn's Hill
  Folly Castle

WEST VIRGINIA